MALAYSIA & SINGAPORE

TOP SIGHTS, AUTHENTIC EXPERIENCES

FIFTYMM99/GETTY IMAGES ©

THIS EDITION WRITTEN AND RESEARCHED BY

Isab… …hwick,
C… …iska,
…s

Ultimate Itinerary

PAUL KENNEDY/GETTY IMAGES ©

This is Lonely Planet's ultimate Malaysia & Singapore itinerary, which ensures you'll see the best of everything these countries have to offer.

For other recommended paths to travel, check out our itineraries section (p26). For inspiration on themed travel, see If You Like... (p20).

Week 1

Singapore to Kuala Lumpur

Fly into **Singapore** (p222) and spend a couple of days dipping into the city's various quarters and sampling its delicious dining and shopping options. Next head across to Peninsula Malaysia and one of the region's oldest cities.

4½ hours, 5½ hours to Melaka

Melaka (p160), an atmospheric time capsule of history and culture, is a great place to explore for a day before moving on to the nation's appealing capital.

2 hours, 3 hours to KL

Sightseeing must-dos in **Kuala Lumpur** (p34) include the Petronas Towers, Batu Caves and Chinatown. Then set your travel compass for the peninsula's interior.

4 hours to Kuala Tembling, then
3 hours to Taman Negara

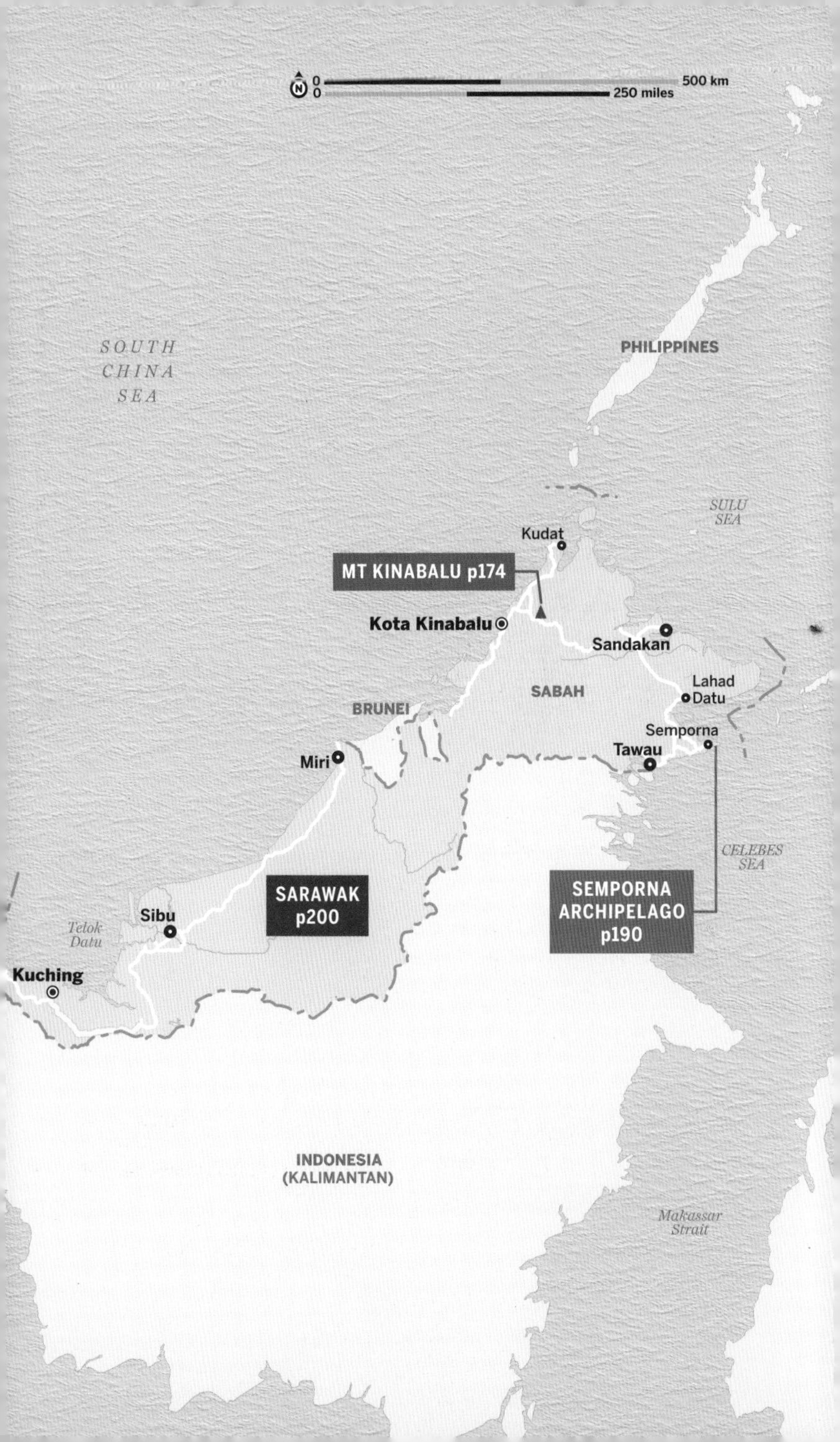

0
0
500 km
250 miles
SOUTH CHINA SEA
PHILIPPINES
SULU SEA
Kudat
MT KINABALU p174
Kota Kinabalu
Sandakan
SABAH
Lahad Datu
BRUNEI
Semporna
Tawau
Miri
CELEBES SEA
SARAWAK p200
SEMPORNA ARCHIPELAGO p190
Sibu
Telok Datu
Kuching
INDONESIA (KALIMANTAN)
Makassar Strait

Welcome to Malaysia & Singapore

Southeast Asia's dynamic duo offer sprawling metropolises, culinary sensations, beautiful beaches, idyllic islands, soaring mountains and national parks packed with wildlife. Equally rich and diverse is the region's fascinating multi-ethnic cultural mix.

Malaysia is home to some of the most ancient ecosystems on earth, with significant areas of primary rainforest protected by national park and conservation projects. The biodiversity is mind-boggling: from the pitcher plants and orchids in the humid lowlands to the conifers and rhododendrons of the high-altitude forests. The most common sightings of wildlife will be a host of insects or colourful birdlife, but you may get lucky and spot a foraging tapir, a silvered leaf monkey or an endearingly downy orangutan. The oceans are just as bountiful, with shoals of tropical fish, paint-box corals, turtles, sharks and dolphins.

City lovers will be thrilled by Singapore, an urban showstopper with elegant colonial buildings, stunning contemporary architecture and world-class attractions. In Malaysia's capital, Kuala Lumpur (KL), Malay *kampung* (village) life hums along cheek by jowl with the 21st-century glitz of the Petronas Towers, and shoppers shuttle from traditional wet markets to air-conditioned megamalls. In sharp contrast to the metropolises, Unesco World Heritage–listed Melaka and George Town (Penang) have uniquely distinctive architectural and cultural townscapes, developed over half a millennium of Southeast Asian cultural and trade exchange, and both should be high on your to-visit list.

sprawling metropolises, culinary sensations, beautiful beaches

Gardens by the Bay (p226), Marina Bay Sands (p240) and Marina Bay, Singapore

THAILAND
CAMBODIA
VIETNAM
Gulf of Thailand
PULAU LANGKAWI p118
CAMERON HIGHLANDS p78
THAILAND
KOTA BHARU p132
Kangar
Alor Setar
Merang
Kuala Terengganu
Gua Musang
GEORGE TOWN p92
TAMAN NEGARA p142
Ipoh
Lumut
Jerantut
Kuantan
Kuala Selangor
KUALA LUMPUR p34
Shah Alam
Putrajaya
Seremban
Port Dickson
Gemas
PULAU TIOMAN p150
MELAKA CITY p160
Johor Bahru
SINGAPORE p222
INDONESIA (SUMATRA)
JAVA SEA

From left: Chinatown hawker stalls (p64), Kuala Lumour; Pantai Cenang (p122); Flying foxes, Taman Negara (p142)

Week 2

Taman Negara to Pulau Langkawi

Make some short jungle hikes in the magnificent national park **Taman Negara** (p142). Then swap steamy jungle for the cool breezes and undulating tea plantations of the **Cameron Highlands** (p78).

4 hours to Cameron Highlands

Return to the west coast and make the short crossing by ferry or bridge to the island of Penang where the World Heritage listed core of **George Town** (p92) awaits urban exploration.

5 hours to Penang

Finish up with some serious beach time on gorgeous **Pulau Langkawi** (p118).

1 hour to Langkawi.

Staying Longer

Kota Bahru to Semporna Archipelago

You'll have to return to Penang or KL to fly to the east coast city **Kota Bahru** (p132). From here the fastest way down the coast to beautiful **Pulau Tioman** (p150) is to fly to Johor Bahru then follow the coast back up to Mersing for the boat.

1 hour to Kota Bahru, then
& 5 hours to Pulau Tioman

Singapore offers good connections to **Kuching** (p204), the natural base from which to arrange expeditions to Sarawak's national parks.

1½ hours to Kuching

Having recovered from the ascent of **Mt Kinabalu** (p174), the roof of Borneo, dive into the tropical marine dreamworld of the **Semporna Archipelago** (p190).

1½ hours to Kota Kinabalu, then
1 hour to Tawau

Contents

NICK GARBUTT/GETTY IMAGES ©

Meerkats, Singapore Zoo (p234)

Plan Your Trip
Malaysia & Singapore's Top 12

Singapore

An ambitious, ever-evolving wonder

Singapore may be small in size, but in touristic terms the island state is a giant. This multicultural nation, one of the wealthiest in the region, offers plenty for the visitor to see and do – from admiring the eye-boggling architecture around Marina Bay to being transfixed by the Bolly beats of Little India or the lush magnificence of the World Heritage–listed Botanic Gardens. And then there's the shopping and the delicious food scene. It's all simply unbeatable. Left: National Orchid Garden (p228), Singapore Botanic Garden; Right: Shophouse facade, Little India (p247)

1

STUART DEE/GETTY IMAGES ©

George Town

Ancient cultures, colonial architecture, street food

George Town has managed to cling to its relatively newfound reign as one of the region's hottest destinations. The 2008 Unesco World Heritage declaration sparked a frenzy of cultural preservation, and the city's charismatic shophouses have been turned into house museums, boutique hotels and chic cafes. George Town is one of the most rewarding cities in Southeast Asia to explore on foot, and it also boasts some of Malaysia's best food. Top: Mini banana pancakes, Gurney Drive Hawker Stalls (p103); Bottom: Staircase in the Blue Mansion (p98)

2

JAVIER GONZÁLEZ/GETTY IMAGES ©

Taman Negara

Step back in time in a primeval jungle

To visit Taman Negara is to experience the land as it was before the modern world rolled through. Inside this shadowy, nigh-impenetrable jungle, ancient trees with gargantuan buttressed root systems dwarf luminescent fungi, orchids, and rare and beautiful flora. Making their home within are elephants, tigers, leopards and deer, as well as smaller wonders such as flying squirrels, lizards, monkeys, tapirs, and serpents of all sorts. Long-tailed macaque

3

AARONLAM/GETTY IMAGES ©

Kuala Lumpur

Cultural diversity and local cuisine

One of Asia's most approachable cities, Kuala Lumpur (KL) offers up an enticing multicultural landscape of fabulously designed mosques, intricate temples, busy night markets, thriving megamalls and soaring contemporary complexes such as the Petronas Towers (pictured). Plus there's a delicious food scene covering everything from freshly made rice noodles at a street stall to haute cuisine and fine wine. Malaysia's capital is also looking back to its 19th-century roots for the ambitious River of Life heritage and landscape project, which is beautifying the areas around Merdeka Square and Chinatown.

6

ROBBIE SHONE/GETTY IMAGES ©

PATRICK GIJSBERS/GETTY IMAGES ©

Sarawak

Natural wonders and cultural riches

Imagine a land where you can search for semi-wild orangutans or a giant rafflesia flower in the morning, spot proboscis monkeys and saltwater crocodiles on a cruise in the South China Sea at dusk, and then dine on superfresh seafood in a bustling, sophisticated city at nightfall. Welcome to Sarawak, in northern Borneo. From Kuching, the capital established by the White Rajas of the Brooke family, it's easy to organise trips to the state's amazing array of nature reserves, including World Heritage–listed Gunung Mulu National Park.

7

Top: Cave in Gunung Mulu National Park (p209); Bottom: Pitcher plants, Bako National Park (p208)

KORAWEE RATCHAPAKDEE/GETTY IMAGES ©

Cameron Highlands

Beautiful vistas, tea plantations and farms

Misty mountains, tea plantations, fragrant highland air, Tudor-themed architecture, 4WDs, warm scones and strawberry farms all converge in this distinctly un–Southeast Asian destination. Activities such as self-guided hiking and agricultural tourism make the Cameron Highlands one of Malaysia's most approachable active destinations. The area also represents a clever escape within a holiday, as the weather tends to stay mercifully cool year-round.

6

MOIRENC CAMILLE/HEMIS.FR/GETTY IMAGES ©

Pulau Langkawi

A tropical paradise

Pulau Langkawi isn't called the Jewel of Kedah for nothing, and its white-sand beaches, isolated resorts, diving opportunities and pristine jungles live up to the sparkling rhetoric. Cheap alcohol and some decent restaurants and bars provide just a hint of a party scene, while a glut of kid-friendly activities make it a great destination for families. And best of all, if you get just a little bit off the beaten track Pulau Langkawi will reveal its endearing rural soul.

7

Temurun Waterfall (p124)

8

Pulau Tioman

Spoiled for choice on pleasure island

What's your pleasure? Swimming off any of the dozens of serenely beautiful beaches that run down the western shore of Pulau Tioman? Taking on the serious surf that pounds the island's eastern beaches at Kampung Juara? Challenging your legs, lungs and internal compass on Tioman's myriad trails? Or perhaps chill out by a waterfall, swing in a hammock all day with a good book, or simply do nothing? All of these goals (and more) are infinitely obtainable on Pulau Tioman. Welcome to paradise. Right: Salang (p154), Pulau Tioman

ALAN COPSON/GETTY IMAGES ©

9

Melaka City

Bustling weekend night market, heritage museums and glitzy trishaws

The biggest party in Melaka is every Friday, Saturday and Sunday night when Jln Hang Jebat hosts the massively popular Jonker Walk Night Market. Start by the river across from the pink Stadthuys building that glows in the street lights and make your way through the crowds towards the karaoke stage at Jln Tokong Besi. Along the way you'll pass stalls selling everything from cheap underwear and trinkets to fresh sugarcane juice. Haggle, nibble and maybe stop by the Geographér Cafe for a cold beer and some people-watching.

PATRIK BLOMQVIST/GETTY IMAGES ©

Mt Kinabalu

Malaysia's first Unesco World Heritage site

It is the abode of the spirits, the highest mountain in Malaysia, the dominant geographic feature of northern Borneo, the granite rock that has worn out countless challengers: Mt Kinabalu is all of this, and it is one of the most popular tourism attractions in Borneo. Don't worry, though, you will still have moments of utter freedom, and, if you're lucky, enjoy a view that stretches to the Philippines. Or it will be cloudy. Whatever: the climb is still exhilarating.

10

Semporna Archipelago

One of the best diving destinations in the world

11

For the amateur diver or the seasoned veteran, the Semporna Archipelago is a dream destination, with the island of Sipadan the ultimate underwater adventure. Sipadan's seawall is filled with the world's most colourful marine life – from hundreds of chromatic coral species to the most utterly alien-looking fish (we're looking at you, frog fish), creatures here seem to have swum through every slice of the colour wheel. Sea slug, Sipadan (p194)

Kota Bharu

Crafts, cuisine and culture

12

In this centre for Malaysian culture and crafts, visitors can lose themselves shopping for traditional items such as batik, *kain songket* (handwoven fabric with gold threads), hand-crafted silverware and hand-carved puppets. The Central Market is a great place to buy local goods. For shoppers inclined to roam, the bikeable road from town to Pantai Cahaya Bulan (PCB) is lined with factories and workshops dedicated to the creation of crafts of all sorts.

Plan Your Trip
Need to Know

When to Go

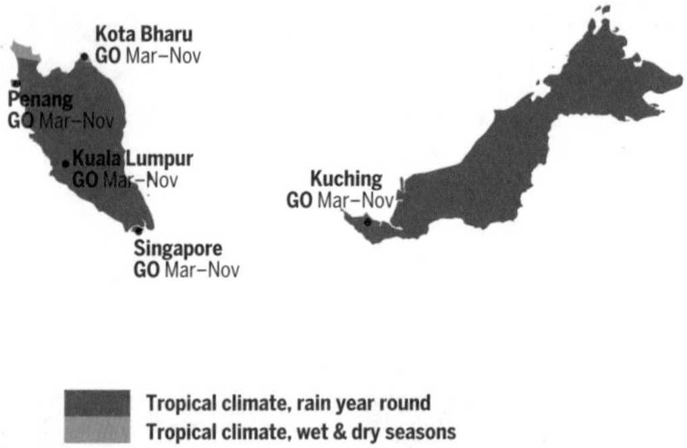

High Season *(Dec–Feb)*

- End-of-year school holidays and Chinese New Year push up prices; book hotels and transport in advance.
- Monsoon season for the east coast of Peninsular Malaysia and western Sarawak.

Shoulder *(Jul–Nov)*

- From July to August, vie with visitors escaping the heat of the Gulf States.
- The end of Ramadan also sees increased travel activity in the region.

Low Season *(Mar–Jun)*

- Avoid the worst of the rains and humidity.
- More chances to enjoy places in relative quietude.
- Be flexible with travel plans.

Currency

Malaysian ringgit (RM) Singapore dollar (S$)

Languages

Bahasa Malaysia, English, Chinese dialects, Tamil

Visas

Mostly not needed for stays under 60 days (Malaysia) and 90 days (Singapore).

Money

ATMs widespread, but check first whether overseas cards are accepted. Credit cards accepted in most hotels and restaurants.

Mobile Phones

Use local SIM cards or set your phone to roaming (but beware expensive charges).

Time

Malaysia and Singapore are eight hours ahead of GMT/UTC (London).

Daily Costs

Budget: Less than RM100/S$150

- Dorm bed: RM15–50/S$20–40
- Hawker-centre and food-court meals: RM5–7/S$3–5
- Metro ticket: RM1–2.50/S$1.60–2.70

Midrange: RM100–400/S$150–350

- Double room in a comfortable hotel: RM100–400/S$100–250
- Two-course meal at a midrange restaurant: RM40–60/S$50
- Cocktails in a decent bar: RM30–40/S$20–30

Top End: More than RM400/S$350

- Luxury double room: RM450–1000/S$250–500
- Meal at a top restaurant: RM200/S$250
- Three-day diving course: RM800–1000

Useful Websites

Tourism Malaysia (www.malaysia.travel) Official national tourist information site.

Your Singapore (www.yoursingapore.com) Official tourism-board site.

Lonely Planet (www.lonelyplanet.com) Information, bookings, forums and more.

Malaysia Asia (http://blog.malaysia-asia.my) Award-winning blog packed with local insider info.

Honeycombers (www.thehoneycombers.com) A good online guide to Singapore, covering events, eating, drinking and shopping.

XE (www.xe.com) For current exchange rates.

Opening Hours

Use the following as a general guide:

Banks 10am to 3pm Monday to Friday, 9.30am to 11.30am Saturday

Bars & clubs 5pm to 5am

Cafes 8am to 10pm

Restaurants noon to 2.30pm and 6pm to 10.30pm

Shopping malls 10am to 10pm

Shops 9.30am to 7pm

Arriving in Malaysia & Singapore

Kuala Lumpur International Airport KLIA Ekspres premium non-stop train to KL Sentral (RM55, 28 minutes, every 15 minutes from 5am to 1am). Taxis from RM75 (one hour to central KL).

Changi International Airport, Singapore Frequent MRT train and public and shuttle buses to town from 5.30am to midnight, S$2.50 to S$9. Taxis cost S$20 to S$40, 50% more between midnight and 6am.

Getting Around

Air Domestic routes from KL, other major Malaysian cities and Singapore are plentiful.

Bus Intercity buses are affordable, comfortable and often frequent; buy tickets at bus stations.

Car It's easy to rent self-drive cars everywhere.

Public transport Singapore's metro and buses are excellent; KL's public transport (metro, monorail, trains and buses) is improving, but is less reliable.

Taxi Singapore's metered taxis are affordable, reliable and honest; KL's are less so.

Train Slow but scenic; popular for overnight trips from the Thai border to Singapore.

For more on **getting around**, see p311

Plan Your Trip
If You Like...

ANTONY GIBLIN/GETTY IMAGES ©

Wildlife

Taman Negara Trek in search of elephants, tigers and tapirs in Malaysia's premier national park. (p142)

Singapore Zoo & Night Safari Possibly the world's best zoo, with wildlife living in open-air enclosures. (p234)

KL Bird Park Fabulous aviary with some 200 species flying beneath an enormous canopy. (p50)

Juara Turtle Project Do your bit on Pulau Tioman to save endangered turtles. (p159)

Semenggoh Wildlife Centre View cute ginger orangutans at this sanctuary in Sarawak. (p209)

Art Galleries

National Gallery Singapore Two historic buildings were connected and revamped for this major new art house. (p232)

National Visual Arts Gallery There's always something interesting showing at this KL-based institution. (p59)

Singapore Art Museum An excellent showcase of Asian contemporary art. (p233)

Art Galleries, Melaka Browse the small galleries scattered around the Unesco World Heritage district. (p167)

Hin Bus Depot Art Centre Hub for George Town's burgeoning art scene, with open-air areas plastered with street art. (p110)

Museums

National Museum of Singapore Interactive ingenuity applied to Singaporean history and culture. (p232)

Asian Civilisations Museum An epic journey through the history, beliefs and creativity of the world's largest continent. (p232)

Islamic Arts Museum In KL, marvel at how Islam has inspired artists and craftspeople to produce gorgeous objects. (p55)

Ethnology Museum Kuching storehouse spotlighting Borneo's incredibly rich indigenous cultures. (p207)

Baba & Nyonya Heritage Museum Lavish Peranakan mansion with lively guided tours shining a light on Melaka's past. (p166)

From left: Ceiling in the Islamic Arts Museum (p55); Singapore Botanic Gardens (p226)

KEVIN CLOGSTOUN / GETTY IMAGES ©

Gardens

Singapore Botanic Gardens World Heritage–listed haven of tropical lushness. (p226)

Gardens by the Bay A triumphant marriage of architecture and horticulture in Singapore. (p226)

KL Forest Eco Park Traverse the new canopy walkway in this pocket of primary rainforest. (p54)

Perdana Botanical Garden Dating back to the 1880s, this serene park has sections devoted to orchids and hibiscus. (p50)

Art & Garden by Fuan Wong Weird and wonderful plants combine with contemporary art in this unique Penang garden. (p110)

Scenic Vistas

Boh Sungei Palas Tea Estate Enjoy your cuppa while gazing over a verdant patchwork of hills and tea plantations. (p82)

Mt Kinabalu You can't beat the view from the top of Malaysia's tallest mountain. (p174)

Penang Hill Look across Penang and on to the mainland from this cool retreat above George Town. (p109)

Menara Kuala Lumpur An open-air observation deck and revolving restaurant with 360-degree views of the city. (p54)

Panorama Langkawi Ride the cable car to the top of Gunung Machinchang for views across the island. (p124)

Crafts & Shopping

Orchard Rd Megamalls, chic boutiques and retro gems fight for space on this legendary shopping strip. (p258)

Main Bazaar, Kuching Shop for handmade Dayak crafts, including textiles, baskets and masks. (p213)

National Textiles Museum Admire skillful weaving, embroidery, knitting and batik printing in KL. (p44)

Central Market Former 1930s wet market in an art-deco KL building that's now a top shopping location. (p62)

Publika Innovative, artsy KL mall with several galleries and a monthly crafts market. (p62)

Plan Your Trip
Month by Month

Lighting lamps for Deepavali (p24)

January

New Year is a busy travel period. It's monsoon season on Malaysia's east coast and Sarawak.

Thaipusam

Enormous crowds converge at the Batu Caves north of KL, Nattukotai Chettiar Temple in Penang and in Singapore for this dramatic Hindu festival involving body piercing. Falls between mid-January and mid-February.

February

Chinese New Year is a big deal throughout the region and a peak travel period. Book transport and hotels well ahead.

Chinese New Year

Dragon dances and pedestrian parades mark the start of the new year, and families hold open house.

Chingay

Singapore's biggest street parade (www.chingay.org.sg), a flamboyant, multicultural event, falls on the 22nd day after Chinese New Year.

April

The light monsoon season ends on Malaysia's west coast, but you should still always be prepared for rain.

Malaysian Grand Prix

Formula One's first big outing of the year in Southeast Asia is held at the Sepang International Circuit over three days, usually at the start of the month or end of March. Associated events and parties are held in KL.

May

This quiet month, prior to the busy school holidays, is a good time to visit the region.

Vesak Day celebrations

Vesak Day

Buddha's birth, enlightenment and death are celebrated with processions in KL, Singapore and other major cities, plus various events including the release of caged birds to symbolise the setting free of captive souls.

Great Singapore Sale

The Great Singapore Sale (www.greatsingaporesale.com.sg) runs from the end of May to the end of July. Retailers around the island cut prices (and wheel out the stuff they couldn't sell earlier in the year). There are bargains to be had if you can stomach the crowds. Go early!

June

School holidays and one of the hottest months, so get ready to sweat it out. Ramadan is also observed through much of this month in 2017 and 2018.

Religious Holidays

Muslim holidays follow a lunar calendar, while dates for Chinese and Hindu religious festivals are calculated using the lunisolar calendar. Muslim holidays fall around 11 days earlier each year, while Hindu and Chinese festivals change dates but fall roughly within the same months.

Dragon Boat Festival

Commemorates the Malay legend of the fishermen who paddled out to sea to prevent the drowning of a Chinese saint, beating drums to scare away any fish that might attack him. Celebrated from June to August, with boat races in Penang.

Gawai Dayak

Held on 1 and 2 June, but beginning on the evening of 31 May, this Sarawak-wide Dayak festival celebrates the end of the rice-harvest season.

Hari Raya Aidilfitri

The end of Ramadan is followed by a month of breaking-the-fast parties, many of which are public occasions where you can enjoy a free array of Malay culinary delicacies. The Malaysian prime minister opens his official home in Putrajaya to the public.

July

Busy travel month for Malaysian Borneo – book ahead for activities, tours and accommodation.

Singapore Food Festival

This month-long celebration of food includes events, cooking classes and food-themed tours.

Rainforest World Music Festival

A three-day musical extravaganza (www.rainforestmusic-borneo.com) held in the Sarawak Cultural Village near Kuching in the second week of July.

August

With a big influx of Arab and European tourists to the region during this time, it pays to book ahead for specific accommodation.

Singapore National Day

Held on 9 August (though dress rehearsals on the two prior weekends are almost as popular), Singapore National Day (www.ndp.org.sg) includes military parades, flyovers and fireworks.

George Town Festival

This outstanding arts, performance and culture festival (www.georgetownfestival.com) in Penang includes international artists and innovative street performances, and also has a fringe component in Butterworth on the mainland.

Hungry Ghosts Festival

Chinese communities perform operas, host open-air concerts and lay out food for their ancestors. Celebrated towards the end of August and in early September.

Malaysia's National Day

Join the crowds at midnight on 31 August to celebrate the anniversary of Malaysia's independence in 1957.

September

Haze from forest and field clearance fires in Indonesia create urban smog across the region.

Formula One Grand Prix

It's Singapore's turn to host the Formula One crowd with a night race (www.singaporegp.sg) on a scenic city-centre circuit. Book well in advance for hotel rooms with a view.

October

Start of the monsoon season on Malaysia's west coast, but it's not so heavy or constant to affect most travel plans.

Deepavali

Tiny oil lamps are lit outside Hindu homes to attract the auspicious gods Rama and Lakshmi. Indian businesses start the new financial year, with Little Indias across the region ablaze with lights.

December

A sense of festivity (and monsoon rains in Singapore and east coast Malaysia) permeates the air as the year winds down. Christmas is a big deal mainly in Singapore, with impressive light displays on Orchard Rd.

Zoukout

Held on Siloso Beach, Sentosa, this annual outdoor dance party (www.zoukout.com) is one of the region's best such events with a 25,000-strong crowd shimmying to international DJs.

Plan Your Trip
Get Inspired

Read

Singapore: A Biography (2010) Mark Ravinder Frost & Yu-Mei Balasingchow's well-written and handsomely illustrated history of Singapore.

Malaysia at Random (2010) Quirky compendium of facts, quotes and anecdotes.

The Garden of the Evening Mists (2012) Tan Twan Eng's tale of intrigue in the Malaysian highlands.

Little Ironies: Short Stories of Singapore (1978) A collection by the doyenne of Singaporean fiction, Catherine Lim.

Urban Odysseys (2010) Short stories set in Kuala Lumpur, edited by Janet Tay and Eric Forbes.

Watch

Ilo Ilo (Anthony Chen; 2013) A 2013 Cannes Film Festival award winner, this touching story is about a troubled Chinese-Singaporean boy and his Filipino maid.

Bunohan (Dain Said; 2012) Moody, slow-moving thriller about a kickboxer on the run and troubled family relations on the Kelantan coast.

The Blue House (2009) Penang's Cheong Fatt Tze Mansion hosts this Singaporean comedy thriller directed by Glen Goei.

881 (2007) Royston Tan's camp musical about *getai* (stage singing).

Sepet (2004) A Chinese boy falls for a Malay girl in Yasmin Ahmad's movie.

Listen

Angin Kencang (Noh Salleh) EP of melodic indie guitar pop by a male vocalist; hailed as one of 2014's best local releases.

Nocturnal (Yuna; www.yunamusic.com) Poster girl for Malaysian young 'hijabsters' with a soulful voice to match her sultry looks.

40th Anniversary Collection (Dick Lee; www.dicklee.com) A Singaporean national treasure, Lee has been making music since the 1970s.

Above: Interior detail, Sri Veeramakaliamman Temple (p247), Singapore

Five-Day Itinerary

Singapore to KL

Singapore is the perfect introduction to the region's rich mix of cultures, Melaka is Malaysia's most historic city, while KL offers another contemporary take on Southeast Asian life.

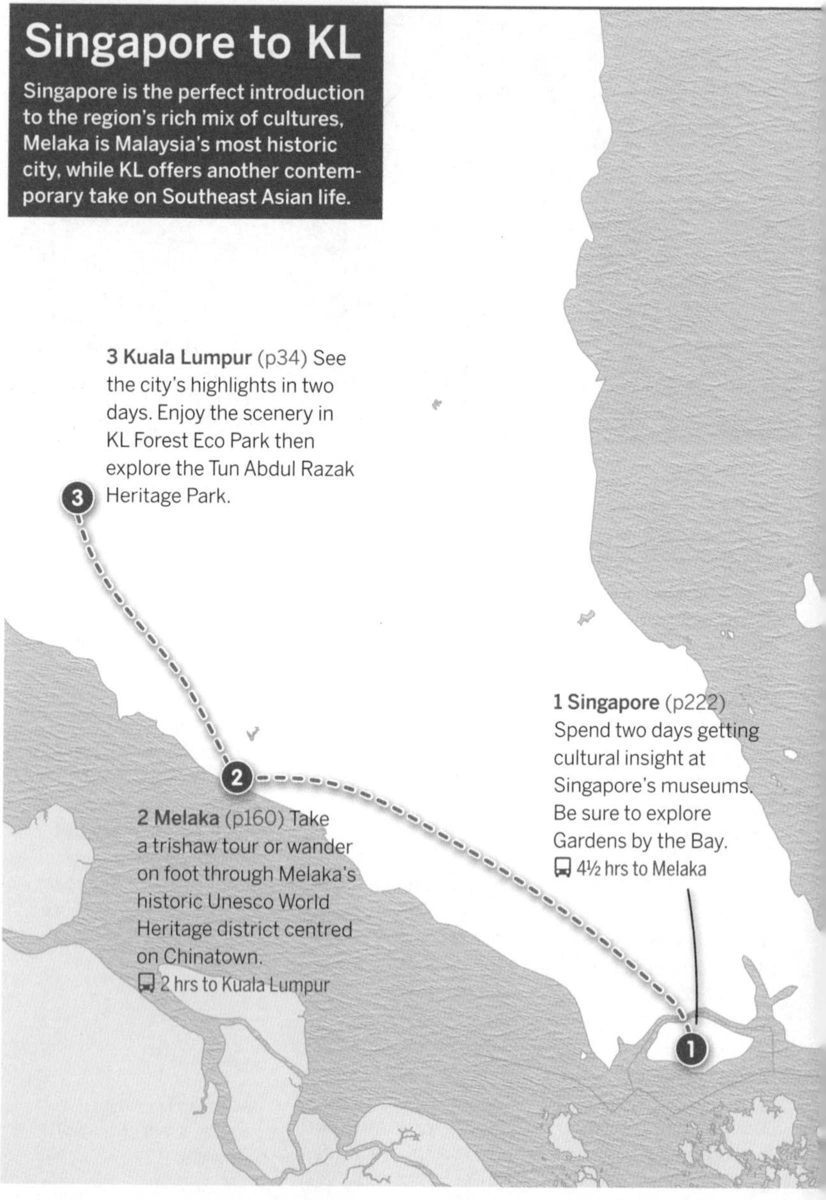

3 Kuala Lumpur (p34) See the city's highlights in two days. Enjoy the scenery in KL Forest Eco Park then explore the Tun Abdul Razak Heritage Park.

1 Singapore (p222) Spend two days getting cultural insight at Singapore's museums. Be sure to explore Gardens by the Bay.
🚌 4½ hrs to Melaka

2 Melaka (p160) Take a trishaw tour or wander on foot through Melaka's historic Unesco World Heritage district centred on Chinatown.
🚌 2 hrs to Kuala Lumpur

1

2

3

Plan Your Trip

Ten-Day Itinerary

Langkawi to Taman Negara

This jaunt around Peninsular Malaysia offers up beautiful beaches, heritage streetscapes, fabulous food, gentle hikes and wildlife spotting.

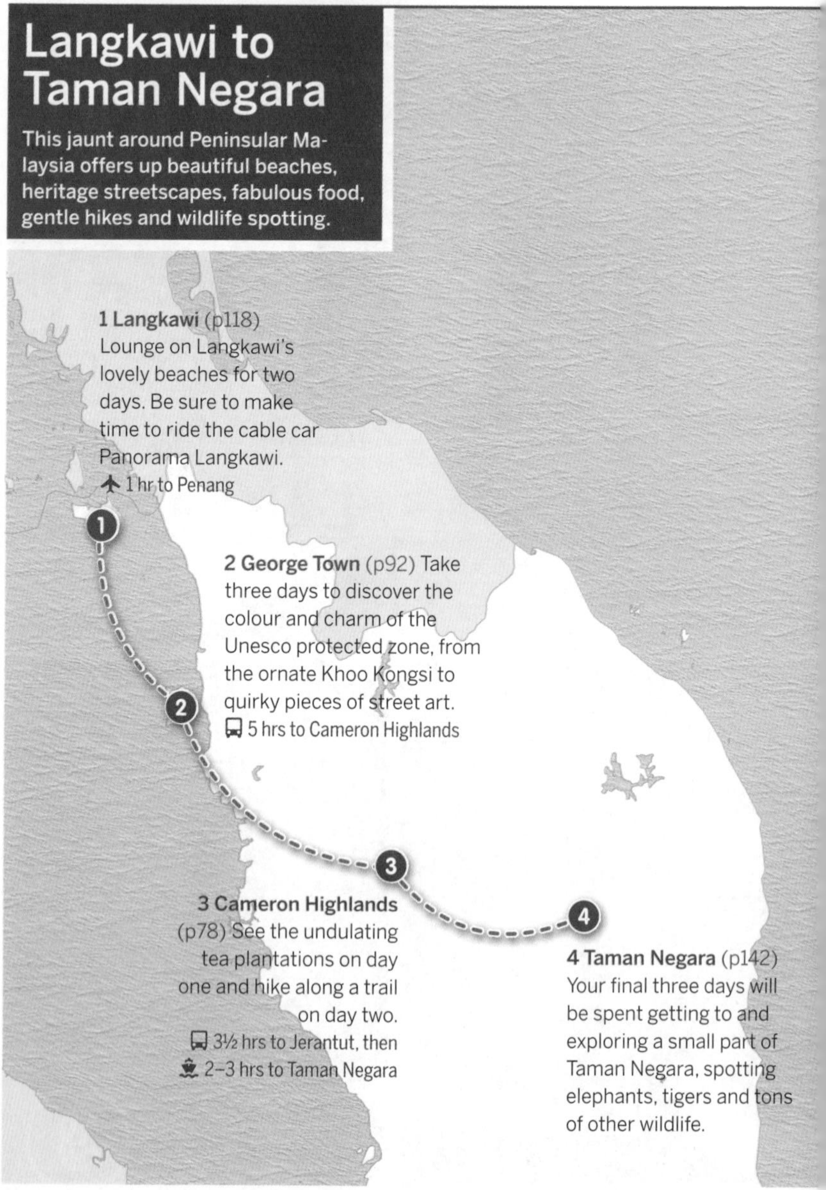

1 Langkawi (p118) Lounge on Langkawi's lovely beaches for two days. Be sure to make time to ride the cable car Panorama Langkawi.
✈ 1 hr to Penang

2 George Town (p92) Take three days to discover the colour and charm of the Unesco protected zone, from the ornate Khoo Kongsi to quirky pieces of street art.
🚌 5 hrs to Cameron Highlands

3 Cameron Highlands (p78) See the undulating tea plantations on day one and hike along a trail on day two.
🚌 3½ hrs to Jerantut, then
⛴ 2–3 hrs to Taman Negara

4 Taman Negara (p142) Your final three days will be spent getting to and exploring a small part of Taman Negara, spotting elephants, tigers and tons of other wildlife.

TOP: TAKEO1775/GETTY IMAGES ©; BOTTOM LEFT: JD DALLET/GETTY IMAGES ©; BOTTOM RIGHT: APEXPHOTOS/GETTY IMAGES ©

Plan Your Trip
Two-Week Itinerary

Kota Bharu to Kuching

If diving, wildlife-spotting and trekking sound like your idea of travel heaven, this activity-packed itinerary is the one to go for.

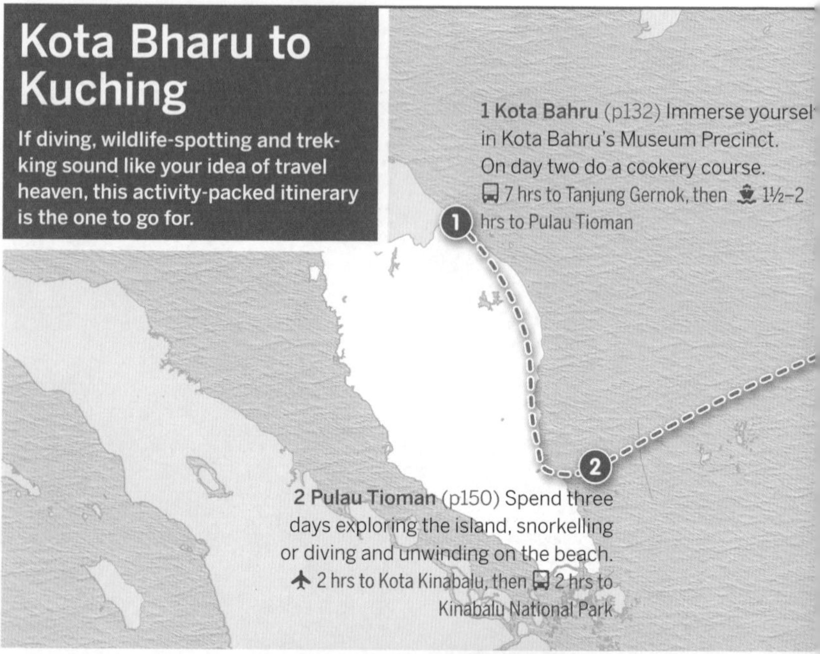
1 Kota Bahru (p132) Immerse yoursel
in Kota Bahru's Museum Precinct.
On day two do a cookery course.
7 hrs to Tanjung Gernok, then 1½–2
hrs to Pulau Tioman
2 Pulau Tioman (p150) Spend three
days exploring the island, snorkelling
or diving and unwinding on the beach.
2 hrs to Kota Kinabalu, then 2 hrs to
Kinabalu National Park

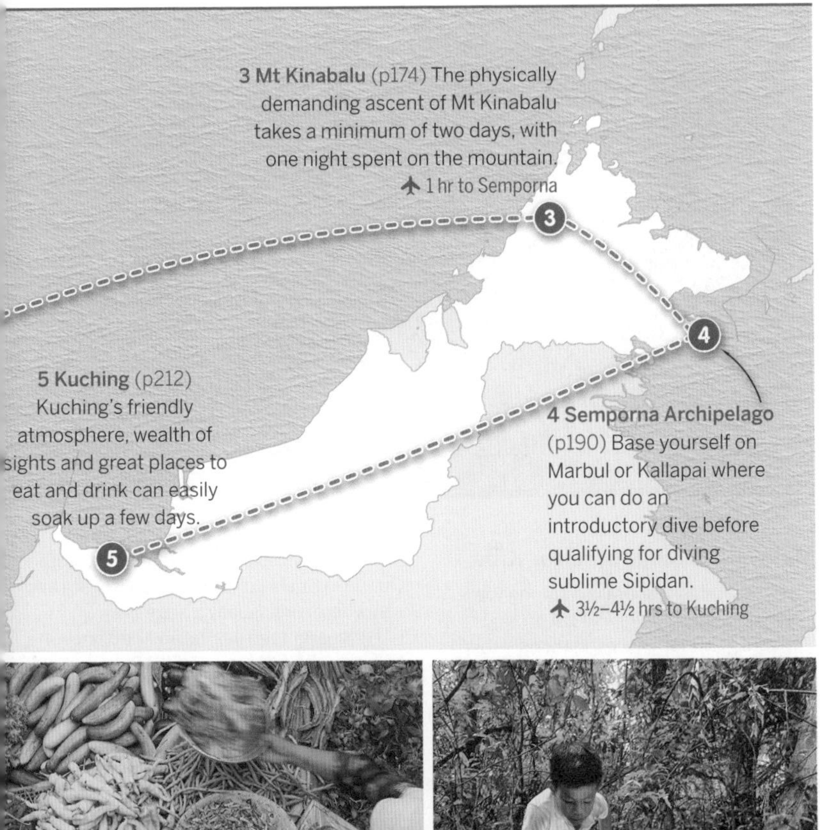

3 Mt Kinabalu (p174) The physically demanding ascent of Mt Kinabalu takes a minimum of two days, with one night spent on the mountain.
✈ 1 hr to Semporna

5 Kuching (p212) Kuching's friendly atmosphere, wealth of sights and great places to eat and drink can easily soak up a few days.

4 Semporna Archipelago (p190) Base yourself on Marbul or Kallapai where you can do an introductory dive before qualifying for diving sublime Sipidan.
✈ 3½–4½ hrs to Kuching

Plan Your Trip
Family Travel

AJPHOTO.GRAPHIC/GETTY IMAGES ©

Malaysia & Singapore for Kids

Malaysia and Singapore are among the easiest countries in Asia to get around. Both are great family destinations – take the kids on trishaw rides, watch temple ceremonies, see wildlife in a world-class zoo or in national parks, and taste some of the best food on the continent. Plus there's access to clean accommodation, modern malls with all the facilities you'll find at home (and more!), and brilliant beaches.

Sights & Activities

Malaysia and Singapore's profusion of gorgeous beach-fringed islands and dense jungles, with soaring trees populated by cheeky monkeys, are straight out of an exotic story land. The cities have verdant parks, often with top-grade play areas.

Those with older children might enjoy some of the jungle parks, including Taman Negara and, over in Sarawak, the Bako and Gunung Mulu National Parks. As long as your kids are not afraid of heights, the canopy walkways strung through the treetops (found in Kuala Lumpur, Taman Negara and elsewhere) are usually a huge hit.

For guaranteed animal and bird encounters also consider the KL Bird Park and Singapore's excellent zoo, night safari and river safari. Snorkelling off some of the safer island beaches will give you a peek at sea life; there are also aquariums in KL, Langkawi and Singapore.

Singapore's museums are super kid-friendly, with creative audio-visual displays. Malaysia's museums are not quite in the same grade, but still worth visiting for cultural and educational background.

Dining Out

Food is a highlight here and there's a lot on offer that kids will love. Contrary to Western impulse, a busy street food stall is usually the safest place to eat – you can see the food being prepared, the ingredients are often very fresh, and there's little chance of harmful bacteria existing in a scalding-hot

Tiger at Singapore Zoo (p234)

wok. Grown-ups can also try more adventurous dishes, while the kids get something more familiar.

Many restaurants attached to hotels and guesthouses will serve familiar Western food; international fast food is everywhere.

Breastfeeding in public should be discreet (Malaysia is a Muslim country, so avoid showing any skin). Local women publicly breastfeed very rarely, using their headscarves for extra coverage.

Local drinks tend to be very sweet and even fresh juices may have sugar added. It's not a bad idea to ask for drinks without sugar or to order bottled water.

Need to Know

Change facilities Available in large malls and some top-end hotels.

Cots By special request at midrange and top-end hotels.

Health Drink a lot of water; wash hands regularly; warn children against playing with animals.

Highchairs Sometimes available in city restaurants as well as resort areas.

Kids' menus Common in cities but usually in Western-style establishments.

Nappies (diapers) Available in supermarkets and convenience stores.

Strollers Bring a compact umbrella stroller.

Toilets Western-style toilets are common, but always carry some toilet paper with you – most will not have any.

Transport Discounted fares are available.

Best Sights & Destinations for Kids

Pantai Cenang (p122)

Sentosa Island (p252)

Taman Negara (p142)

Singapore Zoo (p234)

Menara Kuala Lumpur (p54)

Enjoy spectacular city views from Titiwangsa Lake Gardens (p59)

KUALA LUMPUR

Don't miss the iconic Petronas Towers (p38)

Kuala Lumpur

Malaysia's sultry capital, Kuala Lumpur (KL) is a city of brash juxtaposition, packed with historic monuments, lush parks, mega-sized shopping malls, bustling street markets and trendy nightspots. Its skyline is punctuated by steel-clad skyscrapers, minarets and Mughal-style domes, while its colourful streets are shaded by a leafy canopy of banyan trees.

This city also offers a mouth-watering mix of Asian culinary traditions – everything from superb street food to fine dining with all the trimmings.

Kuala Lumpur in Two Days

Get your bearings from atop **Menara Kuala Lumpur** (p54) and explore the rainforest park at the tower's base. Follow our **walking tour** (p52) of nearby Chinatown and Merdeka Square. On day two immerse yourself in the **Perdana Botanical Gardens** (p50), **KL Bird Park** (p50) and **Islamic Arts Museum** (p55) or **National Museum** (p58). Trawl the night food stalls of **Jalan Alor** (p70).

Kuala Lumpur in Four Days

Explore the Malay area of **Kampung Baru** (p52) and the Indian area of **Brickfields** (p55). The nearby **Thean Hou Temple** (p58) provides great views across KL. On your final day climb the 272 steps at **Batu Caves** (p46) in the morning and visit the **National Visual Arts Gallery** (p59) in the afternoon. Toast the city with a sunset cocktail at **Heli Lounge Bar** (p71).

0 1 km
0 0.5 miles

PETRONAS TOWERS

KLCC
KLCC is the vast development anchored by the Petronas Towers.

Bukit Nanas & Chinatown
You don't have to look too hard to find traces of old KL in Chinatown's shophouse-lined streets.

IATOWN ERDEKA UARE

Tun Abdul Razak Heritage Park & Brickfields
The Tun Abdul Razak Heritage Park remains a lush breathing space in the heart of KL.

Golden Triangle & Around
Golden Triangle is home to major shopping malls and excellent places to eat, including Jln Alor.

Bukit Nanas & Chinatown (p56)
Tun Abdul Razak Heritage Park, Brickfields & Bangsar Baru (p60)
KLCC & Golden Triangle (p66)
Masjid India, Kampung Baru & Titiwangsa (p68)

Menara Kuala Lumpur (p54)

Stroll through Kampung Baru (p52)

BATU CAVES
(8km)

Titiwangsa
The leafy surroun
of Lake Titiwangsa
provide respite fro
the city with parks
the chance to watc
performing arts.

Kampung Baru & Around
Kampung Baru is a Malay village within the heart of the modern city.

Masjid India
Masjid India is KL's second Little India area, teeming with fabric and clothing shops and not to be missed for its Saturday night market.

TUN ABDUL RAZAK HERITAGE PARK

Bangsar & Around
The upscale residential area of Bangsar is one of the top locations in the city in which to shop and eat.

Sungai Gombak
Sungai Klang
Tasik Perdana
Kuala Lumpur
KL Sentral
CH
& M
S
KL Inter

Macaques, Tun Abdul Razak Heritage Park (p48)

Arriving in Kuala Lumpur

Kuala Lumpur International Airport (KLIA) KLIA Ekspres premium non-stop train to KL Sentral (RM55, 28 minutes, every 15 minutes from 5am to 1am) or airport bus to KL Sentral (RM10, one hour, every hour from 5am to 1am). Taxis to central KL from RM75 (one hour).

KL Sentral Train, LRT, monorail, bus and taxi links to the rest of city. Taxi is by prepaid coupon to Chinatown/Golden Triangle (RM13).

Sleeping

Practically all midrange and top-end places offer promotions that substantially slash rack rates; booking online will almost always bring the price down. Room discounts will not apply during public holidays.

For information on where to stay see p77.

DAVID SANTIAGO GARCIA/GETTY IMAGES ©

Petronas Towers

This iconic building anchors the Kuala Lumpur City Centre (KLCC), a 40-hectare development including a tropical park, world-class concert hall and the Suria KLCC shopping mall.

Great For...

☑ **Don't Miss**

The view from the 86th floor of the Petronas Towers.

Petronas Towers

Resembling twin silver rockets plucked from an episode of *Flash Gordon*, the Petronas Towers are the perfect allegory for the meteoric rise of the city from tin-miners' hovel to 21st-century metropolis.

Completed back in 1998, the shimmering stainless-steel-clad towers were designed by Argentinian architect Cesar Pelli as the headquarters of the national oil and gas company Petronas. The 88-storey twin towers are the tallest pair in the world at nearly 452m and their floor plan is based on an eight-sided star that echoes arabesque patterns. Islamic influences are also evident in each tower's five tiers – representing the five pillars of Islam – and in the 63m masts that crown them, calling to mind the minarets of a mosque and the Star of Islam.

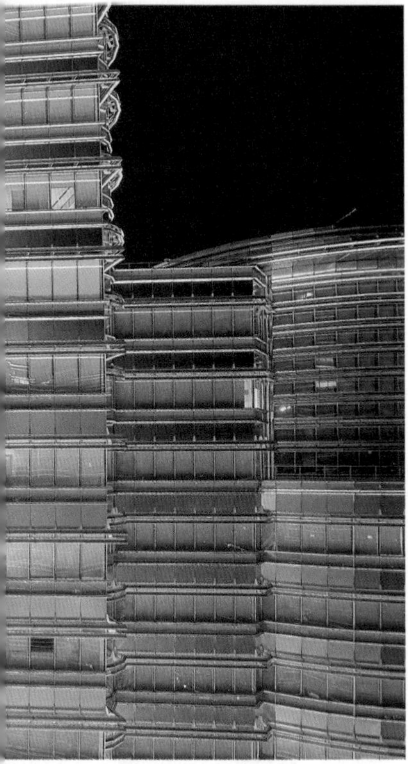

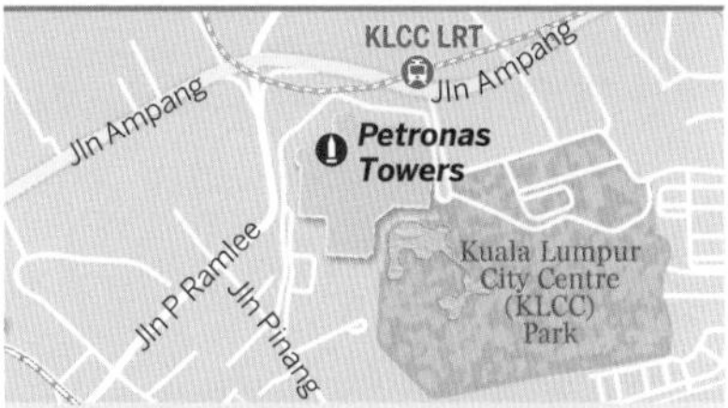

Need to Know

Map p66; ☎03-2331 8080; www.petronas-twintowers.com.my; Jln Ampang; adult/child RM84.80/31.80; ⌚9am-9pm Tue-Sun, closed 1-2.30pm Fri; 👪; Ⓜ KLCC

Take a Break

Suria KLCC (p62) has scores of restaurants and two food courts.

★ Top Tip

At 8pm, 9pm and 10pm the Lake Symphony fountains play in KLCC Park.

They look particularly impressive when illuminated at night.

A 45-minute guided tour takes in the Skybridge connection on the 41st floor and the observation deck on the 86th floor at 370m; half of the 1440 daily tour tickets are sold in advance online.

KLCC Park

This **park** (Map p66; KLCC, Jln Ampang; ⌚7am-10pm; Ⓜ KLCC) is the best vantage point for eyeballing the Petronas Towers. In the early evening, it can seem like everyone in town has come down here to watch the glowing columns punching up into the night sky. A 1.3km soft-surface jogging track winds its way around the park past the excellent children's playground, paddling pool and Masjid Asy-Syakirin.

Aquaria KLCC

The highlight of this impressive **aquarium** (Map p66; ☎03-2333 1888; www.aquariaklcc.com; Concourse, KL Convention Centre, Jln Pinang; adult/child RM53/42; ⌚10.30am-8pm, last admission 7pm; 👪; Ⓜ KLCC) in the basement of the KL Convention Centre is its 90m underwater tunnel, where you can view sand tiger sharks, giant gropers and more up close. Daily feeding sessions for a variety of fish and otters are complemented by ones for arapaima, electric eels and sharks on Monday, Wednesday and Saturday (see website for schedule). Free dives (RM424), cage dives (RM211), and a Sleep with Sharks (RM211) program for kids aged six to 13 are also available.

Galeri Petronas

Swap consumerism for culture at this excellent **art gallery** (Map p66; ☎03-2051 7770; www.galeripetronas.com.my; 3rd fl, Suria KLCC, Jln Ampang; ⌚10am-8pm Tue-Sun; Ⓜ KLCC) FREE showcasing contemporary photography and paintings. It's a bright, modern space with interesting, professionally curated shows that change every few months.

Chinatown & Merdeka Square

Bracketing the confluence of the Gombak and Klang Rivers, these two areas are where KL was born and developed during the latter part of the 19th century. Chinese gang bosses and eminent colonial architects have left their mark in the form of grand secular and religious buildings and in the bustling streetscape, including a colourful night market.

Great For...

Need to Know

These areas are at the heart of KL's ambitious River of Life urban regeneration project.

Sri Mahamariamman Temple (p42)

★ **Top Tip**

There's a great view of Masjid Jamek illuminated at night from the nearby LRT station platform.

Sin Sze Si Ya Temple

Kuala Lumpur's oldest Chinese **temple** (Map p56; Jln Tun HS Lee; 7am-5pm; M Pasar Seni) FREE was built on the instructions of Kapitan Yap Ah Loy and is dedicated to Sin Sze Ya and Si Sze Ya, two Chinese immigrants instrumental in Yap's ascension to Kapitan status. Several beautiful objects decorate the temple, including two hanging carved panels, but the best feature is the almost frontier-like atmosphere.

Sri Mahamariamman Temple

The lively **Sri Mahamariamman Temple** (Map p56; 163 Jln Tun HS Lee; 6am-8.30pm, till 9.30pm Fri; M Pasar Seni) FREE – Malaysia's oldest Hindu temple and rumoured to be the richest – was founded in 1873. Mariamman is the South Indian mother goddess, also known as Parvati. Her shrine is at the back of the complex. On the left sits a shrine to the elephant-headed Ganesh, and on the right one to Lord Murugan. During the Thaipusam festival, Lord Murugan is transported on a silver chariot from the temple to Batu Caves.

Medan Pasar

Pedestrianised Medan Pasar (which translates as Market Square) was once the heart of Chinatown. Kapitan Yap Ah Loy lived here, and in addition to holding the city's wet market, it was a place of brothels and illegal gambling dens (now long gone). In the centre stands an art-deco clock tower built in 1937 to commemorate the coronation of King George VI.

Chinatown market

Central Market

This 1930s art deco building (a former wet market) was rescued from demolition in the 1980s and transformed into a tourist-oriented arts and crafts centre. There are some excellent shops, some good restaurants, and the fascinating private Museum of Ethnic Arts (p62) in the annexe.

Chan She Shu Yuen Clan Association Temple

Opened in 1906 to serve immigrants with the surname Chan, this Cantonese-style **temple** (Map p56; ☎03-2078 1461; Jln Petaling; ⌚9am-6pm; monorail Maharajalela) FREE is a beauty. Decorative panels of 100-year-old Shek Wan pottery adorn the facade and eaves, while side gables swirl like giant waves. Inside the high-ceilinged main hall an altar enshrines the three ancestors of the Chan clan.

☑ **Don't Miss**

The elegant Panggung Bandaraya theatre, which hosts the musical show Mud (p72), about KL's early history.

FEARGUS COONEY/GETTY IMAGES ©

Guandi Temple

Founded in 1886, this atmospheric **temple** (Map p56; Jln Tun HS Lee; ⌚7am-5pm; MPasar Seni) FREE is dedicated to Guandi, a historical Chinese general known as the Taoist god of war, but more commonly worshipped as the patron of righteous brotherhoods: he is in fact patron of both police forces and triad gangs. The temple's high ceilings, red walls, tiled eaves and pointy gable-ends give it a distinctive look that's great for photos.

Masjid Jamek

Gracefully designed in Mughal style by British architect AB Hubback, the onion-domed **Masjid Jamek** (Friday Mosque; Map p56; off Jln Tun Perak; ⌚9am-12.30pm & 2.30-4pm, closed Fri; MMasjid Jamek) FREE is situated at the confluence of the Gombak and Klang Rivers. At the time of writing, the surroundings were being re-landscaped as part of the River of Life project, and the original steps down to the river reinstated. You can visit the interior, outside of prayer times, but dress conservatively and remember to remove your shoes before entering the prayer halls.

Masjid Jamek was the first brick mosque in Malaysia when completed in 1907, and the city's centre of Islamic worship until the opening of the National Mosque in 1965. The small Islamic Experience Centre, on the left as you enter the compound, has some informative displays on Islam.

✕ **Take a Break**

The stalls of Madras Lane Hawkers (p64) serve a tasty selection of local dishes.

KL City Gallery

Pick up brochures and travel information at the **KL City Gallery** (Map p56; ☎03-2691 1382; www.klcitygallery.com; 27 Jln Raja, Merdeka Sq; admission RM5; ⏰9am-6.30pm; Ⓜ Masjid Jamek) set in the former Government Printing Office (built 1898), before exploring the small exhibition on Kuala Lumpur's history. On the 2nd floor there's a large scale model of KL, and you can watch a seven-minute film on the past, present and future of the city.

Sultan Abdul Samad Building

Dominating the eastern side of Merdeka Square, the **Sultan Abdul Samad Building** (Map p56; Jln Raja; Ⓜ Masjid Jamek) was the first public building in Malaysia designed in the Mughal (or Indo-Saracenic) style, and influenced countless others across the city. Built in 1897 as the secretariat for the colonial administration, and designed by AC Norman (an associate of AB Hubback), it now houses a national ministry. The building looks particularly impressive after dark, when its copper domes and 41m clock tower are lit up.

National Textiles Museum

The excellent **National Textiles Museum** (Muzium Tekstil Negara; Map p56; ☎03-2694 3457; www.muziumtekstilnegara.gov.my; Jln Sultan Hishamuddin; ⏰9am-6pm; Ⓜ Masjid Jamek) FREE occupies an elegant Mughal-style building originally constructed for the railway works department. The lower floors cover the history of textiles, in particular Malaysian fabrics such as *songket* (silk or cotton with gold threading), and the traditional process and machinery used in manufacturing. Gorgeous examples of clothing and fabric abound. The upper floors cover Malaysian fabrics and design motifs in greater detail, as well as items for personal adornment such as jewellery and headgear.

St Mary's Anglican Cathedral

This handsome Gothic-revival English country **church** (Map p56; ☎03-2692 8672; www.stmaryscathedral.org.my; Jln Raja; Ⓜ Masjid Jamek) was designed by government architect AC Norman and erected in 1894. It was the first brick church in Malaysia, and it still maintains a small Anglican congregation. Inside is a fine pipe organ built in 1895 by Henry Willis (though since heavily restored), the Englishman responsible for the organ in St Paul's Cathedral in London. It's now dedicated to Sir Henry Gurney, the British high commissioner to Malaya, assassinated in 1951 during the Emergency.

Muzium Musik

The new **Muzium Musik** (Music Museum; Map p56; www.jmm.gov.my; Jln Raja, Merdeka Sq; ⏰9am-6pm; Ⓜ Masjid Jamek) FREE has one floor of exhibits on the history and variety of traditional music from the region. Among the things you'll learn from the displays is that Orang Asli believe music can ward off evil spirits. The building itself, one of the most striking around Merdeka Square, was formerly the Chartered Bank Building, built in 1891.

Dragon statue, Guandi Temple (p43)

Batu Caves

This dramatic limestone crag riddled with caverns is both a natural marvel and a religious site, with its holy Hindu shrines, multicoloured dioramas and giant gilded statue of Murugan.

Great For...

☑ Don't Miss

The Thaipusam festival in late Jan or early Feb – hundreds of thousands of pilgrims attend.

Temple Cave

In 1890, K Thambusamy Pillai, founder of the Sri Mahamariamman Temple in KL, placed a statue of Lord Murugan inside the main Batu cavern, the so-called **Temple Cave** (8am-8.30pm; Batu Caves) FREE – actually two enormous caverns joined by a short flight of stairs.

At the foot of the 272 steps leading to the main dome-shaped cavern stands a 42.7m golden statue of Murugan. It was erected in 2006 and is said to be the largest in the world.

Ramayana Cave

No cave at Batu is more spectacularly over-embellished and enjoyable to visit than the **Ramayana Cave** (admission RM5; 8.30am-6pm; Batu Caves), which boasts gaudy dioramas of the Indian epic Rama-

Murugan statue

PAUL KENNEDY/GETTY IMAGES ©

Need to Know

Trains run from KL Sentral to Batu Caves (RM2.60, 30 minutes).

Take a Break

There's a block of food outlets on the right at the foot of Batu Caves.

★ Top Tip

The Batu Caves limestone outcrop is also one of Malaysia's major rock-climbing locations.

yana. Near the entrance, look for the giant statue of Kumbhakarna, brother of Ravana and a deep sleeper (he once snoozed for six months). At the top of the towering cave interior is a shrine to a naturally occurring linga. This phallic-like stalagmite is a symbol of Shiva.

Dark Cave

At step 204, on the way up to the Temple Cave, branch off to the **Dark Cave** (012-371 5001; www.darkcavemalaysia.com; adult/child RM35/25; 10am-5pm Tue-Fri, 10.30am-5.30pm Sat & Sun; Batu Caves) to join a 45-minute guided tour along 800m of the 2km of surveyed passageways within the cave complex. The tour takes you through seven different chambers where you can witness dramatic limestone formations (including gorgeous flowstones), see pits used for guano extraction, and possibly spot two species of bat and hundreds of other life forms, including the rare trapdoor spider.

Tours run every 20 minutes and are organised by the Malaysian Nature Society. To get further into the cave on the three- to four-hour Adventure Tour you need a minimum of 10 people (RM80 per person); bookings must be made at least one week in advance.

Zoo Negara

A trip to Batu Caves can easily be combined with a visit to **Zoo Negara** (National Zoo; 03-4108 3422; www.zoonegaramalaysia.my; adult/child RM53/27, giant pandas RM85/43; 9am-5pm). Laid out over 62 hectares around a central lake, the zoo, 13km northeast of KL, is home to a wide variety of native wildlife, including tigers and animals from other parts of Asia and Africa. One of the most popular new exhibits is the giant panda enclosure. Although some of the enclosures could definitely be bigger, this is one of Asia's better zoos.

Tun Abdul Razak Heritage Park

Once known as the Lake Gardens, this verdant recreation area is now named after the country's second prime minister. The botanical garden laid out during British days remains at the park's heart and is flanked by one of the city's top attractions, the KL Bird Park. The Islamic Arts Museum and National Museum are also nearby.

Great For...

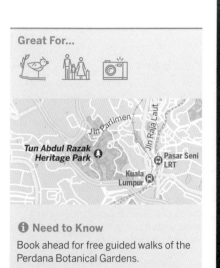

Need to Know

Book ahead for free guided walks of the Perdana Botanical Gardens.

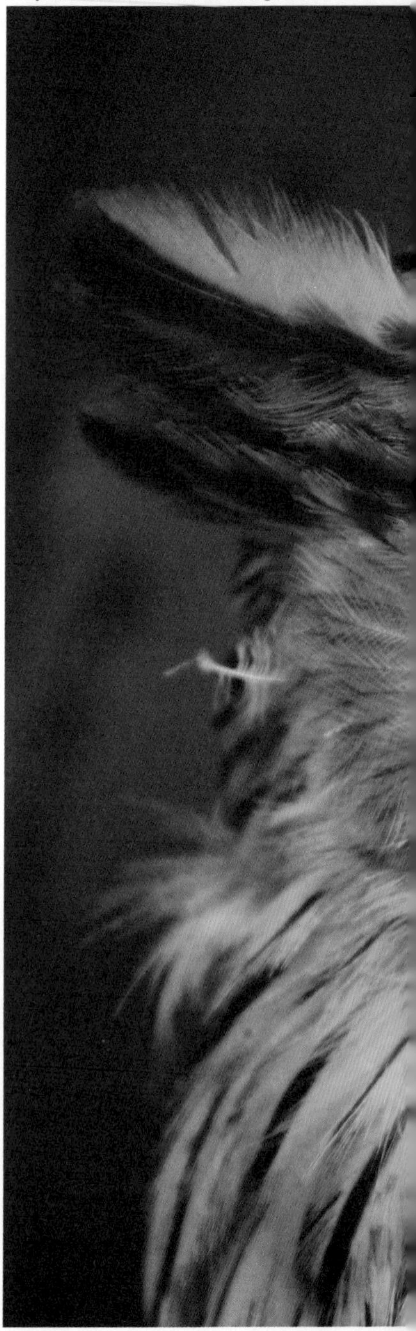
Buffy fish owl, Tun Abdul Razak Heritage Park

★ **Top Tip**

Use the electric tram (RM4/2 per adult/child) to get around the park.

KL Bird Park

This fabulous 21-hectare **aviary** (Map p60; 03-2272 1010; www.klbirdpark.com; Jln Cenderawasih; adult/child RM50/41; 9am-6pm; Kuala Lumpur) houses some 3000 birds comprising 200 species of (mostly) Asian birds. The park is divided into four sections: in the first two, birds fly freely beneath an enormous canopy. Section three features the native hornbills (so-called because of their enormous beaks), while section four offers the less-edifying spectacle of caged species.

Feeding times are scattered throughout the day (see the website for times) and there are bird shows at 12.30pm and 3.30pm.

Perdana Botanical Gardens

The vast **Perdana Botanical Garden** (Map p60; 03-2617 6404; www.klbotanicalgarden.gov.my; 7am-8pm; ; Kuala Lumpur) FREE is planted with a wide variety of native and overseas plants, trees and shrubs. Sections are dedicated to rare fruit trees, herbs, heliconias, ferns and cycads, among other species. Contact the park to book onto a free guided walk (8am and 10am Sunday).

The park has recently undergone major renovations. New features include more specialised gardens, an ornamental waterfall, a visitors centre and a rebuilt amphitheatre.

Orchids, Perdana Botanical Gardens

The **Orchid & Hibiscus Gardens** (Taman Orkid; Map p60; Jln Cenderawasih; admission Sat & Sun RM1, Mon-Fri free; 9am-6pm; Kuala Lumpur) are adjacent to the Botanical Garden. Among the 800-odd species of orchid are Vandas and exotic hybrids. There's also a stall where you can buy orchids. The hibiscus is Malaysia's national flower and the garden has more than 200 colourful hybrids – with names such as Miniskirt and Hawaiian Girl – that flower year-round.

☑ Don't Miss

The excellent children's playground at the park's north end and, near the lake, the deer park, home to mouse deer and spotted deer.

TOM COCKREM/GETTY IMAGES ©

National Monument

At the north end of the park, across Jln Parlimen, the hugely impressive **National Monument** (Map p60; Plaza Tugu Negara, Jln Parlimen; 7am-6pm; M Masjid Jamek, then taxi) FREE commemorates the defeat of the communists in 1950 and provides fine views across the park and city. The giant militaristic bronze sculpture was created in 1966 by Felix de Weldon, the artist behind the Iwo Jima monument in Washington, DC, and is framed beautifully by an azure reflecting pool and graceful curved pavilion.

Nearby is a cenotaph to the Malay fighters who died in WWI and WWII, and at the foot of the hill a quirky sculpture garden commemorating the 20th anniversary of the founding of the Association of South East Asian Nations (ASEAN).

KL Butterfly Park

Billed as the largest enclosed butterfly garden in the world, the **KL Butterfly Park** (Taman Rama Rama; Map p60; 03-2693 4799; www.klbutterflypark.com; Jln Cenderasari; adult/child RM20/10; 9am-6pm; Kuala Lumpur) is a great place to get up close with a hundred or so of the 1100-plus butterfly species found in Malaysia, including the enormous and well-named birdwings, the elegant swallowtails, and the colourful tigers and jezebels. There's also a bug gallery where you can shudder at the size of Malaysia's giant centipedes and spiders.

Take a Break

Hornbill Restaurant (p70), beside the KL Bird Park's entrance, serves tasty food.

A Stroll Through Kampung Baru

This walk reveals a time capsule of a Malay village in the heart of KL, passing traditional wood houses on stilts, a mosque and a Sikh shrine, as well as great places to snack on local dishes.

Start monorail Chow Kit

Distance 2.4km

Duration 2 hours

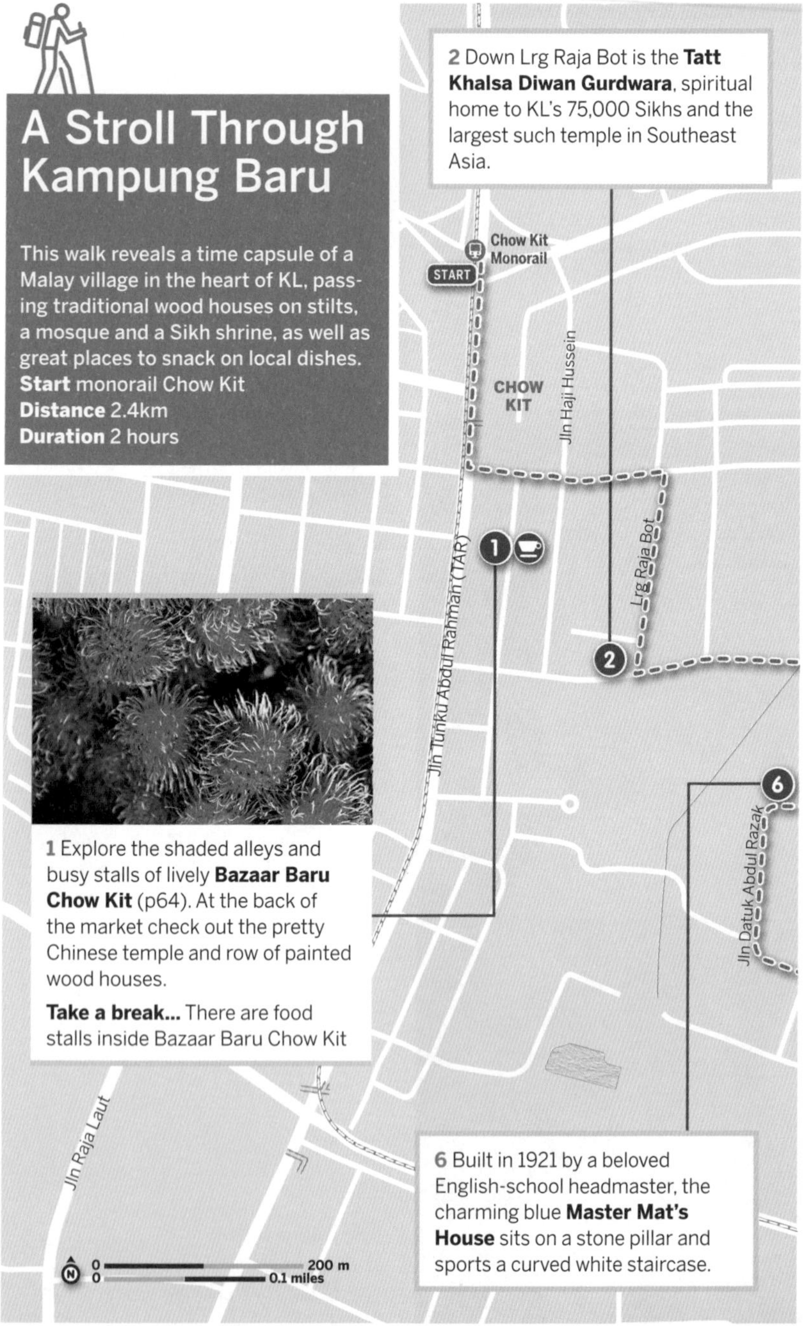

2 Down Lrg Raja Bot is the **Tatt Khalsa Diwan Gurdwara**, spiritual home to KL's 75,000 Sikhs and the largest such temple in Southeast Asia.

1 Explore the shaded alleys and busy stalls of lively **Bazaar Baru Chow Kit** (p64). At the back of the market check out the pretty Chinese temple and row of painted wood houses.

Take a break... There are food stalls inside Bazaar Baru Chow Kit

6 Built in 1921 by a beloved English-school headmaster, the charming blue **Master Mat's House** sits on a stone pillar and sports a curved white staircase.

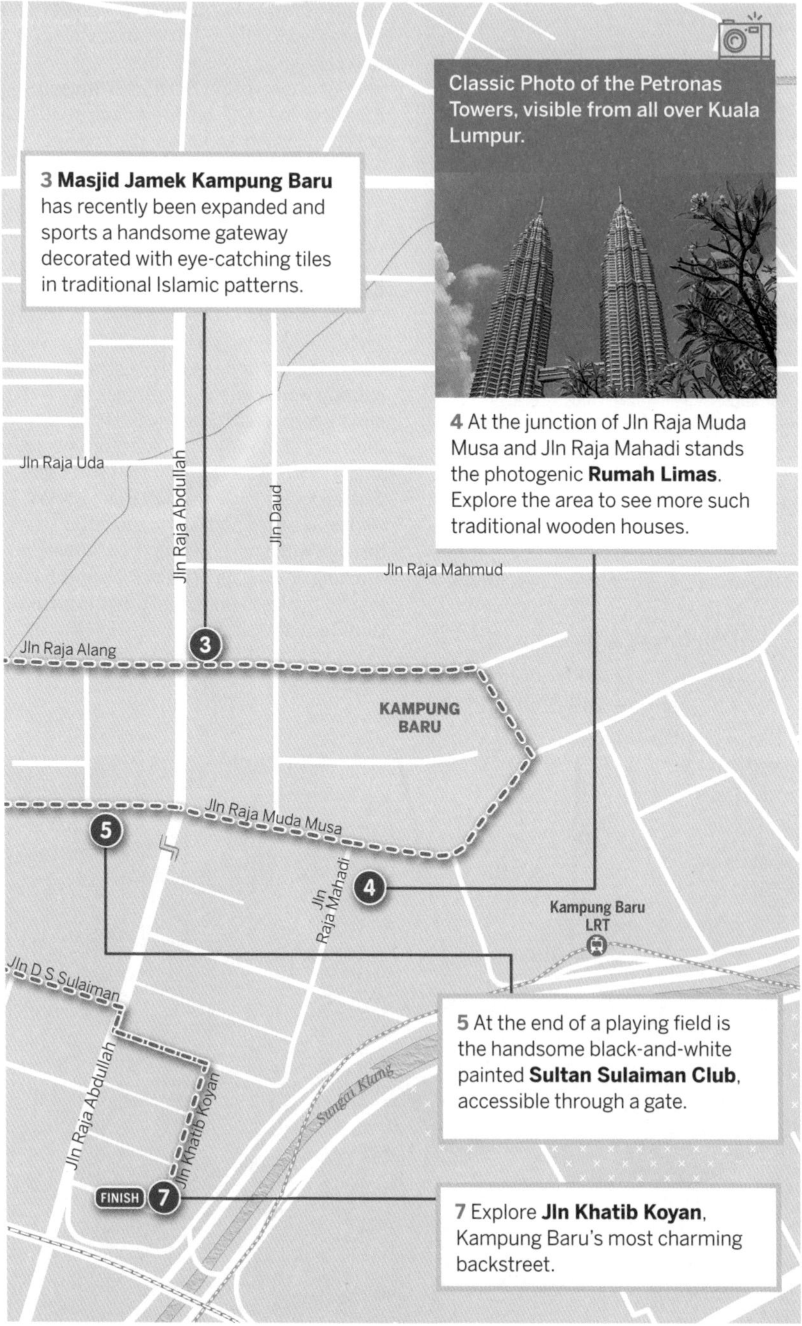

3 Masjid Jamek Kampung Baru has recently been expanded and sports a handsome gateway decorated with eye-catching tiles in traditional Islamic patterns.

Classic Photo of the Petronas Towers, visible from all over Kuala Lumpur.

4 At the junction of Jln Raja Muda Musa and Jln Raja Mahadi stands the photogenic **Rumah Limas**. Explore the area to see more such traditional wooden houses.

5 At the end of a playing field is the handsome black-and-white painted **Sultan Sulaiman Club**, accessible through a gate.

7 Explore **Jln Khatib Koyan**, Kampung Baru's most charming backstreet.

SIGHTS

KL's city centre is surprisingly compact – from Chinatown to Masjid India takes little more than 10 minutes on foot – and some sights are so close together that it's often quicker to walk than take public transport or grab a cab (which can easily become snarled in traffic and KL's tortuous one-way system).

Bukit Nanas

Menara Kuala Lumpur Tower
(KL Tower; Map p56; ☎03-2020 5444; www.menarakl.com.my; 2 Jln Punchak; observation deck adult/child RM52/31, open deck adults only RM105; ⏰observation deck 9am-10pm, last tickets 9.30pm; 🚉KL Tower) Although the Petronas Towers are taller, the 421m Menara KL, rising from the crest of Bukit Nanas, offers the best city views. Surrounded by a pocket of primary rainforest, this lofty spire is the world's fourth-highest telecommunications tower. The bulb at the top (its shape inspired by a Malaysian spinning toy) contains a revolving restaurant, an interior **observation deck** at 276m and, most thrilling of all, an **open deck** at 300m, access to which is weather dependent.

A free **shuttle bus** runs from the gate on Jln Punchak, or you can walk up through the **KL Forest Eco Park** and its new canopy walkway.

"Don't miss traversing the lofty, newly constructed canopy walkway"

KL Forest Eco Park Nature Reserve
(Taman Eko Rimba KL; Map p56; www.forestry.gov.my; ⏰7am-7pm; 🚉KL Tower) Don't miss traversing the lofty, newly constructed **canopy walkway** set in this thick lowland dipterocarp forest covering 9.37 hectares in the heart of the city. The oldest protected jungle in Malaysia (gazetted in 1906), the park is commonly known as Bukit Nanas (Pineapple Hill), and is also threaded through with short trails up from either Jln Ampang or Jln Raja Chulan. Pick up a basic map to the trails from the **Forest Information Centre** (Map p56; ☎03-2026 4741; www.forestry.gov.my; Jln Raja Chulan; ⏰9am-5pm; 🚉KL Tower).

Canopy walkway, KL Forest Eco Park

NEOELLIS/GETTY IMAGES ©

KLCC & Around

ILHAM — Gallery

(Map p66; www.ilhamgallery.com; 3rd & 5th fl, Ilham Tower, 8 Jln Binjai; 11am-7pm Tue-Sat, 11am-5pm Sun; M Ampang Park) FREE KL's latest public art gallery provides an excellent reason to admire close up the slick 60-storey ILHAM Tower designed by Foster + Partners. With a mission to showcase modern and contemporary Malaysian art, ILHAM kicked off in style in August 2015 with a blockbuster show of works by Hoessein Enas (1924–1995). There's no permanent collection, with exhibitions changing every three to four months.

Talks, performances and classes are also planned. Outside the tower the giant copper-clad sculptures are the first permanent public work by Chinese artist Ai Weiwei to be installed in Southeast Asia.

Petrosains — Museum

(Map p66; 03-2331 8181; www.petrosains.com.my; 4th fl, Suria KLCC, Jln Ampang; adult/child/13-17yr RM26.50/15.90/21.20; 9.30am-4pm Tue-Fri, to 5pm Sat & Sun; M KLCC) Fill an educational few hours at this interactive science discovery centre with all sorts of buttons to press and levers to pull. Many of the activities and displays focus on the wonderful things that fuel has brought to Malaysia – no prizes for guessing who sponsors the museum. As a side note, 'sains' is not pronounced 'sayns' but 'science'.

Rumah Penghulu Abu Seman — Historic Building

(Map p66; 2 Jln Stonor; suggested donation RM10; tours 11am & 3pm Mon-Sat; monorail Raja Chulan) This glorious wooden stilt-house was built in stages between 1910 and the 1930s and later moved to the grounds of **Badan Warisan Malaysia** (Heritage of Malaysia Trust; Map p66; 03-2144 9273; www.badanwarisan.org.my; 2 Jln Stonor; 10am-5.30pm Mon-Sat; monorail Raja Chulan) FREE. You can wander around outside tour times (and since it's built with ventilation in mind, you can easily look in). Check out the stunning hand-carved canoe under the house. The boat was used in religious ceremonies in Kelantan and has the head of a fantastic-looking bird carved into the prow.

Free Guided Walks

Visit KL (p73) offers two free guided walks:

Dataran Merdeka 9am to 11.45am Monday, Wednesday and Saturday

Kampung Baru 4.30pm to 7pm Tuesday, Thursday and Sunday

Bookings can be made on 03-2698 0332 or via email at pelancongan@dblk.gov.my, ideally 24 hours in advance.

For self-guided walks, three signposted **heritage walking routes**, part of the River of Life project, are being set up in the Chinatown and Bukit Nanas areas.

Petaling Street Market (p62), Chinatown
TOM BONAVENTURE/GETTY IMAGES ©

Tun Abdul Razak Heritage Park & Brickfields

Islamic Arts Museum — Museum

(Muzium Kesenian Islam Malaysia; Map p60; 03-2274 2020; www.iamm.org.my; Jln Lembah Perdana; adult/child RM14.85/7.40; 10am-6pm; Kuala Lumpur) This outstanding museum is home to one of best collections of Islamic decorative arts in the world. Aside from the quality of the exhibits, which include fabulous textiles, carpets, jewellery and calligraphy-inscribed pottery, the building itself is a stunner, with beautifully decorated domes and glazed tile work. There's a good Middle Eastern restaurant and one of KL's best museum gift shops

Bukit Nanas & Chinatown

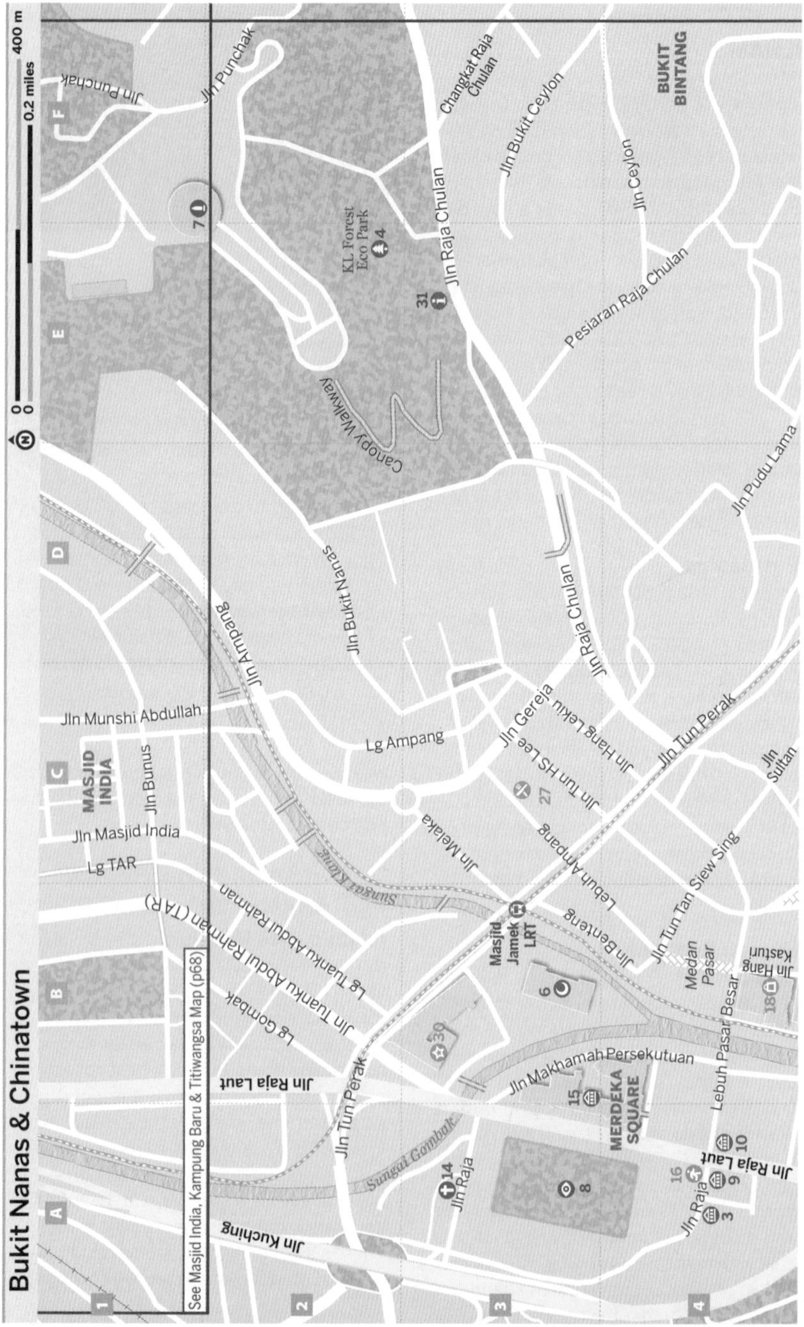

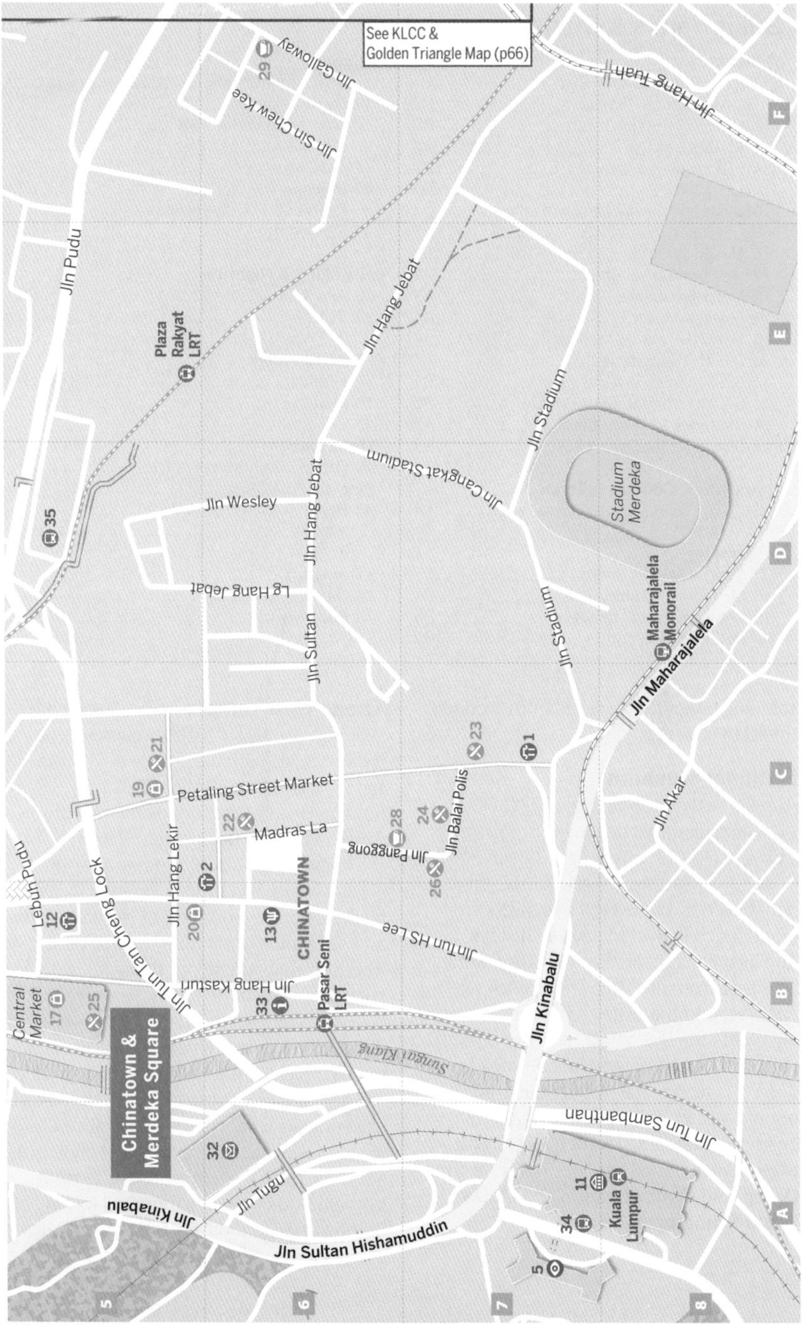
Chinatown & Merdeka Square
See KLCC & Golden Triangle Map (p66)
Jln Galloway
Jln Sin Chew Kee
Jln Pudu
Plaza Rakyat LRT
Jln Hang Jebat
Jln Hang Tuah
Jln Stadium
Jln Cangkat Stadium
Stadium Merdeka
Jln Wesley
Lg Hang Jebat
Jln Sultan
Maharajalela Monorail
Jln Maharajalela
Petaling Street Market
Madras La
Jln Panggong
Jln Balai Polis
Jln Hang Lekir
Lebuh Pudu
Jln Tun Tan Cheng Lock
CHINATOWN
Jln Tun HS Lee
Jln Akar
Jln Hang Kasturi
Central Market
Pasar Seni LRT
Sungai Klang
Jln Kinabalu
Jln Tun Sambanthan
Jln Tugu
Jln Sultan Hishamuddin
Kuala Lumpur
A
B
C
D
E
F
5
6
7
8
1
2
5
11
12
13
17
19
20
21
22
23
24
25
26
28
29
32
33
34
35

Bukit Nanas & Chinatown

Sights

1 Chan She Shu Yuen Clan Association Temple ... C7
2 Guandi Temple ... B6
3 KL City Gallery ... A4
4 KL Forest Eco Park ... E2
Lostgens' ... (see 28)
5 Malayan Railway Administration Building ... A7
6 Masjid Jamek ... B3
7 Menara Kuala Lumpur ... F1
8 Merdeka Square ... A3
9 Muzium Musik ... A4
10 National Textiles Museum ... A4
11 Old KL Train Station ... A7
12 Sin Sze Si Ya Temple ... B5
13 Sri Mahamariamman Temple ... B6
14 St Mary's Anglican Cathedral ... A3
15 Sultan Abdul Samad Building ... B3

Activities, Courses & Tours

16 KL By Cycle ... A4

Shopping

17 Central Market Shops ... B5
18 Museum of Ethnic Arts ... B4
19 Petaling Street Market ... C5
20 Peter Hoe Beyond ... B5

Eating

Atmosphere 360 ... (see 7)
21 Ikan Panggang ... C5
22 Madras Lane Hawkers ... C6
23 Merchant's Lane ... C7
24 Old China Café ... C7
25 Precious Old China ... B5
26 Restaurant Malaya Hainan ... C7
27 Sangeetha ... C3

Drinking & Nightlife

28 Aku Cafe & Gallery ... C6
29 VCR ... F6

Entertainment

Findars ... (see 28)
30 Mud ... B3

Information

31 Forest Information Centre ... E3
32 Main Post Office ... A6
33 Rapid KL Information Booth ... B6
Visit KL ... (see 3)

Transport

34 Nice ... A7
35 Pudu Sentral ... D5

stocking beautiful products from around the Islamic world.

National Museum Museum

(Muzium Negara; Map p60; 03-2282 6255; www.muziumnegara.gov.my; Jln Damansara; adult/child RM5/2; 9am-6pm; Hop-On-Hop-Off Bus Tour, KL Sentral, then taxi) Exhibit quality varies, but overall this museum offers a rich look at Malaysian history. The best exhibits are Early History, with artefacts from neolithic and Bronze Age cultures; and the Malay Kingdoms, which highlights the rise of Islamic kingdoms in the Malay Archipelago. Outside, look for a gorgeous traditional raised house; ancient burial poles from Sarawak; a regularly changing exhibition (extra charge); and two excellent small free side galleries, the **Orang Asli Craft Museum** and **Malay World Ethnology Museum**.

Thean Hou Temple Chinese Temple

(Map p60; 03-2274 7088; www.hainannet.com.my/en; off Jln Syed Putra; 8am-10pm; monorail Tun Sambanthan,) Sitting atop leafy Robson Heights, this imposing multistorey Chinese temple, dedicated to Thean Hou, the heavenly queen, affords wonderful views over Kuala Lumpur. Opened in 1989 by the Selangor and Federal Territory Hainan Association, it serves as both a house of worship and a functional space for events such as weddings. In recent years it's also become a tourist attraction in its own right, especially during Chinese festival times and the birthdays of the various temple gods.

There are great views from the temple's upper decks where you can get close-up views of the mosaic dragons and phoenixes adorning the eaves. To reach the temple, take either a taxi or the monorail to Tun Sambanthan station, cross Jln Syed Putra using the overpass and walk up the hill.

Royal Museum Museum
(Muzium Diraja; www.jmm.gov.my/en/muzium-diraja; Jln Istana; adult/child RM10/5; 9am-5pm;) With the opening in 2011 of the RM800-million new Istana Negara, residence of Malaysia's head of state, in the north of the city, the former Royal Palace has become the Royal Museum. You can tour the first two floors of the mansion, originally built as a family home in 1928 by Chinese tin tycoon Chan Wing. The palace exterior, with its eclectic European style, looks much the same as it was in Chan Wing's day.

Old KL Train Station Historic Building
(Map p56; Jln Sultan Hishamuddin; Kuala Lumpur) One of KL's most distinctive colonial buildings, this 1910 train station (replaced as a transit hub by KL Sentral in 2001) is a grand if ageing structure designed by British architect AB Hubback in the Mughal (or Indo-Saracenic) style. The building's walls are white plaster, rows of keyhole and horseshoe arches provide ventilation on each level, and large chatri and onion domes adorn the roof. In 2014 *Architectural Digest* included it in its list of the 26 most beautiful train stations in the world.

Note that only KTM Komuter trains still stop here. Across from the station is the **Malayan Railway Administration Building** (Map p56; Jln Sultan Hishamuddin; Kuala Lumpur), opened in 1917 and another beautiful piece of Indo-Saracenic architecture.

Sam Kow Tong Temple Chinese Temple
(Map p60; 16 Jln Thambapillai; 7am-5pm; monorail KL Sentral) FREE Established in 1916 by the Heng Hua clan, the 'three teachings' temple has a beautiful Hokkien-style temple roof, with graceful curving ridgelines that taper at the ends like swallowtails. The colourful rooftop dragons and other figures are actually three-dimensional mosaics, another traditional decorative feature of southern Chinese temples (though these are new works). Inside look for photos of the original temple, a simple timber-frame structure with a thatched roof.

Buddhist Maha Vihara Buddhist Temple
(Map p60; 03-2274 1141; www.buddhistmahavihara.com; 123 Jln Berhala, Brickfields; KL Sentral, monorail KL Sentral) Founded in 1894 by Sinhalese settlers, this is one of KL's major Theravada Buddhist temples. It's a particular hive of activity around Wesak Day, the Buddha's birthday, when a massive parade with multiple floats starts from here before winding round the city.

Titiwangsa

National Visual Arts Gallery Gallery
(Balai Seni Lukis Negara; Map p68; 03-4026 7000; www.artgallery.gov.my; 2 Jln Temerloh; 10am-6pm; monorail Titiwangsa) FREE Occupying a pyramid-shaped block, the NVAG showcases modern and contemporary Malaysian art. It's always worth turning up to see a variety of interesting temporary shows of local and regional artists, as well as pieces from the gallery's permanent collection of 4000 pieces, including paintings by Zulkifli Moh'd Dahalan, Wong Hoy Cheong, Ahmad Fuad Osman and the renowned batik artist Chuah Thean Teng. On the ground floor, the National Portrait Gallery also hosts regularly changing exhibitions.

The interior is dominated by a swirly Guggenheim Museum–style staircase that provides access to the main galleries. The side staircases also are used to showcase artworks.

Titiwangsa Lake Gardens Park
(Taman Tasik Titiwangsa; Map p68; Jln Tembeling; monorail Titiwangsa) For a postcard-perfect view of the city skyline, head to Lake Titiwangsa and the relaxing leafy park that surrounds it. If you're feeling energetic, hire a row boat, go for a jog, play some tennis, or explore the nearby neighbourhood of handsome bungalows. The park is a favourite spot for courting Malaysian couples.

Tun Abdul Razak Heritage Park, Brickfields & Bangsar Baru

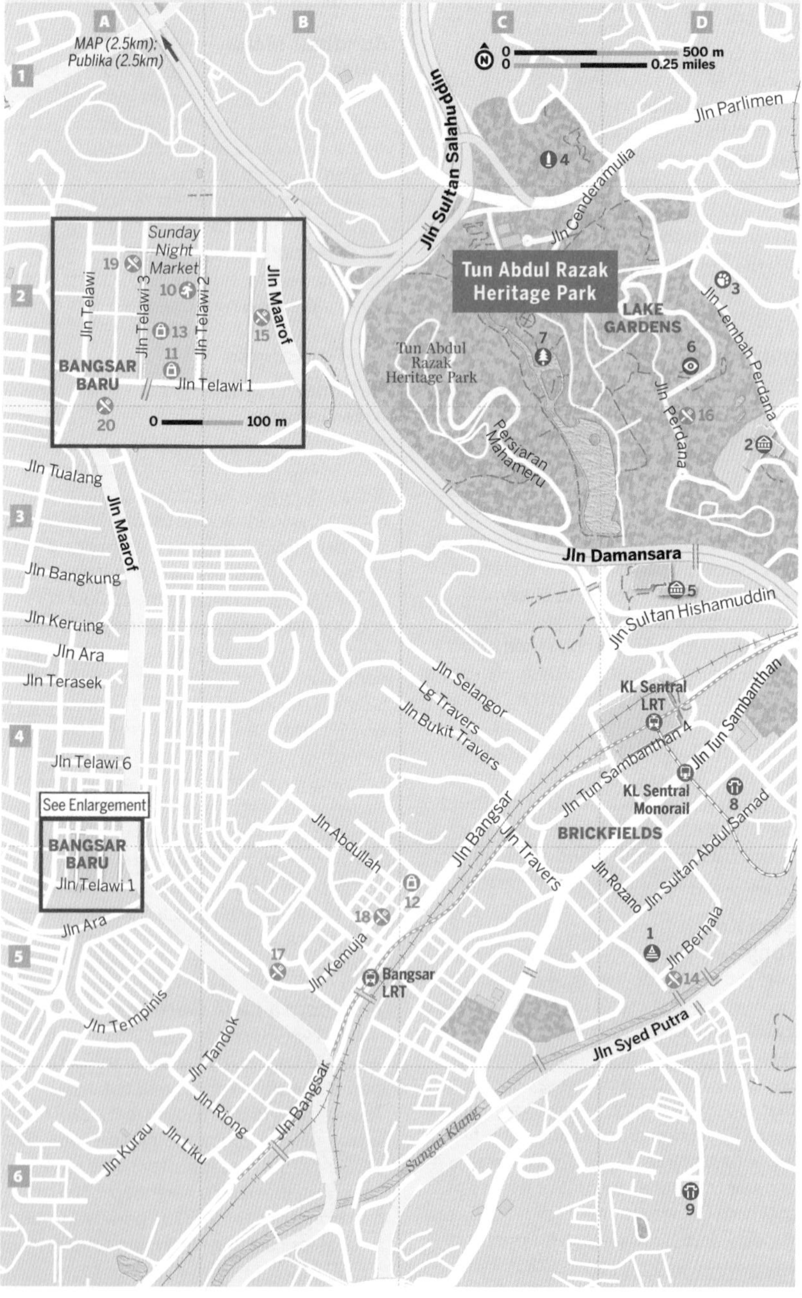

Tun Abdul Razak Heritage Park, Brickfields & Bangsar Baru

It's a 10-minute walk east of the monorail station.

ACTIVITIES

Spa Village Spa

(Map p66; ☎03-2782 9090; www.spavillageresort.org; Ritz Carlton, 168 Jln Imbi; treatments RM350-1000; ⊙10am-10pm; monorail AirAsia-Bukit Bintang) Indoor and outdoor beauty and massage treatments, a sensory room, and a second outdoor pool with waterfalls.

Asianel Reflexology Spa Spa

(Map p66; ☎03-2142 1397; www.asianel.com; Pamper fl, Starhill Gallery, 181 Jln Bukit Bintang; treatments from RM100; ⊙10am-9pm; monorail AirAsia-Bukit Bintang) Upmarket reflexology spa with a particular emphasis on foot treatments, though they also do complete body packages.

Berjaya Times Square Theme Park Amusement Park

(Map p66; ☎03-2117 3118; www.timessquarekl.com/themepark; Berjaya Times Sq, 1 Jln Imbi; adult/child RM51/41; ⊙noon-10pm Mon-Fri, 11am-10pm Sat & Sun; monorail Imbi) Despite the mall location, there's a full-sized looping coaster plus a good selection of thrill rides for teenagers and gentler rides for families. (Avoid the DNA Mixer unless you want to see your *nasi lemak* a second time.)

COURSES

LaZat Malaysian Home Cooking Class Cooking Course

(☎019-238 1198; www.malaysia-klcookingclass.com; Malay House at Penchala Hills, Lot 3196, Jl Seri Penchala, Kampong Sg; ⊙10am-2pm Mon-Sat) A market tour is followed by a hands-on cooking course in a traditional Malay home in the leafy northwestern suburb of Penchala Hills.

School of Hard Knocks Arts, Crafts

(☎03-4145 6122; http://visitorcentre.royalselangor.com/vc2; 4 Jln Usahawan 6, Setapak Jaya; 30-min classes RM63.60; ⊙9am-5pm; Ⓜ Wangsa Maju, then taxi) This famous pewter centre offers entertaining classes where you make your own pewter bowl; advance booking required.

TOURS

Simply Enak Food

(☎017-287 8929; www.simplyenak.com; tours RM200-250) Daily tours to places such as Chow Kit, Petaling St and Kampung Baru to experience authentic Malaysian food with resident experts.

Food Tour Malaysia Food

(www.foodtourmalaysia.com; walking/driving tours RM110/160) Expert guides lead these walking tours around some of KL's best street-food and dining destinations. They

Publika

Art, shopping, dining and social life are all in harmony at KL's most innovative **mall** (www.publika.com.my; 1 Jln Dutamas, Solaris Dutamas; 10am-9pm;), 10 minutes' drive north of Bangsar. **MAP** (03-6207 9732; www.facebook.com/mapkl; Publika, 1 Jln Dutamas, Solaris Dutamas; 10am-9pm;) acts as the cultural anchor, with a wide variety of exhibitions, performances and talks. Free films are screened most Mondays in the central square and there's a good handicrafts market held on the last Sunday of the month.

also offer a full day tour out to the foodie destination of Ipoh, plus food tours in Penang.

SHOPPING

Take your pick from street markets proffering fake-label goods to glitzy shopping malls (all open 10am to 10pm) packed with the real deal. Clothing, camera gear, computers and electronic goods are all competitively priced. You'll also find original handicrafts from all over the country, as well as interesting contemporary art. The shops in the National Textiles Museum (p44) and Islamic Arts Museum (p55) are both packed with appealing items.

Peter Hoe Beyond Arts, Crafts

(Map p56; 03-2026 9788; 2nd fl, Lee Rubber Bldg, 145 Jln Tun HS Lee; 10am-7pm; MPasar Seni) On the 2nd floor of the historic Lee Rubber Building, Peter Hoe's charming emporium is a KL institution. Here you'll find all manner of original fabric products such as tablecloths, curtains and robes (many hand-printed in India directly for Peter Hoe), as well as woven baskets, hanging lanterns, embroidered cushions, silverware, candles, and knickknacks galore. There's also an excellent cafe.

Central Market Shops Arts, Crafts

(Map p56; www.centralmarket.com.my; Jln Hang Kasturi; 10am-10pm; MPasar Seni) This 1930s art deco building houses dozens of shops selling Malaysian arts and crafts including batik clothing and hangings, *songket* (fine cloth woven with silver and gold thread), *wau bulan* (moon kites), baskets, Royal Selangor pewter, as well as vintage items from daily life. Don't miss the fascinating private **Museum of Ethnic Arts** (Map p56; 03-2301 1468; 2nd fl, The Annexe, 10 Jln Hang Kasturi; 11am-7pm; MPasar Seni) in the annexe where most items are for sale.

Petaling Street Market Market

(Map p56; Jln Petaling; noon-11pm; MPasar Seni) Malaysia's relaxed attitude towards counterfeit goods is well illustrated at this heavily hyped night market bracketed by fake Chinese gateways. Traders start to fill Jln Petaling from midmorning until it is jam-packed with market stalls selling everything from fake Gucci handbags to bunches of lychees. Visit in the afternoon if you want to take pictures or see the market without the crowds.

Pavilion KL Mall

(Map p66; www.pavilion-kl.com; 168 Jln Bukit Bintang; 10am-10pm; monorail AirAsia-Bukit Bintang) Pavilion sets the gold standard in KL's shopping scene. Amid the many familiar international brands, there are some good local options, including for fashion British India, offering well-made linen, silk and cotton clothing for men and women; and the more affordable Padini Concept Store. For a quick trip to Japan, head to the Tokyo Street of stalls on the 6th floor.

Suria KLCC Mall

(Map p66; 03-2382 2828; www.suriaklcc.com.my; KLCC, Jln Ampang; 10am-10pm; MKLCC) Even if shopping bores you to tears, you're sure to find something to interest you at this fine shopping complex at the foot of the Petronas Towers. It's mainly international brands but you'll also find some local retailers here too, including Royal Selangor for pewter, Vincci for shoes and accessories and Aseana for designer fashion.

Sungei Wang Plaza Mall

(Map p66; www.sungeiwang.com; Jln Sultan Ismail; ⌚10am-10pm; monorail AirAsia-Bukit Bintang) A little confusing to navigate but jam-packed with youth-oriented fashions and accessories, this is one of KL's more interesting malls, with a focus on street fashion and bargains rather than glitzy international brands. Anchoring one corner is the Parkson Grand department store. There's also a post office, various fast-food outlets and a hawker centre on the 4th floor.

DR.Inc Homewares

(Map p60; ☎03-2283 4698; http://naladesigns.com; 8 Jln Kemuja; ⌚9am-7pm; 📶; Ⓜ Bangsar) Lisette Scheers is the creative force behind the Nala brand of homewares, stationery, accessories and other arty items. All her products embody a contemporary but distinctly local design aesthetic and are beautifully displayed at this Instagram dream of a concept shop and super cool cafe.

She also runs drawing and printing classes here – see the website for details.

Bangsar Village I & II Mall

(Map p60; www.bangsarvillage.com; cnr Jln Telawi 1 & Jln Telawi 2, Bangsar Baru; ⌚10am-10pm; Ⓜ Bangsar) These twin malls are linked by a covered bridge and offer upmarket fashions, including local designers such as Richard Tsen at Dude & the Duchess, shoemaker Thomas Chan, and Desiree for women's clothing with a touch of Chinese styling. There's also a playcentre for kids, the excellent **Hammam Spa** (Map p60; ☎03-2282 2180; www.hammamspas.com; 3rd fl, Bangsar Village II, Jln Telawi 1; treatments from RM168; ⌚10am-10.30pm; Ⓜ Bangsar), and **Silverfish Books** (Map p60; ☎03-2284 4837; www.silverfishbooks.com; 2nd fl, Bangsar Village II, Jln Telawi 1, Bangsar Baru; ⌚10am-10pm;

"this imposing multistorey Chinese temple affords wonderful views over KL"

Thean Hou Temple (p58)

Ⓜ Bank Rakyat-Bangsar) stocking local titles and holding talks.

Bazaar Baru Chow Kit Market
(Chow Kit Market; Map p68; 469-473 Jln TAR; ⏲8am-5pm; monorail Chow Kit) This daily, chaotic wet-and-sundry market serves the Chinese and Malay working class of Chow Kit. It's a warren of tight paths and hangers loaded with fruit, veggies, and all manner of cheap clothing and electronic items. You can also sample hawker and *kopitiam* food and drinks here in hole-in-the-wall outlets that haven't changed in decades.

EATING

KL is a nonstop feast. You can dine in incredible elegance or mingle with locals at street stalls, taking your pick from a global array of cuisines. Ingredients are fresh, the cooking high quality and hygiene standards are excellent. Most vendors speak English and the final bill is seldom heavy on the pocket.

Bukit Nanas & Chinatown

Madras Lane Hawkers Hawker $
(Map p56; Madras Lane; noodles RM5-6; ⏲8am-4pm Tue-Sun; Ⓜ Pasar Seni) Enter beside the Guandi Temple to find this alley of hawker stalls. It's best visited for breakfast or lunch, with standout operators including the one offering 10 types of *yong tau fu* (vegetables stuffed with tofu and a fish and pork paste). The *bah kuh teh* (pork and medicinal herbs stew) and curry laksa stalls are also good.

Sangeetha Indian $
(Map p56; ☎03-2032 3333; 65 Lebuh Ampang; meals RM10; ⏲8am-11pm; 🖉; Ⓜ Masjid Jamek) This well-run vegetarian restaurant serves lots of South Indian delights such as *idli* (savoury, soft, fermented-rice-and-lentil cakes) and *masala dosa* (rice-and-lentil crepes stuffed with spiced potatoes).

Merchant's Lane Fusion $$
(Map p56; ☎03-2022 1736; Level 1, 150 Jln Petaling; mains RM20-30; ⏲10.30am-6pm Thu & Sun-Tue, to 10pm Fri & Sat; 📶; monorail Maharajalela) Look for the narrow doorway at the end of the block for the stairs leading up to this high-ceilinged charmer of a cafe. The vibe is relaxed, the staff young, hip and friendly and the food a very tasty mash up of Eastern and Western dishes, such as Italian chow mein and their take on a Japanese savoury pancake *okonomiyaki*.

Old China Café Malaysian $$
(Map p56; ☎03-2072 5915; www.oldchina.com.my; 11 Jln Balai Polis; mains RM11-21; ⏲11am-11pm; Ⓜ Pasar Seni) Housed in an old guild hall of a laundry association, this long-running restaurant continues to not only conjure retro charm but also serve good-value Peranakan food. Try the beef rendang, the succulent Nonya fried chicken, and tasty appetisers such as the top hats (a small pastry shaped like a hat and stuffed with veggies).

The same company runs the similar **Precious Old China** (Map p56; ☎03-2273 7372; mezzanine fl, Central Market, Jln Hang Kasturi; dishes RM11-30; ⏲11am-11pm; Ⓜ Pasar Seni) in Central Market.

Ikan Panggang Hawker $$
(Map p56; ☎019-315 9448; Jln Hang Lekir; mains RM15; ⏲5-11pm Tue-Sun; Ⓜ Pasar Seni) Tuck into spicy fish and seafood dishes and luscious chicken wings from this stall labelled only Ikan Panggang (which means grilled fish) outside Hong Leong Bank. Order ahead – it generally takes 20 minutes for your foil-wrapped pouch of seafood to cook, allowing time to explore the market.

Restaurant Malaya Hainan Malaysian $$
(Map p56; ☎019-329 7899; lot 16, section 24, Jln Panggong; mains RM12.50-17.50; ⏲10am-10pm; Ⓜ Pasar Seni) It's good to see this long-shuttered mock-Tudor-meets-the-Tropics post office revamped as an appealing restaurant with a choice of breezy open-air and retro themed indoor dining areas. Pick from a good range of colonial Hainanese and Nonya dishes such as roast chicken, sambal prawns and sweet sour fish.

Atmosphere 360 Malaysian, International $$$

(Map p56; ☎03-2020 2020; www.atmosphere360.com.my; Menara Kuala Lumpur, 2 Jln Puncak; buffet lunch/afternoon tea/dinner RM92/60/208; ⏱11.30am-3pm & 6.30-11pm; 🚌KL Tower) There are 360-degree views from this tower-top revolving restaurant. The lunch and dinner buffets offer ample choice of Malay dishes, though they can be hit and miss. Book ahead (you can do this online) for meals, especially sunset dining, but you can usually just drop in for high tea. Note there's a smart-casual dress code.

Golden Triangle

Imbi Market Hawker $

(Pasar Baru Bukit Bintang; Map p66; Jln Kampung; dishes RM5-10; ⏱6am-1pm Tue-Sun; 🚗) Breakfast is a cheerful affair in the courtyard of this walled traditional market. Time-tested stalls include Sisters Crispy Popiah for wraps; Teluk Intan Chee Cheung Fun for oyster-and-peanut congee and egg pudding and Ah Weng Koh Hainan Tea for coffee or tea.

At the time of research the market is slated to move in 2017 as the area's developed into the Tun Razak Exchange financial district.

Bijan Malaysian $$$

(Map p66; ☎03-2031 3575; www.bijanrestaurant.com; 3 Jln Ceylon; mains RM30-90; ⏱4.30-11pm; monorail Raja Chulan) One of KL's best Malaysian restaurants, Bijan offers skilfully cooked traditional dishes in a sophisticated dining room that spills out into a tropical garden. Must-try dishes include *rendang daging* (dry beef curry with lemongrass), *masak lemak ikan* (Penang-style fish curry with turmeric) and *ikan panggang* (grilled skate with tamarind).

KLCC & Around

Nasi Kandar Pelita Mamak $

(Map p66; www.pelita.com.my; 149 Jln Ampang; dishes RM3-9; ⏱24hr; Ⓜ KLCC) There's round-the-clock eating at the Jln Ampang branch of this chain of excellent *mamak* (Muslim Indian-Malay) food courts. Among the scores of dishes available from the various stalls are magnificent *roti canai* (flat, flaky bread) and *hariyali tikka* (spiced chicken with mint, cooked in the tandoor).

Little Penang Kafé Malaysian $

(Map p66; ☎03-2163 0215; level 4, Suria KLCC, Jln Ampang; mains RM12-16; ⏱11.30am-9.30pm; Ⓜ KLCC) At peak meal times expect a long line outside this mall joint serving authentic food from Penang, including specialities

Weekend Night Markets

Masjid India Pasar Malam (Night Market; Map p68; Lg Tuanku Abdul Rahman; street food RM5-10; ⏱3pm-midnight Sat; Ⓜ Masjid Jamek) From around 3pm until late every Saturday, stalls pack out the length of Lg Tuanku Abdul Rahman, the alley between the Jln TAR and Masjid India. Amid the headscarf and T-shirt sellers are plenty of stalls serving excellent Malay, Indian and Chinese snacks and colourful soya- and fruit-based drinks.

Bangsar Sunday Market (Pasar Malam; Map p60; carpark east of Jln Telawi 2; hawker food RM4-6; ⏱1-9pm Sun; Ⓜ Bangsar) This weekly market, though mostly for fresh produce, is also a fine hawker food-grazing zone. Stalls sell satay, and a variety of noodles including *asam laksa* (laksa with a prawn paste and tamarind-flavoured gravy), *chee cheong fun* (rice noodles) and fried *kway teow*.

Stall vendor

TOM COCKREM/GETTY IMAGES ©

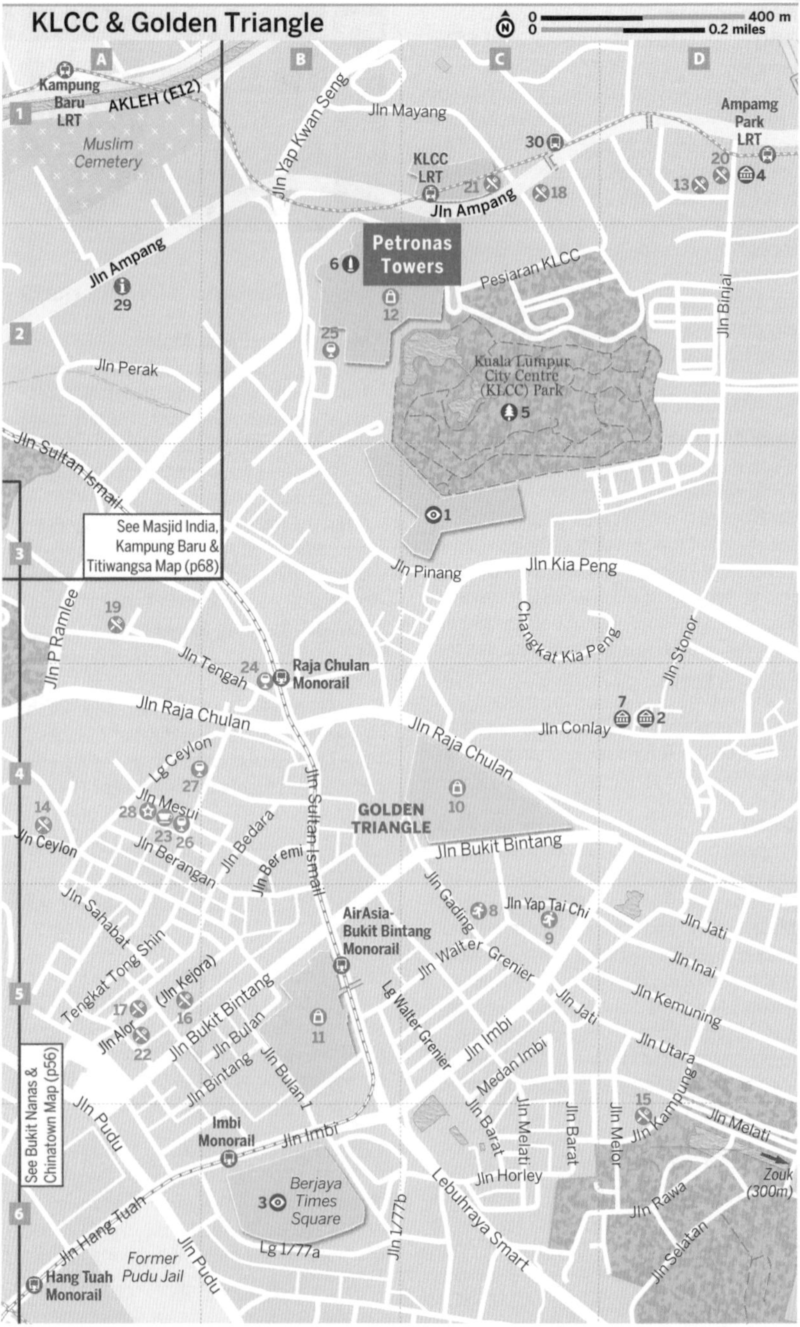
KLCC & Golden Triangle
0 400 m
0 0.2 miles
A
B
C
D
1
2
3
4
5
6
Kampung Baru LRT
AKLEH (E12)
Muslim Cemetery
Jln Yap Kwan Seng
Jln Mayang
KLCC LRT
Jln Ampang
Ampamg Park LRT
Petronas Towers
Pesiaran KLCC
Jln Binjai
Jln Perak
Kuala Lumpur City Centre (KLCC) Park
Jln Sultan Ismail
See Masjid India, Kampung Baru & Titiwangsa Map (p68)
Jln Pinang
Jln Kia Peng
Changkat Kia Peng
Jln Stonor
Jln P Ramlee
Jln Tengah
Raja Chulan Monorail
Jln Raja Chulan
Jln Conlay
Lg Ceylon
Jln Mesui
Jln Ceylon
Jln Berangan
Jln Bedara
Jln Beremi
Jln Sultan Ismail
GOLDEN TRIANGLE
Jln Bukit Bintang
Jln Gading
Jln Yap Tai Chi
Jln Jati
Jln Inai
Jln Sahabat
Tengkat Tong Shin
(Jln Kejora)
AirAsia-Bukit Bintang Monorail
Jln Walter Grenier
Lg Walter Grenier
Jln Kemuning
Jln Utara
Jln Alor
Jln Bukit Bintang
Jln Bulan
Jln Bintang
Jln Bulan 1
Jln Imbi
Medan Imbi
Jln Barat
Jln Melati
Jln Melor
Jln Kampung
Jln Melati
See Bukit Nanas & Chinatown Map (p56)
Jln Pudu
Imbi Monorail
Jln Imbi
Berjaya Times Square
Jln 1/77b
Lebuhraya Smart
Jln Horley
Jln Rawa
Zouk (300m)
Jln Hang Tuah
Former Pudu Jail
Jln Pudu
Lg 1/77a
Jln Selatan
Hang Tuah Monorail
1
2
3
4
5
6
7
8
9
10
11
12
13
14
15
16
17
18
19
20
21
22
23
24
25
26
27
28
29
30

KLCC & Golden Triangle

such as curry *mee* (spicy soup noodles with prawns).

Acme Bar & Coffee International $$
(Map p66; ☎03-2162 2288; www.acmebarcoffee.com; unit G1 The Troika, 19 Persiaran KLCC; mains RM30-60; ⊙11am-midnight Mon-Thu, to 1am Fri, 9.30am-1am Sat, to midnight Sun; Ⓜ Ampang Park) Blink and you might be in a chic bistro in New York, Paris or Sydney. There are tasty nibbles such as root vegetable truffled fries and chilled sugar snap peas if you're not so hungry, and bigger dishes such as lamb shoulder marinated in *kicap* (a type of soy sauce) for larger appetites. It's a great choice for a lazy weekend brunch.

Sushi Hinata Japanese $$$
(Map p66; ☎03-2022 1349; www.shin-hinata.com; St Mary Residence, 1 Jln Tengah; lunch/dinner set meals from RM77/154; ⊙noon-3pm & 6-11pm Mon-Sat; monorail Raja Chulan) It's quite acceptable to use your fingers to savour the sublime sushi, served at the counter one piece at a time, by expert Japanese chefs from Nagoya. There are also private booths for more intimate dinners. The *kaiseki*-style full course meals are edible works of art.

Troika Sky Dining French, Italian $$$
(Map p66; ☎03-2162 0886; www.troikaskydining.com; level 23a, tower B, The Troika, Persiaran KLCC; 🖋; Ⓜ Ampang Park) Sophisticated dining with outstanding views of KLCC's glittering highrises are the highlights of the Troika complex of restaurants and bars. Try **Cantaloupe** (Map p66; set lunch/dinner RM140/from RM290; ⊙noon-2pm Mon-Fri, 6.30pm-10.30pm) for modern French, and **Strato** (Map p66; set lunch from RM50, pizza RM30-50; ⊙noon-3pm & 6-11pm) for Italian that aims for homely authenticity (though we don't ever recall Mama making us Wagyu beef cheek and trotter ravioli).

Masjid India, Kampung Baru & Titiwangsa

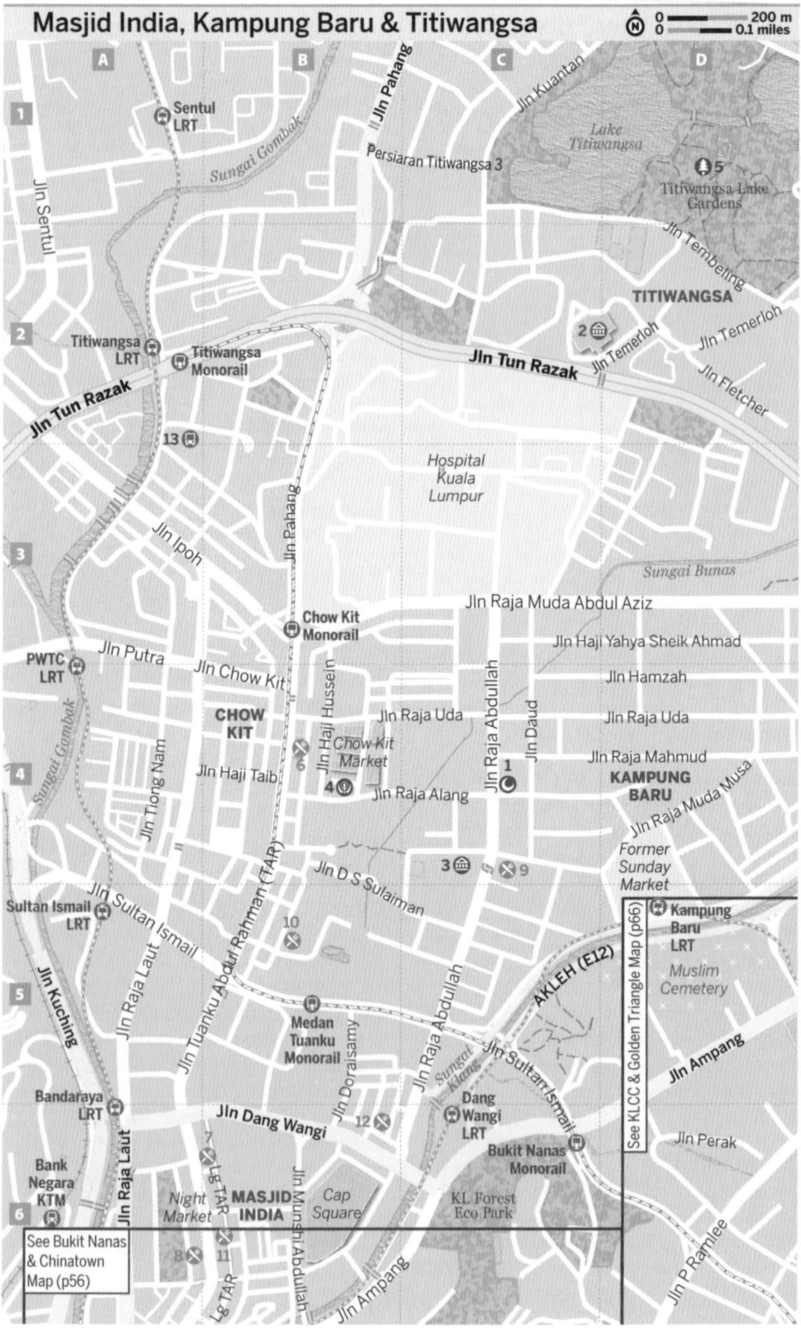

Masjid India, Kampung Baru & Titiwangsa

Sights

1	Masjid Jamek Kampung Baru	C4
2	National Visual Arts Gallery	C2
3	Sultan Sulaiman Club	C4
4	Tatt Khalsa Diwan Gurdwara	B4
5	Titiwangsa Lake Gardens	D1

Eating

6	Bazaar Baru Chow Kit	B4
7	Capital Café	B6
8	Coliseum Cafe	A6
9	Ikan Bakar Berempah	C4
10	Kin Kin	B5
11	Masjid India Pasar Malam	B6
12	Yut Kee	B6

Transport

13	Pekeliling Bus Station	A2

Masjid India, Kampung Baru & Around

Kin Kin Chinese $

(Map p68; 40 Jln Dewan Sultan Sulaiman; noodles RM7.50; ⏲7.30am-6.30pm; monorail Medan Tuanku) This bare-bones shop is famous throughout the city for its chilli *pan mee*. These 'dry' noodles, topped with a soft boiled egg, minced pork, *ikan bilis* (small, deep-fried anchovies), fried onion and a special spicy chilli sauce, are a taste sensation. If you don't eat pork, staff do a version topped with mushrooms.

Capital Café Malaysian $

(Map p68; 213 Jln TAR; dishes RM4-6; ⏲10am-8pm Mon-Sat; M Bandaraya) Since it opened in 1956, this truly Malaysian cafe has had Chinese, Malays and Indians all working together, cooking up excellent renditions of Malay classics such as mee goreng, *rojak* (salad doused in a peanut-sauce dressing) and satay (only available in the evenings).

Ikan Bakar Berempah Hawker $

(Map p68; Jln Raja Muda Musa; meals RM5-10; ⏲7am-10pm; M Kampung Baru) This excellent barbecued-fish stall sits within a hawker-stall market covered by a zinc roof and is one of the best places to eat in Kampung Baru. Pick your fish off the grill and add *kampung*-style side dishes to it off the long buffet.

Yut Kee Chinese, International $

(Map p68; ☎03-2698 8108; 1 Jln Kamunting; meals RM6-15; ⏲8am-5pm Tue-Sun; monorail Medan Tuanku) A new location for this beloved *kopitiam* (in business since 1928) but still much of the same old furnishings and classic Hainanese and colonial-era food: try the chicken chop, *roti babi* (French toast stuffed with pork), toast with homemade *kaya* (coconut-cream jam), or Hokkien mee.

Coliseum Cafe International $$

(Map p68; ☎03-2692 6270; 100 Jln TAR; dishes RM13-49, weekday set lunches RM24-29; ⏲10am-10pm; M Masjid Jamek) Little seems to have changed at Malaysia's longest-running Western restaurant (in business since 1921) since Somerset Maugham tucked into its famous sizzling steaks and Hainan Chicken Chops. Thoroughly retro, it's locally loved and the comfort food truly hits the spot. Even if you're not hungry, it's worth dropping by its attached bar, which is also a colonial time capsule.

Tun Abdul Razak Heritage Park & Brickfields

Annalakshmi Vegetarian Restaurant Indian $

(Map p60; ☎03-2274 0799; www.facebook.com/AnnalakshmiVegetarianRestaurantKuala Lumpur; Temple of Fine Arts, 116 Jln Berhala; dinner mains RM10-15; ⏲11.30am-3pm & 6.30-10pm Tue-Sun; 🌿; 🚉KL Sentral, monorail KL Sentral) Inside the fancy main hall at the Temple of Fine Arts, this well-regarded vegetarian restaurant has set prices at night and a daily lunch buffet for RM16; or you can choose to eat at the humbler Annalakshmi Riverside next to the car park behind the main building, where it's 'eat as you wish, give as you feel'.

Jalan Alor

The collection of roadside restaurants and stalls lining **Jln Alor** (Map p66; Jln Alor; ⏲5pm-late; monorail Bukit Bintang) is the great common denominator of KL's food scene, hauling in everyone from sequined society babes to penny-strapped backpackers. From around 5pm until late every evening, the street transforms into a continuous open-air dining space with hundreds of plastic tables and chairs and rival caterers shouting out to passers-by to drum up business. Most places serve alcohol and you can sample pretty much every Malay Chinese dish imaginable, from grilled fish and satay to *kai-lan* (Chinese greens) in oyster sauce and fried noodles with frogs' legs. Thai food is also popular.

Recommended options:

Kedai Makanan Dan Minuman TKS (Map p66; 32 Jln Alor; small mains RM15-35; ⏲5pm-4am; monorail AirAsia-Bukit Bintang) For mouth-tingling Sichuan dishes.

Restoran Beh Brothers (Map p66; 21a Jln Alor; dishes RM5-10; ⏲24hr) One of the few places open from 7am for breakfast – sister-stall Sisters Noodle serves delicious 'drunken' chicken *mee* (noodles) with rice wine, and there's also a good Hong Kong–style dim sum stall.

Wong Ah Wah (Map p66; 1-9 Jln Alor; small dishes RM10-15; ⏲5pm-4am) Unbeatable for addictive spicy chicken wings, as well as grilled seafood, tofu and satay.

Hornbill Restaurant International $$

(Map p60; ☎03-2693 8086; www.klbirdpark.com; KL Bird Park, 920 Jln Cenderawasih; mains RM13-27; ⏲9am-8pm; 📶; 🚉Kuala Lumpur) Providing a ringside view of the feathered inhabitants of KL Bird Park, this rustic place offers good food without fleecing the tourists too much. Go local with its *nasi lemak* (rice boiled in coconut milk, served with fried anchovies and peanuts) and fried noodles, or please the kids with fish and chips or the homemade chicken or beef burgers.

Bangsar & Around

Rebung Malaysian $$

(Map p60; ☎03-2283 2119; www.restoranrebungdatochefismail.com; 4-2 Lg Maarof; buffet lunch/high-tea/dinner RM40/35/50; ⏲noon-10pm; ❄📶; Ⓜ Bangsar) The flamboyant celebrity chef Ismail runs the show at this excellent Malay restaurant, one of KL's best, respected for its authenticity and consistency. The buffet spread is splendid with all kinds of dishes that you'd typically only be served in a Malay home, several, such as *onde onde* (glutinous rice balls filled with jaggery), made freshly.

Sri Nirwana Maju Indian $$

(Map p60; ☎03-2287 8445; 43 Jln Telawi 3; meals RM10-20; ⏲10am-1.30pm; Ⓜ Bangsar) There are far flashier Indian restaurants in Bangsar, but who cares about the decor when you can tuck into food this good and cheap? Serves it all from roti for breakfast to banana-leaf curries throughout the day.

Wondermama Malaysian $$

(Map p60; ☎03-2284 9821; http://wondermama.co; Bangsar Village I, 1 Jln Telawi 1; mains RM16-26; ⏲9am-11pm Mon-Thu, to 11.30pm Fri & Sat, to 10.30pm Sun; 📶; Ⓜ Bangsar) Traditional meets contemporary at this family-friendly two-level restaurant serving Malaysian food with a modern twist. There's also a branch, **Wondermama X** (Map p66; ground flr, Ave K, 156 Jln Ampang; mains RM16-26; ⏲10am-10pm; Ⓜ KLCC), opposite the Petronas Towers.

Southern Rock Seafood Seafood $$

(Map p60; ☎03-2856 2016; www.southernrockseafood.com; 34 Jln Kemuja; mains RM35-52; 📶; Ⓜ Bangsar) The fishmonger to some of KL's top restaurants has opened its own operation and it's a corker. The fish and seafood – in particular a wide range of oysters – is top quality, simply prepared to allow the flavours to sing. The blue-and-white decor suggests nights spent on

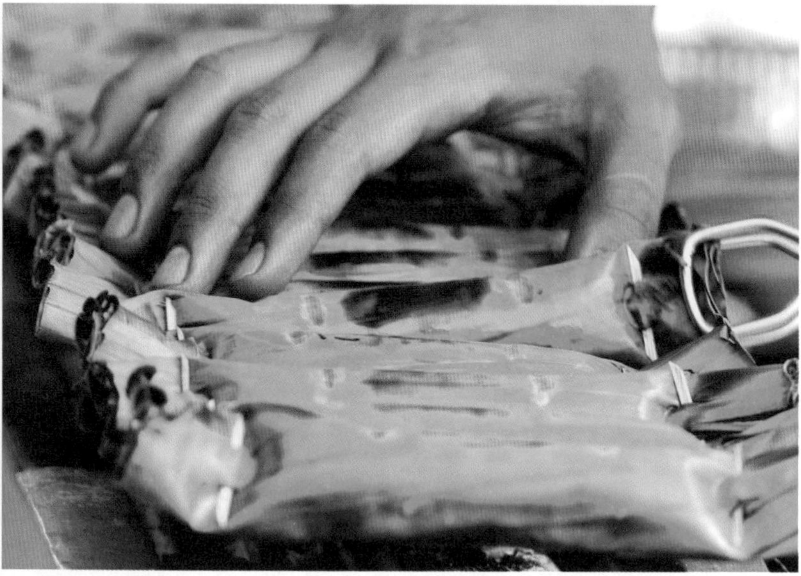
Grilled sticky rice in banana leaves

the sparkling Med rather than the muddy Sungai Klang.

DRINKING & NIGHTLIFE

TREC (www.trec.com.my) is a major new complex of restaurants, cafes and bars on Jln Tun Razak where you'll find the mega-club Zouk (p72).

Heli Lounge Bar Cocktail Bar

(Map p66; ☎03-2110 5034; www.facebook.com/Heliloungebar; level 34, Menara KH, Jln Sultan Ishmail; ⏲5pm-midnight Mon-Wed, to 3am Thu-Sat; 📶; monorail Raja Chulan) If the weather's behaving, this is easily the best place for sundowners in KL. Nothing besides your lychee martini and the cocktail waiter stands between you, the edge of the helipad and amazing 360-degree views. Steady your hands as you have to buy your first drink at the somewhat cheesy bar below and carry it up yourself. Weekends entry often requires your group to stump for a bottle.

Marini's on 57 Bar

(Map p66; ☎03-2386 6030; www.marinis57.com; Level 57, Menara 3, Petronas KLCC; ⏲5pm-1.30am Sun-Thu, to 3am Fri & Sat; Ⓜ KLCC) This is about as close as you can get to eyeballing the upper levels of the Petronas Towers from a bar. The stellar views are complemented by a sleek interior design and attentive service. When booking (advised) be aware that it's the lively bar not the laid-back whisky lounge that has the view of the towers. There's also a dress code.

Fuego Bar

(Map p66; ☎03-2162 0886; www.troikaskydining.com; level 23a, Tower B, The Troika, Persiaran KLCC; ⏲6.30pm-midnight; Ⓜ Ampang Park) Part of the Troika complex, Fuego shares the same sophisticated ambience and jaw-dropping views across the KLCC Park as the fine-dining restaurants. The bar specialises in innovative cocktails and tapas, while its sister venue, **Claret**, open from 4pm to 1am, offers a curated wine list.

Aku Cafe & Gallery Cafe

(Map p56; ☎03-2857 6887; www.oldchina.com.my/aku.html; 1st fl, 8 Jln Panggong; ⏱11am-8pm Tue-Sun; 📶; Ⓜ Pasir Seni) This relaxed coffee haunt serves good hand-drip brews starting at RM10. There are also flavoured drinks such as mint and lemon iced coffee, cakes, and light *kopitiam*-style meals. Exhibitions change on a monthly basis and there are some nice local craft souvenirs for sale.

Keep climbing the stairs to find the contemporary arts space **Lostgens'** (Map p56; www.facebook.com/lostgens; 3rd fl, 8c Jln Panggung; ⏱1-7pm Tue-Sun; Ⓜ Pasar Seni) FREE and, a floor above, the edgy performance space **Findars** (Map p56; www.facebook.com/FINDARS; 4th fl, 8c Jln Panggung; Ⓜ Pasar Seni).

VCR Cafe

(Map p56; ☎03-2110 2330; www.vcr.my; 2 Jln Galloway; ⏱8.30am-10pm; 📶; monorail Hang Tuah) Set in an airy pre-war shophouse, VCR serves first-rate coffee, excellent all-day breakfast and desserts. The crowd is young and diverse, but anyone will feel welcome here. Behind the shop, check out Jln Sin Chew Kee, a photogenic row of colourful shophouses.

Taps Beer Bar Microbrewery

(Map p66; www.tapsbeerbar.my; One Residency, 1 Jln Nagasari; ⏱5pm-1am Mon-Sat, noon-1am Sun; 📶; monorail Raja Chulan) Taps specialises in ale from around the world, with some 80 different microbrews on rotation, 14 of them on tap. There's live music Thursday to Saturday at 9.30pm and an all-day happy hour on Sundays. Taps also serves pub grub (with a few Malaysian dishes) and a Sunday roast.

Feeka Coffee Roasters Cafe

(Map p66; www.facebook.com/feeka.coffee roasters; 19 Jln Mesui; ⏱9am-10pm Mon-Thu, to 11pm Fri-Sun; 📶; monorail Raja Chulan) Set in a minimally remodelled shophouse on hip Jln Mesui, Feeka delivers both on its premium coffee (choose from microlot beans or espresso-based drinks) and its food (from omelettes and pulled-pork sandwiches to cakes). There's a lovely tree-shaded patio area and a gallery space upstairs, making this a place to linger.

Zouk Club

(www.zoukclub.com.my; 436 Jln Tun Razak; admission from RM50; ⏱9pm-3am Tue-Sun; monorail Bukit Bintang, then taxi) If you're going to visit one club in KL, make it this one. Not only does Zouk's new location at the emerging TREC entertainment complex offer no fewer than around nine DJ spaces, bars and a cafe, if you bring your passport as a tourist you gain free entry to some of the enormous complex. Cover charges vary between venues.

Pisco Bar Bar

(Map p66; ☎03-2142 2900; www.piscobarkl.com; 29 Jln Mesui; ⏱5pm-late Tue-Sun; monorail Raja Chulan) Take your pisco sour in the cosy, exposed-brick interior or the plant-filled courtyard of this slick tapas joint. The chef is half Peruvian, so naturally the ceviche here is good. DJs regularly man the decks at the upstairs dance space on Friday and Saturday nights.

ENTERTAINMENT

Dewan Filharmonik Petronas Concert Venue

(Map p66; ☎03-2051 7007; http://mpo.com.my; Box Office, Tower 2, Petronas Towers, KLCC; ⏱box office 10am-6pm Mon-Sat; Ⓜ KLCC) Don't miss the chance to attend a show at this gorgeous concert hall at the base of the Petronas Towers. The polished Malaysian Philharmonic Orchestra plays here (usually Friday and Saturday evenings and Sunday matinees, but also other times), as do other local and international ensembles. There is a smart casual dress code.

Mud Theatre

(Map p56; www.mudKL.com; Panggung Bandaraya, Jln Raja; tickets RM60; ⏱performances 3pm & 8.30pm; Ⓜ Masjid Jamek) A government-funded project, this lively musical show mixes a modern 1Malaysia theme with historical vignettes from KL's early days. The young, talented cast give it their all and there's some fun to be had with audience participation. It's staged in a beautiful historic theatre, the intimate auditorium based on the shape of a Malaysian kite.

No Black Tie Live Music

(Map p66; ☎03-2142 3737; www.noblacktie.com.my; 17 Jln Mesui; cover RM50; ⊙5pm-1am Mon-Sun; monorail Raja Chulan) Blink and you'd miss this small live-music venue, bar and Japanese bistro, as it's hidden behind a grove of bamboo. NBT, as it's known to its faithful patrons, is owned by Malaysian concert pianist Evelyn Hii, who has a knack for finding the talented singer-songwriters, jazz bands and classical-music ensembles who play here from around 9.30pm.

Kuala Lumpur Performing Arts Centre Performing Arts

(KLPAC; ☎03-4047 9000; www.klpac.org; Jln Strachan, Sentul Park; 🚉Sentul) Part of the Sentul West regeneration project, this modernist performing-arts complex puts on a wide range of progressive theatrical events including dramas, musicals and dance. Also on offer are performing arts courses and free screenings of art-house movies (non-censored). Combine a show with a stroll in the peaceful leafy grounds and dinner. Sentul Park is 2.5km west of Titiwangsa Lake Gardens.

INFORMATION

INTERNET ACCESS

Internet cafes are rare these days, but if you're travelling with a wi-fi enabled device, you can get online at hundreds of cafes, restaurants, bars and many hotels for free.

MEDIA

Juice (www.juiceonline.com) Free clubbing-oriented monthly magazine available in top-end hotels, restaurants and bars.

Time Out Kuala Lumpur (www.timeoutkl.com) What's on in KL.

Poskod Malaysia (www.poskod.my) Excellent online magazine about the city and Klang Valley area.

Local Food Blogs

KLites have strong opinions about their favourite places to eat – and they're very happy to share them online:

Fried Chillies (www.friedchillies.com) Spot-on reviews by some fantastically enthusiastic foodies, as well as video clips.

Eat Drink KL (http://eatdrinkkl.blogspot.co.uk) Hundreds of reviews for KL and Klang Valley, plus an app that gives you discounts at selected outlets.

Popiah

SEET YING LAI PHOTOGRAPHY/GETTY IMAGES ©

MONEY

Most banks and shopping malls provide international ATMs (typically on the mall's ground floor or basement level). Moneychangers offer better rates than banks for changing cash and (at times) travellers cheques; they're usually open later and at weekends and are found in shopping malls.

POST

Main Post Office (Map p56; www.pos.com.my; Jln Raja Laut; ⊙6am-11.30pm; Ⓜ Pasar Seni) Across the river from the Central Market. Packaging is available for reasonable rates at the post-office store.

TOURIST INFORMATION

Visit KL (Map p56; ☎03-2698 0332; www.visitkl.gov.my; KL City Gallery, Merdeka Sq; ⊙9am-6.30pm; 📶; Ⓜ Masjid Jamek) Official city tourism office at the KL City Gallery. In addition to tons of useful brochures and maps, it runs free walking tours of Merdeka Sq and Kampung Baru.

Malaysian Tourism Centre (Map p66; ☎03-9235 4800; www.matic.gov.my/en; 109 Jln Ampang; ⌚8am-10pm; monorail Bukit Nanas) Information on KL and tourism across Malaysia. There's also a free traditional dance and music show staged at the theatre here (3pm to 3.45pm Monday to Saturday), plus a branch of the chocolate emporium Cocoa Boutique. The main office is housed in a handsome bungalow built in 1935 for rubber and tin tycoon Eu Tong Sen.

GETTING THERE & AWAY

AIR

Kuala Lumpur International Airport (p311) is 55km south of the city centre at Sepang, while the SkyPark Subang Terminal (p311) is around 20km west of the centre.

BUS

Aeroline (Map p66; ☎03-6258 8800; www.aeroline.com.my; MKLCC) Services to Singapore (RM95, six daily), Penang (RM60, twice daily) and Johor Bahru (RM60, daily) leave from outside the Corus Hotel, Jln Ampang, just northeast of KLCC.

Nice (Map p56; ☎013-220 7867; www.nice-coaches.com.my; Kuala Lumpur) Services run from outside the old KL Train Station on Jln Sultan Hishamuddin to Singapore (from RM82, seven daily), Penang (from RM74, up to six daily) and Melaka (from RM33, three daily).

Pekeliling Bus Station (Map p68; Jln Pekeliling; MTitiwangsa, monorail Titiwangsa) Bus station serving central Pahang towns including Jerantut, Temerloh and Kuala Lipis, as well as east-coast destinations such as Kuantan.

Pudu Sentral (Map p56; Jln Pudu; MPlaza Rakyat) Pudu Sentral Bus Station on the edge of Chinatown serves KLIA, and many northbound destinations around peninsular Malaysia, as well as Thailand. It's a crowded place, with pushy touts. Plaza Rakyat LRT Station is just behind the terminal. At the rear is a left-luggage counter.

Terminal Bersepadu Selatan (TBS; ☎03-9051 2000; www.tbsbts.com.my; Bandar Tasik Selatan; MBandar Tasik Seletan, Bandar Tasik Seletan) Serving destinations to the south and northeast of KL.

From left: Milky stork, KL Bird Park (p50); Menara Kuala Lumpur (p54); Local cuisine; Burning incense at Sin Sze Si Ya Temple (p42)

ANDERS BLOMQVIST/GETTY IMAGES ©

TRAIN

All long-distance trains depart from KL Sentral, hub of the **KTM** (Keretapi Tanah Melayu Berhad; ☎1300 885862; www.ktmb.com.my; ⊙info office 9am-9pm, ticket office 6.30am-9.30pm) national railway system. The information office in the main hall can advise on schedules and check seat availability.

There are daily connections with Butterworth (for Penang), Wakaf Baharu (for Kota Bharu and Jerantut), Johor Bahru and Thailand; fares are cheap, especially if you opt for a seat rather than a berth (for which there are extra charges), but journey times are slow.

The opulent Eastern & Oriental Express (www.orient-express.com) also stops in KL Sentral, connecting with Singapore, Butterworth and Bangkok.

GETTING AROUND

TO/FROM THE AIRPORTS

KLIA

The fastest way to the city is on the comfortable KLIA Ekspres (www.kliaekspres.com), with departures every 15 to 20 minutes from 5am to 1am. From KL Sentral you can transfer to your final destination by monorail, LRT, KTM Komuter train or taxi.

The Airport Coach (www.airportcoach.com.my) takes an hour to KL Sentral; for RM18 it will take you to any central KL hotel from KLIA and pick you up for the return journey for RM25. The bus stand is clearly signed from inside the terminal.

Taxis from KLIA operate on a fixed-fare coupon system. Purchase a coupon from a counter at the arrivals hall and use it to pay the driver. Standard taxis cost RM75.

SKYPARK SUBANG TERMINAL

Taxis from the city centre to Subang take between 30 minutes and one hour depending on traffic and cost RM40 to RM50. **Trans MVS Express** (☎019-276 8315; http://klia2airporttransfer.com) runs buses on the hour from KL Sentral to Subang (RM10, one hour) between 9am and 9pm, and from Subang to KLIA 1 & 2 (RM10, one hour) roughly every two hours between 5am and 11pm.

NAZRA ZAHRI/GETTY IMAGES ©

JOHN SONES SINGING BOWL MEDIA/GETTY IMAGES ©

BICYCLE

Cycling Kuala Lumpur (http://cyclingkl.blogspot.co.uk) is a great resource, with a map of bike routes and plenty of detail on how to stay safe on KL's roads.

KL By Cycle (Map p56; ☎03-2691 2382; www.myhoponhopoff.com; Dataran Merdeka Underground Mall, Merdeka Sq; per hour RM10, deposit RM100; ⏰9am-6pm; Ⓜ Masjid Jamek) Rents basic bikes at the information desk in the underground mall across from the KL City Gallery. Rentals include a helmet.

PUBLIC TRANSPORT

You can happily get around much of central KL on a combination of rail and monorail services.

MyRapid (www.myrapid.com.my) cards are valid on Rapid KL buses, the monorail and the Ampang and Kelana Jaya LRT lines. It costs RM20 (including RM5 in credit) and can be bought at monorail and LRT stations. Just tap at the ticket gates or when you get on the bus and the correct fare will be deducted. RapidKL also offers the Rapidpass Flexi Touch 'n Go valid from one to 30 days (RM10 to RM150).

Touch 'n Go (www.touchngo.com.my) cards can be used on all public transport, at highway toll booths across the country and at selected parking sites. The cards, which cost RM10 and can be reloaded with values from RM10 to RM200, can be purchased at My News outlets.

KL TravelPass (www.kliaekspres.com/deals/kl-travelpass) cards are essentially a Touch 'n Go card that includes a one-way/return trip on the KLIA Ekspres train plus RM10 of credit (RM50/RM85). They can be bought at KLIA and KL Sentral.

BUS

Most buses are provided by either **Rapid KL** (☎03-7885 2585; www.rapidkl.com.my) or Metrobus (☎03-5635 3070). There's an **information booth** (Map p56; ⏰7am-9pm) at the Jln Sultan Mohammed bus stop in Chinatown. The fare is RM2 to RM3; have the correct change ready when you board. There's an information booth near Pasir Seni station in Chinatown, where you can also board the free Go KL City Bus (www.gokl.com.my) services to the Golden Triangle, KLCC and Titiwangsa areas.

KL MONORAIL

The air-conditioned monorail zips from KL Sentral to Titiwangsa, linking up many of the city's sightseeing areas.

KTM KOMUTER TRAINS

KTM Komuter (www.ktmb.com.my) trains use KL Sentral as a hub. There are two lines: Tanjung Malim to Sungai Gadut and Batu Caves to Pelabuhan Klang. Trains run every 15 to 20 minutes from approximately 6am to 11.45pm. Tickets start from RM1 for one stop.

LIGHT RAIL TRANSIT

The user-friendly Light Rail Transit (www.myrapid.com.my) system is composed of the Ampang/Sentul Timur, Sri Petaling/Sentul Timur and Kelana Jaya/Terminal Putra lines.

TAXI

Air-conditioned taxis are plentiful and you can usually flag one down easily during non-peak, non-rainy hours. The red-and-white regular taxis (*teksi bajet*), charge RM3 for the first three minutes and 25 sen for each additional 36 seconds. Blue taxis are newer and more comfortable and start at RM6 for the first three minutes and RM1 for each additional 36 seconds. From midnight to 6am there's a surcharge of 50% on the metered fare of either type of taxi.

Some drivers have a limited geographical knowledge of the city and some also refuse to use the meter, even though this is a legal requirement. Taxi drivers lingering outside luxury hotels or tourist hot spots are especially guilty of this behaviour.

KL Sentral and some large malls such as Pavilion and Suria KLCC have a coupon system for taxis where you pay in advance at a slightly higher fee than the meter.

Download the My Teksi booking app to your smart phone or tablet. My Teksi drivers have to use the meter and the service lets you know before you book the approximate fare. You can get right across the centre of town for RM10 on the meter even in moderate traffic.

Where to Stay

There are many international hotel chains in KL and you can often grab great online deals. Budget sleeps are plentiful, too, but the best places fill up quickly, so book ahead – especially over public holidays.

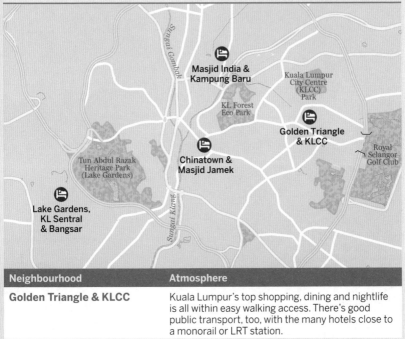

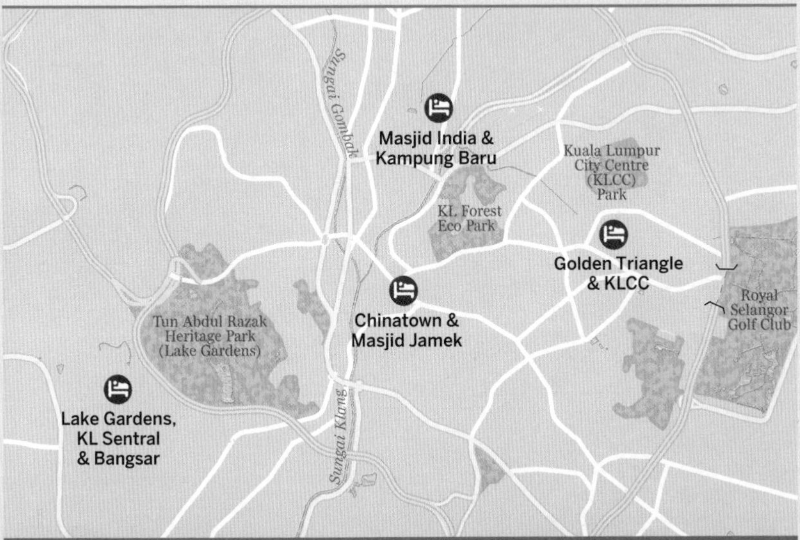

Neighbourhood	Atmosphere
Golden Triangle & KLCC	Kuala Lumpur's top shopping, dining and nightlife is all within easy walking access. There's good public transport, too, with the many hotels close to a monorail or LRT station.
Chinatown & Masjid Jamek	Best location for quality hostels and hanging out with other budget travellers. Good public transport, and great food and local atmosphere on the doorstep.
Masjid India & Kampung Baru	Worth looking online for homestay options in Kampung Baru. Reasonably good public transport links as well as excellent eating options.
Lake Gardens, KL Sentral & Bangsar	Prime access to Kuala Lumpur International Airport (KLIA) and the rest of the city from KL Sentral. Interesting and lively Brickfields area a short walk away, as well as Lake Gardens.

SIMONLONG/GETTY IMAGES ©

CAMERON HIGHLANDS

In this Chapter

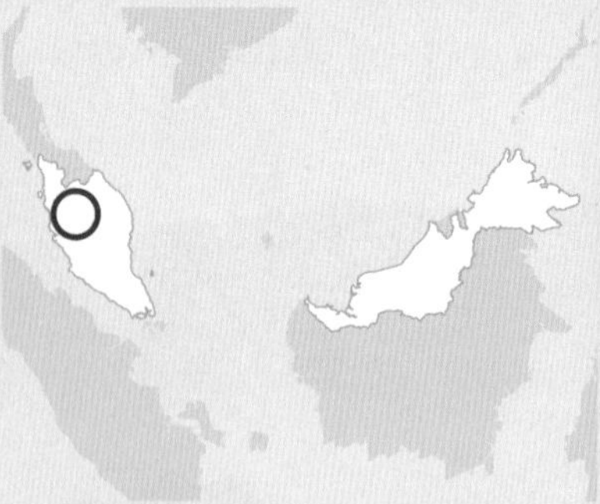

Cameron Highlands

With your first lungful of fragrant highland air, stress and sweat evaporate. In Malaysia's largest hill-station area, the breeze is freshened by eucalyptus, fuzzy tea plantations roll into the distance, and strawberry farms snooze under huge awnings.

Named after explorer Sir William Cameron, who mapped the area in 1885, the highlands were developed during the British colonial period. Tourism is big business today, but the highlands' combination of tea culture, hiking trails and mild temperatures remains irresistible. With eco-conscious trekking, unexplored forests and some interesting temples, there is serenity to be found amid the touristic hubbub.

Cameron Highlands in Two Days

Start by exploring the plantations of **Boh Sungei Palas Tea Estate** (p82), followed by a cuppa in their cafe. Take the afternoon to marvel at the **Sam Poh Temple** (p86) and pick strawberries at the **Kok Lim Strawberry Farm** (p86). Spend the second day striking out on a hiking trail or going on a nature tour with **Eco Cameron** (p87).

Cameron Highlands in Four Days

On day three there are more tea plantations and more strawberry farms, as well as the **Ee Feng Gu Honey Bee Farm** (p86) and **Cameron Highlands Butterfly Farm** (p86) to discover. On your last day return to the lowlands where you can gorge on food highlights in revamped **Ipoh** (p91), from chicken and bean sprouts to excellent Indian cuisine.

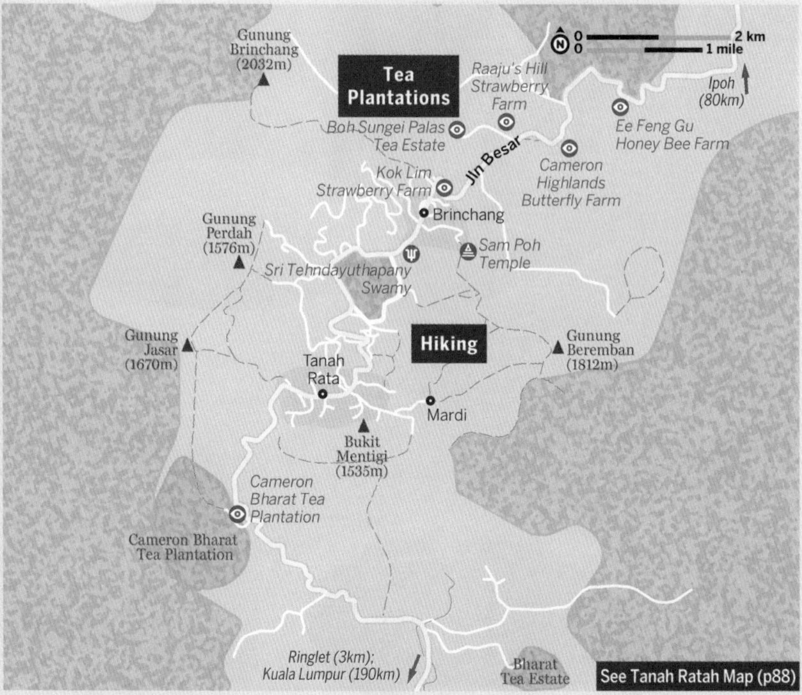

Arriving in the Cameron Highlands

Terminal Freesia The main bus station is located at the eastern end of Jln Besar in the Highlands' transport hub, Tanah Rata. There are daily connections to Kuala Lumpur (four hours), Melaka (six hours), Penang (five hours), Ipoh (two hours) and Singapore (10 hours). Daily bus and boat transfer packages also reach Taman Negara and the Perhentian Islands.

Sleeping

Tanah Rata is the most popular place to stay in the Cameron Highlands, with its huge spread of hotels and proximity to endless restaurants and tour providers. Brinchang, 4km north, also has plenty of hotels, though most places are targeted at domestic tourists. Study a map before booking, as many hotels, especially outside Tanah Rata, are only suited to travellers with a car.

The Highlands are at their busiest during the school holidays in April, August and December. During these times, book well in advance. Prices go up by around 25% at weekends and during holidays.

Tea at Cameron Bharat Tea Plantation

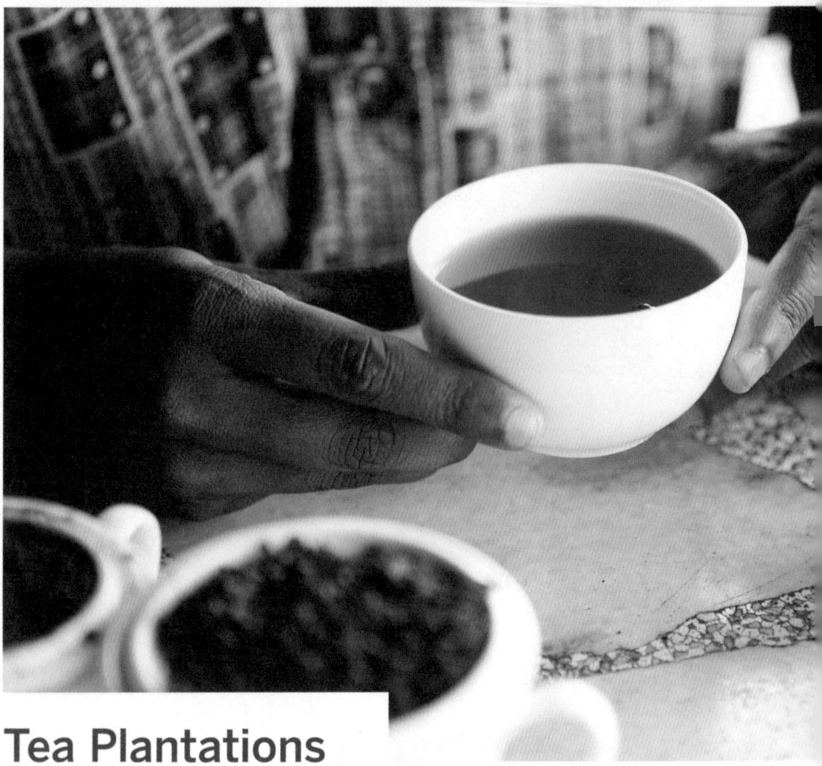

Tea Plantations

The fresh climate of the Cameron Highlands, with temperatures rarely topping 30°C, is perfect for growing tea. Visit two of the region's plantations to admire beautiful vistas and sample the brews.

Great For...

☑ Don't Miss

Sungei Palas' **Tea Appreciation Tours** (adult RM37.10; ⌚9am & 11am Tue-Sun) – tea enthusiasts should call ahead to book.

Boh Sungei Palas Tea Estate

Malaysia's tea industry was born in the Cameron Highlands in 1929 when a couple of British entrepreneurs, JA Russell and AB Milne, saw the area's potential for growing the plant. The pair started a business that now produces 4 million kilograms of tea per year (70% of all tea produced in Malaysia) from four plantations including the breathtakingly beautiful **Boh Sungei Palas Tea Estate** (☎05-496 2096; www.boh.com.my; ⌚9am-4.30pm Tue-Sun) FREE, an almost otherworldly green patchwork of hills and tea plants.

The narrow approach road leads past worker housing and a Hindu temple (tea pickers are predominantly Indian) to the modern visitor centre, where you can witness tea production first-hand, and a

cafe (9am-4.30pm Tue-Sun) where you can sip a cuppa while gazing at the plantations below. Free 15-minute tours showing the tea-making process are conducted during opening hours.

The estate is located in the hills north of Brinchang, off the road to Gunung Brinchang. Public buses running between Tanah Rata and Kampung Raja pass the turn-off to Gunung Brinchang. From there it's 4km along the winding road, after which it's another 15 minutes' walk downhill to the visitor centre.

Cameron Bharat Tea Plantation

Located at the side of the road around 4km south of Tanah Rata, the views over the **Cameron Bharat Tea Plantation** (http://bharattea.com.my; 8.30am-7pm) FREE are

Need to Know

Boh has another impressive **estate** (9am-4.30pm Tue-Sun) FREE southeast of Tanah Rata and 7km off the main road.

Take a Break

Both Boh Sungei Palas and Cameron Bharat tea estates have pleasant cafes.

★ Top Tip

The simplest way to access the tea plantations is by taxi from Tanah Rata.

breathtaking. The plantation was started in 1933 by Shuparshad Bansal Agarwal, an immigrant to Malaysia from Agra in India, and is still run by the same family four generations on. There are no guided tours here, but you can wander around parts of the plantation, and there's a tea house, attractively set overlooking the estate. There's another **branch** (7.30am-6pm), likewise equipped with a cafe, located 12km away on the main road heading northeast from Brinchang, although the views aren't as impressive.

Mossy Forest

Hiking the Cameron Highlands

Rippling hills and pleasant temperatures make the Cameron Highlands an ideal hiking destination. Nature-lovers will also appreciate peeping at orchids and pitcher plants along the way.

Great For...

☑ Don't Miss

Kok Lim Strawberry Farm (p86) and the attached Time Tunnel (p86), near the start of Trail 1.

Yellow-and-black signboards mark the trails, but many aren't maintained very well and can be slippery and unclear. Before setting out on any trail, always ask locally about its safety; the folk at **Father's Guest House** (☎016-566 1111; www.fathersguest-house.net; 4 Jln Mentigi, Tanah Rata) are seriously on the ball when it comes to the trails, routes and trekking safety. Let your guesthouse know your planned route and predicted return time. Better yet, arrange a local guide.

At the time of writing, hikers were being urged to avoid Trails 9 and 9A, as they were not considered safe due of a series of robberies and assaults targeting tourists.

Trail 1

This difficult trail officially starts at white stone marker 1/5 on the summit of Gunung

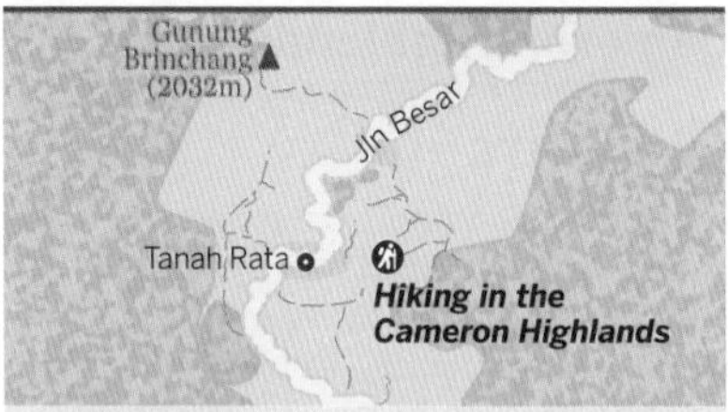

Need to Know

Ensure you carry water, some food, and rain gear to guard against unpredictable weather.

Take a Break

Rest your tired limbs at one of Tanah Rata's eateries.

★ Top Tip

Eco Cameron (p87) has exclusive access to a trail through part of the Mossy Forest.

Brinchang (2032m), but Trail 1 is steep, muddy, overgrown and often closed for repairs – it is not advisable to make the descent via this trail. Instead, start your walk at the end point of the trail, at white stone marker 1/48 just north of Cactus Valley. This section of the trail should take about 2½ hours to complete. From the summit take the 7km-long sealed road back to Brinchang through the tea plantations, about a two-hour walk.

Trail 4

One of the more popular trails starts next to the river, just past Century Pines Resort in Tanah Rata. It leads to Parit Falls, but garbage from the nearby village finds its way here and it's not the most bucolic spot. The falls can also be reached from the main road leading south from the southern end of the golf course. Both hikes are about half a kilometre.

Trail 8

This trail splits off Trail 9 just before Robinson Falls and is another steep three-hour approach to Gunung Beremban. Only experienced hikers should attempt this strenuous trail.

Mossy Forest

If you're more partial to a stroll than a steep hike, an easy boardwalk wends through a short stretch of the Mossy Forest. Find the beginning at a pagoda 2km south of Gunung Brinchang's peak. At the time of writing, the boardwalk was closed to tourists because of littering, but it was due to reopen after lying fallow for a few months.

Cameron Highlands

SIGHTS

Many attractions around the Cameron Highlands are glorified souvenir shops, peddling lavender or honey without much of a visitor experience. Tea plantations are as worthwhile for the views as the brews.

Sam Poh Temple Buddhist Temple
(Brinchang) FREE As unexpected sites in the hills go, a temple dedicated to a Chinese eunuch and naval officer just about tops the list. This temple, just below Brinchang about 1km off the main road, is a brilliant pastiche of imperial Chinese regalia, statuary dedicated to medieval admiral and eunuch Zheng Ho and, allegedly, the fourth-largest Buddha in Malaysia.

Kok Lim Strawberry Farm Farm
(Brinchang; 9am-5pm) Just north of Brinchang, RM30 gets you the chance to be a labourer for a while and go home with half a kilo of hand-picked strawberries.

Time Tunnel Museum
(adult/child RM5/3; 9am-6pm) Less a museum, more a nostalgic array of items from the Cameron Highlands' past, the Time Tunnel (adjoining Kok Lim Strawberry Farm) has English language displays on Malaysia's history amid rusty Horlicks signs, old barber's chairs and 1970s postcards of local towns.

Ee Feng Gu Honey Bee Farm Farm
(www.eefenggu.com; Brinchang; 8am-7pm) FREE A working apiary about 3km northeast of Brinchang, with an indoor maze (adult/child RM3/2) for the kids and a royal selection of honey-themed gifts to take home.

Cameron Highlands Butterfly Farm Farm
(http://cameronbutterflyfarm.com.my; Kea Farm; adult/child RM5/3; 9am-6pm Mon-Fri, 8am-7pm Sat & Sun) This popular attraction is home to a fluttering collection of tropical butterflies, including the majestic Raja Brooke, and some rather depressed-looking reptiles.

From left: Butterfly, Cameron Highlands Butterfly Farm; strawberries; Bo Sungei Palas Tea Estate (p82)

DINOZAVER/GETTY IMAGES ©

JEAN-BERNARD CARILLET/GETTY IMAGES ©

Raaju's Hill Strawberry Farm Farm
(☎019-575 3867; Brinchang; ⊙8.30am-6.30pm) Locals whisper that Raaju has the sweetest strawberries in town. It's believed that the way the evening mist hits this valley-tucked berry farm is the reason its fruit tastes so good. If berry picking (RM30 for two people for half a kilo of strawberries) sounds like too much hard work, you're sure to find something – between tea and scone sets (RM16) and thick strawberry juice (RM6) – to tempt you in Raaju's cafe.

Sri Tehndayuthapany Swamy Hindu Temple
(Brinchang; ⊙6am-6pm) Located just south of Brinchang is this colourful Hindu place of worship. On our visit the temple's Tamil Nadu–style sculptures had enjoyed some recent renovation.

TOURS

The distance between sights plus infrequent public transport makes guided tours popular in the Cameron Highlands. Most are half-day tours that focus on the tea-plantation, strawberry-picking and flower-farm highlights of the area.

Eco Cameron Tour
(☎05-491 5388; www.ecocameron.com; 72-A Psn Camellia 4, Tanah Rata; tours RM50-120; ⊙8am-9.30pm) This outfit specialises in nature tours of the Cameron Highlands: hiking, orchid walks, birdwatching and insect-spotting. Most enthralling are guided hikes through the Mossy Forest – Eco Cameron has exclusive access to a protected trail.

Jason Marcus Chin Tour
(☎010-380 8558; jason.marcus.chin@gmail.com; half/full-day tour from RM50/90) Exceptional nature guide Jason Marcus Chin leads guided hikes on request, sharing superlative knowledge of flora and fauna along the way.

CS Travel & Tours Tour
(☎05-491 1200; www.cstravel.com.my; 47 Jln Besar, Tanah Rata; ⊙7.30am-7.30pm) This agency leads popular half-day 'countryside tours' of the Highlands, departing at 8.45am and 1.45pm (adult/child RM25/20). Longer tours, such as the full-day 'adventure tour'

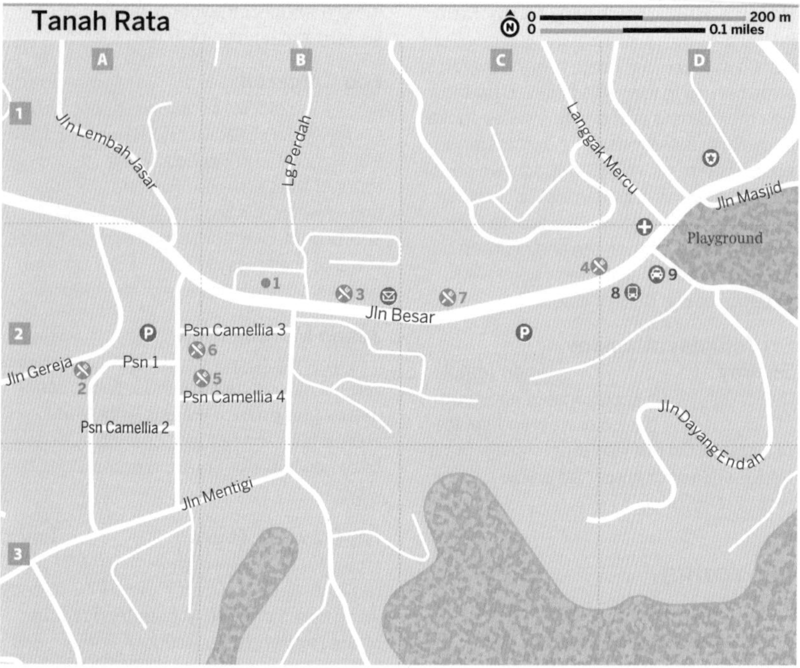

Tanah Rata

Activities, Courses & Tours
1 CS Travel & Tours B2
Eco Cameron .... (see 5)

Eating
2 Barracks Cafe A2
3 KouGen B2
4 Lord's Cafe C2
5 May Flower B2
6 Restaurant Bunga Suria A2
7 Restoran Sri Brinchang C2

Transport
8 Bus Station D2
9 Taxi Station D2

(adult/child RM80/70), take in Gunung Brinchang and an Orang Asli village.

EATING

Tanah Rata is home to the majority of the area's restaurants, with Chinese, Indian and Malay flavours jostling for attention alongside the colonial hangover of English breakfasts and scones. More upmarket fare can be found in hotel restaurants, though Tanah Rata's offerings have upped their game in recent years.

Restaurant Bunga Suria Indian $
(66a Persiaran Camellia 3, Tanah Rata; set meals RM6-10; 7am-10pm;) The most crowd-pleasing (yet least manic) of Tanah Rata's Indian canteens has great-value banana leaf meal specials and a good selection of curries. But where it really excels is at breakfast, when fresh *idli* (savoury, soft, fermented-rice-and-lentil cakes) pop out of the steamer, ready to surrender to a dunking in coconut chutney.

Restoran Sri Brinchang Indian $

(25 Jln Besar, Tanah Rata; mains RM4-20; 7am-10pm;) This busy place heaps spiced aubergine, papadums and rice onto banana leaves for its filling lunches; it prides itself on spring chicken served straight from the tandoor.

Lord's Cafe Cafe $

(Jln Besar, Tanah Rata; mains RM2.50-4.90; 10am-9pm Wed-Fri & Mon, 10am-6pm Sat) Despite the neon threat from Tanah Rata's controversial new Starbucks, Lord's Cafe, reassuringly decorated like your grandma's living room, lives on. Specialities include thick mango and banana lassis and apple pie, the standout star on a menu of cakes and ice cream sundaes. Find the cafe by following the Christian signage to the floor above Marrybrown fast food.

Barracks Cafe Fusion $$

(011-1464 8883; 1 Jln Gereja; mains RM15; 10am-9pm Tue-Sun) This brand-new restaurant within a converted British military barracks suffers from an enjoyable identity crisis. Marble tables encircle a babbling fountain, and corrugated iron walls are emblazoned with a mural of soldiers blasting butterflies from guns. Matching this eclectic decor are menu choices ranging from Indian masala lamb to burgers. The yoghurt smoothies and mason jar mocktails (RM7.90) are exceptional.

KouGen Japanese, Korean $$

(012-377 0387; 35 Jln Besar, Tanah Rata; mains RM13-20; noon-9pm) A border-crossing selection of Japanese and Korean recipes are whipped up in the open kitchen of this friendly Tanah Rata eatery. Choose from sushi, *bibimbap* (a hot bowl of rice, egg, meat, veggies and more), fried rice in *kimchi* (fiery fermented cabbage) and a slurpable range of noodle dishes, topping them up with sides like *yakitori* (grilled chicken skewers) and freshly steamed soy beans.

May Flower Chinese $$

(491 4793; 81a Psn Camellia 4, Tanah Rata; hotpot per person RM16, mains RM7-24; lunch & dinner;) This place does a few versions of the hotpot (referred to as steamboat), so take your pick of seafood, meat and vegetarian options – ingredients are as varied as oyster, jellyfish and tofu – and set them simmering in the broth.

Royal Belum State Park

Perak's northernmost tip is home to Peninsular Malaysia's largest expanse of virgin jungle, the Belum-Temenggor Rainforest.

Within this green dream of wilderness is the 117.5-hectare Royal Belum State Park. The park is excellent for birdwatching, with all 10 species of hornbill cawing from its ancient trees. Tapirs, sun bears, tigers and panthers also make their home here. Spotting Belum's larger animals is a matter of luck, and odds are low unless you secure a guide for dawn or dusk. But even when the wildlife is shy, Belum's magic is revealed through the majesty of its forest, where tangled tree roots harbour orchids, and hand-sized katydids (crickets) zoom across the glades.

Driving offers the best flexibility when reaching Belum. Visiting the park itself requires guided tours by boat. Packages with accommodation, excursions and a park permit can be touristy, but offer good value. Common offerings include nature hikes and visits to the rafflesia site and Orang Asli village (only one village in the area receives visitors).

FAKRUL JAMIL PHOTOGRAPHY/GETTY IMAGES ©

Street art in Ipoh

> *Renewed enthusiasm for Ipoh's heritage is seeing old shophouses restored*

INFORMATION

The post office, hospital and police station are all found on Jln Besar in Tanah Rata.

GETTING THERE & AWAY

BUS

Tanah Rata's bus station, known as Terminal Freesia, is located at the eastern end of Jln Besar. Daily bus and boat transfer packages also reach Taman Negara and the Perhentian Islands. Bus timetables are subject to change, but at the time of writing, daily (or more) services were operating to Brinchang (RM2, 20 minutes), Ipoh (RM18, two hours), Kuala Lumpur (RM35, four hours), Melaka (RM65, six hours), Penang (RM32, five hours) and Singapore (RM125 to RM140, 10 hours).

TAXI

Taxis also wait at Terminal Freesia. At the time of writing, long-distance fares were set at RM160 to Ipoh, RM350 to KL and RM360 to Penang (Butterworth). A noticeboard lists standard fares for a number of destinations.

GETTING AROUND

While we never recommend hitchhiking, some travellers do so to get between Tanah Rata, Brinchang and the tea plantations beyond.

BUS

Buses run between Tanah Rata and Brinchang between 6.30am and 6.30pm every two hours or so.

TAXI

Taxi services from Tanah Rata include Brinchang (RM8), Ringlet (RM25) and Boh (RM40); for prices on additional destinations, including hiking trailheads and tea estates, see the price list posted at the taxi stop at Terminal Freesia. For touring around, a taxi costs RM25 per hour.

Ipoh

A convenient gateway for travel to the Cameron Highlands, Ipoh is undergoing a quiet renaissance. Renewed enthusiasm for Ipoh's heritage is seeing old shophouses restored, while new cafes and craft shops are springing up within historic buildings. Meanwhile, the ribbon is being cut on brand-new accommodation, from hostels to luxury hotels.

The key to enjoying Ipoh is tackling it by neighbourhood. Start with the old town's charismatic laneways and revived period buildings. Grab a trail map to seek out the best heritage structures and street art. South of here, Ipoh's Little India has glittering shops and some fine eateries.

East of the river in Ipoh's new town, a cluster of canteens serve up regional classics like *ayam tauge* and some of the creamiest beancurd pudding around. Just north of this foodie hub are the city's more upmarket hotels, alongside the shiny Parade shopping mall.

It's easy to get to Ipoh by bus, train and long-distance taxi from major urban centres. There are also flights to the local airport from Singapore and Johor Bahru.

Kuala Kangsar

Seat of the sultan of Perak, Kuala Kangsar (KK) is an easy day trip from Ipoh. The busy town, birthplace of Malaysia's rubber industry and site of the first Durbar, or conference of Malay sultans, in 1897, still gleams with Perak's most ostentatious buildings. Colonial constructions are dotted around hectic central KK, while southeast of the town luxuriant royal palaces and a gold-topped mosque steal the spotlight.

Don't miss the **Masjid Ubudiah** (Ubudiah Mosque; Jln Istana; admission by donation; ⌚9am-noon, 3-4pm & 5.30-6pm), a small but magnificent mosque designed by AB Hubbock, the architect of many of Ipoh's colonial edifices, and the **Malay College** (Jln Tun Abdul Razak), the first Malay school to provide English education for Malays destined for the civil service.

Frequent buses connect KK to Ipoh, and the town is also on the Kuala Lumpur–Butterworth train line.

LAURIE NOBLE/GETTY IMAGES ©

GEORGE TOWN

The Blue Mansion (p98)

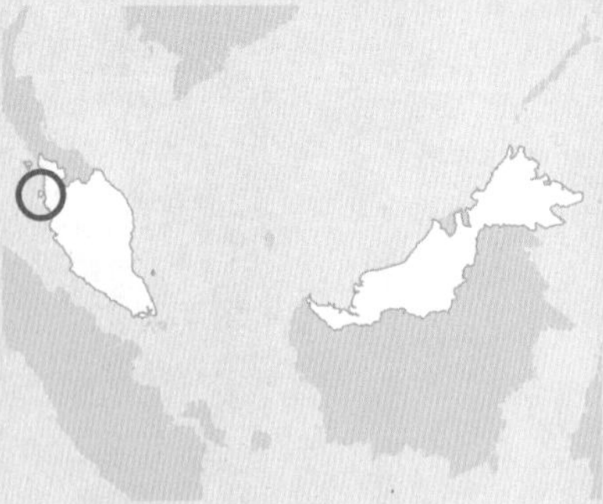

George Town

Combine three distinct and ancient cultures, indigenous and colonial architecture, shake for a few centuries, garnish with a burgeoning art scene, and you've got the tasty urban cocktail that is George Town. The eclectic jumble means that this is a city that rewards explorers. Get lost in the maze of chaotic streets and discover shrines decorated with strings of paper lanterns and fragrant shops selling Indian spices.

The greatest reward of all comes at the end of all this exploration: George Town is Malaysia's, if not Southeast Asia's, food capital. Home to five distinct cuisines, it's the kind of place that can boast both quality and quantity.

George Town in Two Days

Follow our **walking tour** (p104) through George Town's World Heritage zone. Get a virtual crash-course in Feng Shui at the **Blue Mansion** (p98) and start digging into the city's never-ending spread of **hawker food**. On day two enjoy the cool breezes and fantastic views of the island from atop **Penang Hill** (p109) and explore **Kek Lok Si Temple** (p109), Malaysia's largest Buddhist temple.

George Town in Four Days

Spend another day in George Town food-grazing and spotting the street art, including a visit to **Hin Bus Depot Art Centre** (p110). On the final day, head to Penang's northwest corner to the gorgeous **Tropical Spice Garden** (p110), and the lush **Art & Garden by Fuan Wong** (p110), a winning combo of botanicals and contemporary art.

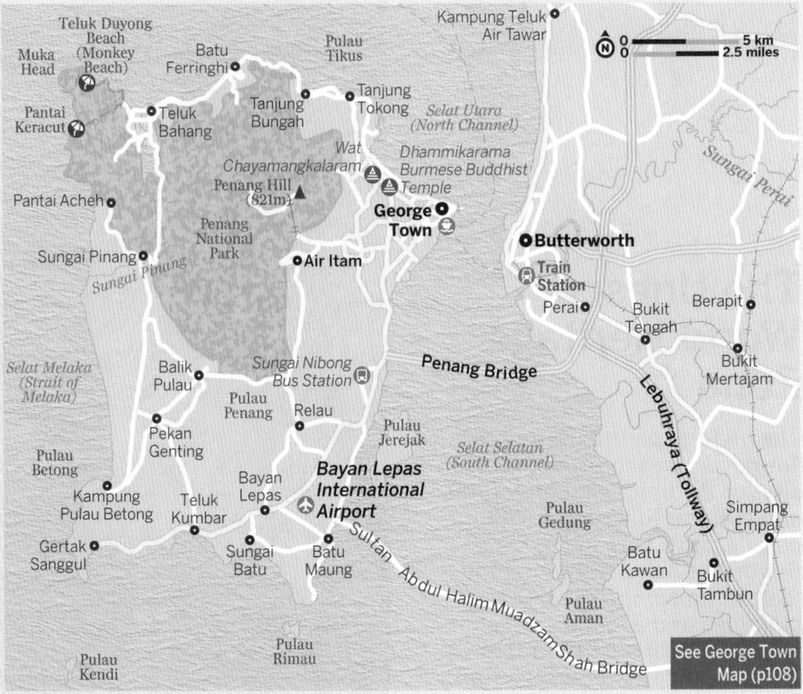

Arriving in George Town

Bayan Lepas International Airport Located 18km south of George Town.

Sungei Nibong Bus Station Just to the south of Penang Bridge; arrival point for long-distance buses.

Two road bridges and a ferry connect Penang to the mainland. Butterworth on the mainland is also where you'll find Penang's train station.

Sleeping

George Town has all the accommodation options you would expect of a tourism destination, from the grungiest hostels to the swankiest hotels, and some really charming boutique properties.

The bulk of the city's budget hotels are located along Love Lane and Jln Muntri. If your budget is under RM100, that most likely means you'll be sleeping in a dorm bed. Moving up to midrange, dozens of George Town's shophouses have been converted into small 'heritage' hotels, although this moniker can mean just about anything nowadays. The top end is where George Town excels, with an impressive selection of unique and atmospheric small hotels.

Yap Kongsi (p104)

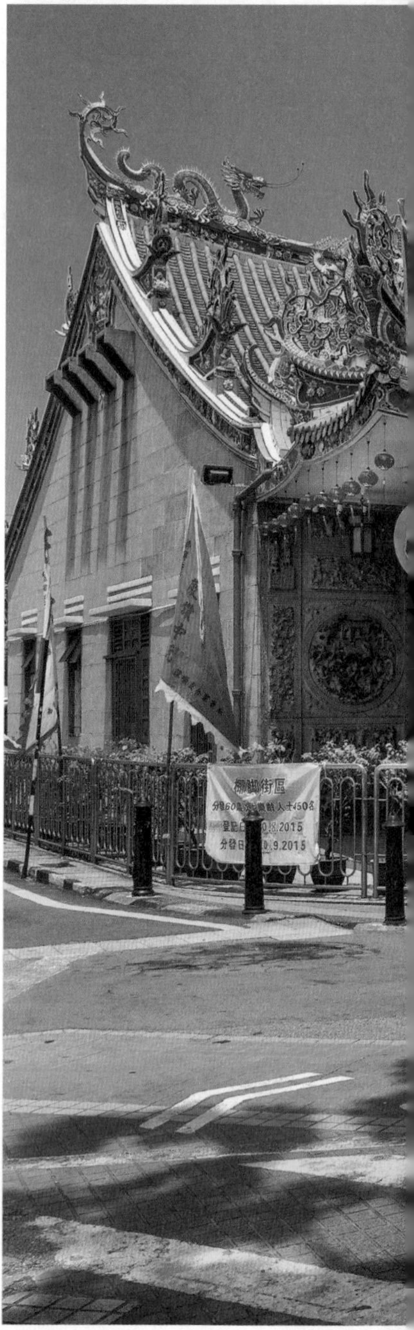

The Unesco World Heritage Zone

The historic centre of George Town is a Unesco World Heritage site for its 'unique architectural and cultural townscape without parallel anywhere in East and Southeast Asia'. The protected 'core' area comprises 1700 buildings and a 'buffer', which together span east from the waterfront to as far west as Jln Transfer and Jln Dr Lim Chwee Leong.

Great For...

Need to Know

Visit **George Town World Heritage Inc. Headquarters** (www.gtwhi.com.my; 116-118 Lebuh Acheh; 8am-1pm & 2-5pm Mon-Thu, 8am-12.15pm & 2.45-5pm Fri).

★ Top Tip

Look out for the series of cartoon steel art pieces across town.

SIMONLONG/GETTY IMAGES ©

You could spend several days meandering around the World Heritage zone and still have plenty left to see – the following are the highlights.

Particularly notable are the clanhouses. Between the mid-1800s and the mid-1900s Penang welcomed a huge influx of Chinese immigrants, primarily from China's Fujian province. To help the new arrivals, the Chinese formed clan associations and built clanhouses, known locally as *kongsi*, to create a sense of community, provide lodging, and help find employment for newcomers. In addition to functioning as 'embassies' of sorts, clanhouses also served as a deeper social, even spiritual, link between an extended clan, its ancestors and its social obligations.

As time went on, many clan associations became extremely prosperous and their buildings became more ornate. Clans – called 'secret societies' by the British – began to compete with each other over the opulence and number of their temples. Due to this rivalry, George Town today has one of the densest concentrations of clan architecture found outside China.

Blue Mansion

The magnificent 38-room, 220-window **Blue Mansion** (www.thebluemansion.com.my; 14 Lebuh Leith; adult/child RM16/8; ⏲tours 11am, 2pm & 3.30pm) was built in the 1880s and rescued from ruin in the 1990s. It blends Eastern and Western designs with louvred windows, art-nouveau stained

glass and beautiful floor tiles, and is a rare surviving example of the eclectic architectural style preferred by wealthy Straits Chinese (Baba-Nonya). Its distinctive (and once-common in George Town) blue hue is the result of an indigo-based lime wash.

Hour-long guided tours (included in the admission fee) provide a glimpse of the interior of the mansion commissioned by Cheong Fatt Tze, a Hakka merchant-trader who left China as a penniless teenager. He eventually established a vast financial empire throughout east Asia, earning himself the dual sobriquets 'Rockefeller of the East' and the 'Last Mandarin'.

☑ Don't Miss

The fascinating guided tours of the Blue Mansion, which provide an insight into traditional Chinese architecture.

MANADO/GETTY IMAGES ©

Pinang Peranakan Mansion

This ostentatious, mint-green **structure** (www.pinangperanakanmansion.com.my; 29 Lebuh Gereja; adult/child RM21.20/10.60; ⌚9.30am-5.30pm) is among the most stunning restored residences in George Town. A self-guided tour reveals that every door, wall and archway is carved and often also painted with gold leaf; the grand rooms are furnished with majestic wood furniture with intricate mother-of-pearl inlay; there are displays of charming antiques; and bright-coloured paintings and fascinating black-and-white photos of the family in regal Chinese dress grace the walls.

The house belonged to Chung Keng Quee, a 19th-century merchant, secret society leader and community pillar, as well as being one of the wealthiest Baba-Nonyas of that era.

After visiting the house, be sure to also check out **Chung Keng Kwi Temple**, the adjacent ancestral hall.

Khoo Kongsi

The Khoo are a successful clan, and their eponymous **clanhouse** (www.khookongsi.com.my; 18 Cannon Sq; adult/child RM10/1; ⌚9am-5pm) is the most impressive in George Town.

Guided tours begin at the stone carvings that dance across the entrance hall and pavilions, many of which symbolise, or are meant to attract, good luck and wealth. The interior is dominated by incredible murals depicting birthdays, weddings and, most impressively, the 36 celestial guardians. Gorgeous ceramic sculptures of immortals,

✕ Take a Break

The World Heritage zone is packed with appealing places to eat. Try Jawi House (p114) for unique local fare or Yin's Sourdough (p114) for some on-the-go goodness.

carp, dragons, and carp becoming dragons dance across the roof ridges.

Cheah Kongsi

Cheah Kongsi (Lebuh Pantai; ⌚9am-5pm) FREE is home to the oldest Straits Chinese clan association in Penang. Besides serving as a temple and assembly hall, this building has also been the registered headquarters of several secret societies. Each society occupied a different portion of the temple, which became a focal point during the inter-clan riots that flared up in 1867. The fighting became so intense that a secret passage existed between here and Khoo Kongsi for a quick escape.

Teochew Temple

This 1870 **clanhouse** (Han Jiang Ancestral Temple; Lebuh Chulia; ⌚9am-5pm) FREE was renovated in 2005 by Chinese artisans and features informative displays on the immigration and culture of the eponymous Chinese group.

Chew Jetty

During the late 18th and early 19th centuries, George Town's Pengkalan Weld was the centre of one of the world's most thriving ports and provided plentiful work for the never-ending influx of immigrants. Soon a community of Chinese grew up around the quay, with floating and stilt houses built along rickety docks; these docking and home areas became known as the clan jetties. The largest and most intact of these remaining today is **Chew Jetty** (Pengkalan Weld).

Today, Chew Jetty consists of 75 elevated houses, a few Chinese shrines, a community hall and lots of tourist facilities, all linked by elevated wooden walkways. It's a fun place to wander, with docked fishing boats, folks cooking in their homes and kids running around. If you like the vibe, there is also a homestay option here.

Penang Museum

Penang's state-run **museum** (www.penangmuseum.gov.my; Lebuh Farquhar; admission RM1; ⌚9am-5pm Sat-Thu) includes exhibits on the history, customs and traditions of the island's various ethnic groups, with photos, videos, documents, costumes, furniture and other well-labelled, engaging displays. Upstairs is the history gallery, with a collection of early-19th-century watercolours by Captain Robert Smith, an engineer with the East India Company, and prints showing landscapes of old Penang.

Dr Sun Yat Sen's Penang Base

Dr Sun Yat Sen was the leader of the 1911 Chinese revolution, which established China as the first republic in Asia. He lived in George Town with his family for about six months in 1910; this **house** (120 Lebuh Armenian; admission RM5; ⌚10am-5pm Mon-Sat) was the central meeting place for his political party. Today the structure is a museum documenting Dr Sun Yat Sen's time in Penang, and even if you're not interested in history, it's worth a visit simply for a peek inside a stunningly restored antique shophouse.

★ Further Reading

Value Your Built Heritage, available at the George Town World Heritage Inc. Headquarters, is an informative and entertaining pocket guide to George Town's shophouse styles. Another excellent guide to the city's buildings is the *George Town World Heritage Site Architectural Walkabout* brochure, available at the Penang Heritage Trust (p117).

Door at the Teochew Temple

RICHARD I'ANSON/GETTY IMAGES ©

Gurney Drive Hawker Stall food

Hawker Stalls

Eating at a hawker stall in George Town is something you simply have to do. There are oodles of them to choose from – the following are our pick of the best.

Great For...

☑ Don't Miss

The exquisite Hainanese chicken rice (steamed chicken with broth and rice) at **Kafe Kheng Pin** (80 Jln Penang; mains from RM4; ⌚7am-3pm Tue-Sun).

Lg Baru (New Lane) Hawker Stalls

Ask locals what their favourite hawker stalls are, and they'll almost always mention this night-time street **extravaganza** (cnr Jln Macalister & Lg Baru; mains from RM3). Just about everything's available here, but one standout is the *char koay kak* stall, which in addition to spicy fried rice cakes with seafood, also does great *otak otak* (spicy fish paste grilled in banana leaves).

Lg Baru intersects with Jln Macalister about 250m northwest of the intersection with Jln Penang.

Joo Hooi Cafe

The hawker centre equivalent of one-stop shopping, this tiny **shophouse** (cnr Jln Penang & Lebuh Keng Kwee; mains from RM3; ⌚11am-5pm) has all of Penang's best

dishes in one location: laksa, *rojak* (a mixed vegetable dish with a thick, shrimp-based sauce), *char kway teow* noodles and the city's most famous vendor of *cendol* (a sweet snack of squiggly noodles in shaved ice with palm sugar and coconut milk).

Lebuh Presgrave Hawker Stalls

A famous Hokkien mee vendor draws most folks to this open-air **hawker convocation** (cnr Lebuh Presgrave & Lebuh Mcnair; 4.30pm-midnight Fri-Wed), but there's lots to keep you around for a second course, from *lor bak* (deep-fried meats dipped in sauce) to a stall selling hard-to-find Peranakan/Nonya dishes.

Gurney Drive Hawker Stalls

Penang's most famous **food area** (Persiaran Gurney; mains from RM3; 5pm-midnight) sits amid modern high-rise buildings bordered by the sea. It's particularly well known for its laksa stalls (try stall 11) and the delicious *rojak* at Ah Chye.

Persiaran Gurney is about 3km west of George Town. A taxi here will set you back at least RM20.

Lg Selamat Hawker Stalls

The southern end of this eponymous **strip** (cnr Jl Macalister & Lg Selamat; noon-7pm Wed-Mon) is largely associated with Kafe Heng Huat, lauded for doing the city's best *char kway teow,* but adjacent stalls sell *lor bak, rojak, won ton mee* (wheat- and egg-noodle soup) and other Chinese Penang staples.

Lg Selamat intersects with Jln Macalister about 500m northwest of the intersection with Jln Penang.

Need to Know

Hawker-stall vendors run flexible schedules, so don't be surprised if one isn't there during your visit.

Take a Break

A unique location and excellent food make **Sea Pearl Lagoon Cafe** (off Jln Tanjong Tokong; mains from RM8; 5-10pm Thu-Tue) worth the 7km trip from the city.

★ Top Tip

Many hawker vendors tend to stay at home on Mondays and Thursdays.

George Town Walking Tour

This walk will give you a glimpse of George Town's cultural mix: English, Indian, Malay, Baba-Nonya and Chinese.
Start Penang Museum
Distance 1.5km
Duration 3 to 4 hours

2 Pass the **Supreme Court** to a statue of **James Richardson Logan**, advocate for non-whites during the colonial era.

1 Begin at state-run **Penang Museum** (p100), where there are exhibits on the history, customs and traditions of the island.

7 On the corner of Jln Masjid Kapitan Keling is the Hokkien clanhouse **Yap Kongsi**, originally built in 1924 Straits Eclectic–style and today painted a distinct shade of light green.

Classic Photo of Khoo Khongsi: don't leave without it.

8 Duck into the magnificently ornate **Khoo Kongsi** (p99), the most impressive kongsi in the city.

6 You can't miss **Little Children on a Bicycle**, the most popular of the street-art works by Lithuanian artist, Ernest Zacharevic.

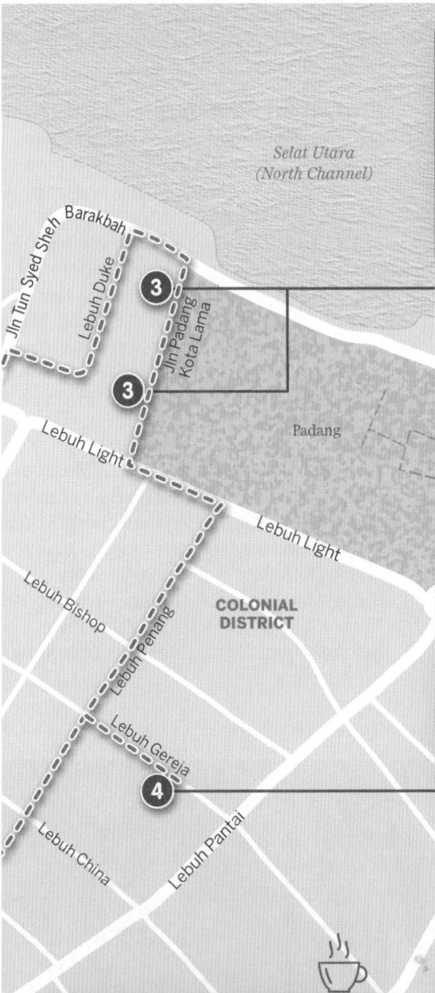

3 Stroll along the waterfront passing the vast *padang* (field) and grandiose architecture of the **City Hall** and **Town Hall**.

4 Along Lebuh Gereja is the impressive **Pinang Peranakan Mansion** (p99), the former digs of one of George Town's great Straits Chinese merchant barons.

Take a Break... Pause for an excellent coffee at China House (p115).

5 Stroll past restored shophouses until you reach **Cheah Kongsi** (p100), home to the oldest Straits Chinese clan association in Penang.

SIGHTS

Inside the Unesco Protected Zone

Camera Museum Museum

(www.penangcameramuseum.com; 49 Jln Muntri; adult RM20, child RM5-10; ⏲9.30am-6.30pm) This fun new museum specialises in just about everything photographic, from ground-floor photo exhibitions to informative displays that span the history of the camera, as well as interactive exhibits ranging from a camera obscura to a model dark room.

House of Yeap Chor Ee Museum

(www.houseyce.com; 4 Lebuh Penang; adult/child RM13/free; ⏲10am-6pm Mon-Fri) This museum, housed in an exquisitely restored three-storey shophouse mansion, is dedicated to a former resident, itinerant barber-turned-banker Yeap Chor Ee. In addition to family photos and mementos, the museum has interesting exhibits on Chinese immigration to Penang.

Protestant Cemetery Cemetery

(Jln Sultan Ahmad Shah; ⏲24hr) FREE Under a canopy of magnolia trees you'll find the graves of Captain Francis Light and many others, including governors, merchants, sailors and Chinese Christians who fled the Boxer Rebellion in China (a movement opposing Western imperialism and evangelism), only to die of fever in Penang. Also here is the tomb of Thomas Leonowens, the young officer who married Anna – the schoolmistress to the King of Siam, made famous by *The King and I*.

Acheen St Mosque Mosque

(Lebuh Acheh; ⏲7am-7pm) FREE Built in 1808 by a wealthy Arab trader, the Acheen St Mosque was the focal point for the Malay and Arab traders in this quarter – the oldest Malay *kampung* (village) in George Town. It's unusual for its Egyptian-style minaret – most Malay mosques have Moorish minarets.

> *Kek Lok Si is a cornerstone of the Malay-Chinese community*

Kek Lok Si Temple (p109)

Hainan Temple Chinese Temple
(Jln Muntri; ⌚9am-6pm) FREE Dedicated to Mar Chor Poh, the patron saint of seafarers, this temple was founded in 1870 but not completed until 1895. A thorough remodelling for its centenary in 1995 refreshed its distinctive swirling dragon pillars and brightened up the ornate carvings.

Fort Cornwallis Historic Site
(Lebuh Light; adult/child RM20/10; ⌚9am-7pm) It was here that Captain Light first set foot on the virtually uninhabited island of Penang in 1786 and established the free port where trade would, he hoped, be lured from Britain's Dutch rivals.

Between 1808 and 1810, convict labour replaced the then-wooden fort with stone; the unique star-profile shape of the walls allowed for overlapping fields of fire against enemies. Yet for all its size, the contemporary fort isn't particularly impressive; only the outer walls stand, enclosing a rather spare park within.

Sri Mariamman Temple Hindu Temple
(Jln Masjid Kapitan Keling; ⌚7am-7pm) FREE Sri Mariamman was built in 1883 and is George Town's oldest Hindu house of worship. For local south Indians, the temple fulfils the purpose of a Chinese clanhouse; it's a reminder of the motherland and the community bonds forged within the diaspora. It is a typically south Indian temple, dominated by the *gopuram* (entrance tower).

Penang's **Thaipusam procession** (⌚Jan-Feb) begins here, and in October a wooden chariot takes the temple's deity for a spin around the neighbourhood during Vijayadasami festivities.

Masjid Kapitan Keling Mosque
(cnr Lebuh Buckingham & Jln Masjid Kapitan Keling; ⌚7am-7pm) FREE Penang's first Indian Muslim settlers (East India Company troops) built Masjid Kapitan Keling in 1801. The mosque's domes are yellow, in a typically Indian-influenced Islamic style, and it has a single minaret. It looks sublime at sunset. Mosque officials can grant permission to enter.

George Town Street Names

Finding your way around George Town can be slightly complicated since many roads have both a Malay and an English name. While many street signs list both, it can still be confusing. We use primarily the Malay name. Some of the main roads, with their English alternatives, include Lebuh Gereja (Church St), Jln Masjid Kapitan Keling (Pitt St), Jln Tun Syed Sheh Barakbah (The Esplanade), Lebuh Pantai (Beach St) and Lebuh Pasar (Market St).

To make matters worse, Jln Penang may also be referred to as Jln Pinang or as Penang Rd – but there's also a Penang St, which may also be called Lebuh Pinang! Similarly, Chulia St is Lebuh Chulia, but there's also a Lorong Chulia, and this confuses even the taxi drivers.

FRASER HALL/ROBERTHARDING ©

Kuan Yin Teng Buddhist Temple
(Temple of the Goddess of Mercy; Jln Masjid Kapital Keling; ⌚24hr) FREE This temple is dedicated to Kuan Yin – the goddess of mercy, good fortune, peace and fertility. Built in the early 19th century by the first Hokkien and Cantonese settlers in Penang, the temple isn't so impressive architecturally, but it's very central and popular with the Chinese community, and seems to be forever swathed in smoke from the outside furnaces where worshippers burn paper money, and from the incense sticks waved around inside.

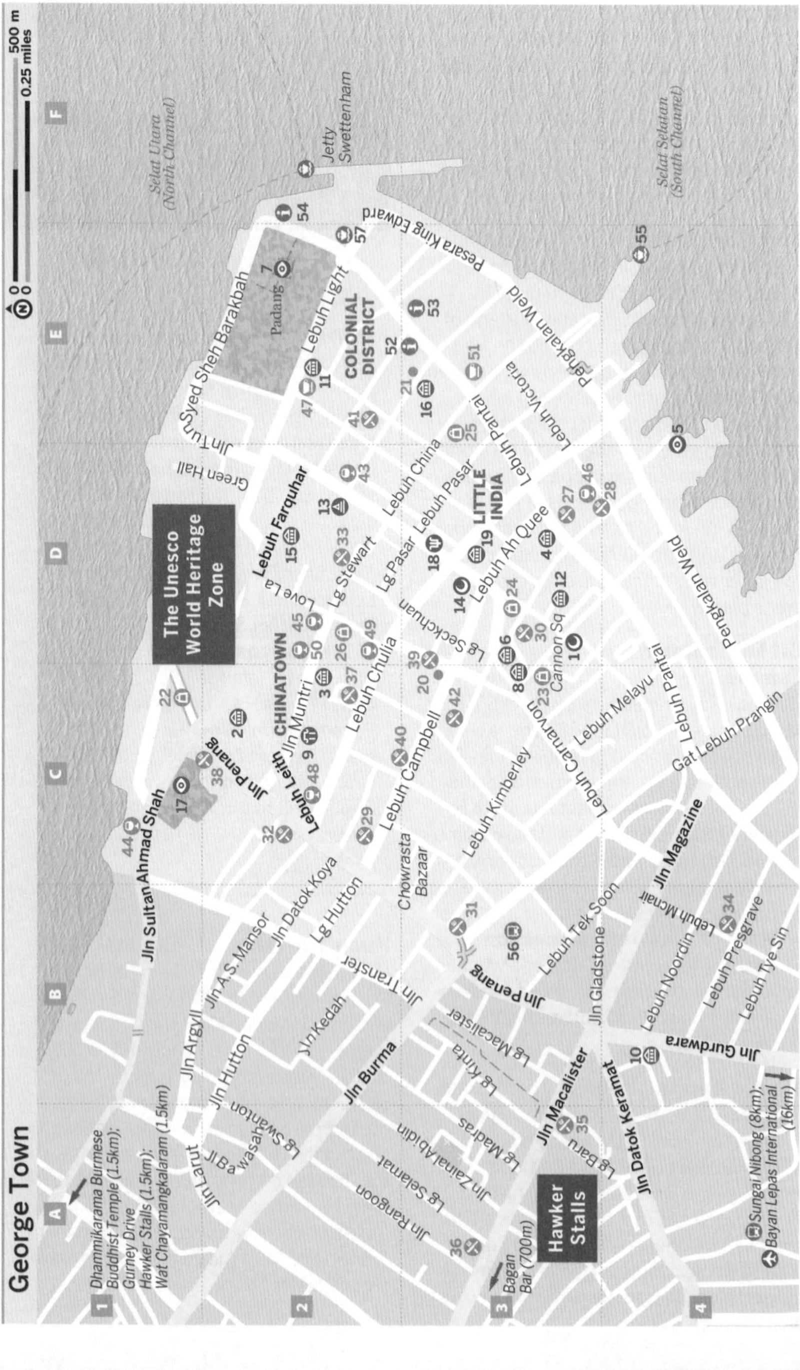
George Town
The Unesco World Heritage Zone
Hawker Stalls
CHINATOWN
LITTLE INDIA
COLONIAL DISTRICT
Selat Utara (North Channel)
Selat Selatan (South Channel)
Jetty
Swettenham
Padang
Dhammikarama Burmese Buddhist Temple (1.5km); Gurney Drive Hawker Stalls (1.5km); Wat Chayamangkalaram (1.5km)
Bagan Bar (700m)
Sungai Nibong (8km); Bayan Lepas International (16km)
0.25 miles
500 m
Jln Sultan Ahmad Shah
Jln Penang
Lebuh Leith
Jln Muntri
Love La
Lebuh Farquhar
Lg Stewart
Lebuh Chulia
Lebuh Campbell
Lg Seckchuan
Lg Pasar
Lebuh Pasar
Lebuh China
Lebuh Ah Quee
Cannon Sq
Lebuh Carnarvon
Lebuh Kimberley
Lebuh Melayu
Lebuh Pantai
Gat Lebuh Prangin
Pengkalan Weld
Lebuh Victoria
Pesara King Edward
Lebuh Light
Syed Sheh Barakbah
Jln Tun
Green Hall
Chowrasta Bazaar
Jln Datok Koya
Lg Hutton
Jln A.S. Mansor
Jln Transfer
Jln Argyll
Jln Hutton
Jln Kedah
Jln Burma
Lg Macalister
Lg Kinta
Jln Macalister
Lg Madras
Jln Zainal Abidin
Lg Selamat
Jln Rangoon
Lg Swatow
Jl Bawasah
Jln Larut
Lg Baru
Jln Datok Keramat
Jln Gurdwara
Jln Gladstone
Lebuh Tek Soon
Jln Magazine
Lebuh Mcnair
Lebuh Noordin
Lebuh Presgrave
Lebuh Tye Sin

George Town

Sights

1	Acheen St Mosque	D3
2	Blue Mansion	C2
3	Camera Museum	C2
4	Cheah Kongsi	D3
5	Chew Jetty	E4
6	Dr Sun Yat Sen's Penang Base	D3
7	Fort Cornwallis	E2
8	George Town World Heritage Inc. Headquarters	C3
9	Hainan Temple	C2
10	Hin Bus Depot Art Centre	B4
11	House of Yeap Chor Ee	E2
12	Khoo Kongsi	D3
13	Kuan Yin Teng	D2
14	Masjid Kapitan Keling	D3
15	Penang Museum	D2
16	Pinang Peranakan Mansion	E3
17	Protestant Cemetery	C1
18	Sri Mariamman Temple	D3
19	Teochew Temple	D3

Activities, Courses & Tours

20	Nazlina Spice Station	C3
21	Penang Heritage Trust	E3

Shopping

22	Little Penang Street Market	C1
23	Rozanas Batik	C3
24	Shop Howard	D3
25	Tropical Spice Garden In Town	E3
26	Unique Penang	D2

Eating

	BTB	(see 27)
27	China House	D3
28	Da Shu Xia Seafood House	D3
29	Hameediyah	C2
30	Jawi House	D3
31	Joo Hooi Cafe	B3
32	Kafe Kheng Pin	C2
33	Kebaya	D2
34	Lebuh Presgrave Hawker Stalls	B4
35	Lg Baru (New Lane) Hawker Stalls	A3
36	Lg Selamat Hawker Stalls	A3
37	Sky Cafe	C2
38	Sup Hameed	C2
39	Teksen	D3
40	Tho Yuen Restaurant	C2
41	Veloo Villas	E2
42	Yin's Sourdough Bakery	C3

Drinking & Nightlife

43	Alabama Shake	D2
44	Beach Blanket Babylon	C1
45	Behind 50 Love Lane	D2
46	Canteen	D3
47	Constant Gardener	E2
48	Georgetown Wines	C2
	Kopi C	(see 27)
49	Micke's Place	D2
50	Mish Mash	D2
51	Ten Yee Tea Trading	E3

Information

52	Penang Global Tourism	E3
	Penang Heritage Trust	(see 21)
53	Tourism Malaysia	E3
54	Tourism Malaysia	F2

Transport

55	Ferry	E4
56	Komtar Bus Station	B3
57	Langkawi Ferry Service	E2

Outside the Unesco Protected Zone

Penang Hill Hill

(www.penanghill.gov.my; funicular adult/child RM30/15; 6.30am-11pm) The top of Penang Hill, 821m above George Town, provides a spectacular view over the island and across to the mainland.

The top is reached by a funicular, and on weekends and public holidays lines can be horrendously long, with waits of up to 30 minutes. From Weld Quay, Komtar or Lebuh Chulia, you can catch the frequent bus 204 (RM2.70) to Air Itam. A taxi here from the centre of George Town will set you back about RM25.

It's generally about 5°C cooler here than at sea level, providing a convenient retreat from the sticky heat below. There are some gardens, a food court, an exuberantly decorated Hindu temple and a mosque as well as David Brown's, a colonial-style British restaurant serving everything from beef Wellington to high tea. From the road that extends from the upper funicular station, you can walk the 5km to the Botanical Gardens in about 1½ hours.

Kek Lok Si Temple Buddhist Temple

(www.kekloksitemple.com; 7am-9pm) FREE The 'Temple of Supreme Bliss' is also the largest Buddhist temple in Malaysia and one of the most recognisable buildings

Penang's Gardens

The **Botanical Gardens** (www.botanicalgardens.penang.gov.my; Waterfall Rd; 5am-8pm) FREE, founded in 1884, cover 30 hectares and include a fern rockery, an orchidarium, a lily pond and even some jungle. The gardens are located about 8km northeast of George Town. To get there, take bus 10 (RM2.70) from Komtar or Weld Quay; a taxi will cost at least RM25.

Between Teluk Bahang and Batu Ferringhi is the **Tropical Spice Garden** (04-881 1797; www.tropicalspicegarden.com; Jl Teluk Bahang; adult/child RM26/15, incl tour RM35/20; 9am-6pm), an oasis of tropical, fragrant fecundity of more than 500 species of flora, with an emphasis on edible herbs and spices. Explore the grounds on your own, or join one of four daily guided tours at 9am, 11.30am, 1.30pm and 3.30pm. The garden also offers **cooking courses** (04-881 1797; www.tropicalspicegarden.com; Jl Teluk Bahang; adult/child RM233.20/116.60; lessons 9am-1pm Mon-Sat), there's a good shop, the restaurant is worth a visit, and just across from the gardens there's a beautiful roadside white-sand beach. To get here by public transport, take any Teluk Bahang–bound bus (RM4).

A short drive further west is **Art & Garden by Fuan Wong** (adult/child RM30/15; 9am-5.30pm Thu-Mon). This amazing conceptual garden marries a superb collection of weird and wonderful plants with Fuan Wong's glass sculptures and installations. Creative works by other artists are dotted throughout the garden, which also has a cafe, gift shop and breathtaking views of Penang Hill.

in the country. Built by an immigrant Chinese Buddhist in 1890, Kek Lok Si is a cornerstone of the Malay-Chinese community, who provided the funding for its two-decade-long building (and ongoing additions).

The temple is in Air Itam, 8km from the centre of George Town. A taxi starts at about RM25, or you can hop on bus 204 (RM2.70).

To reach the entrance, walk through a maze of souvenir stalls, past a tightly packed turtle pond and murky fish ponds, until you reach **Ban Po Thar** (Ten Thousand Buddhas Pagoda; admission RM2), a seven-tier, 30m-high tower. The design is said to be Burmese at the top, Chinese at the bottom and Thai in between. A **cable car** (one way/return RM3/6; 8.30am-5.30pm) whisks you to the highest level, which is presided over by an awesome 36.5m-high bronze statue of Kuan Yin, goddess of mercy.

There are several other temples in this complex, as well as shops and a **vegetarian restaurant** (mains from RM5; 10am-7pm Tue-Sun;).

Hin Bus Depot Art Centre — Gallery

(www.facebook.com/hinbusdepot; 31A Jln Gurdwara; noon-7pm) FREE This gracefully crumbling former bus terminal has become a centre for George Town's burgeoning art scene. The open-air areas are bedecked with street art, and the covered area spans exhibitions that change every couple of months, and a cafe. Peruse the centre's Facebook page to see what's on when you're in town.

Wat Chayamangkalaram — Buddhist Temple

(Temple of the Reclining Buddha; Lg Burma; 7am-6pm) FREE The Temple of the Reclining Buddha is a typically Thai temple with its sharp-eaved roofs and ceiling accents. Inside it houses a 33m-long reclining Buddha draped in a gold-leafed saffron robe.

The temple is located about 2.5km northwest of central George Town; a taxi here will cost RM15.

Dhammikarama Burmese Buddhist Temple — Buddhist Temple

(Lg Burma; 7am-6pm) FREE A rare instance of a Burmese Buddhist temple outside

Burma (now Myanmar). There's a series of panel paintings on the life of the Buddha lining the walkways, the characters dressed in typical Burmese costume, while inside typically round-eyed, serene-faced Burmese Buddha statues stare out at worshippers. This was Penang's first Buddhist temple, built in 1805; it has been significantly added to over the years.

The temple is located about 2.5km northwest of central George Town; a taxi here will cost RM15.

COURSES

Nazlina Spice Station Cooking Course

(☎012-453 8167; www.penang-cooking-class.com; 2 Lebuh Campbell; classes from RM180; ⊙lessons 7.30am-12.30pm & 2.30-5.30pm) The bubbly and enthusiastic Nazlina will teach you how to make those dishes you've fallen in love with while in Penang. A course begins with a visit to a morning market and a local breakfast, followed by instruction in three or four dishes. Afternoon lessons are vegan/vegetarian.

Penang Homecooking School Cooking Course

(www.penanghomecookingschool.com; classes RM270-320; ⊙Mon, Wed & Fri) Three times a week, Pearly and Chandra open their home to teach visitors how to make Indian, Nonya and street dishes. Courses are flexible in terms of scope and time (see the website), and the fee varies depending on how many dishes you want to make. A half-day course includes transportation and a visit to a market.

TOURS

There's a huge variety of self-guided tours of George Town, from food walks to those focusing on traditional trades or architecture – pick up a pamphlet of the routes at the state tourist office or from the Penang Heritage Trust (p117). Likewise, the Penang Global Ethic Project (www.globalethicpenang.net) has put together a World Religion Walk that takes you past

Spices

MICHAEL RHEAULT - MADFIRE@GMAIL.COM/GETTY IMAGES ©

Penang laksa

the iconography and houses of worship of Christians, Muslims, Hindus, Sikhs, Buddhists and Chinese traditional religions.

If walking isn't your thing, consider the city route of the **Hop-On Hop-Off Bus** (www.myhoponhopoff.com/pg; adult/child per 24hrs RM45/24, per 48hrs RM79/43; 9am-8pm), which winds its way around the perimeter of the Unesco-protected zone. It's a good way to get a quick overview of the town, and you can get on and off at one of 17 stops.

George Town Heritage Walks Walking Tour
(016-440 6823; joannkhaw@gmail.com; tours from RM180) Discover George Town – and beyond – with Joann Khaw, a Penang native and heritage expert who also leads architecture, food and inland Penang tours, among others. Excursions require at least two people and advance notice.

Penang Heritage Trust Walking Tour
(PHT; 04-264 2631; www.pht.org.my; 26 Lebuh Gereja; tours RM200; 9am-5pm Mon-Fri, 9am-1pm Sat) This conservation-minded entity leads well-regarded walking tours of George Town. There are four different walks, ranging from a religious-themed meander to an exploration of George Town's Little India, all led by experienced guides. Walks require at least two people, usually last around three hours, and need advance booking.

SHOPPING

Little Penang Street Market Market
(www.littlepenang.com.my; 10am-5pm last Sun of month) On the last Sunday of every month, the pedestrian section of upper Jln Penang hosts an open-air market, with wares including Malaysian arts and crafts (think dolls, batik, pottery, T-shirts and painted tiles), as well as items like bottled chutney.

Unique Penang Handicrafts
(www.uniquepenang.com; 62 Love Lane; 6pm-midnight Sun-Fri, 9pm-midnight Sat) This shophouse gallery features the work of the

friendly young owners, Clovis and Joey, as well as the colourful paintings of the latter's young art students. As the couple point out, paintings are notoriously hard to squeeze in a backpack, so nearly all of the gallery's art is available in postcard size.

Tropical Spice Garden In Town Handicrafts
(Lebuh China; ⏲9am-5pm) Linked with Batu Ferringhi's Tropical Spice Garden (p110), this fragrant shop sells soaps, essential oils, dried spice and other spice-related goods.

Shop Howard Handicrafts
(154 Jln Masjid Kapitan Keling; ⏲10am-6pm) Unique postcards, art, photos, handicrafts and books on local topics, all made by local artists.

Rozanas Batik Handicrafts
(81B Lebuh Acheh; ⏲noon-6pm Mon-Sat) A shophouse workshop featuring the owner's beautiful handmade batik items. If you want to learn more about this craft, take a walk-in two-hour class in the adjacent studio (RM25 to RM100).

Straits Quay Mall
(www.straitsquay.com; Jln Seri Tanjung Pinang, Tanjung Tokong; ⏲10.30am-10pm) Penang's flashiest mall, built on reclaimed land just outside the city centre. If you're not into shopping, it's also home to the Performing Arts Centre of Penang (www.penangpac.org) and there are a couple of decent restaurants and bars.

Straits Quay is located about 7km northwest of George Town. Buses 101 and 104 pass the mall (RM4), and a taxi here will cost about RM25.

EATING

We're just going to come out and say it: George Town is the best food city in Southeast Asia. It's easily the most diverse: in one block alone you can find Malay, regional Chinese, *mamak* (halal Indian/South Asian), regional Indian, Peranakan or Nonya (a blend of Chinese, Malay and sometimes Thai), and other unique blends of local and

Hi, Tea!

Penang's English, Chinese and Indian legacies have left an appreciation for tea that remains strong today. More recent immigrants to George Town have imported an enviable Western-style cafe culture (with good coffee to boot).

For the ultimate English tea experience, head to **Suffolk House** (www.suffolkhouse.com.my; 250 Jln Ayer Itam; high tea for two RM90; ⏲2.30-6pm), about 6.5km west of George Town. In this 200-year-old Georgian-style mansion, high tea, featuring scones and cucumber sandwiches, can be taken inside or in the garden. A taxi here will cost around RM25.

David Brown's Tea Terrace (www.penanghillco.com.my; Penang Hill; afternoon tea RM24-70; ⏲9am-6pm), located at the top of Penang Hill, is probably the island's most atmospheric destination for colonial-style high tea (from 3pm to 6pm).

For Chinese tea try **Ten Yee Tea Trading** (33 Lebuh Pantai; ⏲9.30am-6.30pm Mon-Sat). For RM20 you choose a tea (which you can share with up to five people), then Lim, the enthusiastic owner, shows you how to prepare it the proper way.

If coffee is more to your taste, go for Kopi C (p115), which also boasts some excellent cakes and ice creams, or **Constant Gardener** (www.constantgardener.coffee; 9 Lebuh Light; ⏲9am-6pm), which brews its lattes with coveted beans from Malaysia and beyond, and serves some pristine-looking pastries.

Chinese cuisines. And, best of all, the quality's also there, and the locals are as crazy about the food as the visitors.

Veloo Villas Indian $
(22 Lebuh Penang; mains from RM2, set meals RM5-9.50; ⏲7am-10pm; ✎) For one meal, set aside notions of service – and ambience – and instead focus on the vibrant, fun southern Indian cuisine. Come from approximately 11am to 4pm for hearty and diverse rice-based set meals, or outside of these hours for *dosa* (paper-thin rice-and-lentil crêpes) and other snacks.

Sup Hameed Malaysian $
(48 Jln Penang; mains from RM3; ⏲24hr) On the surface, this is very much your typical *nasi kandar* (South Asian Muslim-influenced) shop found all over Malaysia, and we don't particularly recommend eating here during the day. But come night, Hameed sets out tables on the street and serves his incredibly rich and meaty soups (try *sup kambing* – goat soup), served with slices of white bread.

Sky Cafe Chinese $
(Lebuh Chulia; mains RM1-6; ⏲11am-2pm) This gem sits in the middle of the greatest concentration of travellers in George Town, yet is somehow almost exclusively patronised (in enthusiastic numbers) by locals. Come on the early side of the three-hour open window for *char siew* (barbequed pork) and *siew yoke* (pork belly) that are considered among the best in town.

Hameediyah Malaysian $
(164 Lebuh Campbell; mains RM5-35; ⏲10am-11pm Sat-Thu, 10am-12.30pm & 2-11pm Fri) Dating back to 1907 and allegedly the oldest *nasi kandar* in Malaysia, Hameediyah looked its age until a recent and much-needed face-lift. In addition to rich curries served over rice, try the *murtabak*, a *roti prata* (flaky, flat bread) stuffed with minced mutton, chicken or vegetables, egg and spices.

Yin's Sourdough Bakery Bakery $
(11 Pesara Claimant; mains RM4.50-25; ⏲7am-6pm Mon-Fri, to 2pm Sat; ❄✎) Tired of rice? Weary of noodles? Head here for some of the city's best bread, served in the form of creative sandwiches, pastries and breakfasts.

Tho Yuen Restaurant Chinese $
(92 Lebuh Campbell; dim sum RM1-5; ⏲6am-3pm Wed-Mon) Our favourite place for dim sum. It's packed with newspaper-reading loners and chattering groups of locals all morning long, but you can usually squeeze in somewhere. Servers speak minimal English but do their best to explain the contents of their carts.

Teksen Chinese $$
(18 Lebuh Carnarvon; mains RM10-28; ⏲noon-3pm & 6-9pm Wed-Mon) There's a reason this place is always packed with happy locals: it's one of the tastiest, most consistent restaurants in town (and in a place like George Town that's saying a lot). You almost can't go wrong here, but don't miss the favourites – the 'double roasted pork with chilli padi' is obligatory and delicious – and be sure to ask about the daily specials.

Jawi House Malaysian $$
(www.jawihouse.com; 85 Lebuh Armenian; mains RM16-27; ⏲11am-10pm Wed-Mon; ❄) This cosy, shophouse restaurant specialises in the type of unique Muslim dishes you'd be hard-pressed to find outside of a local home or celebration. We loved the fragrant, meaty 'Jawi briyani', but you may like the 'lemuni rice', which is seasoned with a type of flower.

Da Shu Xia Seafood House Chinese $$
(Tree Shade Seafood Restaurant; cnr Gat Lebuh Armenian & Lebuh Victoria; mains RM10-50; ⏲11am-3.30pm & 5-10pm Thu-Tue) In new digs that lack the shade of the eponymous tree, this open-air shack remains where locals go for cheap and tasty seafood. Pick your aquatic protein from the trays out front, and the staff will fry, steam, soup or grill it up for you.

ROSMAH ABDUL HAMID/EYEEM/GETTY IMAGES ©

Bibimbap

Nyonya Breeze Desire Peranakan $$

(1st fl, Straits Quay, Tanjung Tokong; mains RM9.90-44.90; ⏲11am-10pm; ❄) This long-standing go-to for Peranakan (or Nonya) cuisine has relocated to a rather charmless setting in a mall. But the food is better than ever, and ranges from several *kerabu* (salads) to staples such as *inche kabin* (deep-fried chicken).

Straits Quay is located about 7km north-west of George Town, in Tanjong Toking; a taxi here from central George Town will set you back about RM25.

China House International $$$

(☎04-263 7299; www.chinahouse.com.my; 153 & 155 Lebuh Pantai; ⏲9am-midnight) Where do we start? This complex of three co-joined shophouses features a dining outlet, a café/bakery, **Kopi C** (www.chinahouse.com.my; China House, 153 & 155 Lebuh Pantai; mains from RM10; ⏲9am-midnight); and a bar, Canteen (p116), not to mention a shop and gallery.

BTB (mains RM44.52-76.32; ⏲6.30-10.30pm; ❄🍷), the flagship dining venue, does a relatively short but exotic-sounding menu of Malaysian-, Middle Eastern- and Mediterranean-influenced dishes; think 'rack of lamb with cumin crust, smoked eggplant puree and eggplant gingerbud sambal'.

Kebaya Peranakan $$$

(☎04-264 2333; www.seventerraces.com; Seven Terraces, Lg Stewart; set dinner RM120; ⏲6-10pm Tue-Sun; ❄) Kebaya sets the scene with a stately dining room decorated with a gorgeous collection of antiques, set to a soundtrack of live piano. The Peranakan-influenced cuisine – available only via a set dinner – is an appropriate visual counter-part, but flavour-wise, tends toward the timid end of the spectrum.

DRINKING & NIGHTLIFE

Between the largely hotel-based bars and some rather grungy pubs and clubs, George Town doesn't have much of a sophisticated bar scene. That said, it's growing, and there are a few fun places for a night out.

Butterworth

Butterworth, the city on the mainland section of Penang (known as Sebarang Perai), is home to Penang's main train station and is the departure point for ferries to Penang Island. Unless you're taking the train or your bus has pulled into Butterworth's busy bus station from elsewhere, you'll probably not need to spend any time here.

If you do find yourself in Butterworth, the cheapest way to get to George Town is via the **ferry** (per adult/car RM1.20/7.70; ⌚5.30am-1am); the terminal is linked by walkway to Butterworth's bus and train stations. Ferries take passengers and cars every 10 minutes from 5.30am to 9.30pm, every 20 minutes until 11.15pm, and hourly after that until 1am. The journey takes 10 minutes and fares are charged only for the journey from Butterworth to Penang; returning to the mainland is free.

If you choose to take a taxi to/from Butterworth (approximately RM50), you'll cross the 13.5km Penang Bridge. There's a RM7 toll payable at the toll plaza on the mainland, but no charge to return. The whopping 24km Sultan Abdul Halim Muadzam Shah Bridge connects Batu Maung at the southeastern tip of the island to Batu Kawan on the mainland. There's a RM8.50 toll payable at the toll plaza on the mainland, but no charge to return.

THE BEST PICTURES COME FROM A SINCERE HEART/GETTY IMAGES ©

Bars are scattered throughout town, but the strip of road at the far northern end of Jln Penang is George Town's rather commercial-feeling entertainment strip. Another lively – if somewhat budget-oriented – nightlife area is the conglomeration of backpacker pubs near the intersection of Lebuh Chulia and Love Lane.

Canteen Bar
(www.chinahouse.com.my; China House, 183B Lebuh Victoria; ⌚9am-11pm) This is about as close as George Town comes to a hipster bar – minus the pretension. Canteen has an artsy/warehouse vibe, there's live music from 9.30pm, and there are great bar snacks. Canteen is also accessible via China House's entrance on Lebuh Pantai.

Mish Mash Bar
(www.mishmashpg.com; 24 Jln Muntri; ⌚2pm-midnight Tue-Sun) Mish Mash has brought some unique booze – not to mention some much needed panache – to George Town's drinking scene. Come for the city's most well-stocked bar, clever cocktails and some great non-alcoholic drinks (try the 'traditional ginger soda'), as well as a full tobacco counter. There's also food, although we hesitate to endorse Mish Mash as a dinner locale.

Alabama Shake Bar
(www.facebook.com/cjalabamashake; 92 Lebuh Gereja; ⌚4pm-late) Just your average American boozer – if your average American bar was located in Malaysia and was run by a gregarious Serbian and a local. Come to think of it, there's little ordinary about this bar, previously known as B@92, but it gets it right, from tasty American-themed cocktails to slow-cooked pulled-pork sandwiches.

Micke's Place Bar
(94 Love Lane; ⌚noon-late) This eclectic bar-restaurant is both the longest-standing and most fun of the area's backpacker bars. Pull up a grafittied chair, bump to the vintage soundtrack, suck on a shisha and make a new friend.

Behind 50 Love Lane Bar

(Lebuh Muntri; ⌚6pm-1am Wed-Mon) Pocket-sized, retro-themed bar-restaurant that draws a largely local following, despite being close to the backpacker strip. There's a classic rock soundtrack and a short menu of Western-style comfort dishes (RM14.90 to RM18.90).

Beach Blanket Babylon Bar

(32 Jln Sultan Ahmad Shah; ⌚noon-midnight) The open-air setting and relaxed vibe contrast with the rather grand building this bar is linked to. Pair your drink and al fresco views over the North Channel with tasty local dishes.

Bagan Bar Bar

(Macalister Mansion, 228 Jln Macalister; ⌚5pm-1am) This sleek, dark, velvet-coated den is probably the most sophisticated bar in town – a fact seemingly verified by the rather strict dress code (no shorts, T-shirts or flip-flops). There's live music from 9pm.

Bagan is located about 1km north of the junction with Jln Penang.

Georgetown Wines Bar

(www.facebook.com/georgetownwines; 19 Lebuh Leith; ⌚5pm-midnight Tue-Sun) Wine bars are the flavour of the moment in George Town, and this one, cleverly built into a former stable, is among the more attractive. Take a walk through the cellar or order house wines by the glass; dinner is best left to another venue.

INFORMATION

Penang Global Tourism (☎04-264 3456; www.mypenang.gov.my; Whiteways Arcade, Lebuh Pantai; ⌚9am-5pm Mon-Fri, to 3pm Sat, to 1pm Sun) This, the visitor's centre of the state tourism agency, is the best all-around place to go for maps, brochures and local information.

Penang Heritage Trust (PHT; ☎04-264 2631; www.pht.org.my; Lebuh Gereja; ⌚9am-5pm Mon-Fri, 9am-1pm Sat) Come to this tiny but excellent centre for information on the history and culture of Penang, conservation projects, self-guided walks, or to arrange one of the organisation's excellent guided tours.

Tourism Malaysia (☎04-262 0066; www.tourism.gov.my/en/my; 10 Jln Tun Syed Sheh Barakbah; ⌚8am-1pm & 2-5pm Mon-Fri) The government tourist office provides general tourism information on the country as a whole; nearby, the agency's Penang **branch** (☎04-262 0202; 11 Lebuh Pantai; ⌚8am-1pm & 2-5pm Mon-Fri) provides state-specific information.

GETTING THERE & AWAY

Penang's **Bayan Lepas International Airport** (☎04-643 4411; www.penangairport.com) is 18km south of George Town.

Buses to destinations in Malaysia can be boarded at **Sungai Nibong** (☎04-659 2099; www.rapidpg.com.my; Jln Sultan Azlan Shah, Kampung Dua Bukit) and, more conveniently, at the **Komtar bus station** (www.rapidpg.com.my; Jln Penang); international destinations only at the latter. Note that transport to Thailand (except to Hat Yai) is via minivan. Transport can also be arranged to Ko Samui and Ko Phi Phi via a transfer in Surat Thani and Hat Yai respectively.

Several providers, including **Langkawi Ferry Service** (LFS; ☎04-264 2088; www.langkawi-ferry.com; PPC Bldg, Lebuh King Edward; ⌚7am-5.30pm Mon-Sat, 7am-3pm Sun), operate a shared ferry service to Langkawi (one-way/return RM69/137, 1¾ to 2½ hours). Boats leave at 8.15am, 8.30am and 2pm. Boats return from Langkawi at 10.30am, 2.30pm and 5.15pm. Book a few days in advance to ensure a seat.

GETTING AROUND

The fixed taxi fare from Penang's airport to most places in central George Town is RM45; taxis take about 30 minutes to the centre of town. Bus 401 runs to and from the airport (RM4) every half hour between 6am and 11pm daily, and stops at Komtar and Weld Quay, taking at least an hour.

VASUKIRAO/GETTY IMAGES ©

PULAU LANGKAWI

In this Chapter

Pulau Langkawi

Langkawi is synonymous with 'tropical paradise'. Since 2008, the archipelago's official title has been Langkawi Permata Kedah (Langkawi, the Jewel of Kedah), no doubt inspired by the island's clear waters, relatively pristine beaches and intact jungle. The district has been duty free since 1987 and pulling in tourists well before that. Even so, these 99 islands, dominated by 478.5-sq-km Pulau Langkawi, have not been overdeveloped beyond recognition.

Get just a little way off the main beaches and this is idyllic rural Malaysia, with traditional kampung (villages) and a laid-back vibe.

Pulau Langkawi in Two Days

Get your bearings of the island and ride the **Panorama Langkawi** (p124) cable car all 708m to the top of Gunung Machinchang to enjoy the spectacular views. Relax on the beach at **Pantai Cenang** (p122) or **Pantai Tengah** (p122), perhaps also squeezing in a massage at **Ishan Spa** (p126). On day two, head inland to cool off in the freshwater pools at **Telaga Tujuh** (p124).

Pulau Langkawi in Four Days

Head to the north of the island for a boat tour around the **Kilim Karst Geoforest Park** (p124), then cool down in the pools and waterfalls at **Durian Perangin** (p124). On your final day join an **island-hopping tour** (p127) to see the lovely Lake of the Pregnant Maiden on Pulau Dayang Bunting and the pristine beach at Pulau Beras Basah.

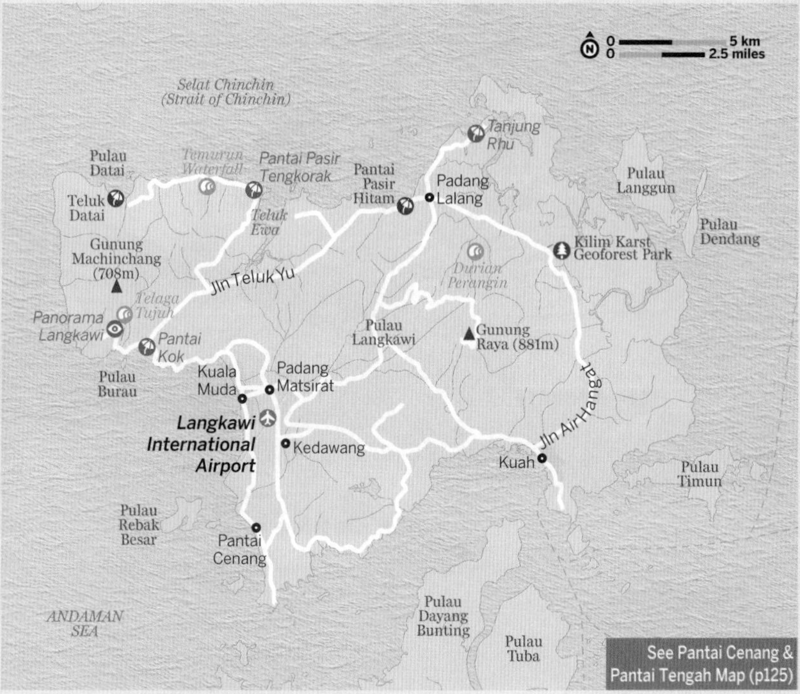

Arriving in Pulau Langkawi

Langkawi International Airport Located in the west of the island near Padang Matsirat, and served by half-a-dozen airlines.

Kuah Jetty Kuah is the island's main town, and all passenger ferries operate out of this busy terminal. Connections include Kuala Perlis, Kuala Kedah, Satun (Thailand), Ko Lipe (Thailand) and George Town.

Sleeping

While there is plenty of decent accommodation on Langkawi, it isn't cheap. Luxury resorts here are some of the best around, but midrange places (and even some of the upscale ones) can feel lacklustre, and there are relatively few budget-oriented hostels and guesthouses.

During school holidays and the peak tourist season (approximately November to February), Pulau Langkawi can become crowded, and advance bookings are generally necessary. At other times of the year supply far outstrips demand and prices are negotiable.

A beach restaurant, Pantai Cenang

Langkawi's Beaches

Beach-lovers rejoice: whatever stretch of sand you're looking for – busy with plenty of facilities or off the beaten track and deserted – chances are Langkawi can deliver.

Great For...

☑ Don't Miss

The beaches at Teluk Datai – arguably some of the island's most beautiful, but only accessible to guests of the area's resorts.

Pantai Cenang

The busiest and most developed beach is the 2km-long strip of sand at Pantai Cenang. The beach is gorgeous: white sand, teal water and green palms. There are water sports on hand and the water is good for swimming, but beware of jellyfish and speeding jet skis ripping past.

There are some very fine top-end resorts at Cenang, as well as the bulk of Langkawi's budget and midrange accommodation. Come night time, the main road is the place to eat, drink, window shop and generally make merry.

Pantai Tengah

Head south and Langkawi gets a little more polished; as the road loops around a rocky headland, you're in upscale Pantai Tengah. It's a slightly smaller, narrower beach,

with less noisy water-sports activity than on Pantai Cenang. There are a few big, all-inclusive resorts here, good restaurants and bars, and a few cheaper hotels, too.

Pantai Kok

On the western part of the island, 12km north of Pantai Cenang, Pantai Kok fronts a beautiful bay surrounded by limestone mountains and jungle. The beach here is popular with locals who picnic under the trees. There are a handful of equidistantly located upscale resorts around here, many with their own small strips of beach.

Tanjung Rhu

On the north coast, Tanjung Rhu is one of Langkawi's wider and better beaches, fronted by magnificent limestone stacks that bend the ocean into a pleasant bay.

Need to Know

There are jellyfish off Langkawi's beaches; stings can be painful, but most are not dangerous.

Take a Break

Langkawi's best selection of restaurants and bars are at Pantai Cenang and Pantai Tengah.

★ Top Tip

To access the more secluded of Langkawi's beaches hire a car or scooter.

On clear days, the sunsets here give the word 'stunning' new meaning. The water is shallow, and at low tide you can walk across the sandbank to the neighbouring islands (except during the monsoon season). Accommodation is provided by two upscale resorts.

Pantai Pasir Tengkorak

This beautiful, secluded public beach, with its soft white sand, clear water, shady trees and jungle backdrop, is popular with locals on weekends; during the week it can be almost empty. The car park and entrance to the beach is on the 161 road, between Langkawi Crocodile Farm and Temurun waterfall. Note that the bathrooms here may or may not be open and there is nowhere to buy food or water.

◎ SIGHTS

Kuah is Langkawi's main town, and aside from a couple of good restaurants the main reason to stop here is for the banks, ferries or duty-free shopping. The main sights are elsewhere on the island.

Underwater World Aquarium

(☑04-955 6100; www.underwaterworldlangkawi.com.my; Pantai Cenang; adult/child RM40/30; ⊙10am-6pm) With an imposing frontage that makes it something of a landmark on the main Cenang strip, this aquarium features 500 species of marine and freshwater creatures as well as Rockhopper penguins. Some exhibits (especially the rainforest walk) are well executed, while others seem small and in need of a clean.

Panorama Langkawi Cable Car

(☑04-959 4225; www.panoramalangkawi.com; Oriental Village, Burau Bay; SkyCab ticket adult/child RM35/25; ⊙9.30am-7pm) Panorama Langkawi encompasses a befuddling number of attractions with individual entrance prices (packages are available). But the star of the show, and one of the island's most worthwhile attractions, is the SkyCab cable car that takes visitors on a vertiginous 20-minute trip to the top of the majestic Gunung Machinchang (708m). There are some incredible views along the way, and at the top, you can walk across the **SkyBridge**, a single-span suspension bridge located 100m above old-growth jungle canopy.

Other attractions here include an F1 simulator, 6D Cinemotion (a 3D movie simulator with splashes of water) and a 3D Art Museum where you can take selfies with murals of famous sights and artworks. Arrive early to avoid long queues at weekends and during school holidays. Once a month the SkyCab is closed for maintenance.

Telaga Tujuh Waterfall

(Seven Wells; Jln Telaga Tujuh) The series of freshwater rockpools at Telaga Tujuh, located at the top of a waterfall inland from Pantai Kok, make a refreshing alternative to splashing about in the ocean. To get here follow the road from Pantai Kok past Oriental Village (SkyCab is well signposted) until it dead-ends at a car park. From here it's a steady 10-minute climb through the rainforest (stay to the right) to the wells at the top of the falls.

Temurun Waterfall Waterfall

(Jln Datai) A brief walk from the main road up to Teluk Datai, the falls here – the island's tallest – are worth a look, though beware of food-stealing monkeys. The turn-off is on the left-hand side as you head east, 1km past Pantai Pasi Tengkorak.

Kilim Karst
Geoforest Park Nature Reserve

(1-4hr tour for a boat of up to 8 people per hr from RM150) The jetty near Tanjung Rhu is the main departure point for boat trips into the extensive mangrove forests with stunning limestone formations that edge much of the northeastern coast of Langkawi. Tours usually include a stop at Gua Kelawar (the bat cave, home to – you've guessed it – a colony of bats), lunch at a floating restaurant and eagle watching.

Unfortunately, to attract eagles and please their camera-toting customers, many tour operators churn chicken fat or other foodstuff into the water behind the boats, disrupting the birds' natural feeding patterns and damaging the ecosystem. Dev's Adventure Tours (p126) is one outfit offering boat and kayaking trips that does not include eagle feeding.

Durian Perangin Waterfall

The swimming pools here are a 10 minutes' walk up paved steps through the forest, with pagoda-like shaded seating areas along the way. The water is always refreshingly cool, but the falls are best seen at the end of monsoon season, from late September and early October. The waterfalls are located 2km off the 112 road, just east of Air Hangat.

Pantai Cenang & Pantai Tengah

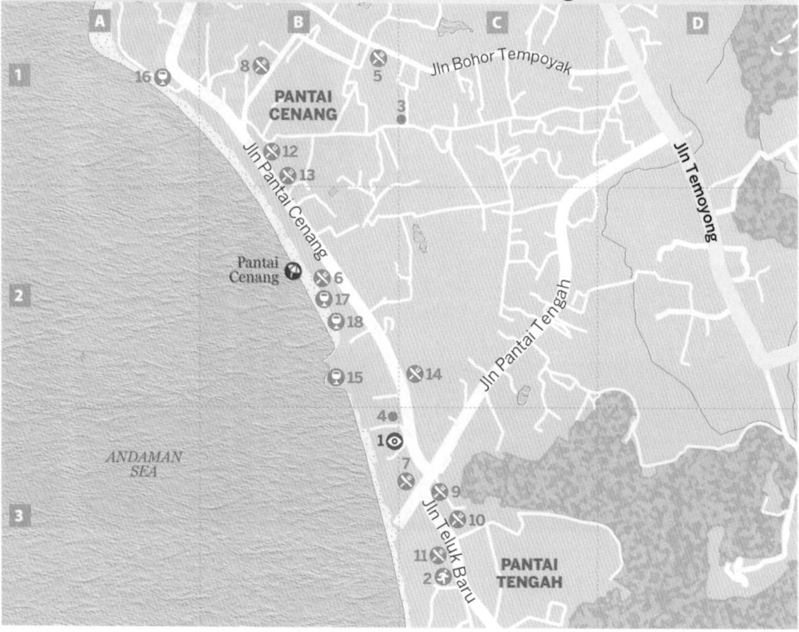

Pantai Cenang & Pantai Tengah

Sights

1 Underwater World B3

Activities, Courses & Tours

2 Alun-Alun Spa C3
3 Crystal Yacht Holidays C1
4 Dev's Adventure Tours B3

Eating

5 Bohor Tempoyak Night Market B1
6 Brasserie B2
7 Istanbul C3
8 Kasbah B1
9 La Chocolatine C3
10 Llawa C3
11 Melayu C3
12 Padang Pasir B1
13 Putumayo B1
14 Red Tomato C2

Drinking & Nightlife

15 Cliff B2
16 La Sal A1
17 Little Lylia's Chill Out Cafe B2
18 Yellow Café B2

Gunung Raya Mountain

The tallest mountain on the island (881m) can be reached by a snaking, paved road through the jungle. It's a spectacular drive to the top with views across the island and over to Thailand from a lookout point and a small teahouse (assuming there's no fog). In the evening there's a good chance of spotting the magnificent great hornbill near the road.

ACTIVITIES

The main strip along Pantai Tengah is home to many of the island's spas. Massages average RM150 per hour, while facials and other treatments start at about RM60. Many spas offer complimentary transfers; call for details.

Panorama Langkawi (p124)

Alun-Alun Spa Spa

(☎04-955 5570; www.alunalunspa.com; Jln Teluk Baru; ⏰11am-11pm) With three branches across the island, Alun-Alun is accessible and gets good reviews. The spa's blended aromatherapy oils are also available for purchase.

Ishan Spa Spa

(☎04-955 5585; www.ishanspa.com; Jln Teluk Baru; ⏰11am-8pm) Some pretty posh pampering is available here with an emphasis on traditional Malaysian techniques – including an invigorating bamboo massage – and natural remedies, such as compresses made with herbs from the garden.

TOURS

Dev's Adventure Tours Adventure Tour

(☎019-494 9193; www.langkawi-nature.com; Lot 1556, Tanjung Mali, Pantai Cenang; tour RM120-220) Cycling, birdwatching, mangrove excursions and jungle walks: this outfit offers a fat menu of options led by knowledgeable and enthusiastic guides. Book online or by phone. Transfers are provided from most hotels.

JungleWalla Adventure Tour

(☎019-590 2300; www.junglewalla.com; 1C, Lot 1392, Jln Tanjung Rhu; tours RM160-250) Since setting up this nature tour company in 1994, Irshad Mobarak has become something of a celebrity naturalist in Malaysia. On offer are birdwatching excursions, jungle walks, and mangrove- and island-hopping trips, all with an emphasis on observing wildlife. Multiday itineraries are available on request.

Langkawi Canopy Adventures Adventure Tour

(☎012-466 8027; www.langkawi.travel; Lubuk Semilang; tour RM80-220) The highlight here is high-adrenalin 'air trekking' through the rainforest along a series of rope courses and zip lines. Excursions must be booked at least a day in advance and you'll need to arrange a taxi to take you to the site at Lubuk Semilang, in the middle of Langkawi.

Blue Water Star Sailing Cruise
(☎04-966 4868; www.bluewaterstarsailing.com; dinner cruise RM450) This outfit runs an infamously boozy dinner cruise every day from 3pm to 8pm. Boats depart from the yacht club in Kuah; transport here is not included.

Crystal Yacht Holidays Cruise
(☎04-955 6545; www.crystalyacht.com; Pantai Cenang; dinner cruise RM280) Operates popular sunset dinner cruises. Boats depart from the pier at Resorts World, south of Pantai Tengah, and transport from most hotels is included.

East Marine Diving
(☎04-966 3966; www.eastmarine.com.my; Royal Langkawi Yacht Club, Jln Pantai Dato Syed Omar, Kuah; snorkelling/diving trips from RM300/320, PADI certification course RM1300) Probably the most reputable diving outfit on the island. East Marine conducts full-day diving and snorkelling excursions to Pulau Payar Marine Park. Strung out like several green jewels in the teal sea are the park's four islands; most trips go to 2km-long Pulau Payar. Enquire about the water conditions before you go, as it can get murky.

Island Hopping

The most popular day trip is the island-hopping tour, offered by most tour and diving companies and costing as little as RM30 per person. Tours usually take in **Dayang Bunting** (Lake of the Pregnant Maiden), located on the island of the same name. It's a freshwater lake surrounded by craggy limestone cliffs and dense jungle, and a good spot for swimming. Other destinations include the pristine beach at **Pulau Beras Basah**, sea stacks and sea caves, and a stop for **eagle watching**. As with the boat trips at Kilim Karst, many operators use food to attract the eagles, which disrupts their natural feeding patterns; the tours offered by JungleWalla (p126) do not include eagle feeding.

Dayang Bunting
EYE UBIQUITOUS/GETTY IMAGES ©

EATING

Pantai Cenang & Around

Padang Pasir Indian $
(☎04-966 6786; Jln Pantai Cenang; mains RM11-16; ⏰7am-1am) This well-positioned food stall with open-air seating on the main Cenang strip sells tempting chicken, lamb and naan bread fresh from the tandoor oven, as well as *nasi kandar* (rice with curry sauces) and rotis. It's open from 7am for breakfast to 1am at night, making it a good place to stop and refuel at any time of day.

Kasbah International $$
(Pantai Cenang; mains RM7-23; ⏰9am-11pm) A relaxed, friendly cafe housed in a spacious, open-sided wooden structure constructed and furnished by the artistic owners using recycled materials. Reggae, hammocks, books and games attract a crowd of happy travellers, as does the menu of decent coffee, breakfasts, salads and sandwiches, and recommended daily Malaysian specials.

Red Tomato International $$
(☎04-955 4055; 5 Casa Fina Ave, Pantai Cenang; mains RM 20-40; ⏰9.30am-10.30pm) Red Tomato is run by expats who crank out some of the best pizza on the island. It's also a popular breakfast spot; options include eggs cooked how you like them and served with homemade bread.

Brasserie Mediterranean $$$
(☎04-955 1927; 27A Jln Pantai Cenang; mains RM24-118; ⏰noon-11pm Tue-Sun) A classy

Shopping

Duty-free shopping in Langkawi is a big draw for Malaysians, who flock here to stock up on cooking utensils, suitcases and chocolate. But unless you're planning to pick up a new set of saucepans or plates you are unlikely to be wildly excited by the duty-free shops.

The best options for handicrafts are the huge complex **Atma Alam Batik Art Vilage** (04-955 1227; www.atmaalam.com; Jln Padang Matsirat, near Petronas fuel station; 9am-6pm), with an emphasis on batik, and **Kompleks Kraf Langkawi** (Langkawi Craft Complex; 04-959 1913; www.malaysiacraft.com.my; Jln Teluk Yu; 10am-6pm), where you can watch demonstrations by craftspeople.

Batik painting
SIMON BRACKEN/GETTY IMAGES ©

beachside restaurant and bar serving modern European food in a breezy, shaded outdoor dining area complete with ocean views and sand underfoot. There's a happy hour on cocktails from 4pm to 6pm.

Nam International $$$
(04-955 6787; Bon Ton Resort, Jln Kuala Muda; mains RM30-94; 11am-11pm;) At Bon Ton resort, Nam boasts a well-executed menu of fusion food, from chargrilled rack of lamb with roast pumpkin, mint salad, hummus and tomato jam, to a nine-dish sampler of Nonya cuisine. There are plenty of veggie options, and at night, amid Bon Ton's starry jungle grounds, the setting is superb. Reservations recommended during peak season (December and January).

Putumayo Asian $$$
(04-953 2233; Lot 1584, Pantai Cenang; mains RM10-100; 1pm-11.30pm) Excellent service (the waiter folds your napkin on your lap) amid a beautiful open-air courtyard. The cuisine ranges from across Asia, looping from Malaysia through Thailand to China with fresh fish and seafood (including prawns the size of your hand) priced by weight.

Pantai Tengah & Around

Melayu Malaysian $
(04-955 4075; Jln Teluk Baru; mains RM5-10; 3-10.30pm) The comfortable dining room, pleasant outdoor seating area and efficient service here belie the reasonable prices. A good place to go for cheap, authentic Malaysian food in the evening, since most of the island's local restaurants are lunchtime buffets. Alcohol isn't served but you can bring your own for no charge.

Llawa Malaysian $$
(04-955 3608; Lot 2863 Jln Teluk Baru; mains RM26-75; 3-11pm Fri-Wed) First impressions of the 'dining lounge' at Llawa – low lighting, generously sized chairs with colourful cushions – are promising, and fortunately the ambience is matched by the flavoursome Malaysian food served here. We recommend the decadently rich beef rendang and the *udang percik* (grilled king prawns). The menu also features steaks and the like for the less adventurous.

Istanbul Turkish $$
(04-955 2100; hungry_monkey@hotmail.com; Jln Pantai Tengah; mains RM22-60; 6pm-midnight;) Istanbul features a cosy dining room, friendly service and a menu that extends far beyond doner kebab. We loved the Adana lamb with eggplant dip that was filling and tasty, but if that doesn't sate your appetite try the 1m-long kebab served with rice, bread, a mixed mezze plate, barbecue tomato and chilli (RM250).

Nonya cuisine

La Chocolatine French $$

(☎04-955 8891; 3 Jln Teluk Baru; mains RM15-30; ⏱9am-9pm; ❄) Excellent French desserts – croissants, tarts and éclairs – as well as light salads, sandwiches and quiches. Did we mention coffees, teas and real hot chocolate? A sophisticated, air-conditioned snack stop.

Unkaizan Japanese $$$

(☎04-955 4118; www.unkaizan.com; Jln Teluk Baru; mains RM30-100; ⏱6-11pm, closed 2nd Wed of each month) Lauded Japanese food, with seating in a cosy bungalow and on an open patio. The menu spans all that Japan is known for, but don't forget to ask for the specials board, which often includes dishes made with imported Japanese seafood. Reservations recommended.

DRINKING & NIGHTLIFE

Langkawi's duty-free status makes it one of the cheapest places to buy booze in Malaysia, and alcohol at many restaurants and hotels is half the price that it is on the mainland. There are some decent beach-style bars along Pantai Cenang, including some informal candlelight and deckchair affairs that pop up on the sand as the sun goes down. Like the island itself, the bar scene here is pretty laid-back, and those looking to party hard may be disappointed.

Little Lylia's Chill Out Cafe Bar

(Pantai Cenang; ⏱noon-1am) This longstanding, chummy bar spills out onto Pantai Cenang until the late hours. The chairs and tables may be practically falling apart, but friendly service and a chilled-out vibe hold the place together.

Yellow Café Bar

(Pantai Cenang; ⏱noon-1am Wed-Mon; 📶) A fun, breezy place with beanbags on the beach and a few imported beers. Come between 4pm and 6pm when beers are buy one get one free.

Cliff Bar

(www.theclifflangkawi.com; Pantai Cenang; ⏱noon-11pm) Perched on the rocky outcrop that divides Pantai Cenang and Pantai Tengah, the Cliff is well located for a sunset cocktail. Expect a full bar, a good wine selection, and an eclectic menu that spans from Europe to Malaysia (mains RM23 to RM72).

La Sal Bar

(www.casadelmar-langkawi.com; Casa del Mar, Pantai Cenang) This open-air restaurant and cocktail bar has some creative drinks – who fancies a five-spiced poached apple and cinnamon mojito? Tom yam martini, anyone? Come evening, tables in the sand and torchlight make La Sal a sexy sunset drink destination.

INFORMATION

The only banks are at Kuah and Telaga Harbour Park, but there are ATMs at the airport, the jetty, at Cenang Mall and at Underwater World. There are a couple of moneychangers at Pantai Cenang.

GETTING THERE & AWAY

AIR

Langkawi International Airport is well stocked with ATMs, currency-exchange booths, car-rental agencies, travel agencies and a Tourism Malaysia office.

BOAT

All passenger ferries operate from the busy terminal at Kuah jetty. **Langkawi Ferry Service** (LFS; ☎04-966 9439; www.langkawi-ferry.com) and other operators offer a daily (or more) shared ferry service to Kuala Perlis (RM18, 1¼ hours), Kuala Kedah (RM23, 1¾ hours), Satun (Thailand; RM30, 1¼ hours) and George Town (RM69, 2¾ hours). Twice-daily ferries to Ko Lipe (Thailand; RM118, 1½ hours) are operated by **Tropical Charters** (☎012-588 3274; www.tropicalcharters.com.my; Pantai Tengah; cruises from RM260).

During the wet season, from July to September, you may want to shelve any notions of taking the ferry to Langkawi, particularly from Penang. At this time of year the seas are typically very rough and the ferry ride can be a terrifying

“*for fans of Malay eats there's a rotating* pasar malam *(night market)*”

Night market

and quite literally vomit-inducing experience. Consider yourself warned.

GETTING AROUND

TO/FROM THE AIRPORT

Fixed taxi fares from the airport include Kuah jetty (RM30), Pantai Cenang or Pantai Kok (RM20), Tanjung Rhu (RM45) and Teluk Datai (RM70). Buy a coupon at the desk before leaving the airport terminal and use it to pay the driver.

CAR

Cars can be rented cheaply, and touts from the travel agencies at the Kuah jetty will assail you upon arrival. Rates start at around RM70 per day, but drop with bargaining.

MOTORCYCLE & BICYCLE

The easiest way to get around is to hire a motorbike for around RM35 per day. You can do a leisurely circuit of the island (70km) in a day. The roads are excellent, and outside Kuah it's very pleasant and easy riding. Motorbikes can be hired at stands all over the island. Many places also rent bikes for RM15 per day.

TAXI

As there is no public transport in Langkawi, taxis are the main way of getting around, but fares are relatively high, so it can be worthwhile renting your own vehicle. There are taxi stands at the airport, Kuah jetty, Pantai Cenang and Cenang Mall, and Pantai Tengah, at Frangipani Hotel. There are fixed rates for all destinations – displayed at the stand – and no taxi should use a meter. It's also possible to hire a taxi for four hours for RM120.

Langkawi's Roving Night Market

Local food can be tricky to find on Langkawi. Fortunately, for fans of Malay eats there's a rotating *pasar malam* (night market) held at various points across the island. It's a great chance to indulge in cheap, take-home meals and snacks, and is held from about 6pm to 10pm at the following locations:

Monday Jalan Makam Mahsuri Lama, in the centre of the island, not far from the Mardi Agro Technology Park.

Tuesday Kedawang, just east of the airport.

Wednesday & Saturday Kuah, opposite the Masjid Al-Hana; this is the largest market.

Thursday Bohor Tempoyak, at the northern end of Pantai Cenang.

Friday Padang Lalang, at the roundabout near Pantai Pasir Hitam.

Sunday Padang Matsirat, near the roundabout just north of the airport.

KOTA BHARU

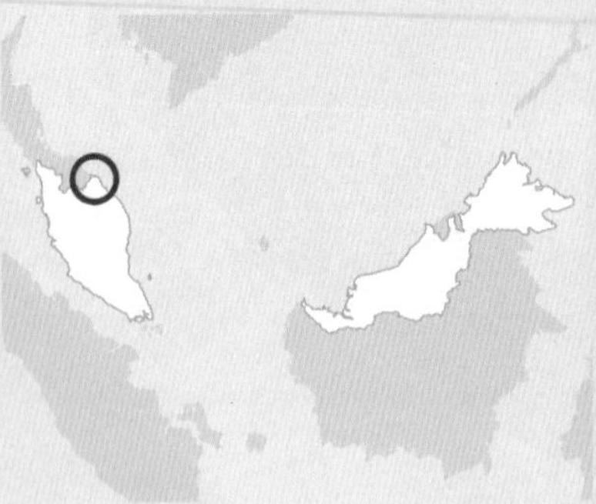

Kota Bharu

Malaysia's east coast is beautiful, containing many lovely beaches and bucolic kampung (villages). Kota Bharu (KB), the capital of Kelantan, boasts the energy of a mid-sized city, the compact feel and friendly vibe of a small town, superb food and a good spread of accommodation. The state's villages are within day-tripping distance, and its crafts, cuisine and culture are present in the city itself.

Kota Bharu in Two Days

Become an expert in Malay history and culture by immersing yourself in KB's **Museum Precinct** (p136). Also check to see what's going on at the **Gelanggang Seni** (p138) cultural centre. After dark hit KB's **night market** (p138) for delicious local food. On day two, indulge in a **cookery course** (p138).

Kota Bharu in Four Days

Leave the bustle of town behind and head to Kuala Besut where you can board a boat to **Pulau Perhentian** (p141). Whichever of the pair of islands you are based on – Kecil (Small) or Besar (Large) – you will be guaranteed gorgeous beaches, tropical waters that are ideal for diving and snorkelling, and gentle hiking along sandy, palm-shaded tracks.

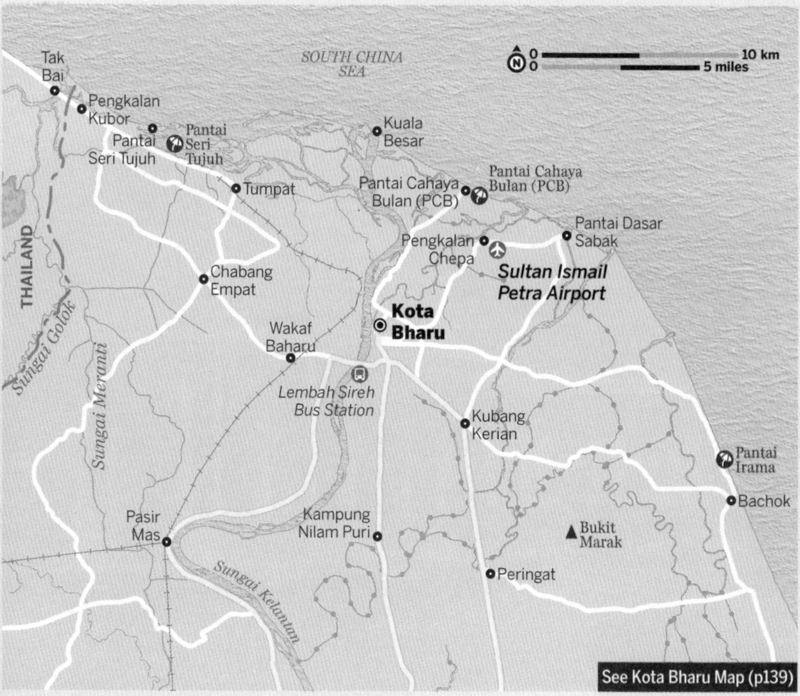

See Kota Bharu Map (p139)

Arriving in Kota Bharu

Sultan Ismail Petra Airport KB's airport is 10km northeast of the city centre.

There are plenty of buses to the city from around Malaysia and nearby Thailand. Trains terminate at Wakaf Baharu, around 10km west of KB.

Sleeping

There's plenty of cheap accommodation around Kota Bharu. Midrange and luxury options are aimed at business travellers.

Istana Jahar

Museum Precinct

Gathered around KB's grassy Padang Merdeka is a cluster of excellent museums focused on Malay history and culture. Nearby are good restaurants and shopping opportunities for between-exhibition downtime.

Great For...

☑ Don't Miss

The small museum displaying various crafts in **Kampung Kraftangan** (Handicraft Village; Jln Hilir Kota; village admission free, museum adult/child RM2/1; ⌚museum 8.30am-4.45pm Sat-Thu).

Istana Jahar

KB's best museum, both in terms of exhibits and structure, is **Istana Jahar** (Royal Ceremonies Museum; Jln Istana; adult/child RM3/1.50; ⌚8.30am-4.45pm Sat-Wed, to 3.30pm Thu). It's housed in a beautiful chocolate-brown building that dates back to 1887, easily one of the most attractive traditional buildings in the city. The interior displays focus on Kelatanese ritual and crafts, from detailed descriptions of batik-weaving to the elaborate ceremonies of coming-of-age circumcision, wedding nights and funerary rights.

Istana Batu

The pale-yellow **Istana Batu** (Royal Museum, Muzium Diraja; Jln Istana; adult/child RM4/2; ⌚8.30am-4.45pm Sat-Wed, to 3.30pm Thu), constructed in 1939, was the crown prince's

Need to Know

Discover more at the Kelantan State Museum Corporation website (www.muzium.kelantan.gov.my).

Take a Break

Restoran Capital (p140) serves Malay specialities. Get there early for an excellent breakfast.

★ Top Tip

If you're short on time, your top priorities should be Istana Jahar and Istana Batu.

palace until donated to the state. The richly furnished rooms give a surprisingly intimate insight into royal life, with family photos and personal belongings scattered among the fine china, chintzy sofas, and the late sultan's collection of hats.

Bank Kerapu

Built in 1912 for the Mercantile Bank of India, the **Bank Kerapu** (WWII Memorial Museum; Jln Sultan; adult/child RM4/2; 8.30am-4.45pm Sat-Wed, to 3.30pm Thu) building is a gem of colonial-era architecture. It was the first stone structure built in Kelantan, and during WWII it was the headquarters of the Kempai Tai, Japan's feared secret police. Today it is also known as the War Museum, thanks to its focus on the Japanese invasion and occupation of Malaya and the 1948 Emergency. Exhibits mainly consist of old photography, rusty guns and other militaria.

Muzium Islam

Muzium Islam (Islamic Museum; Jln Sultan; 8.30am-4.45pm Sat-Wed, to 3.30pm Thu) FREE occupies an old villa once known as Serambi Mekah (Verandah to Mecca) – a reference to its days as Kelantan's first school of Islamic instruction. Nowadays it displays a small collection of photographs and artefacts relating to the history of Islam in the state.

What's Nearby?

One of Malaysia's most colourful and active markets, KB's **central market** (Pasar Besar Siti Khadijah; Jln Hulu; 6am-6pm) is at its busiest first thing in the morning, and has usually packed up by early afternoon. Downstairs is the produce section, while upstairs stalls selling spices, brassware, batik and other goods stay open longer. There's a tasty array of food stalls on the 1st floor, and it's a top spot for breakfast or lunch.

Cheap Eats

One of the great things about Kota Bharu is how well (and cheaply) you can eat without ever setting foot into a restaurant. The most popular spot for delicious, inexpensive Malay food is the town's **night market** (Jln Parit Dalam; mains from RM4; ⏲5-9pm), where stalls are set up in the evening. Specialities include *ayam percik* (marinated chicken on bamboo skewers), *nasi kerabu* (blue rice with coconut, fish and spices), *murtabak* (pan-fried flat bread filled with everything from minced meat to bananas) and squid-on-a-stick. Say *'Suka pedas'* ('I like it hot') to eat as the locals do.

Food courts are another good option and include **Nasi Air Hideng Pok Sen Food Court** (Jln Padang Garong; mains from RM4; ⏲8am-5pm), which has several stalls serving Malay specialities and a self-serve buffet, and the **Medan Selera Kebun Sultan Food Court** (Jln Kebun Sultan; mains from RM4; ⏲noon-11pm).

Satay stall at the night market
PAUL KENNEDY/GETTY IMAGES ©

SIGHTS

KB's main beach was once known as Pantai Cinta Berahi, or the Beach of Passionate Love. In keeping with Islamic sensibilities, it's now known as **Pantai Cahaya Bulan**, or Moonlight Beach, but most people shorten it to PCB. Erosion over recent years has seen the installation of a concrete breakwater, but PCB's sandy sprawl is still worth considering for a seafood lunch and a day's escape from KB's dusty streets.

The road leading to PCB is quite pretty, especially by bicycle, and there are batik shops and workshops along the way. To get here by public transport, take bus 10 (RM1.60) from behind Kampung Kraftangan in KB. Buses also leave from the main bus station.

Gelanggang Seni Cultural Centre

(Cultural Centre; ☎03-744 3124; Jln Mahmud) FREE Local cultural events, including *gasing uri* (top-spinning), *silat* (a Malay martial art), kite-making, drumming and shadow-puppet shows, are held regularly at the Gelanggang Seni. The events are especially kid-friendly, and all totally free. Sessions are held on Monday, Wednesday and Saturday from February to September, between 3.30pm and 5.30pm and 9pm and 11pm. Check with the tourist information centre (p141) for the full timetable.

COURSES

Roselan's Malay Cookery Workshop Cooking Course

(☎012-909 6068; per person RM125, minimum group size of 2) The ever cheerful Roselan runs this popular Malay cookery workshop. Students are invited to a middle-class Malay home (Roselan's own or other locals'), and taught to cook typical Malay dishes. Contact Roselan by phone or ask for him at the tourist information centre. Call ahead for the address.

Zecsman Design Batik Painting

(☎012-929 2822; www.facebook.com/zecsman; Jln Hilir Kota, Kampung Kraftangan; courses half-day RM50-70, full-day RM150; ⏲10am-5pm Sat-Thu) Buy ready-made batik or try your hand at batik painting at Zecsman Design's tutored four- to five-hour classes. Cost depends on the size and fabric used in your work.

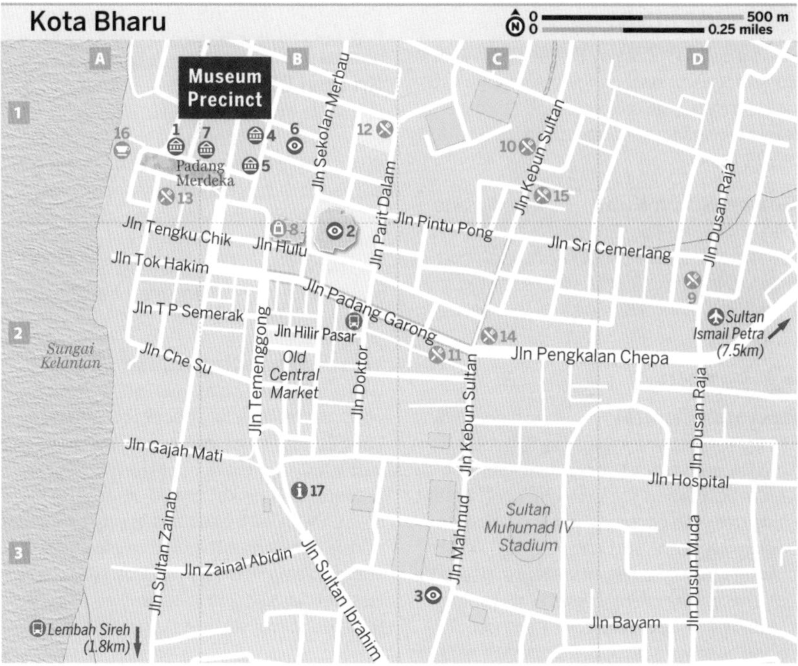

Kota Bharu

Sights

1 Bank Kerapu ... A1
2 Central Market ... B2
3 Gelanggang Seni ... C3
4 Istana Batu ... B1
5 Istana Jahar ... B1
6 Kampung Kraftangan ... B1
7 Muzium Islam ... B1

Activities, Courses & Tours

Roselan's Malay Cookery Workshop ... (see 17)
Zecsman Design ... (see 6)

Shopping

8 Bazaar Buluh Kubu ... B2

Eating

9 Four Seasons ... D2
10 Medan Selera Kebun Sultan Food Court ... C1
11 Nasi Air Hideng Pok Sen Food Court ... C2
12 Night Market ... B1
13 Restoran Capital ... A1
14 Sri Devi Restaurant ... C2
15 West Lake Eating House ... C1

Drinking & Nightlife

16 Bike Station Cafe ... A1

Information

17 Tourist Information Centre ... B3

TOURS

Most hostels and hotels can organise tours for their guests. Possible options include two-day, three-night expeditions into the jungle around Gua Musang (RM280 to RM350), boat trips up small local rivers into sleepy fishing villages where silk kites are made by candlelight (RM65 to RM85), two-hour tours of the Tumpat temples (RM80), half-day craft tours (RM90 to RM115) and short city tours (RM30 to RM40). A recent addition to KB's tour scene is after-dark river journeys to see fireflies.

SHOPPING

KB is a centre for Malay crafts. Batik, *kain songket* (traditional handwoven fabric with gold threads), silverware, woodcarving and kite-making factories and shops are dotted around town.

Bazaar Buluh Kubu Handicrafts
(Jln Hulu; 8am-6pm Sat-Thu) Near the central market, Bazaar Buluh Kubu is a good place to buy handicrafts such as batik, traditional Malay clothing and jewellery.

EATING

Restoran Capital Malaysian $
(Jln Post Office Lama; mains from RM5; 7am-1pm) For our favourite breakfast, get here before 9am when the excellent *nasi kerabu* (blue rice with coconut, fish and spices) usually sells out. Nutty rice combines with a variety of subtle Kelantanese curries, and optional extras include eggs and crunchy crackers. It's also a top spot for an iced coffee or other snacks like *popiah* (fresh spring rolls) from the other stallholders filling the heritage space.

Sri Devi Restaurant Indian $
(4213-F Jln Kebun Sultan; mains from RM5; 7am-9pm;) As popular with locals as it is with tourists, this is a great place for an authentic banana-leaf curry and a mango lassi. They also serve a great *ayam percik* (marinated chicken on bamboo skewers), and terrific *roti canai* (flaky flat bread served with curry) in the morning and evening.

West Lake Eating House Chinese $
(Jln Kebun Sultan; mains from RM5; 10am-8pm;) Don't let the plain decor fool you. West Lake Eating House serves some of the tastiest Chinese fare in Eastern Malaysia. Esoteric dishes like stewed bean curd stuffed with fish cakes and lightly sautéed purple eggplant with garlic sauce share the steam table with more common (but no less delicious) dishes like braised pork ribs, roast duck and stir-fried vegetables.

Shadow-puppet show *(wayang kulit)*

Four Seasons Chinese **$$**
(www.fourseasonsrestaurant.com.my; 5670 Jln Sri Cemerlang; mains from RM15; ⌚noon-2.30pm & 6-10pm) The Four Seasons is packed nightly with locals enjoying seafood dishes like claypot prawn and dry cuttlefish with mango salad. The house speciality, deep fried soft-shell crab, should only set you back about RM40 for two people (it's priced by weight).

DRINKING & NIGHTLIFE

Bike Station Cafe Cafe
(Jln Sultan; ⌚2pm-midnight Thu-Tue) Look forward to elevated river views, a huge menu of hot and cold drinks, a tasty array of local snacks (from RM3), and your best chance to meet some young English-speaking locals. Downstairs you can rent bikes to explore KB's riverfront esplanade (one/two hours RM20/25). The nearby area is often filled with local buskers on weekend afternoons from around 4pm.

INFORMATION

Tourist Information Centre (☎09-748 5534; www.tic-kelantan.gov.my; Jln Sultan Ibrahim; ⌚8am-5pm Sun-Wed, to 3.30pm Thu, to 1.30pm Fri & Sat) Information on homestays, tours and transport.

GETTING THERE & AWAY

Daily flights to major domestic destinations such as Kuala Lumpur depart from KB's **Sultan Ismail Petra Airport** (☎09-773 7400; www.malaysiaairports.com.my; Sultan Ismail Petra Airport Darul Naim). Rental cars are available from **Hawk** (☎773 3824; www.hawkrentacar.com.my; Sultan Ismail Petra Airport) at the airport.

Local buses and Transnasional express buses operate from the **central bus station** (☎09-747 5971, 09-747 4330; Jln Padang Garong). Other express and long-distance buses leave from Lembah Sireh Bus Station near the Kota Bharu Tesco; a taxi from this bus station to the centre of town is around RM15.

The nearest railway station is **Wakaf Baharu** (☎09-719 6986), around 10km west of KB; it can be reached by local buses 17 or 19.

Pulau Perhentian

The gorgeous Perhentians boast waters simultaneously electric teal and crystal clear, jungles thick and fecund, and beaches with blindingly white sand. At night bonfires on the beach and phosphorescence in the water make pin holes in the velvety black, and stars are mirrored above. Most people come to snorkel, dive or do nothing at all.

There are two main islands: **Kecil** (Small), popular with the younger backpacker crowd, and **Besar** (Large), with higher standards of accommodation and a quieter, more relaxed ambience. The quick hop between the two costs around RM20.

While alcohol is available at many restaurants and you can usually find a beach party, the Perhentians are a long way from having a Thai-style party atmosphere.

Note that the islands basically shut down during the monsoon (usually from mid-November to mid-February), although some hotels remain open for hardier travellers. There are no banks or ATMs on the islands, so bring cash.

GETTING AROUND

Taxis from Sultan Ismail Petra Airport to the city centre are around RM35.

Trishaws can still be seen on the city streets, though they are not as common as they once were. Prices are negotiable, but expect to pay around RM5 and upwards for a short journey of up to 1km.

TAMAN NEGARA

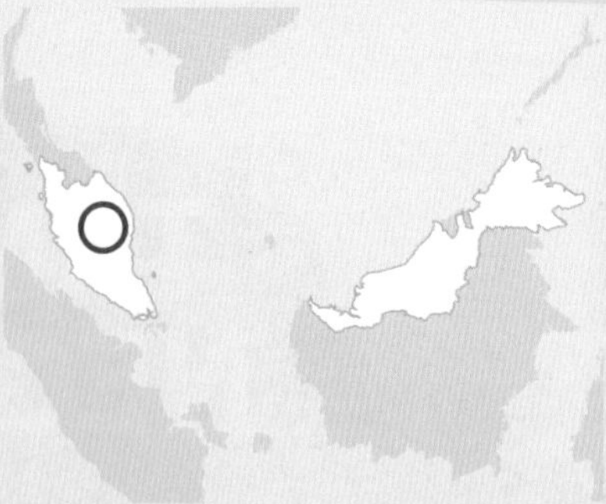

Taman Negara

Taman Negara National Park blankets 4343 sq km in shadowy, damp, impenetrable jungle. Inside this buzzing tangle, ancient trees with gargantuan buttressed root systems dwarf luminescent fungi, orchids, two-tone ferns and even the giant rafflesia (the world's largest flower).

Hidden among the flora are elephants, tigers, leopards, rhinos and flying squirrels, but these animals stay far from the park's trails and sightings are extremely rare. What might be spotted are snakes, lizards, monkeys, small deer, loads of birds and perhaps a tapir or two. Nearly everyone who visits Taman Negara gets an up-close-and-personal meeting with leeches, plus an impressive array of insects.

Taman Negara in Two Days

Either into or out of the park, take the **boat trip** (p149) from Kuala Tembeling (18km north of Jerantut) to Kuala Tahan – it's a beautiful journey and remains a highlight for many visitors. Settle into your accommodation and arrange a **night jungle tour** (p148). Rise early to tackle the **Canopy Walkway** (p146) and continue along the trail to **Bukit Teresik**.

Taman Negara in Four Days

Spend a day following the 9km trail to **Kuala Trenggan** (p147) and then taking a boat back to base along the Sungai Tembeling. On day four pull on your trekking boots again to tackle the easy day hike to **Lata Berkoh** (p147), which passes a swimming hole, or squeeze in a **tour** (p148) to an Orang Asli settlement.

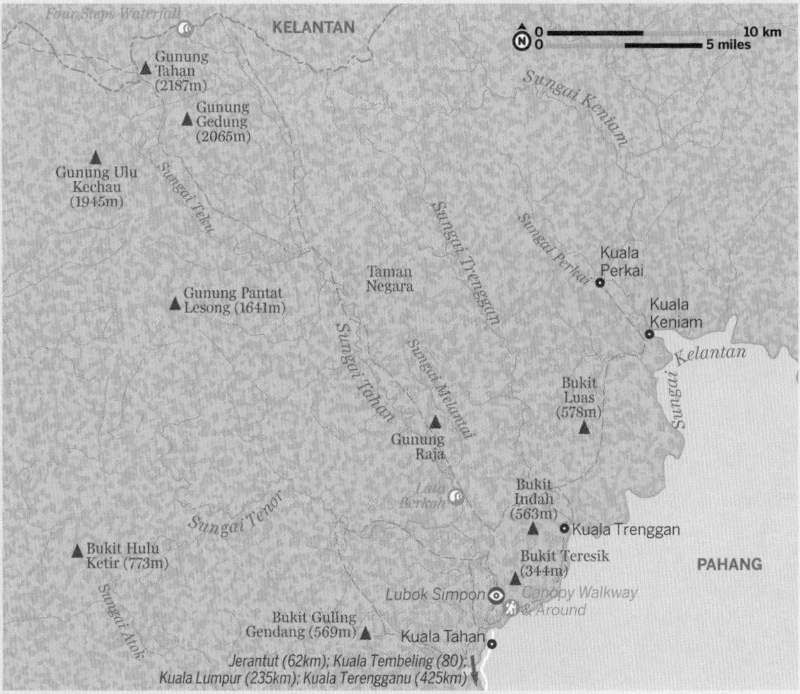

Arriving in Taman Negara

Kampung Kuala Tahan Minibus services go directly from several tourist destinations around Malaysia to Kampung Kuala Tahan (the main entrance to the park).

Jerantut This mid-sized town is the other main access point; travel from here via the recommended combination of bus and river cruise, or directly by bus or taxi.

Sleeping

The park headquarters and a resort are at Kuala Tahan at the edge of Taman Negara National Park; other accommodation and restaurants are across the Sungai Tembeling at Kampung Kuala Tahan. River taxis buzz between the two sides of the river (RM1 each way) throughout the day.

Canopy Walkway

Jungle Trekking

Taman Negara has a wide variety of trekking possibilities – from an hour's stroll to multiday adventures. Shorten your hiking time by taking riverboat services or tours that include boat transport.

Great For...

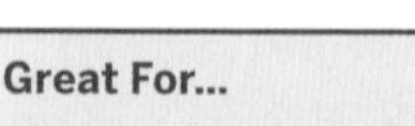

☑ Don't Miss

The Canopy Walkway early in the morning – top for twitchers and wildlife-watchers.

The trails around the park headquarters are convenient but heavily trafficked. Relatively few visitors venture far beyond the headquarters, and longer walks are much less trammelled.

Canopy Walkway & Around

Follow the trail east of park headquarters along the Sungai Tembeling to the **Canopy Walkway** (adult/child RM5/3; ⌚10am-3.30pm Sat-Thu, 9am-noon Fri), 30 minutes away. The walkway is suspended between huge trees and the entire circuit takes around 40 minutes.

From behind the Canopy Walkway a trail leads to **Bukit Teresik** (344m), from the top of which are fine views across the forest. The trail is steep and slippery in parts, but is easily negotiated and takes about an hour up and back. You can descend

back along this trail to the Mutiara Taman Negara Resort or, near the Canopy Walkway, take the branch trail that leads across to **Lubok Simpon**, a swimming area on Sungai Tahan. From here it is an easy stroll back to park headquarters. The entire loop can easily be done in three hours.

Past the Canopy Walkway, a branch of the main trail leads to **Bukit Indah** (563m), another steep but rewarding hill-climb offering fine views across the forest and the rapids in Sungai Tembeling.

Kuala Trenggan

The well-marked main trail along the bank of Sungai Tembeling leads 9km to Kuala Trenggan, a popular trail for those heading to the Bumbun Kumbang hide. Allow five hours. From here, boats go back to Nusa Holiday Village and Kampung Kuala Tahan, or it's a further 2km walk to Bumbun Kumbang.

An alternative longer trail leads inland, back across Sungai Trenggan from Bumbun Kumbang to the camp site at Lubok Lesong on Sungai Tahan, then back to park headquarters (six hours). This trail is flat most of the way and crosses small streams. Check with park headquarters for river levels.

Lata Berkoh

North from park headquarters, this day hike leads to Gunung Tahan, but you can do an easy day walk to Lata Berkoh, the cascading rapids on Sungai Tahan. The trail passes the Lubok Simpon swimming hole and Bumbun Tabing, 1¼ hours from Kuala Tahan.

There is one river crossing before you reach the falls, which can be treacherous if the water is high. Do not attempt the river crossing in high water – you should hail one of the boat operators waiting on the opposite side to ferry you across.

Need to Know

All park visitors need to buy a permit at the Tourist Information Counter (p149).

Take a Break

Bring supplies into the park, or arrange a packed lunch from your accommodation.

★ Top Tip

International travel clinics recommend antimalarial drugs for park visitors.

ACTIVITIES

Though feasible, fleeting visits to Taman Negara only scratch the surface. Consider an overnight trek or at least a long boat trip up one of the park's rivers.

Overnight Treks

Gunung Tahan Hiking

Really adventurous travellers climb Gunung Tahan (2187m), the highest peak in Peninsular Malaysia, 55km from park headquarters. It takes nine days at a steady pace, although it can be done in seven.

A guide is compulsory (RM700 for seven days plus RM75 for each day thereafter). There are no shelters along the way so you have to be fully equipped. Try to organise this trek in advance so you don't have to hang around park headquarters for a couple of days.

Rentis Tenor Hiking

From Kuala Tahan, this trek takes roughly three days, and takes you to remote corners of the park where you are more likely to see wildlife. Hiring a guide for this hike is highly recommended.

Day one: take the trail to Gua Telinga, and beyond, for about seven hours, to Yong camp site. Day two is a six-hour walk to the Rentis camp site. On day three cross Sungai Tahan (up to waist deep) to get back to Kuala Tahan: roughly a six-hour walk, or you can stop over at the Lameh camp site, about halfway.

Fishing

Anglers will find the park a real paradise. Fish found in the park's rivers include the superb fighting fish known in India as the *mahseer* and here as the *kelasa*.

Popular fishing rivers include Sungai Tahan, Sungai Keniam (north of Kuala Trenggan) and the remote Sungai Sepia. Simple fishing lodges are scattered through the park and can be booked at park headquarters. The best fishing months are February, March, July and August. Fishing permits are RM10; rods can be hired across the river for between RM20 and RM30 per day. You can hire a three-day boat tour for up to three people with a guide for about RM1500.

River Bus & Boat Trips

The Mutiara Taman Negara Resort has daily boats that go upriver to Kuala Trenggan at 10am and 2.30pm. In the reverse direction, boats leave Kuala Trenggan at 11.15am and 3.15pm. These services are intended for guests only, but there are boat trips into the park from Mutiara Taman Negara dock that are open to the public, including to Bunbun Yong (RM5, three daily), the Canopy Walkway (RM15, twice daily), Gua Telinga (RM15, four daily) and Kuala Tembeling (RM30, daily).

TOURS

Guides who are licensed by the Wildlife Department have completed coursework in forest flora, fauna and safety. Often the Kuala Tahan tour operators offer cheaper prices than those available at the Tourist Information Counter at Park Headquarters (whose guides are licensed), but talk with these guides first to find out what training they've had. Guides cost RM180 per day (one guide can lead up to 12 people), plus there is a RM100 fee for each night spent out on the trail.

Top tours include canopy and jungle treks that last a couple of hours (RM35 to RM50), night jungle trips with lots of insect viewing (RM25 to RM45), Lata Berkok hike (RM200), and motorboating through Class I rapids (RM40 to RM80).

Many travellers sign up for tours to an Orang Asli settlement. Tribal elders give a general overview and you'll learn how to use a long blowpipe and start a fire. While local guides insist that these tours provide essential income for the Orang Asli, most of your tour money will go to the tour company. A small handicraft purchase in the village will help spread the wealth.

EATING

Floating barge restaurants line the rocky shore of Kampung Kuala Tahan, all selling the same ol' cheap basic noodle and rice meals plus bland Western fare. All are open from morning until late, though most take rest breaks between 2pm and 4pm.

Family Restaurant Malaysian $
(mains RM6-15) This floating restaurant serves a dish called *kerabu*, finely diced meat and vegetables with a light lemongrass sauce that's got way more local cred than the standard banana pancakes. It also serves banana pancakes.

Mutiara Restaurant International $$
(Mutiara Taman Negara Resort; RM20-40; ⏲breakfast, lunch & dinner) Salads, sandwiches/burgers, pizza, local dishes and a small kiddies' menu. Breakfast is filling. This is bit more luxurious than the average, and is also the only place in the area where you can get a beer.

INFORMATION

Information Centre (⏲9am-11pm) At the riverside end of the road in Kuala Tahan. It provides information on onward transport and tours, though it's run by private interests, so selling tours is more important than giving out information.

Tourist Information Counter (north of the river behind Mutiara Resort; park entrance/camera/fishing/canopy/blinds RM1/5/10/5/5; ⏲8am-10pm Sun-Thu, 8am-noon & 3-10pm Fri) Register here before heading off into the park. The counter, located in the building 100m north of the Mutiara Taman Negara Resort's reception, also offers park information and guide services. A short video plays at 10am and 4pm, and there's a small aquarium onsite. Get here by crossing the river with a water taxi (RM1).

GETTING THERE & AWAY

Most people reach Taman Negara by taking a bus from Jerantut to the jetty at Kuala Tembeling, then a river boat to Kampung Kuala Tahan (the main entrance to the park). Many are now opting to head up to Taman Negara by minibus from Jerantut and returning by boat.

Dengue Fever

At the time of writing, dengue fever was on the rise in the deep jungle of Peninsular Malaysia. To avoid this and other mosquito-borne illnesses, such as malaria, the best precaution is to avoid being bitten. Wear light long-sleeved clothes and use a DEET–based insect repellant. Dengue-carrying mozzies generally bite between 6am and 9am and then again between 6pm and 9pm.

BOAT

The river jetty for Taman Negara–bound boats is in Kuala Tembeling, 18km north of Jerantut. Boats (RM35 one-way) depart Kuala Tembeling daily at 9am and 2pm (9am and 2.30pm on Friday). On the return journey, boats leave Kuala Tahan at 9am and 2pm (and 2.30pm on Friday). The journey takes three hours up stream and two hours downstream. Note that the boat service is irregular during the wet season (November to February).

BUS & TAXI

There are buses and taxis from Jerantut to Kuala Tembeling. Han Travel (www.taman-negara.com), **NKS** (☎03-2072 0336; www.tamannegara.nks.com) and **Banana Travel & Tours** (☎04-261 2171; bananapenang.com; Information Centre, Kampung Kuala Tahan) run useful private services, including daily buses to Kuala Lumpur (RM35), a bus/boat combination (RM70), and minibuses to Penang (RM120) and the Cameron Highlands (RM95).

GETTING AROUND

There is a frequent cross-river ferry (RM1) that shuttles passengers across the river from Kuala Tahan to the park entrance and Mutiara Taman Negara Resort.

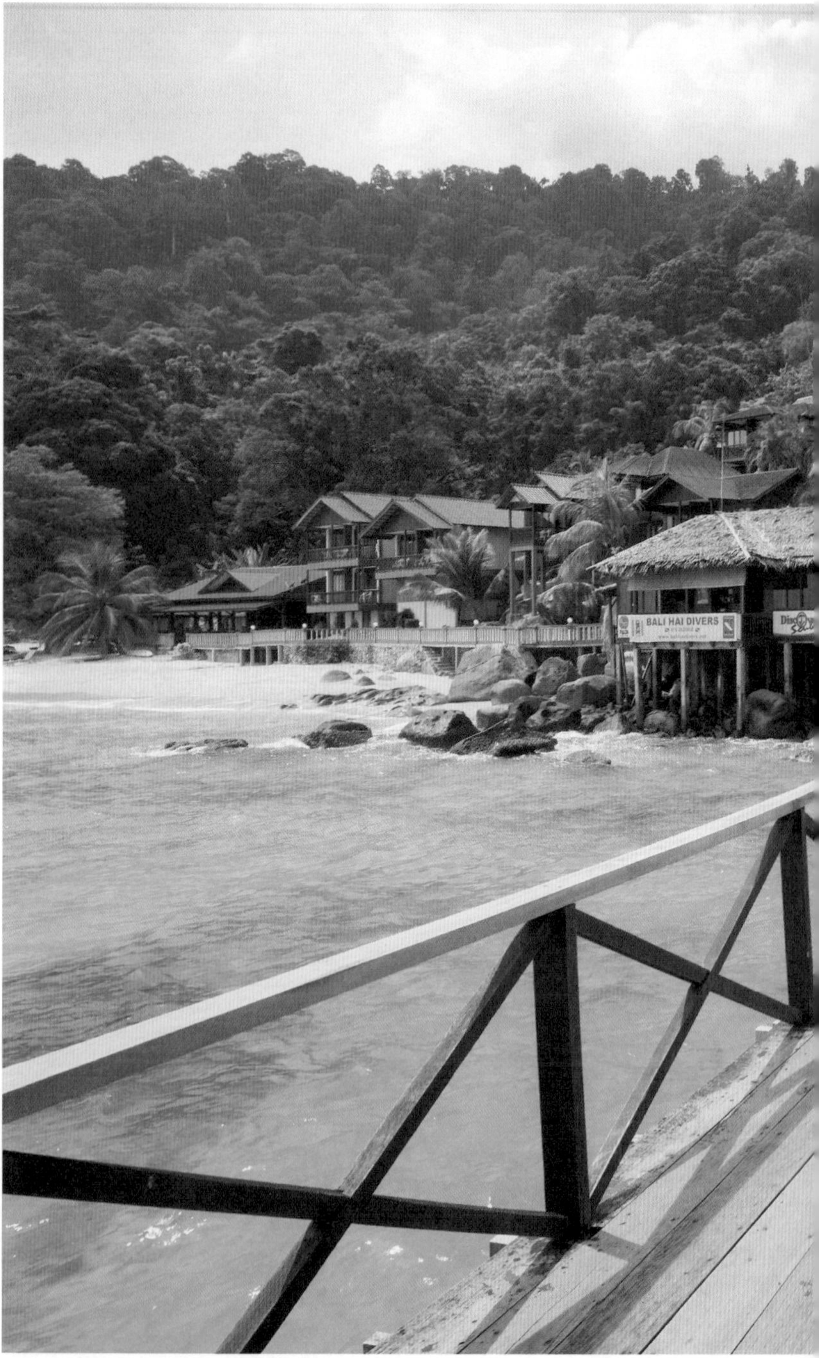
BALI HAI DIVERS

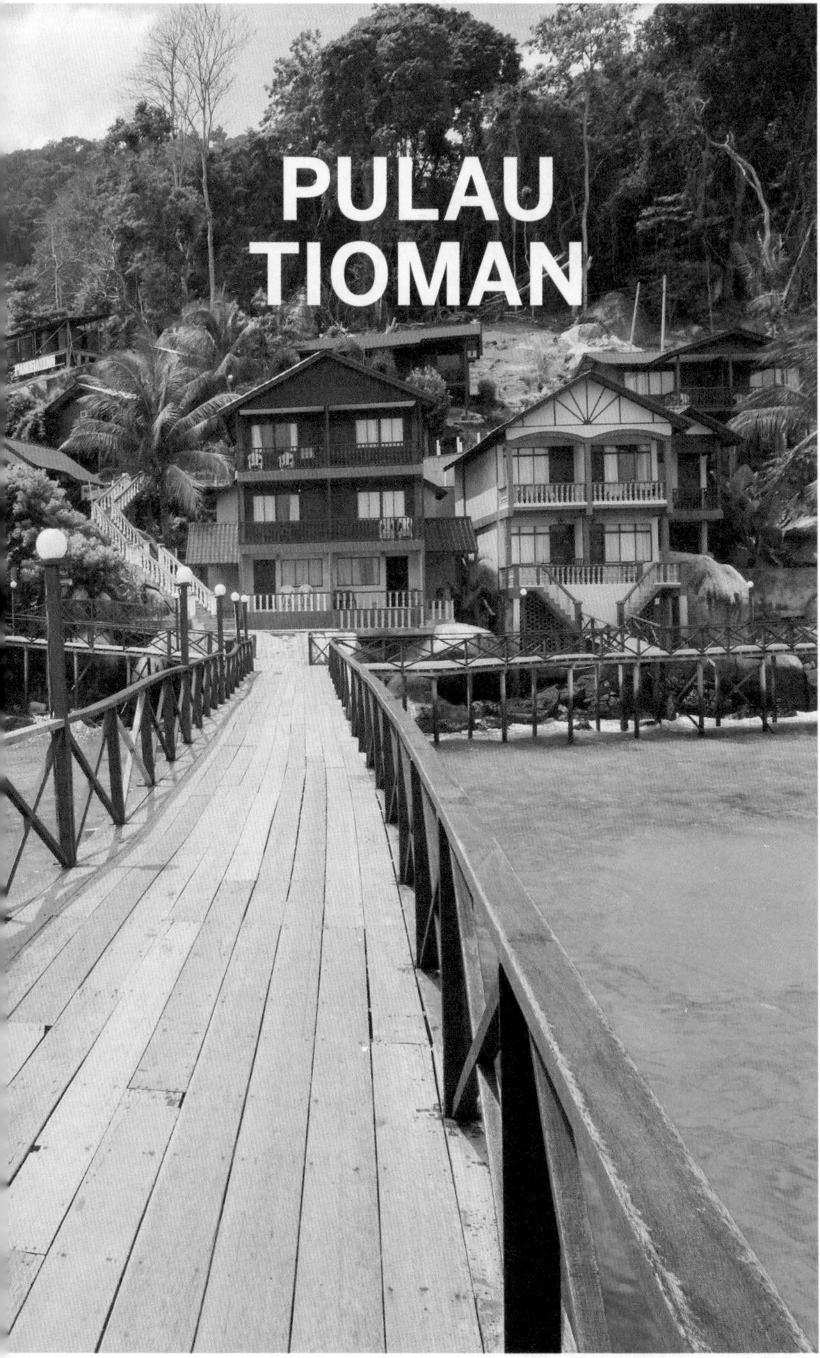

PULAU TIOMAN

Pulau Tioman

Sitting like an emerald dragon guarding the translucent waters of the South China Sea, Tioman Island offers every possible shade of paradise. There's cascading waterfalls, rigorous jungle hikes that take you past orange blossoms under an evergreen canopy, and a wide sampling of laid-back villages that present a tapestry of cultures and curiosities. And then there's that gorgeous sea of green, blue and chartreuse swirls that beckons you to paddle, snorkel, dive and sail.

Despite its growing popularity, Tioman retains an unspoiled feel, with pristine wilderness and friendly, authentic village life.

Pulau Tioman in Two Days

Work up a sweat by crossing the island on the **Tekek to Juara Jungle Walk** (p158) – fine beaches and refreshments await you, whichever direction you decide to go. On day two arrange a diving or snorkelling trip; **Renggis Island** (p156) is ideal for beginners, while **Labas Island and Tiger Reef** (p156) are best for those with experience.

Pulau Tioman in Four Days

Tioman is a great place to learn diving, and with four days in hand you could sign up for a certification course. The already qualified could venture to the **WWII Wreck Sites** (p157). Alternatively, volunteer at the **Juara Turtle Project** (p159) or learn about batik at **Suzila Batik Arts & Crafts Centre** (p158).

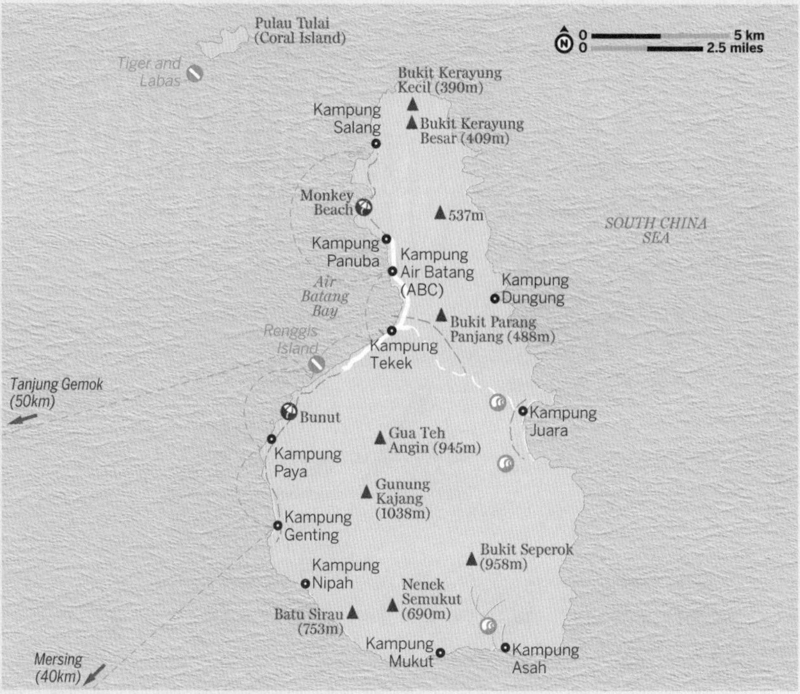

Arriving in Pulau Tioman

Jeti Penumpang Mersing Mersing in Johor is the main access port for Tioman.

Marina Tanjung Gemok Ferries also depart for Tioman from this ferry terminal, 35km north of Mersing near Endau.

Tekek, on the island, has an airport, but there were no commercial flights as of the time of writing.

Sleeping

Budget accommodation largely comprises small wooden 'chalets' (bungalows) and longhouse-style rooms, typically with a bathroom, fan and mosquito net. More expensive rooms have air-con and hot showers. Most operations have larger family rooms for those with children, and many have restaurants.

Tioman resorts have exclusive beaches, pools, restaurants and private jetties. Your best bet for booking most resorts is going through travel aggregators (skip the all-inclusives if you have access to a nearby village). Note that many of these resorts offer amazing deals during the monsoon season (November to February).

ASIATRAVEL/SHUTTERSTOCK ©

Beaches

You're spoiled for choice when deciding which sublime slice of beach on Tioman to make your base. The major options are broken down here, listed counter-clockwise from north to south.

Great For...

☑ Don't Miss

The monstrous monitor lizards that lurk in the river that runs through Salang village.

Salang

Salang has more of a party vibe than elsewhere on the island. A very wide and inviting white-sand beach lies just south of the jetty and is good for swimming. Come to snorkel off nearby Coral Island, stay for the beach parties.

Monkey Beach

It's a 40-minute hike through the rainforest from Salang to Monkey Beach, before the trail continues from the far end of the beach across the next headland to the white-sand beach at Monkey Bay. From here, it's around a two-hour steep climb over the headland to ABC via the tiny beach at Panuba.

ABC (Air Batang)

ABC's beach is usually best at the southern and northern ends, although the sands are constantly shifting, so this is changeable. Most of the beachfront is rocky with little sand. Slightly more upscale than Salang, ABC has a good choice of budget restaurants and accommodation. The narrow trails that lead you through town give the feel of a paradise lost and found again.

Tekek

Tioman's commercial hub is a good central location from which to explore the rest of the island, and the beach at the southern end of town is lovely.

Kampung Paya

The short, wide, white-sand beach is jam-packed with two resorts and a few

Need to Know

Bicycles and mopeds can be hired at guesthouses on all the main beaches.

Take a Break

Stop in at Sunset Corner (p158) for a milkshake or something stronger.

★ Top Tip

The waters of Nipah are home to phosphorescent seaweed that glows at night.

restaurants and food shacks. The rocky seabed and shallow water make it a poor choice for swimming.

Genting

The beach is fairly built up (and caters mostly to the weekend crowds from Singapore and KL), but is surrounded by a local village with an appealing *kampung* atmosphere. A good spot for meeting local fishing folk.

Nipah

Blissful, isolated Nipah Beach is long and white with an unusual stripe of black sand running through it. A river mouth at the southern end creates a deep blue swimming hole that's bordered on one side by a large, flat knuckle of sand with a volleyball pitch. This is the place to come to hang in a hammock, snorkel, or hike in the jungle.

Mukut

This traditional *kampung* may be one of the prettiest towns on the island, and the beach is lovely. If it's traditional Malaysian life you're after, Mukut is your spot.

Juara

This east coast village has the best surfing beach in Tioman and enough restaurants and accommodation to make it well worth the trip. The beachfront bungalows are out of this world.

Diving & Snorkelling

Tioman offers some of the best (and most accessible) diving and snorkelling in Malaysia. There are excellent dive centres, and Open Water Diver (OWD) certification courses are priced competitively.

Great For...

☑ Don't Miss

Learning about Tioman's marine flora and fauna at the Marine Park Information Center (p158).

The leeward side of Tioman offers a remarkable variety of dive and snorkel sites, while the east coast's offerings are more limited. Most dives have a maximum depth of 30m. Tioman is also one of the few places in the country where you have a good chance of seeing pods of dolphins.

Renggis Island

Good for snorkelling and beginner dives, this spot just off the Berjaya Resort pier boasts blacktip reef sharks, turtles and lionfish.

Tiger & Labas

Off Labas Island, advanced divers can spot reef fish, rays and schools of barracuda and jackfish at Tiger Reef.

Coral Island

Head here for stunning soft coral, reef fish and an occasional puffer fish. This is a top half-day boat excursion for snorkellers.

WWII Wreck Sites

Experienced divers won't want to miss two famous WWII–era wreck sites, 45 nautical miles north of Tioman, HMS *Repulse* and HMS *Prince of Wales*. Both sites are astounding for their historical significance and wide array of marine life. They're challenging – best suited for those with more than a few dives under their belts – but you don't need certification aside from your open water.

Dive Operators

B&J Diving
(☎09-419 1218; www.divetioman.com; ABC) This ABC shop is a PADI 5-Star Dive Centre with its own pool and a course director. It offers DSAT Tec and IANTD courses, nitrox blends and other high-end dive options, along with open-water courses (RM1100) and fun dives (RM110).

Ray's Dive Adventures Diving
(☎019-330 8062; http://raysdive.com; ABC) Run by local couple Ray and Chloe, Ray's offers a four-day open-water PADI course for RM1200 and has various dive packages as well.

Tioman Dive Centre Diving
(☎09-419 1228; www.tioman-dive-centre.com; Swiss Cottage Resort, Tekek) This place has a stellar reputation for its very responsible dive practices.

Snorkelling

There is good snorkelling off the rocky points on the west coast of the island, particularly those just north of ABC, but the best snorkelling is around nearby Pulau Tulai, better known as Coral Island. Snorkelling equipment for hire is easy to find (masks and snorkels are typically RM15 per day) at many places on the island. Snorkelling trips with boat transfers cost RM40 to RM100.

Paddleboarding

Above water, you may wish to try your hand at paddleboarding. Swiss Cottage in Tekek rents boards for RM25 for two hours. A round-trip Island Boat Tour costs about RM150.

Need to Know

A PADI OWD course costs RM1100 to RM1200, fun dives RM115 to RM130.

Take a Break

The Malaysian restaurant Delima (p158) has a branch right beside Tekek pier.

Top Tip

Best visibility (15m to 30m) for diving is from March until May and September until November.

SIGHTS

Marine Park Information Center Museum

(Tekek; ⊙8am-1pm & 2-5pm Mon-Fri, 8am-12:15pm & 2:45-5pm Sat; 👪) FREE This centre has a few informative TV programs, a coral display and plenty of information on marine flora and fauna. It's a good stop for families and divers.

ACTIVITIES

Nautical pleasures aside, jungle-swathed Tioman offers plenty of excellent hikes to keep the intrepid landlubber exhausted and happy. You'll see more wildlife than in most of Malaysia's national parks, including black giant squirrels, long-tailed macaques, brush-tailed porcupines and – if you're out with a torch at dawn or dusk and incredibly lucky – the endangered, nocturnal binturong (bear cat).

While you can easily take on most hikes by yourself, guided jungle trips (arranged through your hotel) give you a curated look at the island's unique flora and fauna, and cost RM100 for a half-day. If you're setting out on foot, be wary of entering the jungle after around 4.30pm, as it's easy to get lost in the dark.

Tekek to Juara Jungle Walk Hiking

The 7km Tekek to Juara Jungle Walk offers an excellent feel for the richness of the spectacular interior, not to mention the added bonus of bringing the hiker to beautiful Juara at hike's end. While the walk isn't too strenuous, parts of it are steep, and hiking in tropical heat can be taxing.

COURSES

Genting is the home of Suhadi Mahadi, whose **Suzila Batik Arts & Crafts Centre** (☎013-751 4312; suzilabatik@gmail.com) is just south of the jetty. Suhadi teaches batik making using traditional materials. Tuition varies from RM25 to RM80; a simple batik might take an hour or two to make, while a more complex pattern might take the afternoon. Suhadi also sells ready-made batik (RM30 to RM1200).

EATING

Delima Malaysian $

(Tekek; mains RM7-10) With two locations – one right by the Tekek pier and the other up the road by the Berjaya Resort, this friendly Malaysian joint offers up wholesome fair, big smiles and waterfront views.

Golden Dish Cafe Chinese $

(Genting; dishes from RM6; ⊙10am-midnight; 🅥) 🌿 This might be the only place on Tioman serving its own homegrown organic vegetables. There are also plenty of authentic Chinese seafood specialities and healing herbal drinks and, if that isn't your thing, it serves beer for RM5.

Santai Bistro Malaysian $

(mains RM12-15; ⊙9am-11pm) This bar/restaurant right next to the jetty plays classic rock and serves delights such as sambal prawns, tom yum and mixed vegetable salads. The beers are cold and the views hypnotising.

ABCD Restaurant Malaysian $$

(mains RM10-20; ⊙breakfast, lunch & dinner) This restaurant is packed most nights with travellers who flock to enjoy ABCD's barbecue special (RM20), a tantalising array of freshly caught fish, prawn or squid. For less adventurous eaters, chicken will have to do. Beer is available.

Chinese Sarang Seafood Chinese $$

(☎013-706 6484; mains RM20; ⊙lunch & dinner) This spot does a particularly tasty sizzling hotplate with bean curd and serves beer.

Sunset Corner International $$

(ABC; pizza from RM16; ⊙2pm-late) The last spot before the stairs leading south, Sunset serves beer, booze, milkshakes and pizza. The wildly popular happy hour is from 5pm to 7pm.

INFORMATION

Tioman's sole cash machine is across from Tekek's airport and takes international cards. It's been known to run dry, so consider getting cash in Mersing.

GETTING THERE & AWAY

Tekek has an airport, but at the time of writing there were no commercial operations.

BOAT

Mersing in Johor is the main access port for Tioman. **Island Connection Tours** (☎07-799 2535; return RM70) has an office in Mersing; other operators sell tickets by the jetty for the same price. Boats run from early morning until late afternoon, stopping at Genting, Paya, Berjaya Tioman, Tekek, ABC and Salang, and returning in the reverse order. Decide where you want to get off and tell the ticket inspector. On weekends and holidays it's a good idea to buy your tickets in advance, since the boats fill quickly (queue up or you may miss a spot).

Boat departures during the monsoon season (November to February) can be erratic, with sailings becoming more regular during the low monsoon months (January and February).

Ferries also depart for Tioman from the Tanjung Gemok ferry terminal (return RM70), 35km north of Mersing near Endau. This route is useful if coming from the north. Call ahead and make sure the ferries are running before you arrive.

GETTING AROUND

Sea taxis shunt between the various beaches and towns. Typical fares from Tekek include ABC/Panuba (RM25), Genting (RM50), Nipah (RM120), Mukut (RM150), Paya Beach (RM35) and Salang (RM35).

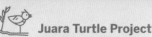

Juara Turtle Project

On the southern end of Juara beach, the **Juara Turtle Project** (☎09-419 3244; www.juaraturtleproject.com; Juara; tour RM10, min 4 nights volunteering with breakfast, lunch & dm RM120; ⏱10am-5pm) works to protect declining sea turtle populations by collecting eggs and moving them to a hatchery, and patrolling the beaches for poachers and predators. Volunteers, who work patrols and give information seminars, get basic dorm accommodation. Extra daily activities, including sea kayaking and trekking, and cooking classes are also offered.

Non-volunteers can tour the facility, check in on the resident turtle, Joe, who is blind and unable to return to the wild, and learn more about the area's turtles, which nest here from February to October, with public releases June through November.

ULLSTEIN BILD/GETTY IMAGES ©

Some sea taxis have a two-person minimum. Most hotels can arrange boat charter. Expect to pay around RM600 for a full day on a boat, and expect waters to be far rougher on the Juara side of Tioman.

Taxis from Tekek to Juara cost RM70 to RM90.

HENTIAN
DATARAN HANG TUAH

MELAKA CITY

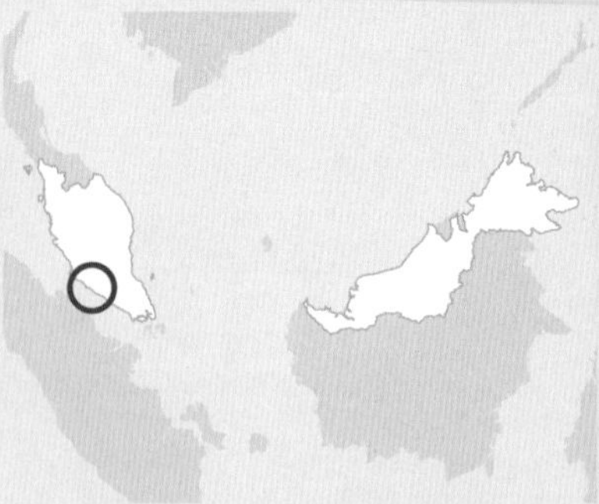

Melaka City

Melaka bloomed from a simple 14th-century fishing village founded by Parameswara, a Hindu prince (or pirate, take your pick) from Sumatra. Its location halfway between China and India, with easy access to the spice islands of Indonesia, soon attracted merchants from all over the East.

Over time it lost favour to Singapore, but this slowdown in trade protected Melaka's ancient architecture from development. When its historic centre was crowned a Unesco World Heritage Site in 2008, it kickstarted a decade of renewal. Modern Melaka swaggers once more, with visitors pouring in to experience the bustling weekend night market, heritage museums and famously glitzy trishaws.

Melaka City in Two Days

Take a trishaw tour or wander on foot through the historic Unesco World Heritage district, including Chinatown, and drop by the **Baba & Nyonya Heritage Museum** (p166) to learn about the city's multicultural past. On day two, sign up for a **cookery course** (p172) and go on a **cruise** (p169) down the Melaka River.

Melaka City in Four Days

Discover more about Melaka's past at the **Maritime Museum & Naval Museum** (p168) and the **Sultanate Palace** (p168). Wander around the atmospheric graveyard on **Bukit China** (p169) and explore the fascinating **Villa Sentosa** (p168). If it's the weekend, dive into the **Jonker Walk Night Market** (p169). Finally, see something of the landscape around the city on an **Eco Bike Tour** (p169).

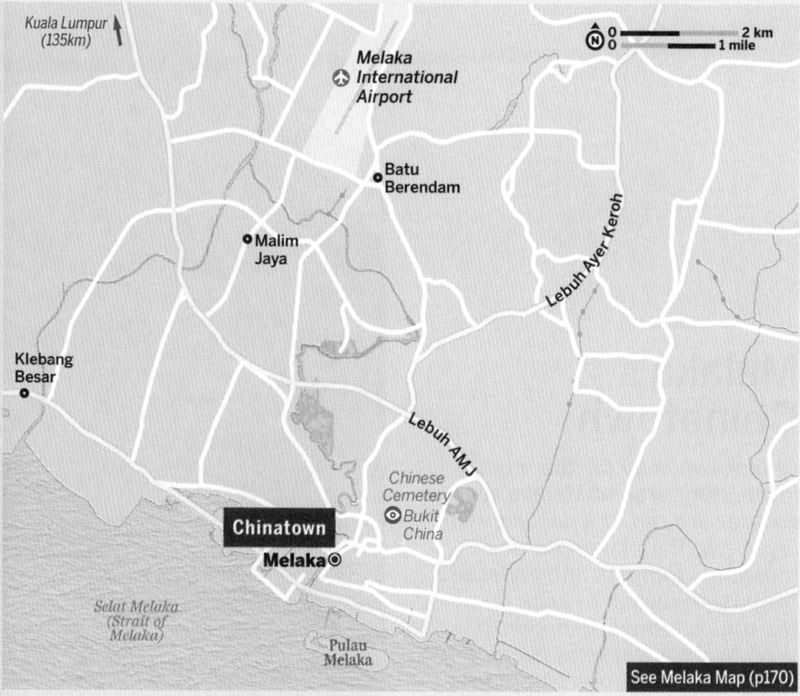

Arriving in Melaka City

Melaka Sentral Located 5km north of the city. There are plenty of bus connections with destinations across Malaysia, as well as Singapore.

Melaka International Airport Twelve kilometres north of Melaka; daily flights to/from Penang and Pekanbaru (Indonesia).

If driving, Melaka is 144km south of Kuala Lumpur.

Sleeping

With new places opening and established hotels rebranding or fading away, accommodation in Melaka is prone to change, though the quality is the best it's been in years.

If you have the option of staying in Chinatown, do it; this is the vibrant historic centre of the city, although it can get both busy and noisy.

The Little India and Bukit China areas allow a glimpse of Melaka's less-touristed side without straying too far from the sights, while the area around Jln Taman Melaka Raya lies in the heart of Melaka's mall shopping zone and is only a short walk to the historic centre and Chinatown.

Melaka's Chinatown

Chinatown is by far the most interesting area of Melaka to wander around. It's packed with lovely old Peranakan homes, mosques, temples and galleries. Stop by midweek to soak up the area's old-world magic, or drop by on a weekend evening to experience the good-humoured elbow-to-elbow razzle-dazzle and tasty street food of the famed Jonker Walk Night Market.

Great For...

Need to Know

The Jonker Walk Night Market (p169) runs Friday to Sunday nights on Jln Hang Jebat.

★ Top Tip

Fuel your night-market excursion with a serve of sweet, *icy cendol* from Jonker 88 (p172).

JOHN S LANDER/GETTY IMAGES ©

Stroll along **Jln Tun Tan Cheng Lock**, formerly called Heeren St, which was the preferred address for wealthy Peranakan traders who were most active during the short-lived rubber boom of the early 20th century. The centre street of Chinatown is **Jln Hang Jebat**, formerly known as Jonker St, that was once famed for its antique shops, but is now more of a collection of clothing and crafts outlets and restaurants. Finally, the northern section of **Jln Tokong Besi** (also known as Harmony St) houses a mosque, a Chinese temple and a handful of authentic Chinese shops.

Baba & Nyonya Heritage Museum

Touring this traditional **Baba-Nonya (Peranakan) townhouse** (☎06-283 1273; http://babanyonyamuseum.com; 48-50 Jln Tun Tan Cheng Lock; adult/child RM16/11; ⏲10am-1pm & 2-5pm Wed-Mon) transports you to a time when women peered at guests through elaborate partitions, and every social situation had its specific location within the house. The captivating museum is arranged to look like a typical 19th-century Baba-Nonya residence. Tour guides enliven the setting with their arch sense of humour. Book ahead or arrive just before the strike of the hour. Last tour of the day is an hour before closing time.

8 Heeren St

This 18th-century Dutch-period **residential house** (8 Jln Tun Tan Cheng Lock; ⏲11am-4pm Tue-Sat) FREE was restored as a model conservation project. The project was partially chronicled in the beautifully designed coffee-table book *Voices from the Street*, which is for sale at the house, along with other titles.

Jln Hang Jebat (Jonker St)

You can also pick up an *Endangered Trades: A Walking Tour of Malacca's Living Heritage* (RM5) booklet and map for an excellent self-guided tour of the city centre. Entry is free but donations are appreciated.

Masjid Kampung Kling

This Chinatown **mosque** (Jln Hang Lekiu) FREE dates to 1748. The 19th-century rebuild you see today mixes a number of styles. Its multi-tiered meru roof (a stacked form similar to that seen in Balinese Hindu architecture) owes its inspiration to Hindu temples, the Moorish watchtower minaret is typical of early mosques in Sumatra, while English and Dutch tiles bedeck its interior. Admission times to go inside vary; dress modestly and, if you're female, bring a scarf.

The proximity of Kampung Kling mosque to Cheng Hoon Teng temple and Hindu temple Sri Poyatha Moorthi has prompted locals to dub this area 'Harmony Street'.

Cheng Hoon Teng Temple

Malaysia's oldest traditional **Chinese temple** (Qing Yun Ting or Green Clouds Temple; 25 Jln Tokong Emas; ⊙7am-7pm) FREE, constructed in 1673, remains a central place of worship for the Buddhist community in Melaka. Notable for its carved woodwork, the temple is dedicated to Kuan Yin, the goddess of mercy.

Sri Poyatha Venayagar Moorthi Temple

One of the first Hindu temples built in Malaysia, **Sri Poyatha Venayagar Moorthi Temple** (Jln Tokong Emas) FREE was constructed in 1781 on the plot given by the religiously tolerant Dutch and dedicated to the Hindu deity Venayagar.

Masjid Kampung Hulu

This is the oldest functioning **mosque** (cnr Jln Masjid & Jln Kampung Hulu) in Malaysia and was, surprisingly, commissioned by the Dutch in 1728. The mosque is made up of predominantly Javanese architecture, with a multi-tiered roof in place of the standard dome. It's not particulary well set up for visitors, but this Chinatown icon is worth admiring from outside.

Melaka's Grassroots Galleries

Chinatown has an impressive concentration of independent galleries and craft workshops. Look out for **Tham Siew Inn Artist Gallery** (www.thamsiewinn.com; 49 Jln Tun Tan Teng Lock; ⊙10am-6pm Thu-Tue), **Red Handicrafts** (Jln Hang Kasturi; ⊙11am-6pm Thu-Tue), **Shihwen Naphaporn Artist Studio** (14 Jln Tun Tan Cheng Lock; ⊙10am-6pm Thu-Tue) and **Hueman Studio** (☑06-288 1795; 9 Jln Tokong Emas; ⊙10.30am-6pm).

LAURIE NOBLE/GETTY IMAGES ©

✕ Take a Break

Nancy's Kitchen (p171) lives up to the hype for its Peranakan (Nonya) cuisine.

SIGHTS

Stadthuys Historic Building

(☎06-282 6526; Dutch Sq; foreign/local visitor RM10/5; ⏰9am-5.30pm Sat-Thu, 9am-12.15pm & 2.45-5.30pm Fri) Melaka's most unmistakable landmark and favourite trishaw pick-up spot is the Stadthuys. This cerise town hall and governor's residence dates to 1650 and is believed to be the oldest Dutch building in the East. The building was erected after Melaka was captured by the Dutch in 1641, and is a reproduction of the former Stadhuis (town hall) of the Frisian town of Hoorn in the Netherlands. Today it's a museum complex, with the **History & Ethnography Museum** as the highlight. Admission covers all the museums. There is no fee for guided tours.

Maritime Museum & Naval Museum Museum

(☎06-283 0926; Jln Quayside; adult/child RM6/2; ⏰9am-5pm Mon-Thu, 9am-8.30pm Fri-Sun) Embark on a voyage through Melaka's maritime history at these linked museums. The most enjoyable of the three (one ticket covers them all) is housed in a huge recreation of the *Flor de la Mar*, a Portuguese ship that sank off the coast of Melaka. The fun of posing on the deck and clambering between floors rather eclipses the displays and dioramas, though the audio guide (RM3) adds engaging detail and a soundtrack of seagulls.

Sultanate Palace Museum

(Jln Kota; adult/child RM2/1; ⏰9am-6pm Tue-Sun) This wooden replica of the palace of Sultan Mansur Shah, who ruled Melaka from 1456 to 1477, houses an open-air cultural museum. The fine recreations were crafted without the use of nails and closely follow descriptions of the original palace from *Sejarah Melayu* (*Malay Annals;* a chronicle of the establishment of the Malay sultanate and 600 years of Malay history).

Villa Sentosa Historic Building

(Peaceful Villa; ☎06-282 3988; Jln Kampung Morten; entry by donation; ⏰hours vary, usually 9am-1pm & 2pm-5pm) Malay village Kampung Morten is nestled right within central Melaka. The highlight of exploring the area,

Night market

with its merry bridge and homes shaded by palm trees, is a visit to this living museum within a 1920s *kampung* house. Visitors (or rather, guests) are welcomed by a member of the household who points out period objects including photographs, Ming dynasty ceramics and a century-old Quran. You're unlikely to leave without a photo-op on plush velvet furniture or a few strikes of the lucky gong.

Christ Church Church
(☎06-284 8804; Jln Gereja; ⊙9am-5pm)
FREE Built in 1753 from pink laterite bricks brought from Zeeland in Holland, this much-photographed church has Dutch and Armenian tombstones in the floor of its rather bare interior. The massive 15m-long ceiling beams overhead were each cut from a single tree.

Bukit China Cemetery
(Jln Puteri Hang Li Poh) More than 12,500 graves, including about 20 Muslim tombs, cover the 25 grassy hectares of serene 'Chinese Hill'. Since the times of British rule, there have been several attempts to acquire Bukit China for road widening, land reclamation or development purposes. Fortunately, Cheng Hoon Teng Temple, with strong community support, has thwarted these attempts.

TOURS

Historic walking tours are offered through several hotels. The **Majestic Malacca** (☎06-289 8000; www.majesticmalacca.com; 188 Jln Bunga Raya) offers an especially good tour (RM150 for non-guests; book ahead) at 10am daily (except Wednesday).

Eco Bike Tour Bicycle Tour
(☎019-652 5029; www.melakaonbike.com; 117 Jln Tiang Dua; per person RM100) Explore the fascinating landscape around Melaka with Alias on his three-hour bike tour (minimum two people) through 20km of oil-palm and rubber-tree plantations and delightful *kampung* communities surrounding town. Flag your level of fitness when you book.

Jonker Walk Night Market

Melaka's weekly **shopping extravaganza** (Jln Hang Jebat; ⊙6-11pm Fri-Sun) keeps the shops along Jln Hang Jebat open late while trinket sellers, food hawkers and the occasional fortune teller close the street to traffic. It has become far more commercial, attracting scores of tourists, but it is an undeniably colourful way to spend an evening shopping and grazing.

Melaka River Cruise Boat Tour
(☎06-281 4322, 06-286 5468; www.melakarivercruise.com; adult/child RM15/7; ⊙9am-11.30pm) Forty-minute riverboat cruises along Sungai Melaka (Melaka River) leave from two locations: one from the 'Spice Garden' on the corner of Jln Tun Mutahii and Jln Tun Sri Lanang in the north of town, and one at the quay near the Maritime Museum. Cruises go 9km upriver past Kampung Morten and old *godowns* (river warehouses) with a recorded narration explaining the riverfront's history.

SHOPPING

Chinatown's shopping spans antiques and cutting-edge art through to novelty flip-flops and keyrings. Best buys include Peranakan beaded shoes and clogs, Southeast Asian and Indian clothing, handmade tiles and stamps, woodblock-printed T-shirts and jewellery. Many shops double as art-and-craft studios, where you can glimpse a painter or silversmith busy at work. Where prices aren't marked, haggle firmly, but always with a smile.

RazKashmir Crafts Accessories
(www.razkashmir.com; 12 Jln Tokong Emas; ⊙10am-7pm) This little boutique is packed floor-to-ceiling with authentic Kashmiri crafts, jewellery and clothing. Peruse embroidered cotton tunics, enamelled teapots and attention-seizing labradorite pendants

Melaka City

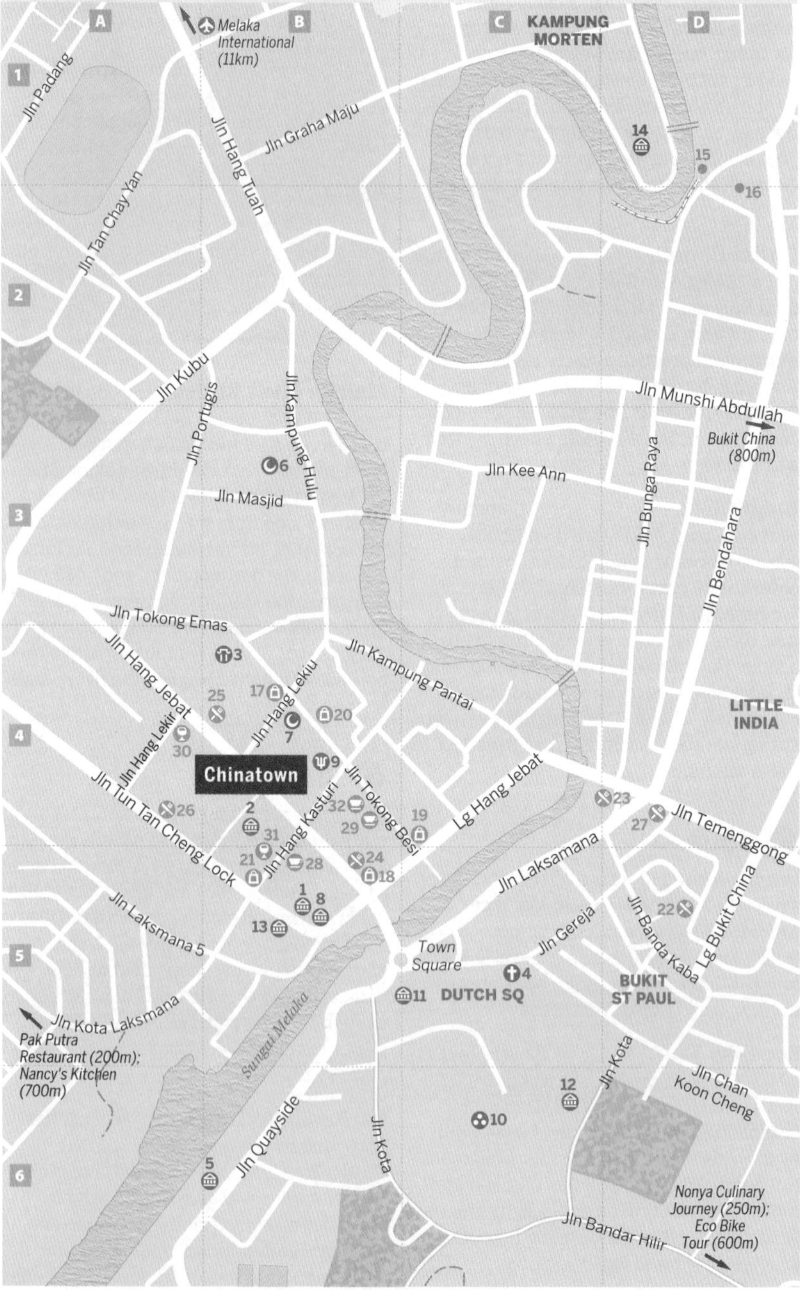

Melaka International (11km)
KAMPUNG MORTEN
Jln Padang
Jln Graha Maju
Jln Hang Tuah
Jln Tan Chay Yan
Jln Kubu
Jln Portugis
Jln Kampung Hulu
Jln Munshi Abdullah
Bukit China (800m)
Jln Kee Ann
Jln Masjid
Jln Bunga Raya
Jln Bendahara
Jln Tokong Emas
Jln Hang Jebat
Jln Kampung Pantai
Jln Hang Lekiu
Jln Hang Lekir
LITTLE INDIA
Chinatown
Jln Tokong Besi
Lg Hang Jebat
Jln Tun Tan Cheng Lock
Jln Hang Kasturi
Jln Temenggong
Jln Laksmana
Jln Laksmana 5
Jln Gereja
Jln Banda Kaba
Lg Bukit China
Town Square
DUTCH SQ
BUKIT ST PAUL
Jln Kota Laksmana
Pak Putra Restaurant (200m); Nancy's Kitchen (700m)
Sungai Melaka
Jln Kota
Jln Chan Koon Cheng
Jln Quayside
Nonya Culinary Journey (250m); Eco Bike Tour (600m)
Jln Bandar Hilir
200 m
0.1 miles

Melaka City

Sights

1	8 Heeren Street	B5
2	Baba & Nyonya Heritage Museum	B4
3	Cheng Hoon Teng Temple	B4
4	Christ Church	C5
5	Maritime Museum & Naval Museum	B6
6	Masjid Kampung Hulu	B3
7	Masjid Kampung Kling	B4
8	Shihwen Naphaporn Artist Studio	B5
9	Sri Poyatha Venayagar Moorthi Temple	B4
10	St Paul's Church	C6
11	Stadthuys	C5
12	Sultanate Palace	C6
13	Tham Siew Inn Artist Gallery	B5
14	Villa Sentosa	D1

Activities, Courses & Tours

15	Melaka River Cruise	D1
16	Peranakan Culinary Journey	D2

Shopping

17	Hueman Studio	B4
18	Jonker Walk Night Market	B5
19	Orangutan House	C4
20	RazKashmir Crafts	B4
21	Red Handicrafts	B5

Eating

22	Capitol Satay	D5
23	Discovery Cafe	D4
24	Hoe Kee Chicken Rice Ball	B5
25	Jonker 88	B4
26	Kocik Kitchen	A4
27	Selvam	D4

Drinking & Nightlife

28	Calanthe Art Cafe	B5
29	Cheng Ho Tea House	B4
30	Geographér Cafe	A4
31	Me & Mrs Jones	B5
32	Ola Lavanderia Café	B4

among the glittering shelves. The laid-back owner is just as pleased to share cultural insights as he is to make a sale. Find it opposite Sri Poyatha temple.

Orangutan House Clothing

(☎06-282 6872; www.absolutearts.com/charlescham; 59 Lg Hang Jebat; ⏲10am-6pm Thu-Tue) Even on colourful Lg Hang Jebat, it's hard to miss the yellow-and-peach orangutan mural above artist Charles Cham's T-shirt store. Spirited designs range from Chinese astrology animals to uplifting slogans and 'play safe' banners above condoms.

EATING

Nancy's Kitchen Peranakan $

(☎06-283 6099; eat@nancyskit.com; 13 Jln KL 3/8, Taman Kota Laksamana; mains RM10; ⏲11am-5pm Wed-Mon) The mouth-watering meals stirred up in this Peranakan (Nonya) restaurant are revered in Melaka, and Nancy's Kitchen lives up to the hype. Local diners crowd this small restaurant, especially at weekends, their bellies rumbling for a taste of signature dishes like candlenut chicken (succulent meat simmered in a nutty sauce, fragrant with lemongrass). The restaurant stays open until 9pm on public holidays.

If you want to take some Peranakan home-cooking flair away with you, call to arrange cooking courses (p172) with Nancy herself.

Pak Putra Restaurant Pakistani $

(☎012-601 5876; Jln Kota Laksmana 4; mains RM8-10; ⏲6pm-1am, closed alternate Mondays; 🌶) Scarlet tikka chickens rotate hypnotically on skewers, luring locals and travellers to this excellent Pakistani restaurant. With aromatic vegetarian dishes, seafood and piquant curries, there's no shortage of choice (try the masala fish). The unchallenged highlights are oven-puffed naan bread and chicken fresh from the clay tandoor. Portions are generous and service is speedy.

Selvam Indian $

(☎06-281 9223; 3 Jln Temenggong; mains RM6-9; ⏲7am-10pm; 🌶) This classic banana-leaf restaurant is excellent value, with efficient and amiable staff. Generous servings of aromatic chicken biryani are eclipsed by the vegetarian offerings, in particular the Friday afternoon veggie special.

Cooking Courses

Peranakan cuisine is the most famous type of cooking in Melaka; it's also known as 'Nonya', an affectionate term for a Peranakan wife (often the family chef). You can learn how to cook key dishes on cooking courses at the following recommended places:

Nancy's Kitchen (☎06-283 6099; 13 Jln KL 3/8, Taman Kota Laksamana; per person RM100)

Peranakan Culinary Journey (☎06-289 8000; www.majesticmalacca.com; Majestic Malacca Hotel, 188 Jln Bunga Raya; per person RM290)

Nonya Culinary Journey (☎06-282 8333; Hotel Equatorial, Jln Parameswara; per person RM115)

AUSTIN BUSH/GETTY IMAGES ©

Jonker 88 Desserts $

(88 Jln Hang Jebat; mains RM6; ⏲11am-10pm Tue-Thu, to 11pm Fri & Sat, to 9pm Sun) Slurp-worthy laksa and decent Peranakan fare are served up at this efficient local canteen. But the highlight of this busy Jonker St eatery is its *cendol* menu. This frosty dessert, a mountain of shaved ice, coconut, pandan noodles, red beans and jaggery syrup, is as rainbow-coloured (and wacky) as it sounds. Jonker 88 has a fabulous selection of flavours and toppings, including sago pearl and durian (from RM5).

Capitol Satay Malaysian $

(☎06-283 5508; 41 Lg Bukit China; mains from RM8; ⏲5pm-midnight; 🗒) Famous for its *satay celup* (a Melaka adaptation of satay steamboat), this place is usually packed and is one of the cheapest outfits in town. Stainless-steel tables have bubbling vats of soup in the middle where you dunk skewers of okra stuffed with tofu, sausages, chicken, prawns and bok choy.

Kocik Kitchen Peranakan $$

(☎016-929 6605; 100 Jln Tun Tan Cheng Lock; mains RM20-30; ⏲11am-6.30pm Mon, Tue & Thu, 11am-5pm & 6-9pm Fri & Sat, 11am-7.30pm Sun) This unassuming little restaurant is hot on the heels of Melaka's other Peranakan (Nonya) specialists; try the creamy *lemak nenas* prawns, swimming in fragrant coconut milk with fresh chunks of pineapple.

Hoe Kee Chicken Rice Ball Chinese $$

(4 Jln Hang Jebat; mains RM20; ⏲8.30am-3pm, closed last Wed of month) This is one of Melaka's top spots for juicy poached chicken served with wadded balls of rice, themselves sticky with chicken stock. A popular pilgrimage place for Hainanese chicken rice, don't expect a menu or deferential service. The queue allows plenty of time to decide if you're hungry enough for a quarter-chicken (RM14) or a whole one (RM40).

DRINKING & NIGHTLIFE

Unlike much of Malaysia, there is no shortage of spots to cool down with a beer in Melaka.

Geographér Cafe Bar

(☎06-281 6813; www.geographer.com.my; 83 Jln Hang Jebat; ⏲10am-1am Wed-Sun; 📶) Some come to socialise, others are drawn by the free wi-fi. Either way, a swinging soundtrack of Eurotrash, jazz and classic pop keeps the beers flowing at traveller magnet Geographér. This well-ventilated cafe-bar, strewn with greenery, feels like a haven despite bordering busy Jonker St. Monday nights have live jazz while Fridays and Saturdays bring a father-daughter vocal-keyboard duet (both 8.30pm).

Calanthe Art Cafe Coffee

(13 States Coffee; 06-292 2960; 11 Jln Hang Kasturi; 10am-11pm;) Full-bodied Johor or classic Perak white? Choose a Malaysian state's favourite coffee and this perky place, also known as '13 States', will have it blended with ice and jelly cubes for a refreshing caffeine kick. Breakfasts are served here too (10am to 11.45am).

Me & Mrs Jones Pub

(016-234 4292; 3 Jln Hang Kasturi; 7pm-12am Tue-Sun) This cosy pub is staunchly un-hip and all the more enjoyable for it. At weekends there is live blues and rock, often with retired co-owner Mr Tan leading a jam session. Relax into the atmosphere and grab a beer or juice (long menus are not the Jones' style).

Cheng Ho Tea House Teahouse

(Jln Tokong Besi; 10am-5pm) In an exquisite setting that resembles a Chinese temple garden courtyard, relax over a pot of fine Chinese tea (from RM15) or nibble on a range of rice and noodle dishes (around RM12).

Ola Lavanderia Café Cafe

(012-612 6665; Jln Tokong Besi; 10am-6pm Mon-Sat;) Backpacker salvation is here, in the form of the holy travel trinity: laundry, wi-fi and caffeine. This friendly Chinatown cafe does coffees (RM7.50) and croissants (RM5), and you can spin your laundry while you sip (RM4.80 per load, RM1 per item ironed).

INFORMATION

Most hotels and guesthouses have wi-fi, and several cafes in Chinatown have a computer for clients and charge around RM3 per hour.

There are plenty of ATMs at the shopping malls, but fewer in Chinatown. Moneychangers can be found throughout Chinatown.

In 2011, Melaka's Chinatown and historic centre was declared a no-smoking zone. It's not heavily enforced, but the air is noticeably more smoke-free than elsewhere in the city.

GETTING THERE & AWAY

AIR

Melaka International Airport (06-317 5860; Lapangan Terbang Batu Berendam) is 12km north of Melaka. At the time of writing, **Malindo Air** (03-7841 5388; www.malindoair.com) offered flights from Melaka to Penang (from RM99, daily) and Pekanbaru (Indonesia; from RM180, daily).

BUS

Melaka Sentral, the huge, modern long-distance bus station, is 5km north of the city. Luggage deposit at Melaka Sentral is RM2 per bag. There is also an ATM and restaurants.

A taxi into town should cost RM20 to RM25, or you can take bus 17 (RM1.40).

A medley of privately run bus companies make checking timetables a herculean feat; you can scout popular routes on www.expressbus-malaysia.com/coach-from-melaka. You can buy bus tickets in advance from downtown Melaka (not a bad idea on busy weekends or if you have a plane to catch) at **Discovery Cafe** (012-683 5606, 06-292 5606; www.discovery-malacca.com; 3 Jln Bunga Raya) – there's a small commission, dependent on the ticket fare.

GETTING AROUND

Melaka is small enough to walk around or, for the traffic-fearless, you can rent a bike for around RM3 per hour from guesthouses around Chinatown. A useful service is town bus 17, running every 15 minutes from Melaka Sentral to the centre of town, past the huge Mahkota Parade shopping complex, to Taman Melaka Raya and on to Medan Portugis. You can find local bus route information at www.panoramamelaka.com.my/routes.

Taking to Melaka's streets by trishaw is a must – by the hour they should cost RM40, or RM15 for any one-way trip within town, but you'll have to bargain.

Taxis should cost around RM15 for a trip anywhere around town.

MT KINABALU

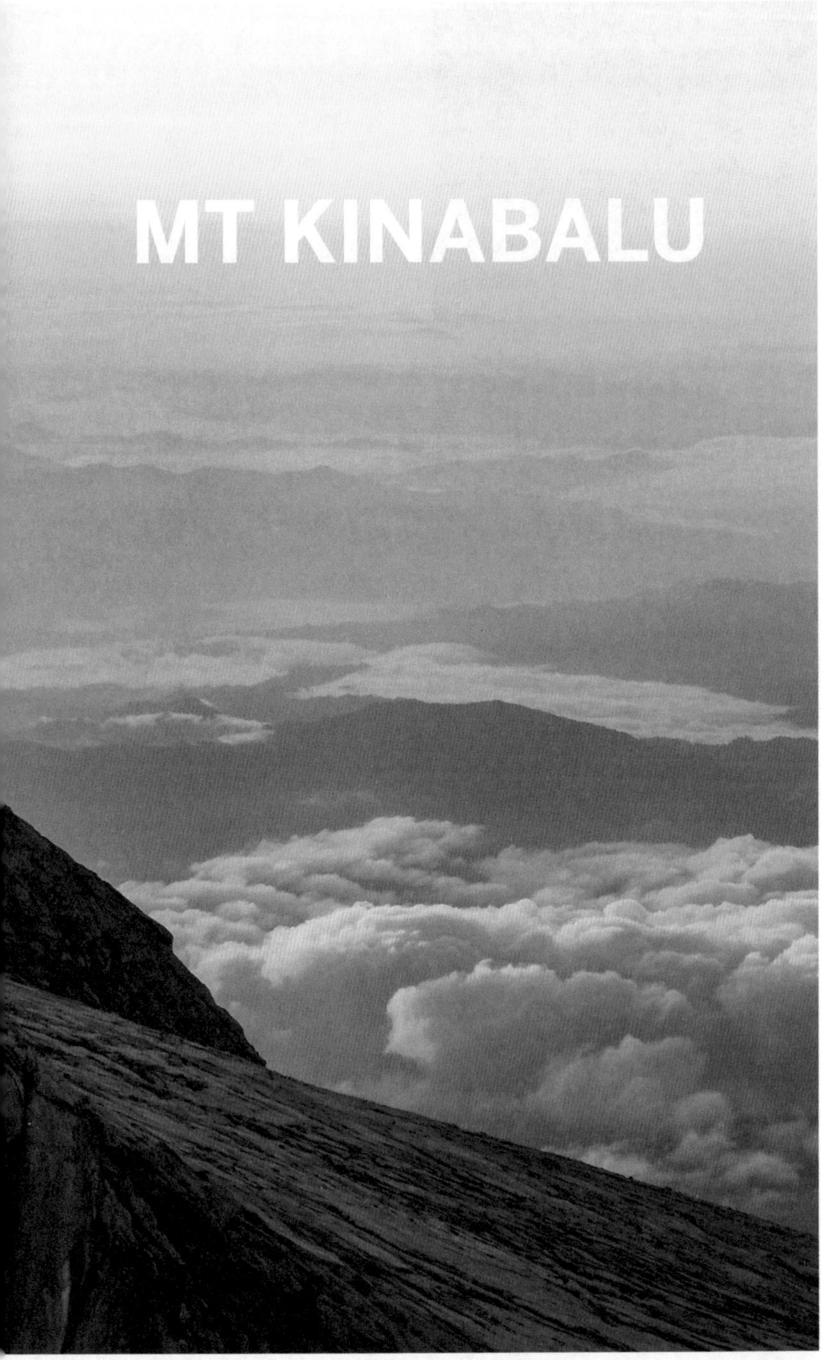

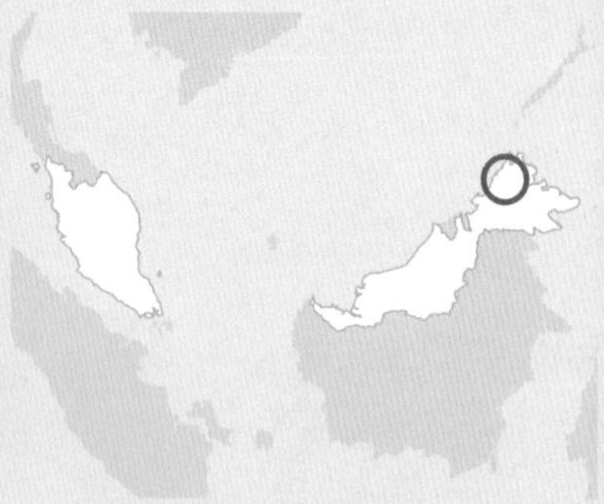

Mt Kinabalu

It is only when you give Gunung Kinabalu, as it is known in Malay, your full attention that you realise how special Malaysia's first Unesco World Heritage site and the region's biggest tourist attraction truly is.

On a clear day you can see the Philippines from Mt Kinabalu's 4095m summit. Usually, though, the mountain is thoroughly wreathed in fog by mid-morning, and, if you're going to get to the top for dawn, you need a minimum of two days to climb, and it's tough going! If you don't feel up to reaching the summit, the base has some worthy attractions, including a large network of nature trails. Also budget time to see sights in and around Sabah's capital, Kota Kinabalu (KK).

Mt Kinabalu in Four Days

The physically demanding **ascent of Kinabalu** takes a minimum of two days, with one night spent on the mountain. In reality you're going to need four days at least for this trip so you can get to and from KK, where you may need to spend time sorting out paperwork and recovering from the climb.

Mt Kinabalu in Six Days

It's worth spending a day exploring the marked trails around park headquarters; do this before you climb the mountain, as chances are you won't really feel like it afterwards. With six days you'll also have time to see some of KK's sights, such as the **Sabah Museum** (p185), the **Night Market** (p188) and the **Kota Kinabalu Wetland Centre** (p186).

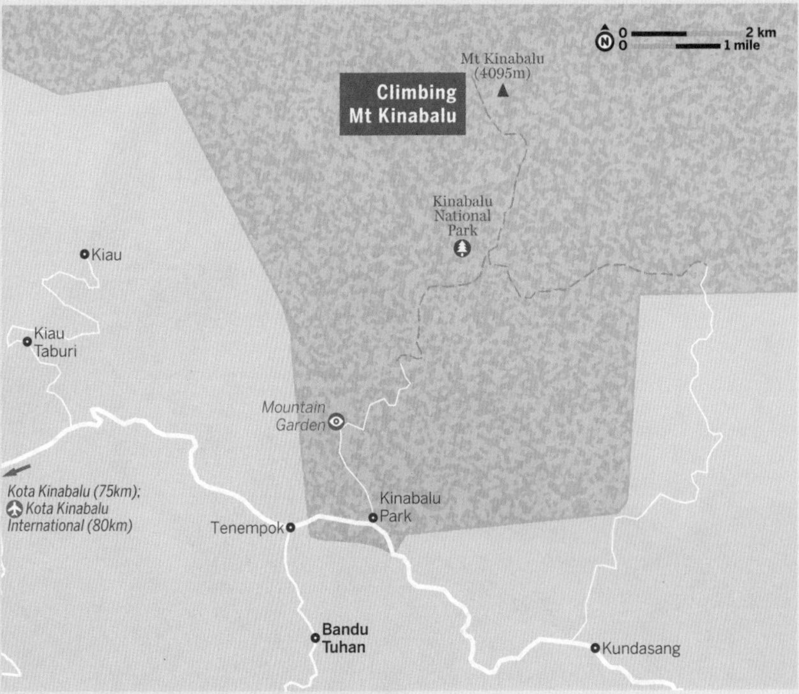

Arriving in Mt Kinabalu

Kota Kinabalu International Airport
Fly to KK from either Peninsular Malaysia, Sarawak or Singapore. Buses, shared taxis and shared jeeps connect KK with the entrance to Kinabalu National Park, which is 88km northeast.

Sleeping

Camping is not allowed on the mountain, and thus access to the summit is limited by availability of the huts on the mountain at Laban Rata. Sleeping options located at the base of the mountain are overpriced compared to sleeping spots just outside the park.

Kota Kinabalu's midrange options are fewer than the many high-end and backpacker choices, but there are deals to be found off-peak. Downtown KK is a convenient base as it's surrounded by restaurants, markets and tour operators.

If you're looking for beachside digs, then consider the resorts at Tanjung Aru or one of the nearby islands.

St John's Peak

Climbing Mt Kinabalu

Mt Kinabalu may not be a Himalayan sky-poker, but it is by no means an easy jaunt – get set for what is essentially a very long walk up a very steep hill.

Great For...

☑ Don't Miss

A descent of Kinabalu using the thrilling *via ferrata* system of rungs and cables.

Although it is commonly believed that local tribesmen climbed Kinabalu many years earlier, it was Sir Hugh Low, the British colonial secretary on Pulau Labuan, who recorded the first official ascent of Mt Kinabalu in 1851. Today Kinabalu's tallest peak is named after him, thus Borneo's highest point is ironically known as Low's Peak.

In those days finding willing local porters was a tricky matter – the tribesmen who accompanied Low believed the spirits of the dead inhabited the mountain. Low was therefore obliged to protect the party by supplying a large basket of quartz crystals and teeth, as was the custom back then. During the subsequent years, the spirit-appeasement ceremonies became more and more elaborate, so that by the 1920s they had come to include loud prayers, gunshots, and the sacrifice of seven eggs

and seven white chickens. These days, the elaborate chicken dances are no more, although climbing the mountain can still feel like a rite of passage.

On June 5, 2015 an earthquake struck the mountain savagely taking the lives of 18 people and leaving 137 people temporarily stranded. The Kadazan-Dusun people believe the earthquake was caused by 'Aki' (the mountain's protectors), who were enraged at the loutish behaviour of 10 Westerners (who allegedly stripped and urinated and insulted their guide while two of their cohort even managed to have sex on their ascent of the mountain) on 30 May.

The trail from Timpohon to Laban Rata reopened to climbers in September 2015, with business as usual, and the trail from Laban Rata to the summit reopened on 1 December.

Need to Know

Check out www.mountkinabalu.com for important information and updates about the climb.

Take a Break

There are restaurants at the park HQ and at Laban Rata on the mountain.

★ Top Tip

The new Ranau trail offers breathtaking views over the Ranau valley.

The Ascent

Most people do a two-day/one-night ascent of the mountain and follow the shorter, easier (but by no means easy) **Timpohon Trail**. You'll want to check in at park headquarters at around 9am (8.45am at the latest for *via ferrata* participants) to pay your park fees, grab your guide and start the ascent (four to six hours) to Laban Rata (3272m), where you'll spend the night before finishing the climb. On the following day you'll start scrambling to the top at about 2.30am in order to reach the summit for a breathtaking sunrise over Borneo.

A climb up Kinabalu is only advised for those in adequate physical condition. The trek is tough, and every step you take will be uphill. You will negotiate several obstacles along the way, including slippery stones, blinding humidity, frigid winds and slow-paced trekkers. Mountain Torq compares the experience to squeezing five days of hiking into a 38-hour trek.

Via Ferrata

Mountain Torq (☎088-268126; www.mountaintorq.com; Low's Peak Circuit RM870, Walk the Torq RM650) has dramatically changed the Kinabalu climbing experience by creating an intricate system of rungs and rails – known as *via ferrata* (literally 'iron road' in Italian) – crowning the mountain's summit.

After ascending Kinabalu in the traditional fashion, participants use the network of rungs, pallets and cables to return to the Laban Rata rest camp area along the mountain's dramatic granite walls. Mountain Torq's star attraction, the Low's Peak Circuit (minimum age 17), is a four- to five-hour scramble down long stretches of sheer rock face. The route's threadlike tightrope walks and swinging planks will have you convinced that the course designers are sadistic, but that's what makes it such fun – testing your limits without putting your safety in jeopardy.

Those who don't want to see their heart leaping out of their chest should try the Walk the Torq route (minimum age 10). This two- to three-hour escapade is an exciting initiation into the world of *via ferrata*, offering dramatic mountain vistas with a few less knee-shaking moments.

Permits, Fees & Guides

A park fee, climbing permit, insurance and a guide fee are *mandatory* if you intend to climb Mt Kinabalu. All permits and guides must be arranged at the **Sabah Parks office** (⏲7am-7pm), which is directly next door to the Sutera Sanctuary Lodges office, immediately on your right after you pass through the main gate of the park. Pay all fees at park HQ before you climb and don't ponder an 'unofficial' climb as permits (laminated cards worn on a string necklace) are scrupulously checked at two points you cannot avoid passing on the way up the mountain. Virtually every tour operator in KK can hook you up with a trip to the mountain; solo travellers are often charged around RM1400. It's possible, and a little cheaper, to do it on your own – but plan ahead. Packages are obviously easier.

Mossy tree frog

All visitors entering the park are required to pay a park entrance fee (RM15/10 per adult/child; Malaysian nationals pay RM3/1). A climbing permit costs RM212/RM85 per adult/child (RM53/RM32 for Malaysian nationals) and climbing insurance costs a flat rate of RM7 per person. Guide fees for the summit trek cost RM230 for a group of one to five people.

Your guide will be assigned to you on the morning you begin your hike. If you ask, the park staff will try to attach individual travellers to a group so that guide fees can be shared. Couples can expect to be given their own guide. Guides are mostly Kadazan from a village nearby and many of them have travelled to the summit several hundred times. Try to ask for a guide who speaks English – he or she (usually he) might point out a few interesting specimens of plant life. The path up the mountain is pretty straightforward, and the guides walk behind the slowest member of the group, so think of them as safety supervisors rather than trailblazers.

★ Top Tip

Advance accommodation bookings are essential if you plan on climbing the mountain.

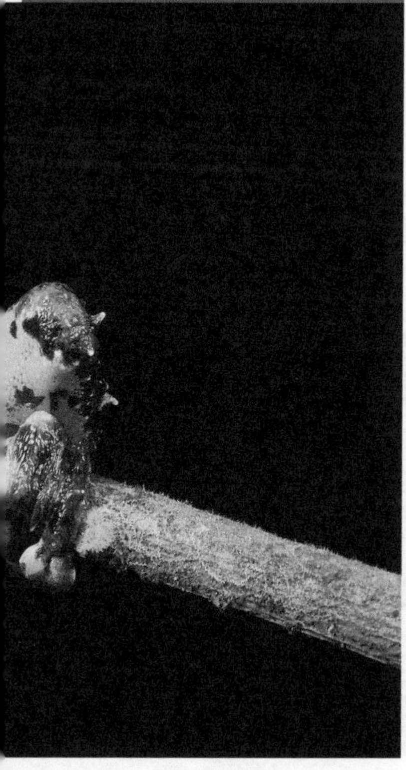

NICK GARBUTT/GETTY IMAGES ©

All this does not include around RM670 for dorm and board (or RM1350 for private room and board) on the mountain at Laban Rata. With said lodging, plus buses or taxis to the park, you're looking at spending around RM900 for the common two-day, one-night trip to the mountain. It's no longer possible to do a one-day hike to the summit.

Optional extra fees include the shuttle bus (RM33 one-way) or taxi (RM18 per person in a group of four) from the park office to the Timpohon Gate, a climbing certificate (RM10) and a porter (RM80 per trip to the summit or RM65 to Laban Rata), who can be hired to carry a maximum load of 10kg.

If you need a helicopter lift off the mountain for emergency reasons, the going rate is RM6000.

Equipment & Clothing

No special equipment is required to successfully summit the mountain, however a headlamp is strongly advised for the predawn jaunt to the top – you'll need your hands free to climb the ropes on the summit massif. Expect freezing temperatures near the summit, not to mention strong winds and the occasional rainstorm. Don't forget a water bottle, which can be refilled at unfiltered (but potable) tanks en route. The average temperature range at Kinabalu Park is 15°C to 24°C. Along the Timpohon (the Summit trail), it's about 6°C to 14°C, and can sometimes drop to as low as 2°C.

Mt Kinabalu & Kinabalu National Park

Mt Kinabalu is ubiquitous in Sabah to the point of being inextricable. It graces the state's flag and is a constant presence at the edge of your eyes, catching the clouds and shading the valleys. The peak and its surrounds were designated as a national park in 1964, protecting a remarkably diverse range of plants, animals and birds (and over 100 species of land snail).

ACTIVITIES

There are various trails and lookouts around park headquarters. The trails interconnect with one another, so you can spend the day, or indeed, days, walking at a leisurely pace through the beautiful forest.

Some interesting plants, plenty of birds and, if you're lucky, the occasional mammal can be seen along the **Liwagu Trail** (6km), which follows the river of the same name. When it rains, watch out for slippery paths and legions of leeches.

At 11am each day a guided walk (per person RM5) starts from the Sabah Parks office and lasts for one to two hours. The knowledgeable guide points out flowers, plants, birds and insects along the way. If you set out from KK early enough, it's possible to arrive at the park in time for the walk.

Many of the plants found on the mountain are cultivated in the **Mountain Garden** (admission RM5; 9am-1pm & 2:30-4pm) behind the visitors centre. Guided tours of the garden depart at 9am, noon and 3pm and cost RM5.

TOURS

The following KK-based agencies can arrange package tours and accommodation within the national park.

Sticky Rice Travel Adventure Tour (088-251 654; www.stickyricetravel.com; 3rd fl, 58 Jln Pantai; 9am-6pm) National

"a constant presence at the edge of your eyes"

View of Mt Kinabalu from Kundasang

NORA CAROL PHOTOGRAPHY/GETTY IMAGES ©

Geographic prefers this outfit for a reason: they're organised, original in their choice of tours and have excellent knowledgeable guides. Responsible community-based tourism; expect adventure, culture and something very different. Sticky Rice will sit down with you and tailor your experience around your interests, fitness and budget; your trip may last four days or a few weeks.

Adventure Alternative Borneo Adventure Tour
(☎019-802 0549; www.aaborneo.com; 1st fl, 97 Jln Gaya; ⏰9am-6pm) Sustainable and ethical travel are key to this British-owned company, which works closely with Sabah Tourist Board, and run tours to Lupa Masa rainforest camp, close to Mt Kinabalu. If you're looking for remote natural immersion, they also operate trips to Orou Sapulot.

Sutera Harbour Trekking
(Sutera Sanctuary Lodges; ☎088-308 914/5; www.suteraharbour.com; ground fl, lot G15, Wisma Sabah, Jln Haji Saman; ⏰9am-6pm) Sutera runs a lot of the tourism activities in Sabah, and has a monopoly on accommodation within Mt Kinabalu park. Make this your first stop in KK if you're planning to climb Kinabalu and didn't book your bed in advance.

EATING

Just outside of the park gates is a roadside restaurant that serves up good Malaysian noodle and rice standards for around RM5 per main.

At Laban Rata the cafeteria-style restaurant in the Laban Rata Resthouse has a simple menu and also offers buffet meals. Most hikers staying at Laban Rata have three meals (dinner, breakfast and lunch) included in their accommodation packages. It is possible to negotiate a price reduction if you plan on bringing your own food (boiling water can be purchased for RM1 if you bring dried noodles). Note: you will have to lug said food up to Laban Rata. Buffet meals can also be purchased individually – dinner costs RM45. A small counter in the dining area sells an assortment of items including soft drinks, chocolate, pain relievers and postcards.

A Growing Mountain

Many visitors to Borneo assume Mt Kinabalu is a volcano, but the mountain is actually a huge granite dome that rose from the depths below some nine million years ago. In geological terms, Mt Kinabalu is still young. Little erosion has occurred on the exposed granite rock faces around the summit, though the effects of glaciers that used to cover much of the mountain can be detected by striations on the rock. There's no longer a snowline and the glaciers have disappeared, but at times ice forms in the rock pools near the summit. Amazingly, the mountain is still growing: researchers have found it increases in height by about 5mm a year.

Restoran Kinabalu Balsam Cafeteria $
(dishes RM5-15; ⏰6am-10pm, to 11pm Sat & Sun) The cheaper and more popular of the two options in the park is this canteen-style spot directly below the park HQ. It offers basic but decent Malaysian, Chinese and Western dishes at reasonable prices. There is also a small but well-stocked shop in Balsam selling tinned and dried foods, chocolate, beer, spirits, cigarettes, T-shirts, bread, eggs and margarine.

Liwagu Restaurant Cafeteria $$
(dishes RM10-30; ⏰6am-10pm, to 11pm Sat & Sun) In the visitors centre, this cafeteria serves a huge range of dishes, including noodles, rice, seafood standards and 'American breakfast'.

GETTING THERE & AWAY

It is highly advised that summit-seekers check in at the park headquarters by 9am, which means

Tunku Abdul Rahman National Park

Whenever one enjoys a sunset off KK, the view tends to be improved by the five jungly humps of Manukan, Gaya, Sapi, Mamutik and Sulug islands. These swaths of sand, plus the reefs and cerulean waters in between them, make up **Tunku Abdul Rahman National Park** (adult/child RM10/6), covering a total area of just over 49 sq km (two-thirds of which is water). Only a short boat ride from KK, the islands are individually quite pretty, but in an effort to accommodate the ever-increasing tourist flow, barbecue stalls and restaurants now crowd the beaches. On weekends the islands can get *very* crowded, but on weekdays you can easily find some serenity. Accommodation tends to be expensive, but most travellers come here for day trips anyway, and there are camping options.

Diving in the park (especially around Gaya and Sapi) – with a dizzying 364 species of fish found here – may bring you into contact with blue-ringed octopus, black-tip reef shark and shape-shifting cuttlefish. And, if you're here between November and February, it's possible you might sight a whale shark. **Borneo Dream** (☎088-244064; www.borneodream.com; F-G-1 Plaza Tanjung Aru, Jln Mat Salleh) and **Downbelow** (☎012-866 1935; www.divedownbelow.com; Lot 67 & 68, 5th fl, KK Times Sq Block; ⌚9am-6pm) both run PADI Open Water diving programs on Pulau Gaya.

Diving in Tunku Abdul Rahman National Park

SCUBAZOO/GETTY IMAGES ©

if you're coming from KK, you should plan to leave by 7am, or consider spending the night somewhere near the base of the mountain.

BUS

Express buses (RM30) leave KK from the Utara Terminal bus station every hour on the hour from 7am to 10am and at 12.30pm, 2pm and 3pm, and leave at the same times in the reverse direction; alternatively take a Ranau-bound minivan (RM25) from central KK at Padang Merdeka bus terminal, asking the driver to drop you outside the gate at Kinabalu National Park. Minivans leave when full and run from early morning till around 2pm. We recommend leaving by 7am for the two-hour trip.

Express buses and minivans travelling between KK and Ranau (and Sandakan) pass the park turn-off, 100m uphill from the park entrance. You can go to Sandakan (RM40) if the bus has room.

TAXI

Share taxis (RM200) leave KK from Inanam and Padang Merdeka Bus Stations.

JEEP

Share jeeps park just outside of the park gates and leave when full for KK (RM200) and Sandakan (RM500); each jeep can hold around five passengers, but they can be chartered by individuals.

Kota Kinabalu

Kota Kinabalu won't immediately overwhelm you with its beauty, but you'll soon notice its friendly locals, breathtaking fiery sunsets, blossoming arts and music scene, and rich culinary spectrum spanning Malay to Japanese, Western to Cantonese, street food to high end. Alongside swanky new malls and condos springing up at every turn, old KK with its markets stocked to the gills with fish, pearls and busy fishermen shuttling about the waterfront, happily endures. This may be a city on the move with the 21st century, but its old-world charm and history are very much alive.

Heritage Village, Sabah Museum

SIGHTS

Some of KK's best attractions are located beyond the city centre, and it's well worth putting in the effort to check them out.

Signal Hill Observatory Platform Landmark

(Jln Bukit Bendera; 8am-midnight) Up on Signal Hill, among the art deco mansions at the eastern edge of the city centre, there's an unmissable UFO-like observation pavilion. Come here to make sense of the city layout below. The view is best as the sun sets over the islands. To reach it, catch a cab (RM15), as there's no bus.

Sabah Museum Museum

(Kompleks Muzium Sabah; 088-253 199; www.museum.sabah.gov.my; Jln Muzium; admission RM15; 9am-5pm Sat-Thu; P) About 2km south of the city centre, this refurbished museum is the best place to go in KK for an introduction to Sabah's ethnicities and environments, with new signage and clear explanations. Expect tribal and historical artefacts including ceramics and a centrepiece whale skeleton, and replica limestone cave. The **Heritage Village** has traditional tribal dwellings, including Kadazan bamboo houses and a Chinese farmhouse, all nicely set on a lily-pad lake.

Mari Mari Cultural Village Museum

(088-260 501; www.traversetours.com/sabah/marimari-cultural-village; Jln Kiansom; adult/child RM160/130; tours at 10am, 2pm & 6pm; P) With three-hour tours at 10am, 2pm or 6pm, Mari Mari showcases various traditional homes of Sabahan ethnic communities – the Bajau, Lundayeh, Murut, Rungus and Dusun – all of which are built by descendants of the tribes they represent. Along the way you'll get the chance to see blow-pipe making, tattooing, fire-starting, and an insight into the mystical belief systems of each of these groups, as well as a notable culinary nibble from each tribe! It's touristy, sure, but good fun – especially for families.

A short dance recital is also included in the visit. The village is a 20- to 30-minute drive north of central KK. There is also a small waterfall – **Kiansom Waterfall** –

Restaurants along Waterfront Esplanade

ANDERS BLOMQVIST/GETTY IMAGES ©

about 400m beyond the cultural village, which is easily accessible by private transport or on foot. The area around the cascade lends itself well to swimming and it's a great place to cool off after a visit to Mari Mari.

Lok Kawi Wildlife Park Zoo

(☎088-765793, 088-765710; Jln Penampang; adult/child RM25/10; ⏰9.30am-5.30pm, last entry at 4.30pm; P) About an hour (20km) from KK, this zoo offers a chance to see Sabah's creatures if you are unable to spot them in their natural environment. We warn you, however, that the tiger and sun bear enclosures are lamentably bare and small, and the orangutans are made to peel coconuts for tourists. Other animals includes tarsiers, proboscis monkeys, pygmy elephants and rhinoceros hornbills. There is also a train that carts you around the park (RM2).

Kota Kinabalu Wetland Centre Bird Sanctuary

(☎088-246 955; www.sabahwetlands.org; Jln Bukit Bendera Upper, Likas District; admission RM15; ⏰8.30am-6pm Tue-Sun; P) The sanctuary features 1.4km of wooden walkways passing through a 24-hectare mangrove swamp. Expect to see scuttling fiddler and mangrove crabs, mud lobsters, mudskippers, skinks, turtles, water monitors and mangrove slugs (sadly, there are also plastic bottles.). For many, the big attraction is a stunning variety of migratory birds. To get here, take the bus towards Likas from the bus stations in front of City Hall or Wawasan Plaza in the city, to Likas Sq. A taxi from KK costs around RM15.

ACTIVITIES

KK Heritage Walk Walking Tour

(☎012-802 8823; www.kkheritagewalk.com; walk incl tea break, batik bandana & booklet RM200; ⏰departs 9am daily) This 2½-hour tour, which can be booked through any of KK's many tour operators (just ask at your hotel front desk), explores colonial KK and its hidden delights. Stops include Chinese herbal shops, bulk produce stalls, a *kopitiam* (coffee shop), and Jln Gaya (known as

Bond St when the British were in charge). Guides speak English, Chinese and Bahasa Malaysia.

SHOPPING

KK is fast becoming a shopaholic's heaven, with leading brands in ubersmart malls across the city.

Cracko Art Gallery Arts
(www.facebook.com/crackoart; cnr Jln Bakau & Jln Gaya; 12-8pm) Made up of a group of brilliantly talented KK artists, high up on the 3rd floor (look for the Cracko sign outside on the street), you'll find a vivid working studio of abstract and figurative art, stunning jewellery, and sculpture from Manga-style figurines to mannequin-art. Affordable and original work, a visit here makes for a great hour.

Oceanus Waterfront Mall Shopping Centre
(Jln Tun Fuad Stephens; 10am-10pm;) The city centre's newest mall, this gleaming palace of consumerism has all the top Western brands, from sunglass shops to coffee-house chains, beauty products to fashion.

Handicraft Market Market
(Filipino Market; Jln Tun Fuad Stephens; 8am-9pm) The Handicraft Market is a good place to shop for inexpensive souvenirs. Offerings include pearls, textiles, seashell crafts, jewellery and bamboo goods, some from the Philippines, some from Malaysia and some from other parts of Asia. Needless to say, bargaining is a must!

EATING

KK is one of the few cities in Borneo with an eating scene diverse enough to refresh the noodle-jaded palate. Besides the ubiquitous Chinese *kedai kopi* (coffee shops) and Malay halal restaurants, you'll find plenty of interesting options around the city centre.

KK's Art Scene

KK is buzzing with festivals and gigs, you just need to keep an eye out for them. While the free and widely available monthly glossy magazine *Sabah* lists upcoming events, it's also worth checking out the website of Sparks (Society of Performing Arts Kota Kinabalu; www.sparks.org.my). Sparks works with the US Embassy to bring world-famous acts here to play gigs in intimate venues, as well as organising the hugely popular Jazz Festival (www.kkjazzfest.com) in June or July, and the KK Arts Festival, which also runs through June and July.

Look out, too, for the new and quirky street market, **Tamutamu**, which is part arts and crafts, part eclectic gathering, with artists, musos and tarot readers. Happening on the third Sunday of every month from 10am to 5pm, it will also feature the work of the brilliant Cracko Art Gallery. Enquire at Biru Biru restaurant.

Print Cafe Cafe $
(013-880 2486; 12 Lg Dewan; mains RM12; 8.30am-10.30pm) In the backpacker street of Lg Dewan, this brilliant cafe is a cool (in both senses of the word) place to catch your breath, read a book or play Jenga at one of its tables. Excellent coffee, papaya and orange shakes, a selection of cakes and waffles, pizza and lovely service. Keep an eye out for ingeniously foamed cappuccinos.

Biru Biru Fusion $
(24 Lg Dewan; mains RM9-13; 9am-late) Based at Borneo Backpackers, this blue joint is Asian fusion galore, with dishes like fish cooked in lime and ginger, huge tacos, and an ever evolving menu. Try the Lihing rice wine (aka, rocket fuel). With its parasols and bikes on the wall, and lovely manager Jules, it's easy to fall in love with this place.

Hawker Centres & Food Courts

As in any Southeast Asian city, the best food in KK is the street food and hawker stalls. If you're worried about sanitation, you really shouldn't be, but assuage your fears by looking for popular stalls, especially those frequented by families.

Night Market (Jln Tun Fuad Stephens; fish/prawn per 100g from RM4/15, satay RM1; 5-11pm) The night market is the best, cheapest and most interesting place in KK for barbecued squid, ray and a vast selection of delicious seafood cooked up right before your eyes.

Centre Point Food Court (basement, Centre Point Shopping Mall, Jln Raya Pantai Baru; mains from RM3; 9am-9.30pm) Your ringgit will go a long way at this popular and varied basement food court in the Centre Point mall. There are Malay, Chinese and Indian options, as well as drink and dessert specialists.

Grace Point (Jln Pantai Sembulan; mains RM2-8; 11am-3pm) Take bus 15 out near Tanjung Aru for some local grub at this KK mainstay. The development is actually quite chic compared to the smoke-swathed food courts in the city centre – KKers joke that the public bathrooms here are Borneo's nicest (and it's true!). Go for the Sabahan food stall (located in the far right corner when facing the row of counters) and try *hinava* (raw fish pickled with fresh lime juice, *chilli padi*, sliced shallots and grated ginger).

Alu-Alu Cafe Seafood $$
(Jessleton Point; mains RM15-30; 10.30am-2.30pm & 6.30-10pm) Drab on the outside, perhaps, but this restaurant wears its stripes in the tastiness of its food, and the fact it gets its seafood from sustainable sources – no shark-fin soup here. Alu-Alu excels in taking the Chinese seafood concept to new levels, with dishes such as lightly breaded fish chunks doused in a mouth-watering buttermilk sauce, or simmered with diced chillies.

Kohinoor Indian $$
(088-235 160; lot 4, Waterfront Esplanade; mains RM17-30; 11.30am-2.30pm & 5.30-11pm) Come to this silk-festooned waterfront restaurant for northern Indian cuisine and classic dishes ranging from chicken tikka masala to prawn biryani and lamb rogan josh. The aromas from its tandoori oven are mouthwatering, the naan bread pillowy-soft, and the service pure old-world charm. You'll be back more than once.

Nagisa Japanese $$$
(088-221 234; Hyatt Regency, Jln Datuk Salleh Sulong; mains RM40-220; noon-10pm) Super-swanky Nagisa exudes class and executes Japanese cuisine with élan, with a wealth of sushi dishes from California *temaki* (crabstick, avocado and prawn roe), *ebi tempura maki* (crispy prawn rolled with rice) to *agemeon* (deep-fried dishes) and noodles. Located in the Hyatt Regency.

DRINKING & NIGHTLIFE

Get ready for loads of karaoke bars and big, booming nightclubs, clustered around the Waterfront Esplanade, KK Times Sq, where the newest hot spots are congregating, and Beach St, in the centre of town, a semi-pedestrianised street cluttered with bars and eateries.

El Centro Bar
(32 Jln Haji Saman; 5pm-midnight, closed Mon) El Centro is understandably popular with local expats and travellers alike; it's friendly, the food is good and it makes for a nice

spot to meet other travellers. Cool tunes, non smokey, and a laid-back vibe, El Centro also hosts impromptu quiz nights, costume parties and live-music shows.

Bed Club
(☎088-251 901; Waterfront Esplanade; admission Fri & Sat incl drink RM20, beer from RM21; ⏲8pm-2am, until 3am Fri & Sat) KK's largest club thunders with pop, gyrating Filipino musicians and shrill teenagers, and boasts guest DJs nightly. It's overcrowded and cheesy, but if you're looking for a party, this is it. Bands play from 9pm.

INFORMATION

Sabah Parks (☎088-486 430, 088-523 500; www.sabahparks.org.my; 1st-5th fl, lot 45 & 46, block H, Signature Office KK Times Sq; ⏲8am-1pm & 2-4.30pm Mon-Thu, 8-11.30am & 2-4.30pm Fri, 8am-12.50pm Sat) Source of information on the state's parks.

Sabah Tourism Board (☎088-212 121; www.sabahtourism.com; 51 Jln Gaya; ⏲8am-5pm Mon-Fri, 9am-4pm Sat, Sun & holidays) Housed in the historic post office building, KK's tourist office has plenty of brochures, maps and knowledgeable staff keen to help you with advice tailored to your needs – they won't just try and sell you a package tour! Their website, packed with helpful information from accommodation to sights, is equally worth a visit. Organised.

GETTING THERE & AWAY

KK is well served by **Malaysia Airlines** (☎1300 883 000; www.malaysiaairlines.com) and **AirAsia** (www.airasia.com; ground fl, Wisma Sabah, Jln Haji Saman; ⏲8.30am-5.30pm Mon-Fri, to 3pm Sat) for flights around Malaysia and the region. Jetstar (www.jetstar.com) and Tiger Airways (www.tigerairways.com) both offer flights to Singapore.

GETTING AROUND

TO/FROM THE AIRPORT

Kota Kinabalu International Airport (KKIA) is 7km south of central KK and takes around 25 to 40 minutes to reach by taxi. Note that the airport's two terminals are not connected, and at rush hour it can take a while to get from one to the other in the event you go to the wrong one. Most airlines operate out of Terminal 1, but an increasing number of carriers, including AirAsia, depart from Terminal 2.

Airport shuttle buses (adult/child RM5/3) leave Padang Merdeka station hourly between 7.30am and 8.15pm daily, arriving first at Terminal 2, then Terminal 1. Public transport runs from 6am to 7pm daily.

Taxis heading from terminals into town operate on a voucher system (RM30) sold at a taxi desk on the terminal's ground floor. Taxis heading to the airport should not charge over RM40, if you catch one in the city centre.

CAR

Major car-rental agencies have counters on the first floor at KKIA and branch offices elsewhere in town. Manual cars start at around RM120 to RM140 per day and most agencies can arrange chauffeured vehicles as well.

MINIVANS

Minivans operate from several stops, including Padang Merdeka Bus Station, Wawasan Plaza, and the car park outside Milimewa Superstore (near the intersection of Jln Haji Saman and Beach St). They circulate the town looking for passengers. Since most destinations in the city are within walking distance, it's unlikely that you'll need to catch a minivan, although they're handy for getting to the airport or to KK Times Square. Most destinations within the city cost RM4 to RM6.

TAXI

Expect to pay a minimum of RM15 for a ride in the city centre (even a short trip). Taxis can be found throughout the city and at all bus stations and shopping centres. There's a stand by Milimewa Superstore and another 200m southwest of City Park.

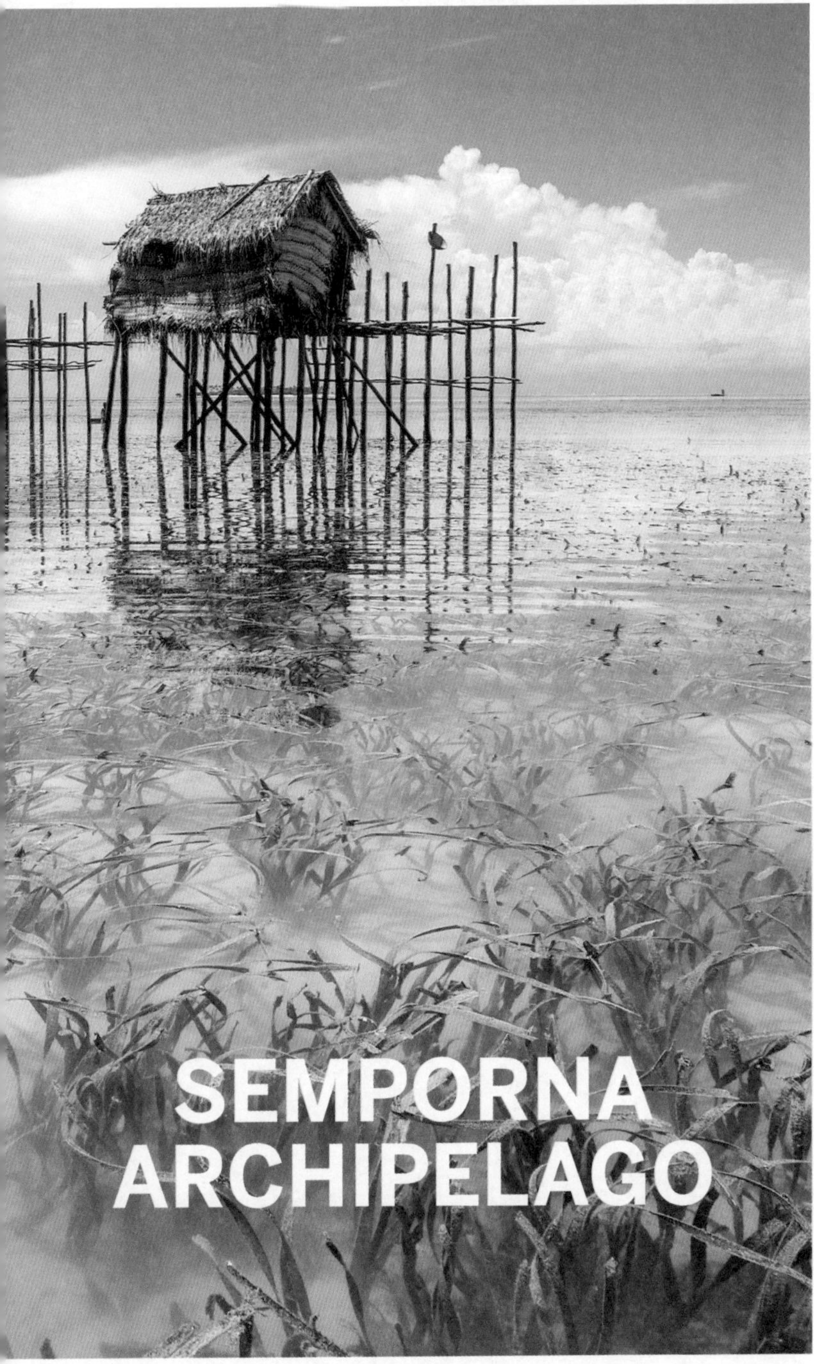
SEMPORNA
ARCHIPELAGO

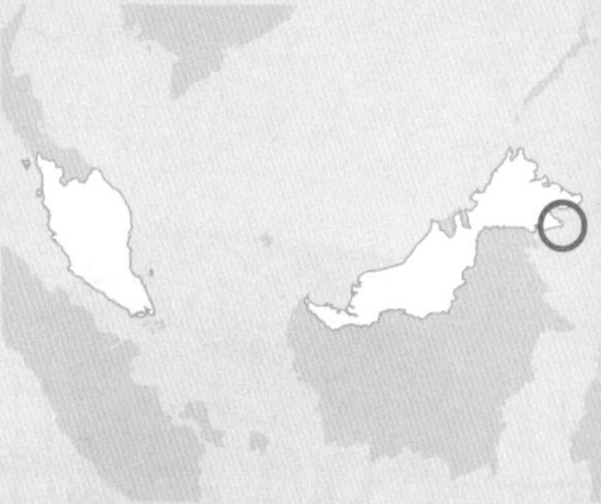

Semporna Archipelago

The stunning Semporna Archipelago is home to copper-skinned Bajau sea gypsies in crayola-coloured boats and lush desert islands plucked from your wildest fantasies. But no one comes this way for the islands, such as they are – rather, it is the sapphire ocean and everything beneath it that appeals, because this is first and foremost a diving destination, consistently voted one of the best in the world.

Semporna's crown jewel is Sipadan, a place that Jacques Cousteau described as 'an untouched piece of art'. A virtual motorway of marine life swims by the island on any given day, including parrotfish; reef, hammerhead and whale sharks; and majestic manta and eagle rays.

Semporna Archipelago in Two Days

Nearly everyone is required to warm up with dives at **Marbul** and/or **Kapalai** before qualifying for one of the limited daily slots to explore the dive and snorkelling site of sublime Sipadan. Also consider the delights of **Pom Pom**, an attractive option for those who want to dive and beach flop.

Semporna Archipelago in Four Days

The glittering prize of **Sipadan** is now within reach. For those who desire dive qualifications, Open Water certifications are available, and advanced coursework is popular for those wanting to increase their skills.

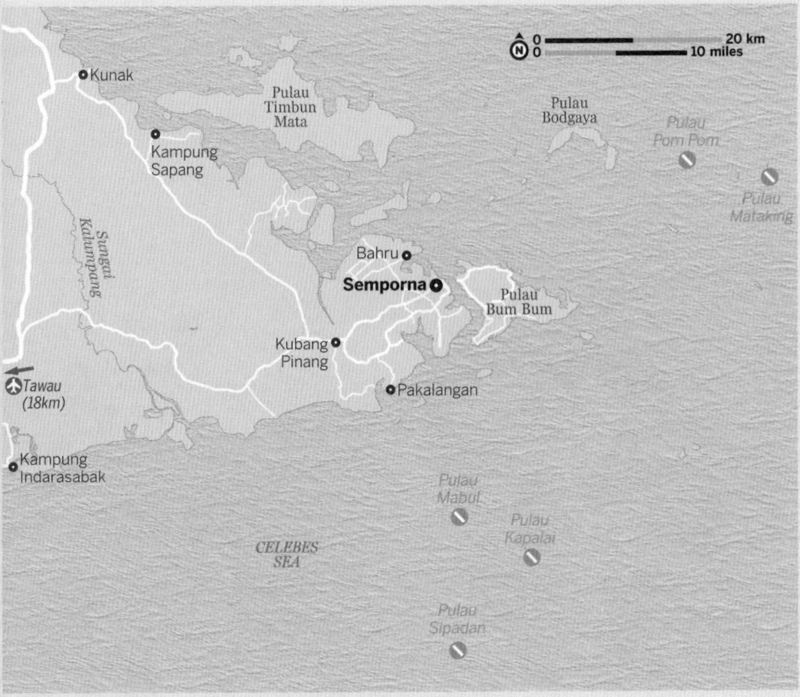

Arriving in the Semporna Archipelago

Tawau Airport The closest airport to the islands is at Tawau. A private taxi from the airport to Semporna (82km away) costs RM100. If you've booked your dive and stay, you'll be picked up from the airport by your respective tour company and spirited straight to Semporna's port to be transferred to your end destination.

Sleeping

From opulent bungalows to ragtag sea shanties, the marine park offers a wide variety of accommodation catering to all budgets, with most clustered on Mabul (Sipadan's closest neighbour), which is now threatening to become over-crowded. No one is allowed to stay on Sipadan. Note that prices rise in August and September. Non-divers are charged at different rates than divers.

Divers and snorkellers can also opt to stay in the town of Semporna. That means slightly better bang for your buck, but no fiery equatorial sunsets. Perhaps more pertinently, it takes at least 30 minutes to get to dive sites from Semporna town.

Diving

Although Sipadan, situated 36km off the southeast coast, outshines the neighbouring dive sites, there are plenty of other reefs and locations in the marine park that are well worth exploring.

The Semporna Islands are loosely divided into two geographical sections: the northern islands (protected as Tun Sakaran Marine Park) and the southern islands. Both areas have desirable diving – Sipadan is located in the southern region, as is Mabul and Kapalai. Mataking belongs to the northern area. If you are based in Semporna, you'll have a greater chance of diving both areas, although most people are happy to stick with Sipadan and its neighbours.

Great For...

☑ Don't Miss

Sipadan's Barracuda Point, where chevron and blacktail barracuda form walls of undulating fish.

Sipadan

In local speak 'Semporna' means perfect, but there is only one island in the glittering archipelago that truly takes this title: Sipadan.

Roughly a dozen delineated dive sites orbit the island – the most famous being **Barracuda Point**. Reef sharks seem attracted

to the strong current here and almost always swing by to say hello. **South Point** hosts the large pelagics such as hammerhead and thresher sharks and manta, as well as bumphead parrotfish. Expect the current to also be strong here. The west side of the island features walls that tumble down to an impossibly deep 2000m.

Note that it is not possible to stay on Sipadan.

Mabul

The macro diving around Mabul (or 'Pulau Mabul') is world-famous, and on any given day you can expect to see blue-ringed octopus, bobtail squid, boxer and orangutan crabs and cardinal fish. In fact, the term 'muck diving' was invented here.

Need to Know

Only 120 passes for diving and snorkelling at Sipadan are available each day.

Take a Break

The island resorts include meals in their accommodation and dive packages.

★ Top Tip

Advance booking for dives is essential for July and August, and over Christmas/New Year.

Kapalai

Set on stilts on the shallow sandbanks of the Ligitan Reefs, this is one of the best macro dive sites in the world; as with Mabul, you'll likely see blue-ring octopus, bobtail squid, cardinal fish and orangutan crabs. Although commonly referred to as an island, Kapalai is more like a large sandbar sitting slightly under the ocean surface. Unlike busy Mabul, there's a sense of escape here, with a long, thin powdery sandbar you can sunbathe on and snorkel from between dives.

Mataking

Mataking is also essentially a sandbar: two little patches of green bookending a dusty tadpole tail of white sand that's home to just one resort. This sandy escape has some beautiful diving – an artificial reef and sunken boats provide haven for plenty of sea life – and has a novel 'underwater post office' at a local shipwreck site. Mataking's eastern shore is a sloping reef and drops to 100m, making it great for sighting macro treasures as well as pelagics. Among the regular visitors large and small, expect to see trevally, eagle ray and barracuda, and pygmy seahorse and mandarin fish.

Pom Pom

About an hour from Semporna, and deep within the Tun Sakaran Marine Park, is this pear-shaped idyll with its perfect azure water and white sand backed by Pom Pom trees. With only two hotels, it's far less crowded here; in fact, many come to get married and explore the underwater treasures as a secondary pursuit. That said, the diving is amazing.

Permits & Costs

The government issues 120 permits (RM40) to Sipadan each day (this number includes divers, snorkellers and day trippers). Bizarre rules and red tape, like having certain gender ratios, make the permit process even more frustrating. Each dive company is issued a predetermined number of passes per day depending on the size of its operation and the general demand for permits. Each operator has a unique way of 'awarding' tickets – some companies place their divers in a permit lottery, others promise a day at Sipadan after a day (or two) of diving at Mabul and Kapalai. No matter which operator you choose, you will be required to do a non-Sipadan intro dive unless you are a Divemaster who has logged a dive in the last six months. Permits to Sipadan are issued by day (and not by dive), so make sure you are getting at least three dives in your package.

A three-dive day trip costs between RM250 and RM500 (some operators include park fees, other do not – be sure to ask), and equipment rental (full gear) comes to about RM50 or RM60 per day. Cameras (around RM100 per day) and dive computers (around RM80 per day) are also available for rent at most dive centres. Top-end resorts on Mabul and Kapalai offer all-inclusive package holidays (plus a fee for equipment rental).

Barracuda, Sipadan

Although most of the diving in the area is 'fun diving', Open Water certifications are available, and advanced coursework is popular for those wanting to take things to the next level. Diving at Sipadan is geared toward divers with an Advanced Open Water certificate (currents and thermoclines can be strong), but Open Water divers should not have any problems (they just can't go as deep as advanced divers). A three-day Open Water course will set you back at least RM975. Advanced Open Water courses (two days) cost the same, and Divemaster certification runs for around RM2800 and takes four weeks.

Security in Semporna

On Marbul armed police patrol the beaches and there's a 6pm curfew to be back in your resort. It's all because of past attacks on and kidnappings of tourists.

Many international embassies recommend reconsidering your need to travel here, yet all through 2015 visitors have been enjoying one of the best dive sites in the world without incident. With the proactively beefed-up police numbers on the islands, the kidnappers are having to look elsewhere for their ransoms.

Furthermore, a recent international assessment of the security situation in the Semporna Archipelago was judged to be positive. For now the curfew remains, but should you choose to come here you will be more than handsomely rewarded for any risks you may have taken by the region's glorious underwater treasures.

Coral around Sipadan

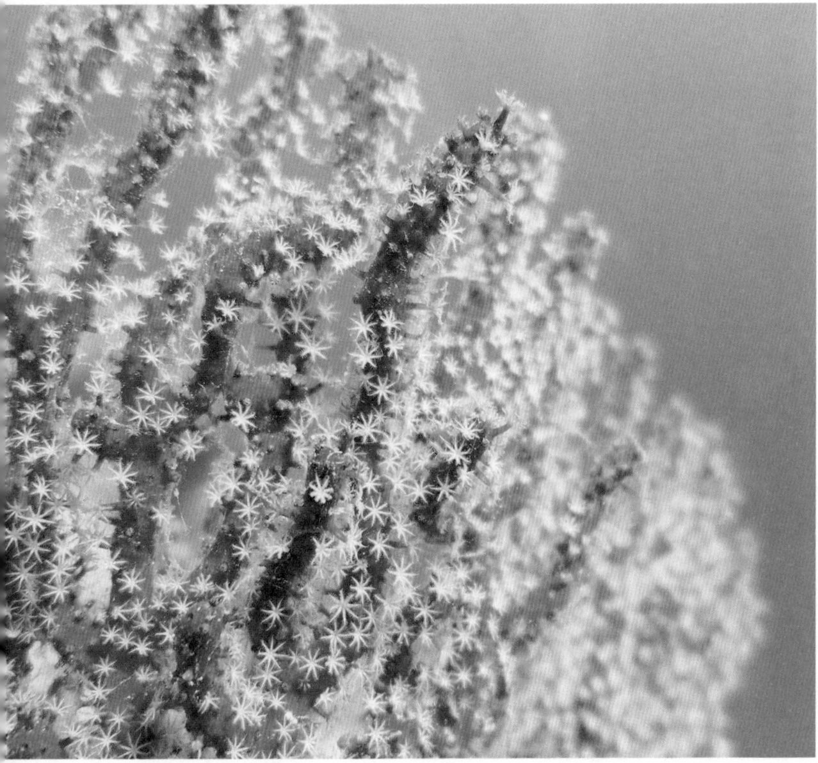

TUNART/GETTY IMAGES ©

SIGHTS

It's worth having a walk around **Mabul**, passing a Bajau graveyard with its salt-worn wood-carved tombstones, and side-stepping giant monitor lizards. Try to be sensitive if taking pictures of local people.

ACTIVITIES

Several dive operators are based at their respective resorts, while others have shopfronts and offices in Semporna and/or Kota Kinabalu.

Many nondivers wonder if they should visit Semporna. Of course you should! If you're travelling in a group or as a couple where some dive and some don't, the Semporna islands are a lot of fun, and divergent dive and snorkelling trips are organised so that groups leave and come back at similar times, so you won't feel isolated from each other. If you're on your own and only want to snorkel, it's still great, but not as world class as the diving experience, and a bit pricey relative to the rest of Malaysia – snorkel trips cost around RM150, and you also have to factor in the relatively high cost of accommodation here and the price of getting out to the islands. Then again, you still have a good chance of seeing sting rays, sea turtles and all sorts of other macro marine wildlife while in the midst of a tropical archipelago, so really, who's complaining?

Borneo Divers Diving
(☎088-222 226; www.borneodivers.net; 9th fl, Menara Jubili, 53 Jln Gaya, Kota Kinabalu) The original and still one of the best dive outfits thanks to their high safety standards, quality equipment, excellent PADI teachers and divemasters. The office is located in Kota Kinabalu; there is also a lovely resort on Mabul. Recommended.

Scuba Junkie Diving
(☎089-785 372; www.scuba-junkie.com; lot 36, block B, Semporna seafront; 4-days & 3-nights on Mabul incl 3 dives per day at Kapilai, Mabul & 4

> *perfect azure water and white sand*

Tun Sakaran Marine Park islands (p194)

dives at Sipadan per person RM2385, snorkelling day trips incl lunch RM120; 9am-6pm) The most proactive conservationists on Mabul, Scuba Junkie employs two full-time environmentalists and recycles much of its profits into its turtle hatchery and rehab centre and 'shark week' initiative. It's also a favourite with Westerners thanks to its excellent divemasters.

EATING

At almost all resorts you're tied to a set schedule of three to five meals broken up by roughly three diving (or snorkelling) trips per day. Meals are included, drinks extra, although tea and coffee are often gratis. High-end resorts have their own bars and restaurants; you may be able to eat and drink there if you're staying in a budget spot and the staff member at the gate is in a good mood, but you'll pay for it.

INFORMATION

Consider stocking up on supplies (sunscreen, mosquito repellent etc) before making your way into the archipelago. Top-end resorts have small convenience stores with inflated prices. ATMs are nonexistent, but high-end resorts accept credit cards (Visa and MasterCard). Mabul has shack shops selling basic foodstuffs and a small pharmacy. Internet is of the wi-fi variety; most resorts now offer it, but service is spotty.

The closest **decompression chamber** (089-783 100, 012-483 9572; www.navy.mil.my; Pangkalan TLDM, Semporna) is at the Semporna Naval Base.

Regatta Lepa

The big annual festival of local Bajau sea gypsies is the Regatta Lepa, held in mid-April. Traditionally, the Bajau only set foot on mainland Borneo once a year; for the rest of the time they live on small islets or their boats. Today the Bajau go to Semporna and other towns more frequently for supplies, but the old cycle of annual return is still celebrated and marked by the regatta. For visitors, the highlight of the festival is the *lepa*-decorating contest held between Bajau families. Their already rainbow-coloured boats are further decked out in streamers, flags (known as *tapi*), bunting, ceremonial umbrellas (which symbolise protection from the omnipresent sun and rain that beats down on the ocean) and *sambulayang*, gorgeously decorated sails passed down within Bajau clans. Violin, cymbal and drum music, plus 'sea sport' competitions like duck catching and boat tug-of-war, punctuate the entire affair. Check www.sabahtourism.com/events for details.

GETTING THERE & AWAY

Your accommodation will arrange any transport needs from Semporna or Tawau Airport (sometimes included, sometimes for an extra fee – ask!), which will most likely depart in the morning. That means if you arrive in Semporna in the afternoon, you will be required to spend the night in town.

RICHARD I'ANSON/GETTY IMAGES ©

SARAWAK

Sarawak

For easy access to Borneo's natural wonders and cultural riches, head to Sarawak. From Kuching, the state's most historic and sophisticated city, pristine rainforests can be visited on day trips. After spotting orangutans, proboscis monkeys, crocodiles and the world's largest flower, the Rafflesia, there's still plenty of time in the evening for a delicious meal and a drink by Kuching's waterfront.

Sarawak in Four Days

Kuching's friendly atmosphere, wealth of sights and great places to eat and drink can easily soak up a couple of days. Budget another two days for doing some trekking and wildlife spotting at **Bako National Park** (p208), and hanging out with the orangutans at **Semenggoh Wildlife Centre** (p209).

Sarawak in Six Days

Fly to Miri, and continue on to **Gunung Mulu National Park** (p209) for challenging trekking plus spectacular caves. Advance bookings are essential, but if you're caught out, a day or overnight trip to the equally amazing caves at **Niah National Park** (p211) will not disappoint.

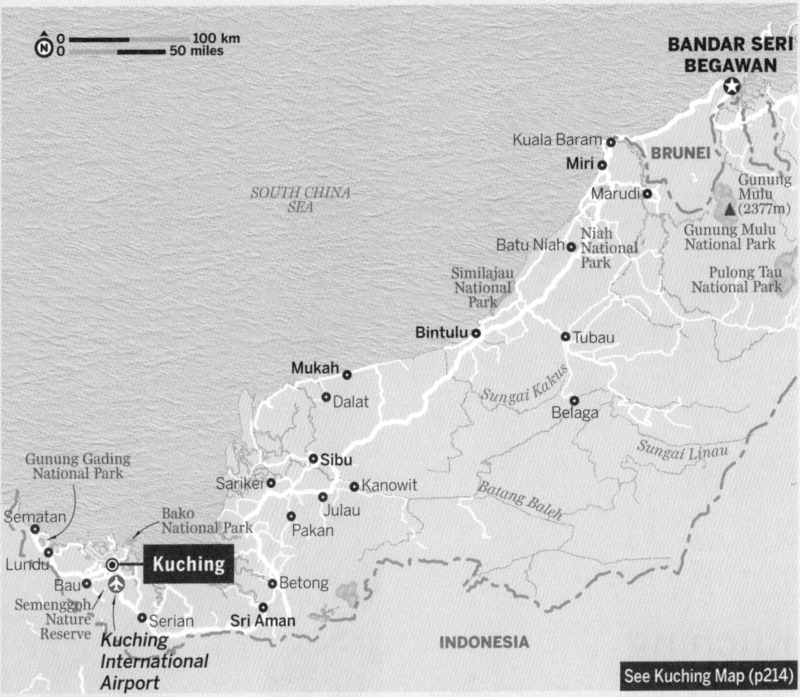

Arriving in Sarawak

Kuching International Airport Located 11km south of Kuching city.

Miri Airport Located 10km south of the town centre.

Flights from Malaysia and Singapore arrive at both Kuching and Miri airports and the two are connected by flights on MASwings.

Sleeping

Kuching's accommodation options range from international-standard suites to windowless, musty cells deep inside converted Chinese shophouses. Many of the guesthouses are on or near Jln Carpenter (Old Chinatown), while the top-end spots are clustered a bit to the east in Kuching's high-rise district, on or near Jln Tunku Abdul Rahman. Cheap Chinese hotels can be found around Jln Padungan and on the lorong (alleys) coming off L-shaped Jln Green Hill.

Miri has some of Sarawak's best backpackers' guesthouses, but if you're on a tight budget, choose your bed carefully as Miri's brothel business booms at some of the shadier bottom-end digs.

Statue at Hong San Si Temple

Kuching

Kuching's bustling streets amply reward visitors with a penchant for aimless ambling. Chinese temples decorated with dragons abut shophouses from the time of the White Rajahs; a South Indian mosque is a five-minute walk from stalls selling half a dozen Asian cuisines; and a landscaped riverfront park attracts families out for a stroll and a quick bite.

Great For...

Need to Know

Sarawak's main museum is undergoing major renovations until 2020.

★ **Top Tip**

Kuching's huge asset is its day-trip proximity to a dozen first-rate nature sites.

BILDAGENTUR ZOONAR GMBH/SHUTTERSTOCK ©

Waterfront Promenade

A promenade runs along the south bank of the Sungai Sarawak. It's a fine place for a stroll any time a cool breeze blows off the river, especially at sunset. In the evening, the waterfront is ablaze with colourful fairy lights and people eating snacks as *tambang* (small passenger ferries) glide past with their glowing lanterns.

Located along the promenade are the **Chinese History Museum** (cnr Main Bazaar & Jln Wayang; 9am-4.45pm Mon-Fri, 10am-4pm Sat, Sun & holidays) FREE, providing an excellent introduction to the nine Chinese communities – each with its own dialect, cuisine and temples – who began settling in Sarawak around 1830; and the Old Court House built in the late 1800s to serve as the city's administrative centre and newly revamped as **ChinaHouse at CourtHouse** (082-417601; www.facebook.com/ChinaHouseK; Jln Tun Abang Haji Openg, noon-midnight; mains from R10;), a happening restaurant, bar, cafe and shopping complex.

Old Chinatown

Lined with evocative, colonial-era shop-houses and home to several vibrantly coloured Chinese temples, Jln Carpenter is the heart of Kuching's Old Chinatown. Along it, look out for **Hong San Si Temple** (Say Ong Kong; cnr Jln Wayang & Jln Carpenter; 6am-6pm) FREE, thought to date back to around 1840 and with intricate rooftop dragons; **Hiang Thian Siang Temple** (Sang Ti Miao Temple; btwn 12 & 14 Jln Carpenter) FREE, which serves the Teochew congregation as a shrine to Shang Di (the Emperor of Heaven); and the easily missed **Hin Ho Bio** (36 Jln Carpenter; 6am-5pm) FREE, a vivid

Sarawak State Assembly across the Sungai Sarawak

little Chinese shrine with rooftop views of Jln Carpenter.

Also in this area, the **Sarawak Textile Museum** (Muzium Tekstil Sarawak; Jln Tun Abang Haji Openg; ⏲9am-4.45pm Mon-Fri, 10am-4pm Sat, Sun & holidays) FREE displays some superb examples of traditional Sarawakian textiles as well as the hats, mats, basketwork, beadwork, silverwork, barkwork, bangles and ceremonial headdresses created by the Iban, Bidayuh and Penan and other Dayak groups.

Jalan India

Once Kuching's main shopping area for imported textiles, brassware and household goods, pedestrianised Jln India is the western continuation of Jln Carpenter. Turn off onto tiny Indian Mosque Lane (Lg Sempit) and you enter another world. About halfway up, entirely surrounded by houses and shops, stands Kuching's oldest **mosque** (Indian Mosque Lane; ⏲6am-8.30pm except during prayers) FREE, a modest structure built of *belian* (ironwood) in 1863 by Muslim traders from Tamil Nadu.

☑ **Don't Miss**

The new museum devoted to the Brooke dynasty at Fort Margherita.

SHAIFULZAMRI.COM/GETTY IMAGES ©

Sarawak Museum

The museums in the area just south of Padang Merdeka (Independence Square) contain a first-rate collection of cultural artefacts that no one interested in Borneo's peoples and habitats should miss.

At the top of the hill, on the eastern side of Jln Tun Abang Haji Openg, the **Ethnology Museum** (www.museum.sarawak.gov.my; Jln Tun Abang Haji Openg; ⏲9am-4.45pm Mon-Fri, 10am-4pm Sat, Sun & holidays) FREE spotlights Borneo's incredibly rich indigenous cultures. Upstairs the superb exhibits include a recreated section of an Iban longhouse, masks and spears; downstairs is an old-fashioned natural-history museum.

At time of writing this heritage building was scheduled to close by the end of 2016 for major renovations, during which time some of the contents may be displayed in nearby buildings. Across Jln Tun Aban Haji Openg, the new state museum, schedule to open in 2020, is under construction.

North Bank of the River

To get to Sungai Sarawak's northern bank, take a *tambang* (river ferry; 50 sen) from one of the docks along the Waterfront Promenade. The key sights here are the old Malay village **Kampung Boyan**, filled with joyously colourful houses and a profusion of flowering plants; and the whitewashed **Fort Margherita** (Kampung Boyan; ⏲9am-4.30pm), built by Charles Brooke in 1879 and named after his wife, Ranee Margaret.

Both the **Astana**, home to Sarawak's governor, and the **Sarawak State Assembly**, an imposing structure with a soaring golden roof, are closed to the public and best viewed from Waterfront Promenade.

Swimmers at Gunung Mulu National Park

Sarawak National Parks

Sarawak's stunning natural beauty is best viewed in the state's many national parks and nature reserves.

Great For...

☑ Don't Miss

Gunung Mulu's so-called Headhunters' Trail, which follows an old tribal war path through the rainforest.

Bako National Park

Occupying a jagged peninsula jutting into the South China Sea, Sarawak's oldest **national park** (Bako terminal 082-370434; www.sarawakforestry.com; RM20; park office 8am-5pm) is just 37km northeast of Kuching, but feels like worlds and aeons away. It's one of the best places in Sarawak to see rainforest animals in their native habitats – especially proboscis monkeys and long-tailed macaques. Bako is also notable for its incredible biodiversity.

The peninsula consists of lovely pocket beaches tucked into secret bays interspersed with wind-sculpted cliffs, forested bluffs and stretches of brilliant mangrove swamp. Hiking trails cross the sandstone plateau that forms the peninsula's backbone, and connect with some of the main

beaches, all of which can be reached by boat from park HQ.

Semenggoh Nature Reserve

One of the best places in the world to see semi-wild orangutans in their natural rainforest habitat, the **Semenggoh Wildlife Centre** (082-618325; www.sarawakforestry.com; Jln Puncak Borneo; admission RM10; 8-11am & 2-4pm, feeding 9am & 3pm) can be visited on a half-day trip from Kuching.

Situated within the 6.8-sq-km Semenggoh Nature Reserve, the centre is home to 25 orangutans. There's a very good chance you'll see some of them during the twice-daily feedings (9am to 10am and 3pm to 4pm) in the rainforest a few hundred metres from park HQ.

Need to Know

Contact the **National Park Booking Offices** (in Kuching 082-248088, in Miri 085-434184) in Kuching and Miri to make accommodation bookings.

Take a Break

Canteens are available in some national parks, but don't count on them.

★ Top Tip

Stay overnight in the parks to really experience their wild beauty.

Gunung Gading National Park

The best place in Sarawak to see the world's largest flower, the renowned Rafflesia, **Gunung Gading National Park** (082-735144; www.sarawakforestry.com; admission RM20; 8am-5pm) makes a fine day trip from Kuching. Its old-growth rainforest covers the slopes of four *gunung* (mountains) – Gading, Lundu, Perigi and Sebuloh – traversed by well-marked walking trails that are great for day hikes.

To find out if a Rafflesia is in bloom – something that happens here only about 25 times a year – and how long it will stay that way (never more than five days), contact the park or call the National Park Booking Office (p217) in Kuching.

Gunung Mulu National Park

Also known as the **Gunung Mulu World Heritage Area** (085-792300; www.mulupark.com; Gunung Mulu National Park; 5-day pass adult/child RM30/10; HQ office 8am-5pm), this 529-sq-km park – a World Heritage site – can only be reached by flights from Miri.

Among the park's remarkable features are its two highest peaks, Gunung Mulu (2376m) and Gunung Api (1710m). In between are rugged karst mountains, deep gorges with crystal-clear rivers, and a unique mosaic of habitats supporting fascinating and incredibly diverse wildlife. Mulu's most famous hiking attractions are the **Pinnacles**, a forest of razor-sharp limestone spires, and the **Headhunters' Trail** down to Limbang.

For almost all of the caves, walks and treks, visitors must be accompanied by a guide licensed by Sarawak Forestry, generally supplied either by the park or by an adventure-tour agency. Tours and activities booked directly through the park are cheaper and are often booked up well in advance (especially the more difficult cave tours and the longer treks); agencies charge considerably more, but also supply extras, such as meals, and can often offer more flexibility when it comes to advance booking.

If you've got your heart set on adventure caving, or on trekking to the Pinnacles or up to the summit of Gunung Mulu, advance reservations – by phone (☎085-792300) or email (enquiries@mulupark.com) – are a must. They're doubly important if you're coming in July, August or September, when some routes are booked out several months ahead, and are essential if your travel dates are not flexible. If this is your situation, don't buy your air tickets until your trek or caving dates are confirmed.

That's not to say a last-minute trip to Mulu is impossible. The park may be able to reassign guides to accommodate you, so it's worth getting in touch.

The park's sleeping options range from five-star luxury to extremely basic.

★ Top Tip

The best time to see swiftlets and bats in Niah National Park is at dusk (5.30pm to 6.45pm).

Bako National Park (p208)

Camping is no longer permitted at park HQ, but you can pitch a tent at some of the guesthouses just outside the park (across the bridge from HQ). If you find accommodation within the park is fully booked, don't panic. There is always a bed of some kind available at one of the informal homestays just outside the park gates.

Niah National Park

The vast limestone caverns of 31-sq-km **Niah National Park** (☎085-737450, 085-737454; www.sarawakforestry.com; admission RM20; ⏲park office 8am-5pm) are among Borneo's most famous and impressive natural attractions. At the heart of the park is the Great Cave, one of the largest caverns in the world.

Niah's caves have provided groundbreaking insights into human life on Borneo way back when the island was still connected to mainland Southeast Asia. Despite its historical significance, Niah has not been overly done-up for tourists. It's possible to visit the caves without a guide, and during the week you may have the place to yourself.

The park is about 115km southwest of Miri and 122km northeast of Bintulu and can be visited as a day trip from either city.

✕ Take a Break

Café Mulu (mains RM12.50-16; ⏲7.30am-8.30pm) serves excellent breakfasts and has a varied menu. Staff are happy to prepare packed lunches.

Green water dragon, Gunung Mulu National Park (p209)

REINHARD DIRSCHERL/GETTY IMAGES ©

Kuching

Sarawak's capital and Borneo's most sophisticated city brings together a kaleidoscope of cultures, crafts and cuisines.

SIGHTS

Tun Jugah Foundation Museum

(☎082-239672; www.tunjugahfoundation.org.my; 4th fl, Tun Jugah Tower, 18 Jln Tunku Abdul Rahman; ⌚9am-noon & 1-4.30pm Mon-Fri) FREE The textile gallery and museum of this charitable foundation, which aims to promote and preserve Iban culture, has excellent exhibits on Iban *ikat* and *sungkit* weaving, as well as beadwork. Iban women come here to make traditional textiles using handlooms.

St Thomas's Cathedral Church

(www.stthomascathedralkuching.org; Jln Tun Abang Haji Openg; ⌚8.30am-6pm Mon-Sat, to 7pm Sun) FREE Facing **Padang Merdeka** (Independence Sq), with its huge and ancient kapok tree, Kuching's Anglican cathedral (1954) has a mid-20th-century look and, inside, a bright red barrel-vaulted ceiling. Enter from Jln McDougall, named after Kuching's first Anglican bishop, who arrived here in 1848.

At the top of the hill, on the other side of the Parish Centre, stands the Bishop's House. Kuching's oldest building, it was constructed – in 1849 with admirable solidness – by a German shipwright.

Orchid Garden Gardens

(Jln Astana Lot; ⌚9.30am-6pm Tue-Sun) FREE Sarawak's state flower, the Normah orchid is just one of the 82 species growing in these peaceful gardens and greenhouse nursery. Other Borneo orchids to look out for are lady's slippers, identifiable by their distinct, insect-trapping pouches.

The easiest way to get here from the city centre is to take a *tambang* across the river to Pengakalan Sapi on the north bank (next to the Sarawak State Assembly building) and walk up the hill.

Medan Niaga Satok Market

(Satok Weekend Market; Jln Matang Jaya; ⌚5.30am-7.30pm) Kuching's biggest and liveliest market has now moved to its spacious new digs 9km west of the city centre. It's open everyday, but the main event is the larger weekend market, which begins around midday on Saturday, when rural folk, some from area longhouses, arrive with their fruits, vegetables, fish and spices. To get here, take the K7 bus.

The air is heady with the aromas of fresh coriander, ginger, herbs and jungle ferns, which are displayed among piles of bananas, mangoes, custard apples and obscure jungle fruits. If you smell something overpoweringly sickly sweet and pungent, chances are it's a durian. Vendors are friendly and many are happy to tell you about their wares, which are often divided into quantities worth RM1 or RM2.

COURSES

Bumbu Cooking School Cooking Course

(☎019-879 1050; http://bumbucookingclass.weebly.com; 57 Jln Carpenter; per person RM150; ⌚9am-1pm & 2.30-7pm) Raised in a Bidayuh village, Joseph teaches the secrets of cooking with fresh, organic ingredients from the rainforest. At the market you'll learn how to spot top-quality jungle ferns; back in the kitchen you'll prepare this crunchy delicacy, along with a main dish and a dessert that's served in a *pandan*-leaf basket you weave yourself. Maximum 10 participants.

The small shop that serves as the entrance to the cooking school is like a mini-museum full of pieces Joseph has collected: blow pipes, rattan baskets (one designed to be used as a baby carrier), a rice mill, and ceremonial blankets and masks from Iban and Orang Ulu longhouses.

TOURS

Borneo Adventure Tour

(☎082-245 175; www.borneoadventure.com; 55 Main Bazaar) Award-winning company that sets the standard for high-end Borneo tours and is the leader in cooperative projects benefitting Sarawak's indigenous peoples. Known for its excellent guides.

Adventure Alternative Borneo Adventure Tour
(082-248000, 019-892 9627; www.aaborneo.com; Lot 37 Jln Tabuan) Offers ethical and sustainable trips that combine 'culture, nature and adventure'. Can help you design and coordinate an itinerary for independent travel to remote areas, including the Penan villages of the Upper Baram.

Rainforest Kayaking Tour
(Borneo Trek & Kayak Adventure; 082-240571, 013-804 8338; www.rainforestkayaking.com) Specialises in river trips, which can be combined with a trip to Semenggoh Nature Reserve.

SHOPPING

If it's traditional Borneo arts and crafts you're after, then you've come to the right place – Kuching is the best shopping spot on the island for collectors and cultural enthusiasts. Don't expect many bargains, but don't be afraid to negotiate either – there's plenty to choose from, and the quality varies as much as the price. Dubiously 'aged' items are common, so be sure to spend some time browsing to familiarise yourself with prices and range.

Most of Kuching's shops are closed on Sunday.

Juliana Native Handwork Handicrafts
(082-230144; ground fl, Sarawak Textile Museum, Jln Tun Abang Haji Openg; 9am-4.30pm) As well as her own Bidayuh beadwork pieces – most of which have been displayed in an exhibition in Singapore – Juliana sells quality rattan mats made by Penan artists (RM490) and *pua kumba* Iban woven cloths. The intricate, 50cm-long beaded table runners she sells (RM680) take her three months to complete.

Kuching Kitties

It's just a coincidence that in Bahasa Malaysia, Kuching means 'cat' (spelled 'kucing'), but the city has milked the homonym for all it's worth, branding Sarawak's capital the 'Cat City' and erecting a number of marvellously kitschy cat statues – such as the **Cat Fountain** (Jln Tunku Abdul Rahman), **Cat Column** (cnr Jln Padungan & Jln Chan Chin Ann) and **Great Cat of Kuching** (Jln Padungan) – to beautify the urban landscape.

There's also the **Cat Museum** (www.dbku.sarawak.gov.my; Jln Semariang, Bukit Siol; camera/video RM4/5; 9am-5pm) FREE, featuring hundreds of entertaining, surprising and bizarre cat figurines – some the size of a cow, others tiny – alongside detailed presentations on 'Cats in Malay Society' and 'Cats in Chinese Art'. By the time you reach the exhibits on 'Cats in Stamps' and 'Cats in Film' (in which Bond villain Blofeld's mog features), you may feel it's all getting a little silly.

Great Cat of Kuching
FOTOSOL/GETTY IMAGES ©

Main Bazaar Handicrafts
(Main Bazaar; some shops closed Sun) The row of old shophouses facing the Waterfront Promenade is chock-full of handicrafts shops, some outfitted like art galleries, others with more of a 'garage sale' appeal, and yet others (especially along the Main Bazaar's western section) stocking little more than kitschy-cute cat souvenirs.

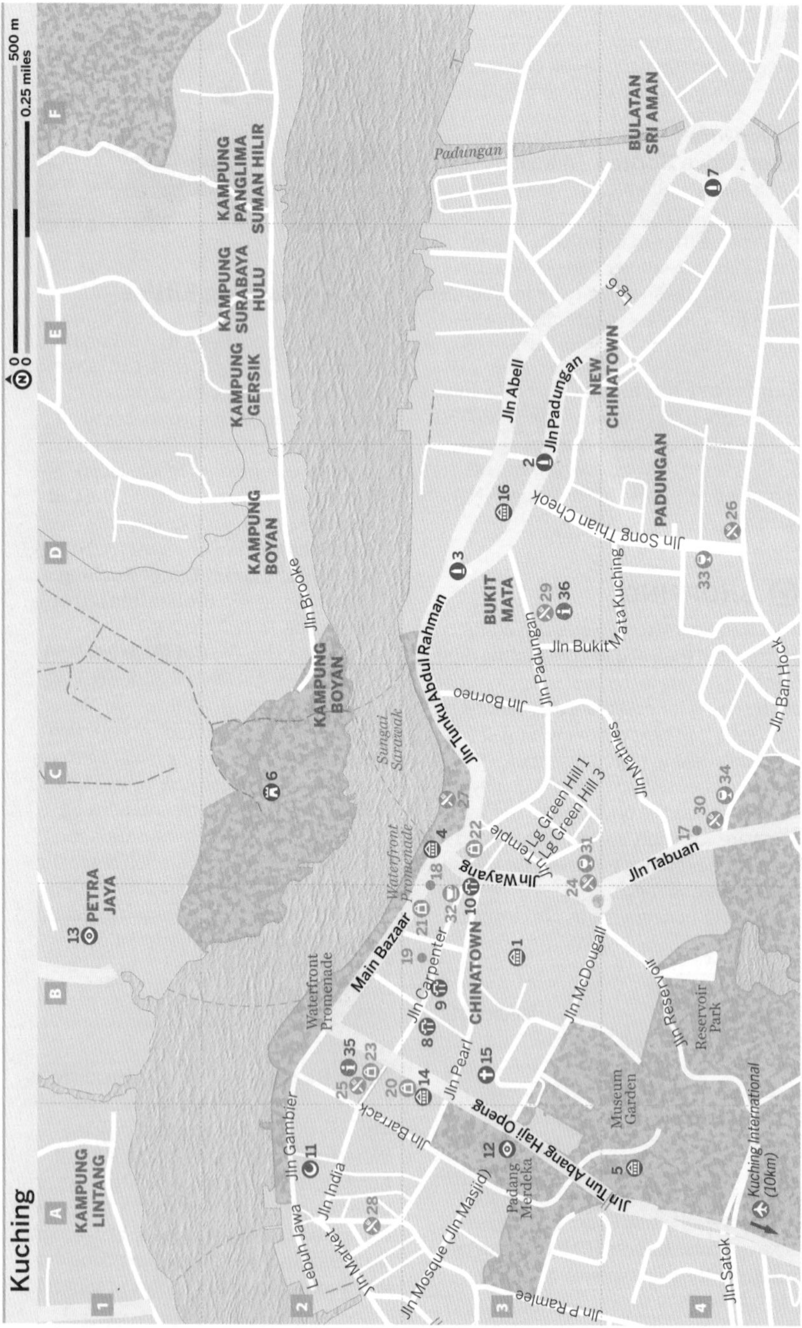
Kuching
0 500 m
0 0.25 miles
KAMPUNG LINTANG
PETRA JAYA
KAMPUNG BOYAN
KAMPUNG GERSIK
KAMPUNG SURABAYA HULU
KAMPUNG PANGLIMA SUMAN HILIR
BULATAN SRI AMAN
NEW CHINATOWN
PADUNGAN
BUKIT MATA
CHINATOWN
Sungai Sarawak
Padungan
Waterfront Promenade
Main Bazaar
Jln Tunku Abdul Rahman
Jln Brooke
Jln Abell
Jln Padungan
Lg 6
Jln Song Thian Cheok
Jln Bukit Mata Kuching
Jln Borneo
Jln Ban Hock
Jln Mathies
Jln Tabuan
Jln Lg Green Hill 1
Jln Lg Green Hill 3
Jln Temple
Jln Wayang
Jln Carpenter
Jln McDougall
Jln Reservoir
Reservoir Park
Museum Garden
Padang Merdeka
Jln Tun Abang Haji Openg
Jln Pearl
Jln Barrack
Jln Gambier
Jln India
Lebuh Jawa
Jln Market
Jln Mosque (Jln Masjid)
Jln P Ramlee
Jln Satok
Kuching International (10km)

Kuching

Sights

1 Bishop's House ... B3
2 Cat Column ... D3
3 Cat Fountain ... D3
4 Chinese History Museum ... C3
5 Ethnology Museum ... A4
6 Fort Margherita ... C2
7 Great Cat of Kuching ... F4
8 Hiang Thian Siang Temple ... B3
9 Hin Ho Bio ... B3
10 Hong San Si Temple ... B3
11 Indian Mosque ... A2
12 Kapok Tree ... A3
13 Orchid Garden ... B1
14 Sarawak Textile Museum ... B3
15 St Thomas's Cathedral ... B3
16 Tun Jugah Foundation ... D3

Activities, Courses & Tours

17 Adventure Alternative Borneo ... C4
18 Borneo Adventure ... B3
19 Bumbu Cooking School ... B3

Shopping

Fabriko ... (see 21)
20 Juliana Native Handwork ... B3
21 Main Bazaar ... B3
22 Nelson's Gallery ... C3
23 Sarawak Craft Council ... B2

Eating

24 Bla Bla Bla ... C3
25 ChinaHouse at CourtHouse ... B2
26 Choon Hui ... D4
27 James Brooke Bistro & Cafe ... C3
28 Open-Air Market ... A2
29 Top Spot Food Court ... D3
30 Zinc ... C4

Drinking & Nightlife

31 Barber ... C3
32 Black Bean Coffee & Tea Company ... B3
33 Monkee Bar ... D4
34 Ruai ... C4

Information

35 National Park Booking Office ... B2
36 Visitors Information Centre ... D3

Handmade items worth seeing (if not purchasing) – many from the highlands of Kalimantan – include hand-woven textiles and baskets, masks, drums, brass gongs, statues (up to 2m high), beaded headdresses, swords, spears, painted shields and cannons from Brunei. At many places, staff enjoy explaining the origin and use of each item.

Fabriko Clothing

(56 Main Bazaar; 9am-5pm Mon-Sat) This fine little boutique has a well-chosen selection of made-in-Sarawak fabrics and clothing in both traditional and modern Orang Ulu–inspired designs, including silk sarongs and men's batik shirts.

Nelson's Gallery Arts

(54 Main Bazaar; 9am-5pm) Upstairs, artist Narong Daun patiently creates vibrant jungle-themed batik paintings on silk.

Sarawak Craft Council Handicrafts

(sarawakhandicraft.com.my; Old Courthouse, Jln Tun Abang Haji Openg; 8.30am-4.30pm Mon-Fri) Run by a non-profit government agency, this shop has a pretty good selection of Malay, Bidayuh, Iban and Orang Ulu handicrafts – check out the cowboy hats made entirely of bark and the conical *terendak* (Melanau hats).

EATING

Kuching is the best place in Malaysian Borneo to work your way through the entire range of Sarawak-style cooking. At hawker centres, you can pick and choose from a variety of Chinese and Malay stalls, each specialising in a particular culinary tradition or dish, while Jln Padungan is home to some of the city's best noodle houses. The question of where to find the city's best laksa is a sensitive subject and one sure to spark a heated debate among Kuchingites. The only way to get a definitive answer is to try them all yourself.

Choon Hui Malaysian $

(34 Jln Ban Hock; laksa RM5-7; 7-11am Tue-Sun) This old-school *kopitiam* (coffee shop) gets our vote for the most delicious laksa in

town, and we're not alone – the place can get crowded, especially at weekends. There is also a stall here selling excellent *popia*, a kind of spring roll made with peanuts, radish and carrot (RM3).

Open-Air Market Hawker $

(Tower Market; Jln Khoo Hun Yeang; mains RM3-6.50; most stalls 6am-4pm, Chinese seafood 3pm-4am) Cheap, tasty dishes to look for include laksa, Chinese-style *mee sapi* (beef noodle soup), red *kolo mee* (noodles with pork and a sweet barbecue sauce), tomato *kway teow* (a fried rice-noodle dish) and shaved ice desserts (ask for 'ABC' at stall 17). The Chinese seafood stalls that open in the afternoon are on the side facing the river.

From early mornings until mid-afternoon there is also a stall selling fish head and duck porridge, if that's your thing.

The market (which isn't strictly speaking open-air) has two sections, separated by a road, on the site of a former fire station; the yellow tower was once used as a fire lookout.

Top Spot Food Court Seafood $$

(Jln Padungan; fish per kg RM30-70, vegetable dishes RM8-12; noon-11pm) A perennial favourite among local foodies, this neon-lit courtyard and its half-a-dozen humming seafooderies sits, rather improbably, on the roof of a concrete parking garage – look for the giant backlit lobster sign. Grilled white pomfret is a particular delicacy. Ling Loong Seafood and the Bukit Mata Seafood Centre are especially good.

James Brooke Bistro & Cafe Western $$

(082-412120; Waterfront Promenade opposite Jln Temple; mains RM10-39; 10.30am-10.30pm, for drinks only to midnight) Gets consistently good reviews both for the cuisine and the lovely river views. Local dishes such as Sarawak laksa (RM12) and its own invention, uniquely flavoursome wild Borneo laksa (RM12), are quite reasonably priced. The beef stroganoff (RM25) has a following.

Dyak Dayak $$

(082-234068; Jln Mendu & Jln Simpang Tiga; mains RM25-35; noon-11pm, last order 8.30pm;) This elegant restaurant is the first to treat Dayak home cooking as true cuisine. The chef, classically trained in a Western style, uses traditional recipes, many of them Iban (a few are Kelabit, Kayan or Bidayuh), and fresh, organic jungle produce to create mouth-watering dishes unlike anything you've ever tasted. Situated 2km southeast of Old Chinatown.

Bla Bla Bla Fusion $$$

(082-233944; 27 Jln Tabuan; mains RM22-90; 6-11.30pm, closed Tue) Innovative and stylish, Bla Bla Bla serves excellent Chinese-inspired fusion dishes that – like the decor, the koi ponds and the Balinese Buddha – range from traditional to far-out. Specialities include *midin* (jungle fern) salad, mango duck (delicious), ostrich and deer, and pandan chicken. The generous portions are designed to be shared.

Zinc Mediterranean $$$

(082-243304; 38 Jln Tabuan; mains RM50-140; 6-10.45pm) Well-to-do Kuchingites celebrated the recent opening of Zinc and its selection of European foods: Spanish Iberico ham, French cheeses and high-end wines that aren't available anywhere else in Borneo. Naturally, the finest imported ingredients don't come cheap, but you don't come to Zinc unless you're prepared to splurge. Often has live music; on Thursdays there's a jazz band.

DRINKING & NIGHTLIFE

Bars can be found along Jln Carpenter and Jln Tabuan.

Ruai Bar

(7F Jln Ban Hock; 6pm-2.30am) This Iban-owned bar has a laid-back, welcoming spirit all its own. Decorated with old photos and Orang Ulu art (and, inexplicably, several Mexican sombreros), it serves as an urban *ruai* (the covered verandah of an Iban longhouse) for aficionados of caving, hiking and running. Has a good selection of *tuak* (local rice wine). Starts to pick up after about 9pm.

Barber Bar
(☎016-658 1052; Jln Wayang; ⏰5-11pm, to 1.30am Fri & Sat, closed Tue) The designers of this successfully repurposed barber's salon made use of the original tiled floor, mirrors and even old hairdryers to create a suitably hip hangout for Kuching's in-crowd. Serves a menu of burgers and American-diner-style food (mains RM16 to RM24) and a good selection of desserts (RM16). Beers are three for RM45 on Sunday, Monday and Wednesday.

Monkee Bar Bar
(www.monkeebars.com; Jln Song Thian Cheok; beer RM6.50-12, spirit & mixer RM13; ⏰3pm-2am) At Monkee Bar, 50% of profits go to the Orangutan Project, a wildlife conservation NGO that works at **Matang Wildlife Centre** (☎082-374869; www.sarawakforestry.com; admission incl Kubah National Park RM20; ⏰8am-5pm, animal encloure trail 8.30am-3.30pm). If the idea of 'drinking for conservation' doesn't entice you, the prices might; Monkee Bar has some of the cheapest drinks in town. It's a smokey joint with a young local crowd interspersed with volunteers enjoying downtime from cage-cleaning.

Black Bean Coffee & Tea Company Cafe
(Jln Carpenter; drinks RM3-4.80; ⏰9am-6pm Mon-Sat; 📶) The aroma of freshly ground coffee assaults the senses at this tiny shop, believed by many to purvey Kuching's finest brews. Specialities, roasted daily, include Arabica, Liberica and Robusta coffees grown in Java, Sumatra and, of course, Sarawak. Also serves oolong and green teas from Taiwan. Has just three tables. Decaf not available.

ℹ INFORMATION

National Park Booking Office (☎082-248088; www.sarawakforestry.com; Jln Tun Abang Haji Openg, Sarawak Tourism Complex; ⏰8am-5pm Mon-Fri, closed public holidays) Sells brochures on each of Sarawak's national parks and can

Jalan India (p207)

ANDREW WATSON/GETTY IMAGES ©

Annah Rais Longhouse

About 40km south of Kuching is **Annah Rais Longhouse** (adult/student RM8/4). Although this Bidayuh longhouse village has been on the tourist circuit for decades, it's still a good place to get a sense of what a longhouse is and what longhouse life is like.

The 500 residents here are as keen as the rest of us to enjoy the comforts of modern life – they love their mobile phones and 3G internet access – but they've made a conscious decision to preserve their traditional architecture and the social interaction it engenders.

They've also decided that welcoming modern tourists is a good way to earn a living without moving to the city, something most young people end up doing.

A taxi from Kuching costs RM90 one-way. A variety of Kuching guesthouses and tour agencies offer four-hour tours to Annah Rais (from RM100 per person).

Rattan weaving, Annah Rais
NYIRAGONGO/GETTY IMAGES ©

supply the latest newsflash on Rafflesia sightings. Telephone enquiries are not only welcomed but patiently answered. Bookings for accommodation at Bako, Gunung Gading and Kubah National Parks and the Matang Wildlife Centre can be made in person, by phone or via http://ebooking.com.my.

Visitors Information Centre (082-410942, 082-410944; www.sarawaktourism.com; UTC Sarawak, Jln Padungan; 8am-5pm Mon-Fri, closed public holidays) Usually located in the atmospheric old courthouse complex, at research time the Visitors Information Centre was about to move to a temporary new home in the UTC building on Jln Padungan while the Old Court House buildings were redeveloped.

The office has helpful and well-informed staff, lots of brochures and oodles of practical information (eg bus schedules).

GETTING THERE & AWAY

Kuching International Airport (www.kuchingairportonline.com), 11km south of the city centre, has direct air links with Singapore, Johor Bahru, Kuala Lumpur, Penang, Kota Kinabalu, Bandar Seri Begawan (Brunei) and Pontianak (Indonesia), as well as with Miri and other destinations within Sarawak.

GETTING AROUND

The regular taxi fare into Kuching from the airport is fixed at RM30, including luggage; the larger *teksi eksekutiv* (executive taxi), painted blue, costs RM35. Coupons are sold inside the terminal next to the car-rental counters.

The only way to get to many nature sites is to hire a taxi or join a tour. Exceptions include Bako National Park and Semenggoh Nature Reserve.

If you do need a taxi, try **Kuching City Radio Taxi** (082-348898, 082-480000). Hiring an official taxi for an eight-hour day should cost about RM300 to RM350, with the price depending in part on distance; unofficial taxis may charge less. If you'd like your driver to wait at your destination and then take you back to town, count on paying about RM20 per hour of wait time.

Miri

Sarawak's second city, a major transport hub, is a thriving oil town that is both busy and modern. There's plenty of money sloshing around, so the eating is good, the broad avenues are brightly lit, there's plenty to do when it's raining, and the city's friendly guesthouses are a great place to meet other travellers.

SIGHTS

Miri is not big on historical sites – it was pretty much destroyed during WWII – but it's not an unattractive city. A walk around the centre is a good way to get a feel for the local vibe. Streets worth a wander include (from north to south) Jln North Yu Seng, Jln South Yu Seng, Jln Maju and Jln High Street.

Miri City Fan Park

(Jln Kipas; 24hr) An attractive open, landscaped park with Chinese- and Malay-style gardens and ponds that is a popular spot for walking and jogging. The complex also comprises a library, an indoor stadium and an Olympic-sized public swimming pool (RM1).

Petroleum Museum Museum

(Bukit Tenaga; 9am-4.45pm Tue-Fri, 10am-4pm Sat & Sun) FREE The Petroleum Museum sits atop **Canada Hill**, a low ridge 2km southeast of the town centre that was the site of Malaysia's first oil well, the **Grand Old Lady**, drilled in 1910. Appropriately, the old derrick stands right outside the museum whose interactive exhibits, some designed for kids, are a good, pro-Big Oil introduction to the hugely lucrative industry that has so enriched Miri (and Malaysia's federal government).

The hill itself is a popular exercise spot, and it's worth coming here at sunset for the views across town to the South China Sea.

Saberkas Weekend Market Market

(Jln Miri Pujut ; 4-11pm Thu-Sat, 8am-noon Sun) One of the most colourful and friendly markets in Sarawak. Vendors are more than happy to answer questions about their produce, which includes tropical fruits and vegetables, barbecued chicken, satay and handicrafts. Situated about 3km northeast of the centre outside the Saberkas Commercial Centre. A taxi here costs RM15 (there is no bus).

ACTIVITIES

Although the waters off Miri are better known for drilling than diving, the area – much of it part of the Miri-Sibuti Coral Reef Marine Park – has some excellent 7m- to 30m-deep scuba sites, including old oil platforms teeming with fish and assorted trawler and freighter wrecks. Water visibility is at its best from March to September.

The corals here are in good condition and the water unpolluted, despite the proximity of heavy industry. When visibility is good you might see giant cuttlefish, whale sharks and sting rays.

Coco Dive Diving

(085-417053; www.cocodive.com.my; Lot 2117 Block 9, Jln Miri Pujut; 2 dives RM320, 3 dives RM370) A well-regarded dive company with a fat programme of dive packages and PADI-certification courses. Gets rave reviews for its friendly, professional staff and solid equipment.

TOURS

Planet Borneo Tours Tour

(085-414300, 085-415582; www.planetborneotours.com; Lot 273, 1st fl Brighton Centre, Jln Temenggong Datuk Oyong Lawai) Established tour operator with a head office in Miri offering a range of tours and activities in northeastern Sarawak and beyond. Longer itineraries include trekking in the highlands from Ba Kelalan to Bario via Gunung Murud (from RM2567) and a visit to a remote Kenyah longhouse in the upper Baram (four days, RM5880).

Borneo Tropical Adventure Trekking

(085-419337; www.borneotropicaladventures.com; Lot 906, Shop 12, ground fl, Soon Hup Tower, Jln Merbau; 9am-6pm) Veteran Miri-based company offering packages including the Headhunters' Trail from Gunung Mulu National Park (five days, from RM1750) as well as longhouse visits and multiday Borneo-wide tours.

Borneo Trekkers Trekking
(☎012-872 9159; www.borneotrekkers.blogspot.com) Guide Willie Kajan specialises in treks to Mulu along the Headhunters' Trail with the possibility of beginning or ending with a night at a longhouse in Limbang. Can also arrange treks in the Kelabit Highlands.

SHOPPING

Miri Handicraft Centre Handicrafts
(cnr Jln Brooke & Jln Merbau; ⏰9am-6pm) Thirteen stalls, rented from the city, sell colourful bags, baskets, sarongs, textiles etc made by Iban, Kelabit, Kenyah, Kayan, Lun Bawang, Chinese and Malay artisans. Stall No 7 has some fine Kelabit beadwork from Bario. Some stalls are closed on Sundays.

EATING

Summit Café Dayak $
(☎019-885 3920; Lot 1245, Centre Point Commercial Centre, Jln Melayu; meals RM8-15; ⏰7am-4pm Mon-Sat; ☑) If you've never tried Kelabit cuisine, this place will open up whole new worlds for your tastebuds. Queue up and choose from the colourful array of 'jungle food' laid out at the counter, including *dure* (fried jungle leaf), minced tapioca leaves, and *labo senutuk* (wild boar). The best selection is available before 11.30am – once the food runs out it closes.

Khan's Islamic Restaurant Indian $
(☎012-878 9640; 229 Jln Maju; mains RM6-12; ⏰6.30am-9pm; ☑) This simple canteen is one of Miri's best North Indian eateries, serving up mouth-watering tandoori chicken (RM12), naan bread and mango lassi (RM4) as well as a variety of curries and vegetarian dishes.

Madli's Restaurant Malaysian $
(☎085-426615; www.madli.net; Lot 1088 ground fl, Block 9, Jln Merpati; mains RM6-18.50; ⏰8am-midnight Sun-Thu, 8am-1am Fri & Sat; ❄) A long-running family business that started off as a satay stall in the 1970s; the first of three restaurants was opened in Miri 1995. As well as lip-smackingly good chicken and lamb satay (RM1 per stick), the menu includes Malaysian dishes like *nasi lemak* (coconut rice) and *kampung* fried rice. Serves roti canai and Western breakfasts until noon.

Rainforest Cafe Chinese $$
(☎085-426967; 49 Jln Brooke; mains RM10-30; ⏰10.30am-2pm & 5-11pm) Often packed with families tucking into a banquet of shared dishes, this breezy, open-air eatery specialises in Chinese-style dishes such as 'braised rainforest bean curd', 'crispy roasted chicken' and 'pork leg Philippine style'.

Meng Chai Seafood Seafood $$
(☎085-413648; 11A Jln Merbau; meals from RM25; ⏰4pm-midnight) Discerning locals crowd this first-rate eatery, housed in two unassuming adjacent buildings. There is no menu here – make your selection from the fishy candidates lined up on ice, decide how you would like it cooked and order any accompaniments such as rice or *midin* (fern). Seawater tanks hold live clams and prawns. Servings of fish are priced by weight.

INFORMATION

For some great tips and an outline of local history, see Miri's unofficial website, www.miriresortcity.com.

ATMs can be found at the airport and all over the city centre.

It's a good idea to stock up on first-aid supplies before heading inland to Gunung Mulu National Park.

National Park Booking Office (☎085-434184; www.sarawakforestry.com; 452 Jln Melayu; ⏰8am-5pm Mon-Fri) Inside the Visitors Information Centre. Has details on Sarawak's national parks and can book beds and rooms at Niah, but not Gunung Mulu.

Visitors Information Centre (☎085-434181; www.sarawaktourism.com; 452 Jln Melayu; ⏰8am-5pm Mon-Fri, 9am-3pm Sat, Sun & public holidays) The helpful staff can provide city maps,

Hawker stall

information on accommodation and a list of licensed guides. Situated in a little park.

GETTING THERE & AWAY

Miri's **airport** (www.miriairport.com; Jln Airport) is 10km south of the town centre.

Long-distance buses use the Pujut Bus Terminal, about 4km northeast of the centre.

About once an hour, buses head to Kuching (RM60 to RM90, 12 to 14 hours, departures from 7.15am to 8.30pm) via the inland (old) Miri–Bintulu highway, with a stop at Batu Niah Junction (access point for Niah National Park; RM10 to RM12, 1½ hours). This route is highly competitive, so it pays to shop around. Taking a spacious 'VIP bus', with just three seats across, is like flying 1st class.

GETTING AROUND

A taxi from the airport to the city centre (15 minutes or 25 minutes in traffic) costs RM25; a *kupon teksi* (taxi coupon) can be purchased at the taxi desk just outside the baggage-claim area (next to the car-rental desks). If you're heading from town to the airport, the fare is RM22. There is no public transport from the airport.

A short cab ride around downtown is RM12, while a ride from the centre to the Pujut Bus Terminal costs RM20. Taxis run by the **Miri Taxi Association** (085-432277; 24hr) can be summoned by phone 24 hours a day.

Most of Miri's guesthouses are happy to organise private transport to area destinations such as Niah National Park (RM240 return).

SINGAPORE

Singapore

The island state is an ambitious, ever-evolving wonder of sci-fi architecture in billion-dollar gardens, of masterpieces in colonial palaces, and of single-origin coffee in flouncy heritage shophouses.

Beyond the new and dynamic simmers the Singapore of old: a spicy broth of Chinese, Malay, Indian and Peranakan traditions. Sure, it might be clean, rich and a stickler for rules, but dig a little deeper and you'll uncover a Singapore far more complex than you ever imagined.

Singapore in Two Days

Stroll around the **Colonial District, Marina Bay and the Quays** (p238) for a glimpse of the British influence left on the city and stunning contemporary architecture. Spend a day getting museumed out at the **National Museum of Singapore** (p232), the **Asian Civilisations Museum** (p232) or the **Peranakan Museum** (p232) – they're all worth your time. Dip into **Chinatown** for its food, shopping, temples and cultural centre.

Singapore in Four Days

There are interesting new heritage centres in both **Little India** (p248) and **Kampong Glam** (p248), as well as great shopping and streetlife. Escape the afternoon heat in the air-conditioned comfort of **Orchard Rd** or under the foliage of the **Botanic Gardens** (p228). Save a day for Singapore's incredible new **Gardens by the Bay** (p228) and some down time on Singapore's pleasure island, **Sentosa** (p252).

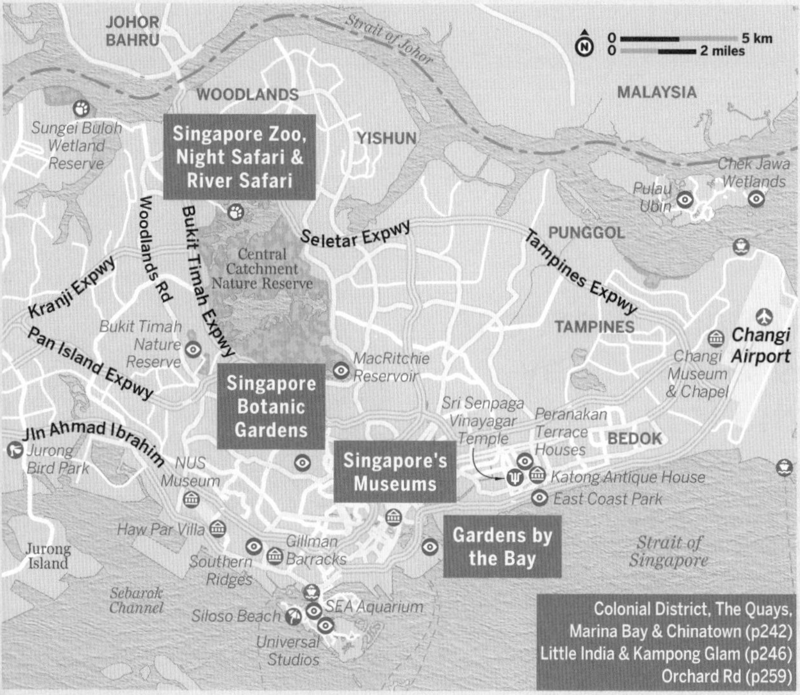

Arriving in Singapore

Changi Airport Located 20km north-east; connected to the city centre by MRT trains, public buses and taxis.

Woodlands Train Checkpoint The shuttle train from Johor Bahru in Malaysia terminates here; direct buses then run to Singapore's Queen Street Bus Terminal.

Ferry services from Malaysia and Indonesia arrive at various ferry terminals in Singapore.

Sleeping

Book way in advance during peak periods, which include the Formula One race. Even average hostels tend to be booked up over the weekends.

For information on the best neighbourhood to stay, see p271.

Botanic Gardens & Gardens by the Bay

For instant stress relief, slip into the Singapore Botanic Gardens – a tranquil, verdant paradise of rolling lawns, themed gardens and glassy lakes. Less than 10km away, the newer Gardens by the Bay, which sprawls across 101 hectares of reclaimed land, is an ambitious masterpiece of urban planning – as thrilling to architecture buffs as it is to nature lovers.

Great For...

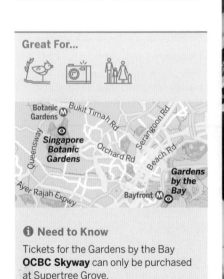

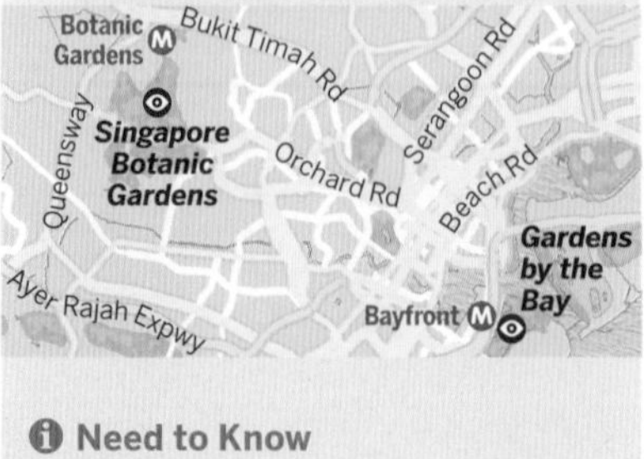

Need to Know

Tickets for the Gardens by the Bay **OCBC Skyway** can only be purchased at Supertree Grove.

Cranes statue, National Orchid Garden (p228)

★ Top Tip

Free, themed guided tours of the Botanic Gardens run on Saturdays (check the website).

GAVIN HELLIER/GETTY IMAGES ©

Singapore Botanic Gardens

Singapore's 74-hectare botanic **wonderland** (☎6471 7361; www.sbg.org.sg; 1 Cluny Rd; garden admission free; ⏰5am-midnight, Healing Garden 5am-7.30pm Wed-Mon, Jacob Ballas Children's Garden 8am-7pm Tue-Sun, last entry 6.30pm; 🚌7, 105, 123, 174, Ⓜ Botanic Gardens) is a Unesco World Heritage site and one of the city's most arresting attractions. Established in 1860, it's a tropical utopia peppered with glassy lakes, rolling lawns and themed gardens.

The Botanic Gardens' now famous orchid breeding began in 1928 and its legacy is the **National Orchid Garden** (adult/child S$5/free; ⏰8.30am-7pm). Its three hectares are home to over 1000 species and 2000 hybrids, around 600 of which are on display – the largest showcase of tropical orchids on Earth.

Located next to the National Orchid Garden, the one-hectare Ginger Garden contains over 250 members of the Zingiberaceae family. It's also where you'll find **Halia** (☎6476 6711; www.halia.com.sg; mains S$28-68, dinner set menu S$88-98, English tea S$28; ⏰noon-4pm & 6-10pm Mon-Fri, 10am-5pm & 6-10pm Sat & Sun; 🌶), which, alongside **Blue Bali** (☎6733 0185; www.bluebali.sg; tapas S$8-20, mains S$16-32; ⏰3pm-midnight Tue-Sun; 📶), just outside the Gardens, delivers one of Singapore's most memorable dining experiences.

Ancient Rainforest & Swan Lake

Hit the boardwalk and escape into this rare patch of dense primeval rainforest, older than the Botanic Gardens themselves. Of the rainforest's 314 species of vegetation, over half are now considered rare in Singapore.

For a touch of romanticism, it's hard to beat Swan Lake. One of three lakes in the Botanic Gardens, it boasts a tiny island cluttered with nibong palms. Look out for the mute swans, imported from Amsterdam.

Gardens by the Bay

Singapore's 21st-century **Gardens by the Bay** (Map p242; ☎6420 6848; www.gardensbythebay.com.sg; 18 Marina Gardens Dr; gardens free, conservatories adult/child under 13yr S$28/15; ⏰5am-2am, conservatories & OCBC Skyway 9am-9pm, last ticket sale 8pm; Ⓜ Bayfront) is a S$1 billion, fantasy-land of space-age biodomes and whimsical sculptures. The most striking feature of the gardens are its **Supertrees**, 18 steel-clad concrete structures adorned with over 162,900 plants. Actually massive exhausts for the Gardens' biomass steam turbines, they're used to generate electricity to cool the conservatories.

For a sweeping view, walk across the 22m-high **OCBC Skyway** (adult/child S$5/3) connecting six Supertrees at Supertree Grove. Each night at 7.45pm and 8.45pm, the Supertrees become the glowing protagonists of Garden Rhapsody, a light-and-sound spectacular.

The **Visitor Centres** offer stroller hire, lockers (S$1 to S$3 depending on size) and audioguides, while a regular shuttle bus

Gardens by the Bay

(9.45am to 5.45pm; two rides S$2) runs between Dragonfly Bridge at Bayfront MRT, Supertree Grove, the domed conservatories, and the taxi stand at Arrival Plaza.

The Conservatories

Housing 217,000 plants from 800 species, the Gardens' asymmetrical conservatories rise like giant paper nautilus shells beside Marina Bay. **Flower Dome** replicates a dry, Mediterranean climate and includes ancient olive trees. **Cloud Forest Dome** is a steamy affair, recreating the tropical montane climate found at elevations between 1500m and 3000m. Its centrepiece is a 35m mountain complete with waterfall.

Heritage Gardens & Sculptures

Directly west of the Supertrees are the Heritage Gardens, four themed spaces inspired by the cultures of Singapore's three main ethnic groups – Chinese, Malay and Indian – as well as its former colonial ruler.

The most visually arresting of the Gardens' numerous artworks is Mark Quinn's *Planet*. The colossal sculpture is a giant seven-month-old infant, fast asleep and seemingly floating above the ground. This illusion is nothing short of brilliant, especially considering the bronze bubba comes in at a hefty seven tonnes. The work was modelled on Quinn's own son.

Children's Garden

If you have kids in tow, head to the Children's Garden, which features a water playground (with shower and changing facilities), as well as a huge tree house and adventure playground.

WSBOON IMAGES/GETTY IMAGES ©

Javanese art, Asian Civilisations Museum (p232)

Singapore's Museums

Among the many things that Singapore does supremely well is its museums and galleries, which shine a light on the cultures and arts of its multi-ethnic population. The following are our pick of the best, although there are many more excellent institutions should you wish to dig deeper.

Great For...

Need to Know

The National Gallery Singapore runs daily guided tours, artist talks, lectures and workshops.

★ **Top Tip**

Entry to the separate gallery 8Q SAM (p233) is free with your SAM ticket.

National Museum of Singapore

Imaginative and immersive, Singapore's rebooted **National Museum** (Map p242; www.nationalmuseum.sg; 93 Stamford Rd; adult/student & senior S$10/5; ⌚10am-6pm; Ⓜ Dhoby Ghaut) is good enough to warrant two visits. At once cutting-edge and classic, the space ditches staid exhibits for lively multimedia galleries that bring Singapore's jam-packed biography to vivid life. It's a colourful, intimate journey, spanning ancient Malay royalty, wartime occupation, nation-building, food and fashion.

Asian Civilisations Museum

This remarkable **museum** (Map p242; ☎6332 7798; www.acm.org.sg; 1 Empress Pl; adult/child under 6yr S$8/free, 7-9pm Fri half-price; ⌚10am-7pm Sat-Thu, to 9pm Fri; Ⓜ Raffles Pl) houses the region's most comprehensive collection of pan-Asian treasures. Its series of thematic galleries explore the history, cultures and religions of Southeast Asia, China, the Asian subcontinent and Islamic West Asia. Exquisite artefacts include glittering Sumatran and Javanese ceremonial jewellery, Thai tribal textiles, Chinese silk tapestries, and astronomical treatises from 14th-century Iran and 16th-century Egypt. Among the more macabre objects is a 17th- or 18th-century Tibetan ritual bone apron, made with human and animal bones.

National Gallery Singapore

Connected by a striking aluminium and glass canopy, Singapore's historic City Hall and Old Supreme Court buildings now form the city's breathtaking **National Gallery** (Map p242; www.nationalgallery.sg; St Andrew's Rd; adult/child S$20/15; ⌚10am-7pm Sun-Thu, to 10pm Fri-Sat; Ⓜ City Hall). Its world-class collection of 19th-century and modern Southeast Asian art is housed in two major spaces, the DBS Singapore Gallery and the UOB Southeast Asia Gallery. The former delivers a comprehensive overview of Singaporean art from the 19th century to today, while the latter focuses on the greater Southeast Asian region.

Beyond them, the Singtel Special Exhibition Gallery is the setting for temporary exhibitions, which include major collaborations with some of the world's highest-profile art museums. Young culture vultures shouldn't miss the National Gallery's Keppel Centre for Art Education, which delivers innovative, multisensory art experiences for kids.

Peranakan Museum

Explore the rich heritage of the Peranakans (Straits Chinese descendants) at this **museum** (Map p242; ☎6332 7591; http://peranakanmuseum.org.sg; 39 Armenian St; adult/child under 7yr S$6/free, 7-9pm Fri half-price; ⌚10am-7pm, to 9pm Fri; Ⓜ City Hall). Thematic galleries cover various aspects of Peranakan culture, from the traditional 12-day wedding ceremony to crafts, spirituality and feasting. Look out for

National Museum of Singapore

intricately detailed ceremonial costumes and beadwork, beautifully carved wedding beds, and rare dining porcelain. An especially curious example of Peranakan fusion culture is a pair of Victorian bell jars in which statues of Christ and the Madonna are adorned with Chinese-style flowers and vines.

Singapore Art Museum

Formerly the St Joseph's Institution – a Catholic boys' school – **Singapore Art Museum** (Map p242; ☎6589 9580; www.singaporeartmuseum.sg; 71 Bras Basah Rd; adult/student & senior S$10/5, 6-9pm Fri free; ⏰10am-7pm Sat-Thu, to 9pm Fri; Ⓜ Bras Basah) now sings the praises of contemporary Southeast Asian art. Themed exhibitions include works from the museum's permanent collection as well as those from private collections, from painting and sculpture to video art and site-specific installations. Free, 45-minute guided tours of the museum are conducted in English two to three times daily; check the website for times.

Round the corner from the museum is its younger sibling, **8Q SAM** (Map p242; www.singaporeartmuseum.sg; 8 Queen St; admission with SAM ticket free; ⏰10am-7pm Sat-Thu, to 9pm Fri; Ⓜ Bras Basah, City Hall), named after its address. Snoop around four floors of contemporary art, taking in quirky installations, video art and mixed-media statements.

☑ Don't Miss

The interactive artwork *GoHead/GoStan: Panorama Singapura* at the National Museum of Singapore, which offers an audiovisual trip through the city-state's many periods.

SENG CHYE TEO/GETTY IMAGES ©

Malayan tiger

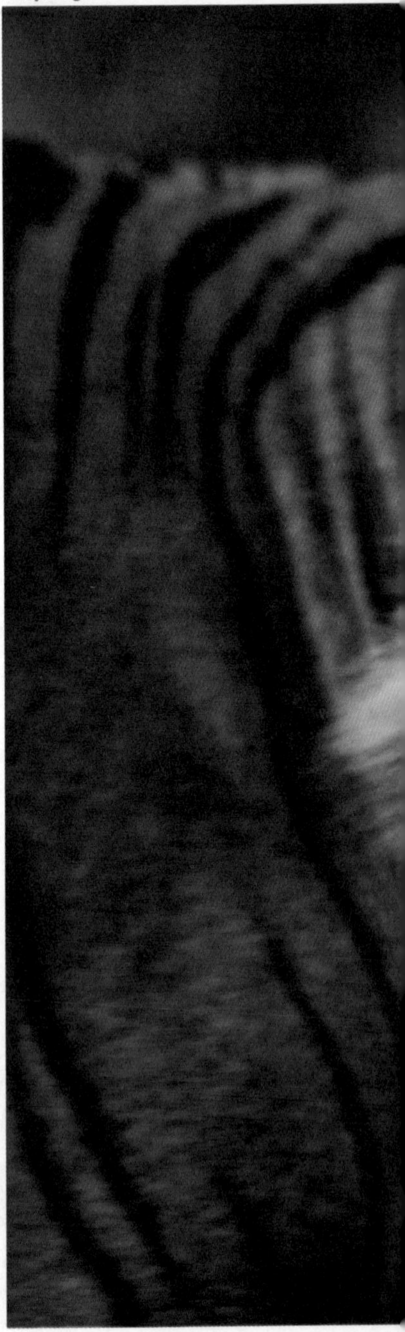

Singapore Zoo, Night Safari & River Safari

A great family attraction, Singapore Zoo is a refreshing mix of spacious, naturalistic enclosures, freely roaming animals and interactive attractions. Next door, the separate Night Safari is also worth a visit in its own right, as is the River Safari, which recreates the habitats of numerous world-famous rivers.

Great For...

Need to Know

6269 3411; 80 Mandai Lake Rd; Ang Mo Kio, then 138

★ Top Tip

Arrive for the Night Safari after 9.30pm to avoid the worst queues.

Singapore Zoo

We're calling it: this is possibly the world's best **zoo** (www.zoo.com.sg; adult/child under 13yr S$32/21; ⌚8.30am-6pm). The open-air enclosures allow for both freedom for the animals to roam and unobstructed visitor views. Get up close to orangutans, dodge Malaysian flying foxes, even snoop around a replica African village. Then there's that setting: 26 soothing hectares on a lush peninsula jutting out into the waters of the Upper Seletar Reservoir.

There are over 2800 residents here, and as far as zoos go, the enclosures are among the world's most comfortable. If you have kids in tow, let them go wild at **Rainforest Kidzworld**, a wonderland of slides, swings, pulling boats, pony rides and farmyard animals happy for a feed. There's even a dedicated wet area, with swimwear available for purchase if you didn't bring your own.

Fragile Forest & Great Rift Valley

The zoo's Fragile Forest is a giant biodome that replicates the stratas of a rainforest. Cross paths with free-roaming butterflies, lories, Malayan flying foxes and ring-tailed lemurs. The pathway leads up to the forest canopy and the dome's most chilled-out locals, the two-toed sloths.

Complete with cliffs and a waterfall, the evocative Great Rift Valley exhibit is home to hamadryas baboons, Nubian ibexes, banded mongooses, black-backed jackals and rock hyraxes. You'll also find replica Ethiopian village huts, which offer insight into the area's unforgiving living conditions.

Green tree python, Singapore Zoo

Night Safari

Next door to the zoo, but completely separate, Singapore's acclaimed **Night Safari** (www.nightsafari.com.sg; adult/child under 13yr S$42/28; ⌚7.30pm-midnight, restaurants & shops from 5.30pm) offers a very different type of nightlife. Home to over 130 species of animals, the park's moats and barriers seem to melt away in the darkness, giving you the feeling of travelling through a jungle filled with the likes of leopards, tigers and alligators. It's an atmosphere further heightened by the herds of strolling antelopes, often passing within inches of the electric shuttle trams that quietly cart you around.

☑ Don't Miss

Taking the kids to the Creatures of the Night show at the Night Zoo.

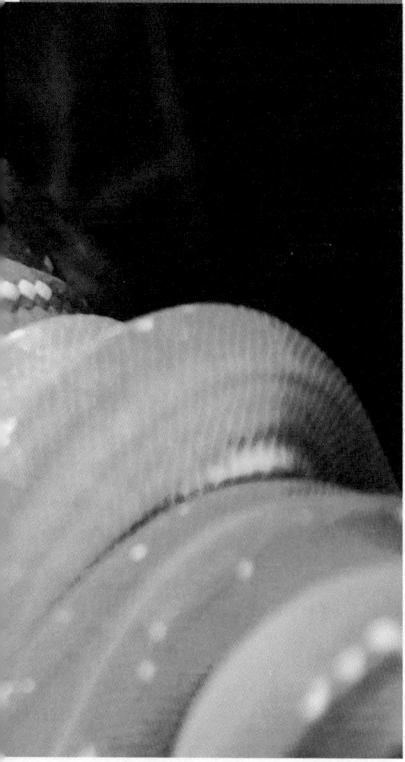

KIMBERLEY COOLE/GETTY IMAGES ©

The 45-minute tram tour comes with a guide whose commentary is a good introduction to the park. Alight at the East Lodge Trail and hit the atmospheric walking paths, which lead to enclosures inaccessible by tram. Among them is the deliciously creepy Giant Flying Squirrel walk-through aviary. Kids will love the intelligent and entertaining 20-minute **Creatures of the Night** (⌚7.30pm, 8.30pm & 9.30pm, plus 10.30pm Fri & Sat) show.

When returning from the safari, you'll need to catch a bus at around 10.35pm to make the last MRT train departing Ang Mo Kio at 11.35pm. Otherwise, there's a taxi stand out front – expect to pay around $20 for a trip back to the CBD.

River Safari

This **wildlife park** (www.riversafari.com.sg; adult/child under 13yr S$28/18, boat ride adult/child S$5/3; ⌚9am-6pm) recreates the habitats of seven major river systems, including the Yangtze, Nile and Congo. While most are underwhelming, the Mekong River and Amazon Flooded Forest exhibits are impressive, their epic aquariums rippling with giant catfish and stingrays, electric eels, red-bellied piranhas, manatees and sea cows. Another highlight is the Giant Panda Forest enclosure, home to rare red pandas and the park's famous black-and-whiters, KaiKai and JiaJia.

Young kids will enjoy the 10-minute Amazon River Quest Boat Ride, a tranquil, theme-park-style tour past roaming monkeys, wild cats and exotic birdlife. The ride begins with a big splash, so if you're sitting in the front row, keep feet and bags off the floor. Boat-ride time slots often fill by 1pm, so go early. River Safari tickets purchased online include a 10% discount.

Take a Break

Enjoy the **Jungle Breakfast with Wildlife** (adult/child S$33/23; ⌚9-10.30am) in the company of orangutans at the zoo.

Singapore Walking Tour

This amble around the old Colonial district and Marina Bay takes you from the Singapore of Sir Stamford Raffles to the the cutting-edge visions of 21st-century architects.
Start MRT City Hall
Distance 3.5km
Duration 4 to 5 hours

1 Step into elegant **St Andrew's Cathedral** (p241), used as an emergency hospital during WWII and a fine example of English Gothic Revival architecture.

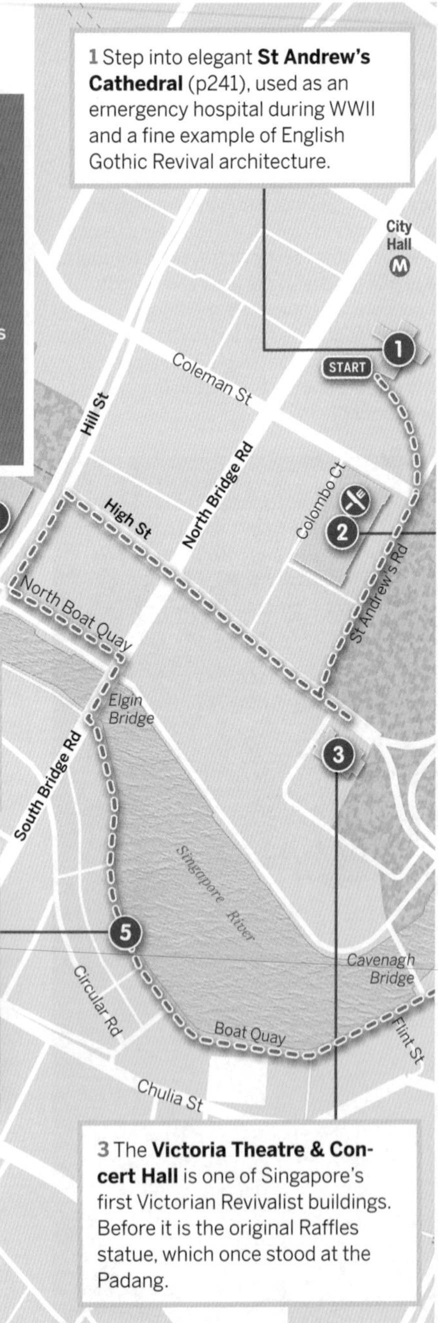

4 Multicoloured **Old Hill St Police Station** was proclaimed a 'sky-scraper' upon completion in 1934. The building now houses several high-end art galleries.

5 The riverfront shophouses in **Boat Quay** (p241) are home to bars, restaurants and snap-happy tourists. Look out for Salvador Dalí's Homage to Newton and other sculptures.

3 The **Victoria Theatre & Concert Hall** is one of Singapore's first Victorian Revivalist buildings. Before it is the original Raffles statue, which once stood at the Padang.

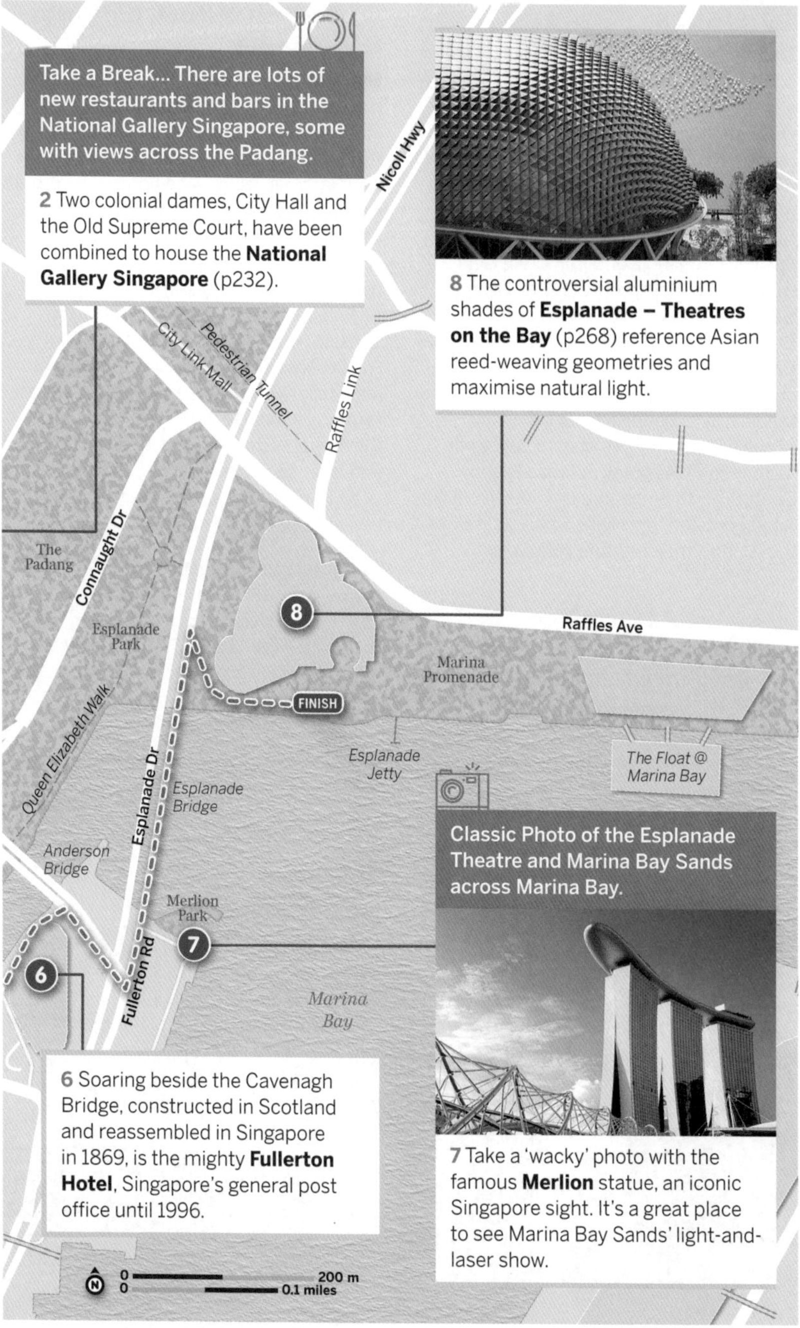

Take a Break... There are lots of new restaurants and bars in the National Gallery Singapore, some with views across the Padang.

2 Two colonial dames, City Hall and the Old Supreme Court, have been combined to house the **National Gallery Singapore** (p232).

8 The controversial aluminium shades of **Esplanade – Theatres on the Bay** (p268) reference Asian reed-weaving geometries and maximise natural light.

Classic Photo of the Esplanade Theatre and Marina Bay Sands across Marina Bay.

7 Take a 'wacky' photo with the famous **Merlion** statue, an iconic Singapore sight. It's a great place to see Marina Bay Sands' light-and-laser show.

6 Soaring beside the Cavenagh Bridge, constructed in Scotland and reassembled in Singapore in 1869, is the mighty **Fullerton Hotel**, Singapore's general post office until 1996.

SIGHTS

Singapore's urban core is located on the south of the island. Here you'll find the Singapore River, flanked by Boat Quay, Clarke Quay and Robertson Quay. South of the river lie the CBD (Central Business District) and Chinatown, while immediately north of the river lies the Colonial District (also referred to as the Civic District). Further north is Little India and Kampong Glam, while east of Kampong Glam you'll find Geylang, Katong (Joo Chiat), East Coast Park and Changi. Northwest of the Colonial District is Orchard Rd, while further west still lie the Singapore Botanic Gardens, and the heavily expat district of Dempsey Hill. At the river's mouth is Marina Bay, while further southwest lies Sentosa Island. Central-north Singapore is where you'll find Singapore Zoo and Night Safari, as well as the island's major nature reserves.

Colonial District, the Quays & Marina Bay

Marina Bay Sands Complex

(Map p242; www.marinabaysands.com; Marina Bay; M Bayfront) Designed by Israeli–North American architect Moshe Safdie, Marina Bay Sands is a sprawling hotel, casino, mall, theatre, exhibition and museum complex. Star of the show is the Marina Bay Sands Hotel, its three 55-storey towers connected by a cantilevered **sky park** (Map p242; level 57, Marina Bay Sands; adult/child under 13yr S$25/17; 9.30am-10pm Mon-Thu, to 11pm Fri-Sun; M Bayfront). Head up for a drink and stellar views at Ce La Vie (the sky bar formerly known as Ku De Ta). Each night, the complex dazzles with its 13-minute light and laser spectacular, Wonder Full.

You'll get the best view of the show from the city side of Marina Bay.

ArtScience Museum Museum

(Map p242; www.marinabaysands.com/museum.html; Marina Bay Sands; average prices adult/child under 13yr S$27/17; 10am-7pm; M Bayfront) Designed by Moshe Safdie and

"the complex dazzles with its 13-minute light and laser spectacular"

Marina Bay Sands

NATAPONG SUPALERTSOPHON/GETTY IMAGES ©

looking like a giant white lotus, the lily-pond-framed ArtScience Museum hosts major international travelling exhibitions in fields as varied as art, design, media, science and technology. Expect anything from explorations of deep-sea creatures to retrospectives of world-famous industrial designers.

St Andrew's Cathedral Church

(Map p242; www.livingstreams.org.sg; 11 St Andrew's Rd; 9am-5pm; City Hall) FREE

Funded by Scottish merchants and built by Indian convicts, this wedding cake of a cathedral stands in stark contrast to the glass and steel surrounding it. Completed in 1838 but torn down and rebuilt in its present form in 1862 after lightning damage, it's one of Singapore's finest surviving examples of English Gothic Revival architecture. Interesting details include the tropics-friendly *porte-cochère* (carriage porch) entrance – designed to shelter passengers – and the colourful stained glass adorning the western wall.

Fort Canning Park Park

(Map p242; www.nparks.gov.sg; Dhoby Ghaut)

When Raffles rolled into Singapore, locals steered clear of Fort Canning Hill, then called Bukit Larangan (Forbidden Hill) out of respect for the sacred shrine of Sultan Iskandar Shah, ancient Singapura's last ruler. These days, the hill is better known as Fort Canning Park, a lush retreat from the hot streets below. Amble through the spice garden, catch an exhibition at **Singapore Pinacothéque de Paris** (Map p242; 6883 1588; www.pinacotheque.com.sg; 5 Cox Tce; Heritage Gallery, Graffiti Walk & Garden Walk free, all galleries adult/student/child under 7yr S$28/19/9; 10am-7.30pm Sun-Thu, to 8.30pm Fri & Sat; Dhoby Ghaut) or ponder Singapore's wartime defeat at the **Battle Box Museum** (Map p242; www.battlebox.com.sg; 2 Cox Tce; adult/child S$8/5; 10am-6pm, last entry 5pm; Dhoby Ghaut).

The former command post of the British during WWII, Battle Box's eerie subterranean rooms explore the fateful surrender to the Japanese on 15 February 1942. Japanese Morse codes are still etched on the walls.

Fort Canning Park hosts several outdoor events and concerts throughout the year, including Shakespeare in the Park

Quays of the City

The stretch of riverfront that separates the Colonial District from the CBD is known as the Quays. The Singapore River – once a thriving entryway for bumboats bearing cargo into the *godown* (warehouses) that lined the riverside – now connects the three quays together. A walk along them offers an eye-opening view to the changes that have impacted Singapore's trade through the years.

Boat Quay (Map p242; Raffles Pl, Clarke Quay) Closest to the former harbour, Boat Quay was once Singapore's centre of commerce, and remained an important economic area into the 1960s. By the mid-1980s, many of the shophouses were in ruins, business having shifted to high-tech cargo centres elsewhere on the island. Declared a conservation zone by the government, the area has reinvented itself as a major entertainment district packed with touristy bars and smooth-talking restaurant touts.

Clarke Quay (Map p242; www.clarkequay.com.sg; Clarke Quay) Named after Singapore's second colonial governor, Sir Andrew Clarke, this is the busiest and most popular of the three quays, its plethora of bars, restaurants and clubs pulling in the pleasure seekers. To its critics, though, this is Singapore at its tackiest and most touristy.

Robertson Quay (Map p242; 64, 123, 143, Clarke Quay) At the furthest reach of the river, Robertson Quay was once used for the storage of goods. It is now home to some of the best eateries and bars along the river.

Colonial District, The Quays, Marina Bay & Chinatown

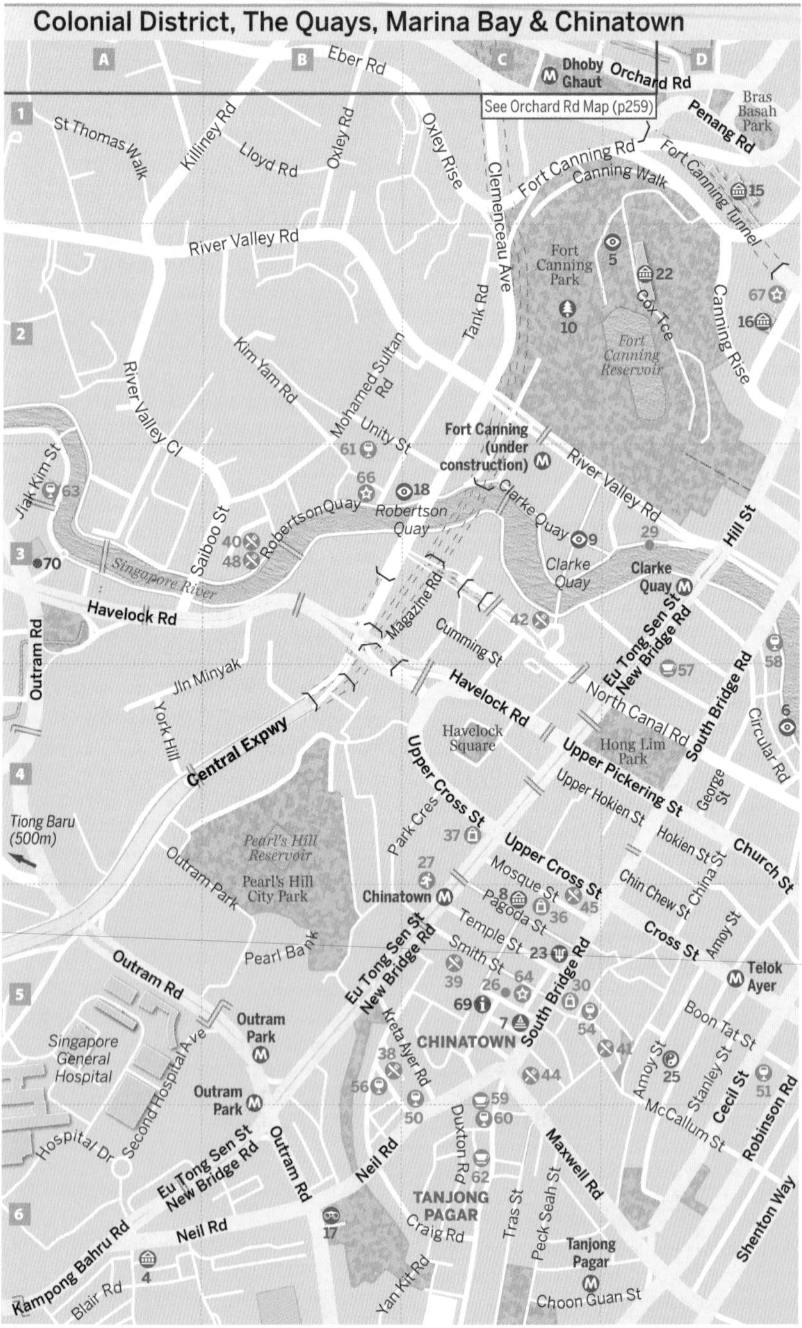

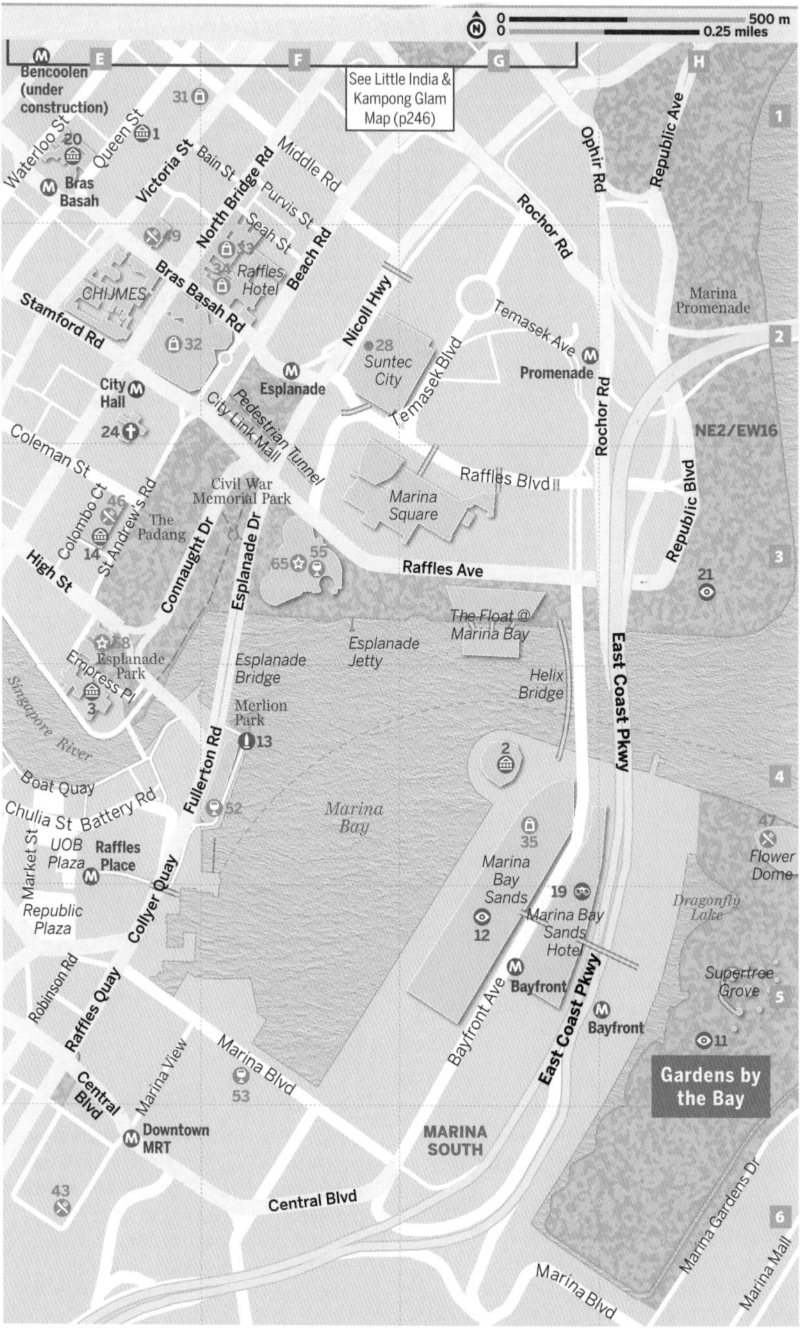

0 500 m
0 0.25 miles
E
F
G
H
1
2
3
4
5
6
See Little India & Kampong Glam Map (p246)
Bencoolen (under construction)
Waterloo St
Queen St
Bras Basah
Victoria St
Bain St
North Bridge Rd
Middle Rd
Purvis St
Seah St
Beach Rd
Raffles Hotel
CHIJMES
Bras Basah Rd
Stamford Rd
Nicoll Hwy
Suntec City
Temasek Blvd
Temasek Ave
Promenade
Rochor Rd
Ophir Rd
Republic Ave
Marina Promenade
NE2/EW16
Republic Blvd
Esplanade
City Hall
Pedestrian Tunnel
City Link Mall
Coleman St
Colombo Ct
St Andrew's Rd
The Padang
Civil War Memorial Park
Connaught Dr
Esplanade Dr
Raffles Blvd
Marina Square
Raffles Ave
High St
The Float @ Marina Bay
Esplanade Jetty
Esplanade Bridge
Esplanade Park
Empress Pl
Singapore River
Merlion Park
Helix Bridge
East Coast Pkwy
Fullerton Rd
Boat Quay
Battery Rd
Chulia St
Market St
UOB Plaza
Raffles Place
Collyer Quay
Republic Plaza
Marina Bay
Marina Bay Sands
Marina Bay Sands Hotel
Flower Dome
Dragonfly Lake
Supertree Grove
Bayfront
Bayfront Ave
Robinson Rd
Raffles Quay
Marina View
Marina Blvd
Gardens by the Bay
Central Blvd
Downtown MRT
MARINA SOUTH
Marina Gardens Dr
Marina Mall

Colonial District, The Quays, Marina Bay & Chinatown

Sights
1 8Q SAM ... E1
2 ArtScience Museum ... G4
3 Asian Civilisations Museum ... E4
4 Baba House ... A6
5 Battlebox ... D2
6 Boat Quay ... D4
7 Buddha Tooth Relic Temple ... C5
8 Chinatown Heritage Centre ... C5
9 Clarke Quay ... C3
10 Fort Canning Park ... C2
11 Gardens by the Bay ... H5
12 Marina Bay Sands ... G5
13 Merlion ... F4
14 National Gallery Singapore ... E3
15 National Museum of Singapore ... D1
16 Peranakan Museum ... D2
17 Pinnacle@Duxton ... B6
18 Robertson Quay ... C3
19 Sands SkyPark Observation Deck ... G5
20 Singapore Art Museum ... E1
21 Singapore Flyer ... H3
22 Singapore Pinacothèque de Paris ... D2
23 Sri Mariamman Temple ... C5
24 St Andrew's Cathedral ... E2
25 Thian Hock Keng Temple ... D5

Activities, Courses & Tours
26 Food Playground ... C5
Mr Lim Foot Reflexology ... (see 27)
27 People's Park Complex ... C4
28 Singapore Ducktours ... F2
29 Singapore River Cruise ... D3

Shopping
Chan Hampe Galleries ... (see 33)
30 Eu Yan Sang ... C5
31 Kapok ... E1
Leica ... (see 33)
Ode to Art ... (see 32)
32 Raffles City ... E2
33 Raffles Hotel Arcade ... F2
34 Raffles Hotel Gift Shop ... F2
35 Shoppes at Marina Bay Sands ... G4
36 Utterly Art ... C5
37 Yue Hwa Chinese Products ... C4

Eating
Bonne Soup ... (see 39)
38 Burnt Ends ... B5
39 Chinatown Complex ... C5
40 Curry Culture ... B3
41 Ding Dong ... D5
42 Jumbo Seafood ... C3
Lian He Ben Ji Claypot Rice ... (see 39)
43 Lobby Lounge at The Westin ... E6
44 Maxwell Food Centre ... C5
45 Momma Kong's ... C5
46 National Kitchen by Violet Oon ... E3
47 Pollen ... H4
Rojak, Popiah & Cockle ... (see 44)
Shi Xiang Satay ... (see 39)
48 Super Loco ... B3
Tian Tian Hainanese Chicken Rice.. (see 44)
49 Wah Lok ... E2

Drinking & Nightlife
50 Backstage Bar ... C5
51 Kyō ... D5
Landing Point ... (see 52)
52 Lantern ... F4
53 Level 33 ... F5
54 Operation Dagger ... C5
55 Orgo ... F3
56 Potato Head Folk ... B5
57 Ronin ... D4
58 Southbridge ... D3
59 Tea Chapter ... C5
60 Tippling Club ... C6
61 Wine Connection ... B3
62 Yixing Xuan Teahouse ... C6
63 Zouk ... A3

Entertainment
64 Chinese Theatre Circle ... C5
65 Esplanade – Theatres on the Bay ... F3
66 Singapore Repertory Theatre ... B3
67 Timbrè @ The Substation ... D2
68 Victoria Theatre & Concert Hall ... E3

Information
69 Chinatown Visitor Centre ... C5

Transport
70 Avis ... A3

(April/May), Ballet under the Stars (June/July) and Films at the Fort (August).

Singapore Flyer Ferris Wheel

(Map p242; ☎6333 3311; www.singaporeflyer.com.sg; 30 Raffles Ave; adult/child under 13yr S$33/21; ⏰ticket booth 8am-10pm, wheel 8.30am-10.30pm, last ride 10pm; Ⓜ Promenade)

Las Vegas' High Roller may have since stolen its 'World's Biggest Observation Wheel' title, but Singapore's 165m-tall ferris wheel continues to serve up a gob-smacking panorama. On a clear day, the 30-minute ride will have you peering out over the Colonial District, CBD and Marina Bay, the high-rise housing sprawl to the east and out to the ship-clogged South China Sea. The wheel's construction is documented in the onsite multimedia display Journey of Dreams. Purchase tickets online for a modest discount.

Chinatown & the CBD

Baba House Museum

(Map p242; ☎6227 5731; www.nus.edu.sg/cfa/museum/about.php; 157 Neil Rd; ⏱1hr tours 2pm Mon, 6.30pm Tue, 10am Thu, 11am Sat; Ⓜ Outram Park) FREE Baba House is one of Singapore's best-preserved Peranakan heritage homes. Built in the 1890s, it's a wonderful window into the life of an affluent Peranakan family living in Singapore a century ago. Its loving restoration has seen every detail attended to, from the carved motifs on the blue facade down to the door screens. The only way in is on a guided tour, held every Monday, Tuesday, Thursday and Saturday, but the tour is excellent and free. Bookings, by telephone, are essential.

Chinatown Heritage Centre Museum

(Map p242; ☎6221 9556; www.chinatownheritagecentre.com.sg; 48 Pagoda St; adult/child S$10/6; ⏱9am-8pm; Ⓜ Chinatown) Delve into Chinatown's gritty, cacophonous backstory at the recently revamped Chinatown Heritage Centre. Occupying several levels of a converted shophouse, its interactive exhibitions shed light on numerous historical chapters, from the treacherous journey of Singapore's early Chinese immigrants to the development of local clan associations to the district's notorious opium dens. It's an evocative place, digging well beneath modern Chinatown's touristy veneer.

Sri Mariamman Temple Hindu Temple

(Map p242; 244 South Bridge Rd; ⏱7am-noon & 6-9pm; Ⓜ Chinatown) FREE Paradoxically in the middle of Chinatown, this is the oldest Hindu temple in Singapore, originally built in 1823, then rebuilt in 1843. You can't miss the fabulously animated, technicolor 1930s *gopuram* (tower) above the entrance, the key to the temple's south Indian Dravidian style. Sacred cow sculptures grace the boundary walls, while the *gopuram* is covered in kitsch plasterwork images of Brahma the creator, Vishnu the preserver and Shiva the destroyer.

Every October the temple hosts the Thimithi festival; devotees queue along South Bridge Rd to hotfoot it over burning coals!

Buddha Tooth Relic Temple Buddhist Temple

(Map p242; www.btrts.org.sg; 288 South Bridge Rd; ⏱7am-7pm, relic viewing 9am-6pm; Ⓜ Chinatown) FREE Consecrated in 2008, this hulking, five-story Buddhist temple is home to what is reputedly the left canine tooth of the Buddha, recovered from his funeral pyre in Kushinagar, northern India. While its authenticity is debated, the relic enjoys VIP status inside a 420kg solid-gold stupa in a dazzlingly ornate 4th-floor room. More religious relics await at the 3rd-floor Buddhism museum, while the peaceful rooftop garden features a huge prayer wheel inside a 10,000 Buddha Pavilion.

Thian Hock Keng Temple Taoist Temple

(Map p242; www.thianhockkeng.com.sg; 158 Telok Ayer St; ⏱7.30am-5.30pm; Ⓜ Telok Ayer) FREE Surprisingly, Chinatown's oldest and most important Hokkien temple is often a haven of tranquility. Built between 1839 and 1842, it's a beautiful place, and once the favourite landing point of Chinese sailors, before land reclamation pushed the sea far down the road. Typically, the temple's design features are richly symbolic: the stone lions at the entrance ward off evil spirits, while the painted depiction of phoenixes and peonies in the central hall symbolise peace and good tidings respectively.

Pinnacle@Duxton Viewpoint

(Map p242; www.pinnacleduxton.com.sg; Block 1G, 1 Cantonment Rd; 50th-floor skybridge S$5; ⏱9am-9pm; Ⓜ Outram Park, Tanjong Pagar) For killer city views at a bargain S$5, head to the 50th-floor rooftop of Pinnacle@Duxton,

Little India & Kampong Glam

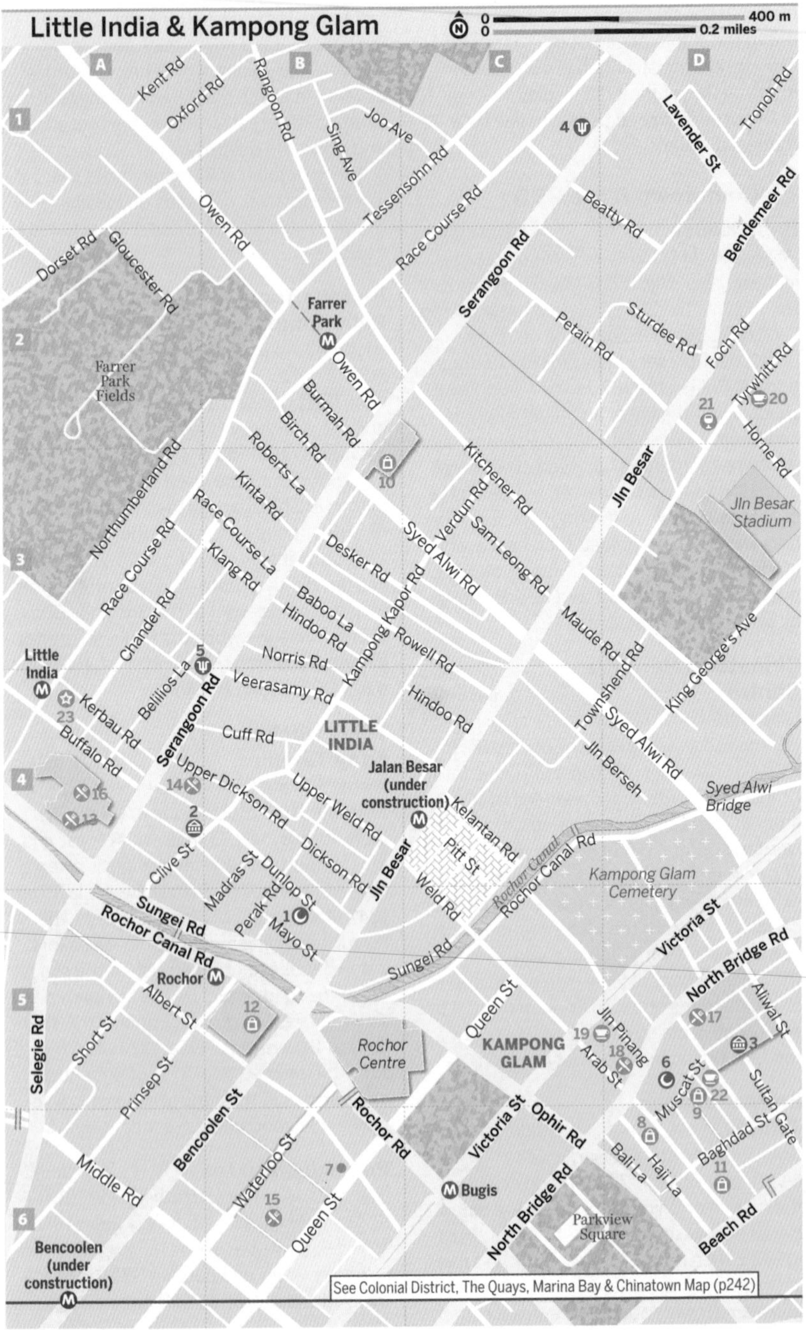

0 400 m
0 0.2 miles
A
B
C
D
1
2
3
4
5
6
Kent Rd
Oxford Rd
Rangoon Rd
Sing Ave
Joo Ave
Tessensohn Rd
Race Course Rd
Lavender St
Tronoh Rd
Beatty Rd
Bendemeer Rd
Owen Rd
Dorset Rd
Gloucester Rd
Serangoon Rd
Farrer Park
Farrer Park Fields
Petain Rd
Sturdee Rd
Foch Rd
Tyrwhitt Rd
Burmah Rd
Birch Rd
Roberts La
Kinta Rd
Northumberland Rd
Kitchener Rd
Jln Besar
Horne Rd
Jln Besar Stadium
Verdun Rd
Sam Leong Rd
Syed Alwi Rd
Race Course La
Klang Rd
Desker Rd
Baboo La
Hindoo Rd
Kampong Kapor Rd
Rowell Rd
Chander Rd
Maude Rd
Townshend Rd
King George's Ave
Little India
Belilios La
Norris Rd
Veerasamy Rd
Kerbau Rd
Buffalo Rd
Cuff Rd
LITTLE INDIA
Jln Berseh
Upper Dickson Rd
Upper Weld Rd
Jalan Besar (under construction)
Kelantan Rd
Syed Alwi Bridge
Clive St
Madras St
Dunlop St
Dickson Rd
Pitt St
Weld Rd
Rochor Canal
Rochor Canal Rd
Kampong Glam Cemetery
Perak Rd
Mayo St
Sungei Rd
Victoria St
North Bridge Rd
Rochor
Albert St
Aliwal St
Selegie Rd
Short St
Rochor Centre
Queen St
KAMPONG GLAM
Jln Pinang
Arab St
Muscat St
Sultan Gate
Prinsep St
Bencoolen St
Rochor Rd
Ophir Rd
Bali La
Haji La
Baghdad St
Middle Rd
Waterloo St
Bugis
North Bridge Rd
Parkview Square
Beach Rd
Bencoolen (under construction)
1
2
3
4
5
6
7
8
9
10
11
12
13
14
15
16
17
18
19
20
21
22
23

See Colonial District, The Quays, Marina Bay & Chinatown Map (p242)

Little India & Kampong Glam

the world's largest public housing complex. Skybridges connecting the seven towers provide a 360-degree sweep of city, port and sea. Although a makeshift ticket booth was operating on our last visit, payment is usually by EZ-Link transport card only; simply rest your EZ-Link card on the ticket machine located at the bottom of Block G to pay, then catch a lift up to the 50th floor.

Chilling out is encouraged, with patches of lawn, modular furniture and sunloungers. For maximum impact, head up just before sunset to catch the sinking sun.

Little India

Sri Veeramakaliamman Temple — Hindu Temple

(Map p246; www.sriveeramakaliamman.com; 141 Serangoon Rd; 8am-noon & 6.30-9pm Mon-Thu & Sat, 8am-noon & 6-9pm Fri & Sun; MLittle India) FREE Little India's most colourful, visually stunning temple is dedicated to the ferocious goddess Kali, depicted wearing a garland of skulls, ripping out the insides of her victims, and sharing more tranquil family moments with her sons Ganesh and Murugan. The bloodthirsty consort of Shiva has always been popular in Bengal, the birthplace of the labourers who built the structure in 1881. The temple is at its most evocative during each of the four daily *puja* (prayer) sessions.

Sri Vadapathira Kaliamman Temple — Hindu Temple

(Map p246; 555 Serangoon Rd; 6am-noon & 4.30-9pm Sun-Thu, 6am-12.30pm & 4.30-9.30pm Fri & Sat; MFarrer Park, Boon Keng) FREE Dedicated to Kaliamman, the Destroyer of Evil, this south Indian temple began life in 1870 as a modest shrine but underwent a significant facelift in 1969 to transform it into the beauty standing today. The carvings here – particularly on the *vimana* (domed structure within the temple) – are among the best temple artwork you'll see anywhere in Singapore.

Abdul Gafoor Mosque — Mosque

(Map p246; 41 Dunlop St; MRochor, Little India) FREE Completed in 1910, the Abdul Gafoor mosque serves up a storybook fusion of Moorish, southern Indian and Victorian architectural styles. Look out for the elaborate sundial crowning its main entrance, each of its 25 rays decorated with Arabic calligraphy denoting the names of 25 prophets. The sundial is the only one of its kind in the world.

Indian Heritage Centre Museum

(Map p246; ☎6291 1601; www.indianheritage.org.sg; 5 Campbell Lane; adult/child under 7yr S$4/free; ⊙10am-7pm Tue-Thu, to 8pm Fri & Sat, to 4pm Sun; Ⓜ Little India, Rochor) Delve into the heritage of Singapore's Indian community at this showpiece museum. Divided into five themes, its hundreds of historical and cultural artefacts explore everything from early interactions between South Asia and Southeast Asia to Indian cultural traditions and the contributions of Indian Singaporeans in the development of the island nation. Among the more extraordinary objects is a 19th-century Chettinad doorway, intricately adorned with 5000 minute carvings.

Inspired by the *baoli* (Indian stepped well), the museum's architecture is equally intriguing. As night falls, the museum's translucent facade transforms into a giant tapestry of sorts, showcasing the richly coloured mural behind it.

Kampong Glam

Sultan Mosque Mosque

(Map p246; www.sultanmosque.org.sg; 3 Muscat St; ⊙10am-noon & 2-4pm Sat-Thu, 2.30-4pm Fri; Ⓜ Bugis) FREE Seemingly pulled from the pages of the *Arabian Nights*, Singapore's largest mosque is nothing short of enchanting, designed in the Saracenic style and topped by a golden dome. It was originally built in 1825 with the aid of a grant from Raffles and the East India Company, after Raffles' treaty with the Sultan of Singapore allowed the Malay leader to retain sovereignty over the area. In 1928, the original mosque was replaced by the present magnificent building, designed by an Irish architect.

Non-Muslims are asked to refrain from entering the prayer hall at any time, and all visitors are expected to be dressed appropriately (cloaks are available at the entrance). Pointing cameras at people during prayer time is never appropriate.

Malay Heritage Centre Museum

(Map p246; ☎6391 0450; www.malayheritage.org.sg; 85 Sultan Gate; adult/child under 6yr S$4/free; ⊙10am-6pm Tue-Sun; Ⓜ Bugis) The Kampong Glam area is the historic seat of Malay royalty, resident here before the arrival of Raffles, and the *istana* (palace) on this site was built for the last sultan of Singapore, Ali Iskander Shah, between 1836 and 1843. It's now a museum, its recently revamped galleries exploring Malay-Singaporean culture and history, from the early migration of traders to Kampong Glam to the development of Malay-Singaporean film, theatre, music and publishing.

Free guided tours run at 11am Tuesday to Friday, while special events include free Malay film nights under the stars – check the museum website for upcoming events.

Orchard Road

Emerald Hill Road Architecture

(Map p259; Ⓜ Somerset) Take time out from your shopping to wander up frangipani-scented Emerald Hill Rd, graced with some of Singapore's finest terrace houses. Special mentions go to No 56 (built in 1902, and one of the earliest buildings here), Nos 39 to 45 (with unusually wide frontages and a grand Chinese-style entrance gate), and Nos 120 to 130 (with art-deco features dating from around 1925). At the Orchard Rd end of the hill is a cluster of popular bars housed in fetching shophouse renovations.

Eastern Singapore

Pulau Ubin Island

(www.pulauubin.com.sg; ⛴ from Changi Village) FREE A chugging 10-minute bumboat ride from Changi Point Ferry Terminal at Changi Village lands you on the shores of Pulau Ubin. There's no timetable; boats depart when 12 people are ready to go.

Singaporeans like to wax nostalgic about Ubin's *kampong* atmosphere, and a small resort aside, it has thus far resisted the lure of cashed-up developers. It remains a rural, unkempt expanse of jungle full of fast lizards, weird shrines and cacophonic birdlife. Tin-roofed buildings bake in the sun, chickens squawk and panting dogs slump in the dust.

The best way to get around is by mountain bike (rental per day S$2 to S$10). Don't bother with the cheaper clunkers as your bum will appreciate proper suspension. Veer right from the jetty to the Pulau Ubin information kiosk, pick up a map, and sniff around the exhibition on Ubin's culture, history and wildlife.

Trundle off on your bike and see where the road takes you. For those keen on scraping their knees, there's **Ketam Mountain Bike Park**, with over a dozen trails of varying difficulty. You can also take a trip to the **Chek Jawa Wetlands** (⌚8.30am-6pm) in the island's east. A 1km coastal boardwalk takes you out to sea and loops back through the mangrove swamp, and the 20m-high **Jejawi Tower** offers stunning views of the area.

There are several places to eat near the ferry terminal – complete your island adventure with some chilli crab and Tiger beer as the Bee Gees wail shamelessly from the stereo.

For those inclined to stay on the island, you can rent a basic but pricey chalet run by the Marina Country Club. Beach camping is allowed.

Changi Museum & Chapel Museum
(☎6214 2451; www.changimuseum.sg; 1000 Upper Changi Rd N; audioguide adult/child S$8/4; ⌚9.30am-5pm, last entry 4.30pm; Ⓜ Tanah Merah, then 🚌2) FREE The Changi Museum & Chapel poignantly commemorates the WWII Allied POWs who suffered horrific treatment at the hands of the invading Japanese. The museum includes full-size replicas of the famous Changi Murals painted by POW Stanley Warren in the old POW hospital and a replica of the original Changi Chapel built by inmates as a focus for worship and as a sign of solidarity.

East Coast Park Park
This 15km stretch of seafront park is where Singaporeans come to swim, windsurf, wakeboard, kayak, picnic, bicycle, inline skate, skateboard, and, of course, eat. You'll find swaying coconut palms, patches of

Sultan Mosque

Tiong Bahru

Those with finely tuned hipster radars will most likely end up in Singapore's Tiong Bahru neighbourhood. Yet this epicentre of independent cool – where you can sip artisan coffee at **40 Hands** (www.40handscoffee.com; 78 Yong Siak St; ⌚8am-7pm Tue-Sun; Ⓜ Tiong Bahru) and browse the works of local writers at **BooksActually** (www.booksactually.com; 9 Yong Siak St; ⌚10am-8pm Tue-Sat, to 6pm Mon & Sun; Ⓜ Tiong Bahru) – is more than just its idiosyncratic boutiques, cafes and bakeries: it's also a rare heritage asset. Distinctly low-rise, the area was Singapore's first public housing estate and its streetscapes of whitewashed, 'walk-up' Moderne apartment buildings are an unexpected architectural treat.

For a taste of pre-gentrification, the **Tiong Bahru Market & Food Centre** (83 Seng Poh Rd; ⌚8am-late, individual stalls vary; Ⓜ Tiong Bahru) remains staunchly old-school, right down to its orange-hued exterior, the neighbourhood's original shade. Whet your appetite exploring the wet market, then head upstairs to the hawker centre for *shui kueh* (steamed rice cake with diced preserved radish) at **Jian Bo Shui Kueh** (stall 02-05; shui kueh from S$2; ⌚7am-9.30pm; Ⓜ Tiong Bahru) and luscious *kway teow* (fried noodles with cockles, sliced fish cake and Chinese sausage) at **Tiong Bahru Fried Kway Teow** (stall 02-11; dishes S$2-4; ⌚11am-9.30pm Fri-Tue; Ⓜ Tiong Bahru).

Kway teow

bushland, a lagoon, sea-sports clubs, and some excellent eateries.

Renting a bike from kiosks like **CycleMax** (☎6445 1147; www.facebook.com/cyclemax.sg; 01-03, 1018 East Coast Parkway; 2hr bike hire S$8; ⌚9am-9pm Mon-Fri, 9am-10pm Sat, 8am-9pm Sun; Ⓜ Bedok, then 🚌197 or 401), enjoying the sea breezes, watching the veritable city of container ships out in the strait, and capping it all off with a beachfront meal is one of the most pleasant ways to spend a Singapore afternoon.

Peranakan Terrace Houses — Architecture

(Koon Seng Rd & Joo Chiat Pl; 🚌16, 33, Ⓜ Eunos) Just off Joo Chiat Rd, these two streets feature Singapore's most extraordinary Peranakan terrace houses, joyously decorated with stucco dragons, birds, crabs and brilliantly glazed tiles. *Pintu pagar* (swinging doors) at the front of the houses are another typical feature, allowing cross breezes while retaining privacy. Those on Koon Seng Rd are located between Joo Chiat and Tembeling Rds, while those on Joo Chiat Pl run between Everitt and Mangis Rds.

Sri Senpaga Vinayagar Temple — Hindu Temple

(19 Ceylon Rd; ⌚6.15am-noon & 6.30-9pm; 🚌10, 12, 14, 32, 40) FREE Easily among the most beautiful Hindu temples in Singapore, Sri Senpaga Vinayagar's interior is adorned with wonderfully colourful devotional art, all labelled in various languages. Another feature is the temple's *kamala paatham*, a specially sculpted granite footstone found in certain ancient Hindu temples. Topping it all off, literally, is the roof of the inner *sanctum sanctorum*, lavishly covered in gold.

Katong Antique House — Museum

(☎6345 8544; 208 East Coast Rd; 🚌10, 12, 14, 32, 40) Part shop, part museum, the Katong Antique House is a labour of love for owner Peter Wee, a fourth-generation Baba Peranakan. A noted expert on Peranakan history and culture, Peter will happily regale you with tales as you browse an intriguing collection of Peranakan antiques, artefacts and other objets d'art. By appointment only, though it's sometimes open to the public (try your luck).

Northern & Central Singapore

MacRitchie Reservoir Nature Reserve

(☎1800 471 7300; www.nparks.gov.sg; Lornie Rd; ⏰7am-7pm, TreeTop Walk 9am-5pm Tue-Fri, 8.30am-5pm Sat & Sun; Ⓜ Toa Payoh, then 🚌157) MacRitchie Reservoir makes for a calming, evocative jungle escape. Walking trails skirt the water's edge and snake through the mature secondary rainforest spotted with long-tailed macaques and huge monitor lizards. You can rent kayaks at the **Paddle Lodge** (☎6258 0057; www.scf.org.sg; per hour S$15; ⏰9am-noon & 2-6pm Tue-Sun, last hire 4.30pm; Ⓜ Toa Payoh, then bus 157), but the highlight is the excellent 11km walking trail – and its various well-signposted offshoots. Aim for the **TreeTop Walk** (⏰9am-5pm Tue-Fri, 8.30am-5pm Sat & Sun), the highlight of which is traversing a 250m-long suspension bridge, perched 25m up in the forest canopy.

Trails then continue through the forest and around the reservoir, sometimes on dirt tracks, sometimes on wooden boardwalks. It takes three to four hours to complete the main circuit. From the service centre (which has changing facilities and a small cafe), near where bus 157 drops you off, start walking off to your right (anti-clockwise around the lake) and you'll soon reach the Paddle Lodge. Treetop Walk is about 3km or 4km beyond this.

Bukit Timah Nature Reserve Nature Reserve

(☎1800 471 7300; www.nparks.gov.sg; 177 Hindhede Dr; ⏰6am-7pm, visitor-centre exhibition 8.30am-5pm; 🚌67, 75, 170, 171, 173, 184, 852, 961, Ⓜ Beauty World) Singapore's steamy heart of darkness is Bukit Timah Nature Reserve, a 163-hectare tract of primary rainforest clinging to Singapore's highest peak, Bukit Timah (163m). The reserve holds more tree species than the entire North American continent, and its unbroken forest canopy shelters what remains of Singapore's native wildlife, including long-tailed macaques (monkeys), pythons and dozens of bird species. Due to major repair work, only the sealed Summit Trail was accessible when we visited, and only on weekends. Check the website for updates.

Sungei Buloh Wetland Reserve Wildlife Reserve

(☎6794 1401; www.sbwr.org.sg; 301 Neo Tiew Cres; ⏰7.30am-7pm Mon-Sat, 7am-7pm Sun; Ⓜ Kranji, then 🚌925) Sungei Buloh's 202 hectares of mangroves, mudflats, ponds and secondary rainforest are a bird-spotter's paradise, with migratory birds including egrets, sandpipers and plovers joining locals like herons, bitterns, coucals and kingfishers. The reserve is also a good spot to see monitor lizards, mudskippers, crabs and – if you're very lucky – an estuarine crocodile. Free guided tours run every Saturday at 9.30am.

The reserve is one of the few remaining mangrove areas in Singapore, and its lush, tranquil walking trails – which include a Migratory Bird Trail (1.9km) and a Coastal Trail (1.3km) – are dotted with bird-viewing huts and lookouts. Also on site is a Visitor Centre complete with cafe and mangrove exhibition gallery (open 8.30am to 5.30pm), shedding light on the reserve's wildlife and botany. To get here, catch bus 925 from Kranji MRT station and alight at Kranji Reservoir Carpark B, directly opposite the reserve's entrance on Kranji Way. On Sunday, bus 925 also stops at the reserve's other entrance on Neo Tiew Cres.

Southern & Western Singapore

Jurong Bird Park Bird Sanctuary

(www.birdpark.com.sg; 2 Jurong Hill; adult/child under 13yr S$28/18; ⏰8.30am-6pm; 👪; Ⓜ Boon Lay, then 🚌194 or 251) Home to some 600 species of feathered friends – including spectacular macaws – Jurong is a great place for young kids. Highlights include the wonderful Lory Loft forest enclosure, where you can feed colourful lories and lorikeets, and the interactive High Flyers (11am and 3pm) and Kings of the Skies (10am and 4pm). We must note, however, that some birds are made to perform for humans, which is discouraged by animal-welfare groups.

Young ones can splash about at the Birdz of Play (open 11am to 5.30pm weekdays, 9am to 5.30pm weekends), a wet and dry play area with a shop selling swimwear. There's a guided tram to cart you around the park when energy levels are low.

NUS Museum Museum

(www.nus.edu.sg/museum; University Cultural Centre, 50 Kent Ridge Cres; ⏱10am-7.30pm Tue-Sat, to 6pm Sun; MKent Ridge, then A2, the university shuttle bus) FREE Located on the verdant campus of the National University of Singapore (NUS), this museum is one of the city's lesser-known cultural delights. Ancient Chinese ceramics and bronzes, as well as archaeological fragments found in Singapore, dominate the ground-floor Lee Kong Chian Collection; one floor up, the South and Southeast Asian Gallery showcases paintings, sculpture and textiles from the region. The Ng Eng Teng Collection is dedicated to Ng Eng Teng (1934–2001), Singapore's foremost modern artist, best known for his figurative sculptures.

Lee Kong Chian Natural History Museum Museum

(http://lkcnhm.nus.edu.sg; 2 Conservatory Dr; adult/child under 13yr S$21/12; ⏱10am-7pm Tue-Sun, last entry 5.30pm; MKent Ridge, then A2 (university shuttle) What looks like a giant rock bursting with greenery is actually Singapore's high-tech, child-friendly natural-history museum. The main Biodiversity Gallery delves into the origin of life using a stimulating combo of fossils, taxidermy and interactive displays. Hard to miss are Prince, Apollonia and Twinky: three 150-million-year-old Diplodocid sauropod dinosaur skeletons, two with their original skull. Upstairs, the Heritage Gallery explores the collection's 19th-century origins, with an interesting section on Singapore's geology to boot.

Haw Par Villa Museum, Park

(6872 2780; 262 Pasir Panjang Rd; ⏱9am-7pm, Ten Courts of Hell exhibit 9am-5.45pm; MHaw Par Villa) FREE The refreshingly weird and kitsch Haw Par Villa was the brainchild of Aw Boon Haw, the creator of the medicinal salve Tiger Balm. After Aw Boon Haw built a villa here in 1937 for his beloved brother and business partner, Aw Boon Par, the siblings began building a Chinese-mythology theme park within the grounds. Top billing goes to the Ten Courts of Hell, a walk-through exhibit depicting the gruesome torments awaiting sinners in the underworld.

Gillman Barracks Gallery

(www.gillmanbarracks.com; 9 Lock Rd; ⏱11am-7pm Tue-Sat, to 6pm Sun; MLabrador Park) Built in 1936 as a British military encampment, Gillman Barracks is now a rambling art outpost, with 11 galleries scattered around verdant grounds. Among these is New York's **Sundaram Tagore** (www.sundaramtagore.com; 01-05, Gillman Barracks; ⏱11am-7pm Tue-Sat, to 6pm Sun; MLabrador Park) FREE, whose stable of artists includes award-winning photographers Edward Burtynsky and Annie Leibovitz. Also on site is the **NTU Centre for Contemporary Art** (http://ntu.ccasingapore.org; Block 43, Malan Rd; ⏱noon-7pm Tue-Thu, Sat & Sun, to 9pm Fri; MLabrador Park) FREE, a forward-thinking art-research centre hosting art talks, lectures and contemporary exhibitions from dynamic regional and international artists working in a variety of media.

To reach Gillman Barracks, catch the MRT to Labrador Park station and walk north up Alexandra Rd for 800m; the entry to Gillman Barracks is on your right. A one-way taxi fare from the CBD will set you back around S$10.

Sentosa Island

Sentosa Island charges a small entry fee, based on the form of transport you take. If you walk across from VivoCity, the fee is S$1. If you ride the frequent Sentosa Express monorail, it is S$4, which you can pay using your EZ-Link or Nets transport

Sri Veeramakaliamman Temple (p247)

card. Ride the Mt Faber Line cable car and the entrance fee is included in the price of your cable-car ticket. If arriving by taxi, the fee varies according to the time of day: the peak price is S$6 (2pm to 5pm weekdays, 7am to 5pm weekends).

Once on Sentosa, it's easy to get around, either by walking, taking the Sentosa Express (7am to midnight), riding the free 'beach tram' (shuttling the length of all three beaches, 9am to 10.30pm, to midnight Saturday) or by using the three free colour-coded bus routes that link the main attractions (7am to 10.30pm, to midnight Saturday). The island now also operates a dedicated cable car line (Sentosa Line), with stops at Siloso Point, Imbiah Lookout and Merlion.

SEA Aquarium Aquarium
(www.rwsentosa.com; Resorts World; adult/child under 13yr S$32/22; ⏲10am-7pm; Ⓜ Harbourfront, then monorail to Waterfront) You'll be gawking at over 800 species of aquatic creatures at Singapore's impressive, sprawling aquarium. The state-of-the-art complex recreates 49 aquatic habitats

> *Little India's most colourful, visually stunning temple*

found between Southeast Asia, Australia and Africa. The Open Ocean habitat is especially spectacular, its 36m-long, 8.3m-high viewing panel one of the world's largest. The complex is also home to an interactive, family-friendly exhibition exploring the history of the maritime Silk Route.

Universal Studios Amusement Park
(www.rwsentosa.com; Resorts World; adult/child under 13yr S$74/54; ⏲10am-6pm; Ⓜ Harbourfront, then monorail to Waterfront) Universal Studios is the top-drawer attraction in Resorts World. Shops, shows, restaurants, rides and roller-coasters are all neatly packaged into fantasy-world themes based on blockbuster Hollywood films. Top draws include Transformers: The Ride, a next-generation thrill ride deploying 3D animation, and Battlestar Galactica: Human vs Cylon, the world's tallest duelling roller-coasters. Opening times are subject

to slight variations at different times of the year, so always check the website before heading in.

Siloso Beach Beach

(MHarbourFront, then monorail to Beach) The most popular of Sentosa's three beaches is jam-packed with beach activities, eateries and bars.

ACTIVITIES

People's Park Complex Massage

(Map p242; 1 Park Cres; MChinatown) Heady with the scent of Tiger Balm, Singapore's oldest mall is well known for its cheap massage joints. Our favourite is **Mr Lim Foot Reflexology** (Map p242; 03-53 & 03-78 People's Park Complex, 1 Park Cres; 1hr foot reflexology S$25; 10am-11pm; MChinatown), where your robust rubdown comes with televised local and Taiwanese soaps.

Tomi Foot Reflexology Massage

(Map p259; B1-114, Lucky Plaza, 304 Orchard Rd; 30min foot reflexology S$30; 10am-10pm; MOrchard) Yes, that's Sting in the photo – even he knows about this no-frills massage joint, lurking in the basement of '70s throwback Lucky Plaza. Head in for one of the best rubdowns in town, provided by a tactile team in matching pink polos. Techniques include acupressure and shiatsu, all approved by Jesus and Mary, hanging on the wall.

Remède Spa Spa

(Map p259; 6506 6896; www.remedespasingapore.com; St Regis Hotel, 29 Tanglin Rd; 1hr massage from S$180; 9am-midnight; MOrchard) Reputed to have the best masseurs in town, the St Regis Hotel's in-house spa is also home to the award-winning Pedi:Mani:Cure Studio by renowned pedicurist Bastien Gonzalez. Remède's wet lounge – a marbled wonderland of steam room, sauna, ice fountains and spa baths – is a perfect prelude to standout treatments like the 90-minute warm jade stone massage (S$290).

COURSES

Food Playground Cooking Course

(Map p242; 9452 3669; www.foodplayground.com.sg; 24A Sago St; 3hr class from S$99; 9.30am-12.30pm Mon-Sat; MChinatown) You've been gorging on Singapore's famous food, so why not learn to make it? This fantastic hands-on cooking school explores Singapore's multicultural make-up and sees you cook up classic dishes like laksa, *nasi lemak* (coconut rice) and Hainanese chicken rice. Courses usually run for three hours and can be tailored for budding cooks with dietary restrictions.

Cookery Magic Cooking Course

(9665 6831; www.cookerymagic.com; 117 Fidelio St; 3hr classes from S$100; MEunos, then 28) Ruqxana conducts standout cooking classes in her own home. Options span numerous regional cuisines, including Chinese, Malay, Indian, Peranakan and Eurasian. She also conducts classes in a century-old *kampong* home on the bucolic island of Pulau Ubin, as well as one-hour courses (S$50) for foodies in a hurry.

TOURS

Singapore Ducktours Boat Tour

(Map p242; 6338 6877; www.ducktours.com.sg; 01-330, Suntec City Mall, Nicoll Hwy; adult/child under 13yr $37/27; 10am-6pm; MEsplanade) An informative, kid-friendly, one-hour romp in the 'Wacky Duck', a remodelled WWII amphibious Vietnamese war craft. The route traverses land and water, with a focus on Marina Bay and the Colonial District. You'll find the ticket kiosk and departure point in Tower 5 of Suntec City, directly facing the Nicoll Hwy.

Singapore River Cruise Boat Tour

(Map p242; 6336 6111; www.rivercruise.com.sg; bumboat river cruise adult/child S$25/15; MClarke Quay) Runs 40-minute bumboat tours of the Singapore River and Marina Bay. Boats depart about every 15 minutes from various locations, including Clarke

Quay, Boat Quay and Marina Bay. A cheaper option is to catch one of the company's river taxis – commuter boats running a similar route; see the website for stops. River-taxi payment is by EZ-Link transport card only.

Original Singapore Walks
Walking Tour

(☑6325 1631; www.singaporewalks.com; adult S\$35-55, child 7-12yr S\$15-30) Conducts irreverent but knowledgeable off-the-beaten-track walking tours through Chinatown, Little India, Kampong Glam, the Colonial District, Boat Quay, Haw Par Villa and war-related sites. Rain-or-shine tours last from 2½ to 3½ hours. Bookings are not necessary; check the website for departure times and locations.

🔓 SHOPPING

Bangkok and Hong Kong might upstage it on the bargain front, but when it comes to choice, few cities match Singapore. Mall-heavy, chain-centric **Orchard Rd** is Singapore's retail queen, with no shortage of department stores, luxury boutiques and High Street chains, as well as a smaller smattering of boutiques selling independent local and foreign designers.

For computers and electronics, hit specialist malls such as **Sim Lim Square** (Map p246; www.simlimsquare.com.sg; 1 Rochor Canal Rd; ⊙10.30am-9pm; MRochor). Good places for antiques include **Tanglin Shopping Centre** (Map p259; www.tanglinsc.com; 19 Tanglin Rd; ⊙10am-10pm; MOrchard), Dempsey Hill and Chinatown. For fabrics and textiles, scour Little India and Kampong Glam. Kampong Glam is also famous for its perfume traders, as well as for independent fashion boutiques (of varying quality) on pedestrianised Haji Lane. Southwest of Chinatown, Tiong Bahru delivers a handful of interesting retailers, selling everything from local literature and art tomes, to fashion accessories, homewares and records.

🚶 Walk the Southern Ridges

Made up of a series of parks and hills connecting West Coast Park to Mt Faber, the **Southern Ridges** (www.nparks.gov. sg; MPasir Panjang) will have you walking through the jungle without ever really leaving the city. While the entire route spans 9km, the best stretch is from Kent Ridge Park to Mt Faber. Not only is it relatively easy, this 4km section offers forest-canopy walkways, lofty skyline vistas, and the chance to cross the spectacular Henderson Waves, an undulating pedestrian bridge suspended 36m above the ground.

CHRISTIAN KOBER/GETTY IMAGES ©

🏛 Colonial District, the Quays & Marina Bay

Shoppes at Marina Bay Sands
Mall

(Map p242; www.marinabaysands.com; 10 Bayfront Ave; 🚇; MBayfront) From Miu Miu pumps and Prada frocks to Boggi Milano blazers, this sprawling temple of aspiration gives credit cards a thorough workout. Despite being one of Singapore's largest luxury malls, it's relatively thin on crowds – great if you're not a fan of the Orchard Rd pandemonium. The world's first floating Louis Vuitton store is also here, right on Marina Bay.

Raffles City
Mall

(Map p242; www.rafflescity.com.sg; 252 North Bridge Rd; MCity Hall) Atrium-graced

Raffles City includes a three-level branch of fashion-savvy Robinsons department store, flip-flop shop Havaianas, and a string of fashionable bag and luggage retailers, including Coach, Tumi and Kate Spade. You'll find kids' boutiques on level three. For high-end art by established and emerging Asian and Western artists, drop into **Ode to Art** (Map p242; ☑6250 1901; 01-36 Raffles City Shopping Centre, North Bridge Rd; ☺11am-9pm Sun-Thu, to 10pm Fri & Sat; Ⓜ City Hall) gallery. Hungry? Trawl the decent basement food court.

Raffles Hotel Arcade Mall

(Map p242; www.raffles.com; 328 North Bridge Rd; Ⓜ City Hall) Part of the hotel complex, Raffles Hotel Arcade is home to a handful of notable retailers. You'll find quality, afforda- ble souvenirs (the vintage hotel posters are great buys) at **Raffles Hotel Gift Shop** (www.raffleshotelgifts.com; ☺8.30am-9pm) and high-end Singaporean art from emerging talent at **Chan Hampe** (www.chanhampegal- leries.com; ☺11am-7pm Tue-Sun). And even if you can't afford its cameras, **Leica** (www. leica-store.sg; ☺10am-8pm) usually has a

free, high-quality photographic exhibition on show.

Kapok Gifts

(Map p242; ☑6339 7987; www.ka-pok.co; 01-05, National Design Centre, 111 Middle Rd; ☺shop 11am-9pm; Ⓜ Bugis) Inside the National Design Centre, Kapok showcas- es beautifully designed products from Singapore and beyond. Restyle your world with local recycled jewellery from ATGAB, artisanal fragrances from Code Deco, and wristwatches from HyperGrand. Imports include anything from seamless Italian wallets to French tees and Nordic courier bags. When you're shopped out, recharge at the on-site cafe.

🔒 Chinatown

Utterly Art Artworks

(Map p242; ☑9487 2006; www.utterlyart.com. sg; level 3, 20B Mosque St; ☺usually 2-8pm Mon- Sat, noon-5.30pm Sun; Ⓜ Chinatown) Climb the stairs to this tiny, welcoming gallery for works by contemporary Singaporean, Filipino and, on occasion, Cambodian

Shophouse on Kerbau Rd, Little India

artists. While painting is the gallery's focus, exhibitions dabble in sculpture and ceramics on occasion, with artworks priced from around S$500 (depending on the exhibition). Opening times can be a little erratic, so always call ahead if making a special trip.

Eu Yan Sang Chinese Medicine

(Map p242; www.euyansang.com.sg; 269 South Bridge Rd; shop 9am-6.30pm Mon-Sat, clinic 8.30am-6pm Mon-Fri, to 7.30pm Sat; M Chinatown) Get your *qi* back in order at Singapore's most famous and user-friendly Chinese-medicine store. Pick from traditional remedies that are said to assist with a wide range of ailments. You'll find herbal teas, soups and oils, and you can even consult a practitioner of Chinese medicine at the clinic next door (bring your passport).

Yue Hwa Chinese Products Department Store

(Map p242; www.yuehwa.com.sg; 70 Eu Tong Sen St; 11am-9pm Sun-Fri, to 10pm Sat; M Chinatown) With a deco facade paging Shanghai, this multi-level department store specialises in all things Chinese. Downstairs you'll find medicine and herbs, clothes and cushions. Head up the escalator for silks, food and tea, arts and crafts and household goods, before ending up in a large, cluttered sea of furniture.

Little India, Kampong Glam & Bugis

Sifr Aromatics Beauty

(Map p246; www.sifr.sg; 42 Arab St; 11am-8pm Mon-Sat, to 5pm Sun; M Bugis) This Zen-like perfume laboratory belongs to third-generation perfumer Johari Kazura, whose exquisite creations include the heady East (50mL S$140), a blend of oud, rose absolute, amber and neroli. The focus is on custom-made fragrances (consider calling ahead to arrange an appointment), with other heavenly offerings including affordable, high-quality body balms, scented candles, and vintage perfume bottles.

Little Shophouse Handicrafts

(Map p246; 43 Bussorah St; 10am-5pm; M Bugis) Traditional Peranakan beadwork is a dying art, but it's kept very much alive in this quaint shop and workshop. The shop's colourful slippers are designed by craftsman Robert Sng and hand-beaded by his sister, Irene. While they're not cheap (circa S$1000), each pair takes a painstaking 100 hours to complete. You'll also find Peranakan-style tea sets, crockery, vases, handbags and jewellery.

Haji Lane Fashion, Homewares

(Map p246; Haji Lane; M Bugis) Narrow, pastel Haji Lane harbours a handful of quirky, indie boutiques. Female fashion blogerati favourites include Dulcetfig, a good spot for cool local and foreign frocks and accessories, including high-end vintage bags and jewellery. Girly threads get a little indie edge at Soon Lee, while concept store Mondays Off stocks anything from contemporary local ceramics and funky cushions to art mags and geometric racks to store them on.

Tyrwhitt General Company Gifts

(Map p246; www.thegeneralco.sg; 150A Tyrwhitt Rd; noon-5pm Tue-Thu, to 7pm Fri-Sun; M Lavender) After a caffeine fix at Chye Seng Huat Hardware, duck upstairs to this shop-workshop for hip, beautifully crafted accessories, jewellery and knickknacks from Singapore and beyond. Bag anything from graphic-print ceramics and striking totes to handsome leather wallets. Check the website for upcoming workshops, usually run on Sunday afternoon and mainly focused on leather craft.

Mustafa Centre Department Store

(Map p246; www.mustafa.com.sg; 145 Syed Alwi Rd; 24hr; M Farrer Park) Little India's bustling 24-hour Mustafa Centre is a magnet for budget shoppers, most of them from the subcontinent. It's a sprawling place, selling everything from electronics and garish gold jewellery to shoes, bags, luggage and beauty products. There's also a large supermarket with a great range of Indian foodstuffs. If you can't handle crowds, avoid the place on Sunday.

Orchard Road

ION Orchard Mall Mall

(Map p259; www.ionorchard.com; 430 Orchard Rd; 10am-10pm; M Orchard) Rising directly above Orchard MRT Station, futuristic ION is the cream of Orchard Rd malls. Basement floors focus on mere-mortal high-street labels like Zara and Uniqlo, while upper-floor tenants read like the index of *Vogue*. Dining options span food-court bites to posher nosh, and the attached 56-storey tower offers a top-floor viewing gallery, **ION Sky** (Map p259; www.ionorchard.com/en/ion-sky.html; 3-6pm, last entry 5.30pm) FREE.

Ngee Ann City Mall

(Map p259; www.ngeeanncity.com.sg; 391 Orchard Rd; 10am-9.30pm; M Somerset) It might look like a forbidding mausoleum, but this marble-and-granite behemoth promises retail giddiness on its seven floors. International luxury brands compete for space with sprawling bookworm nirvana **Kinokuniya** (Map p259; www.kinokuniya.com.sg; 04-20/20B/20C, Ngee Ann City, 391 Orchard Rd; 10am-9.30pm Sun-Fri, to 10pm Sat; M Somerset) and upmarket Japanese department store **Takashimaya** (Map p259; www.takashimaya.com.sg; Ngee Ann City, 391 Orchard Rd; 10am-9.30pm; M Somerset), home to Takashimaya Food Village, one of the strip's best food courts.

Robinsons Department Store

(Map p259; www.robinsons.com.sg; 260 Orchard Rd; 10.30am-10pm; M Somerset) The flagship for Singapore's top department store offers sharp fashion edits, pairing well-known 'It' labels like Chloe, Bruno Magli and Manolo Blahnik with street-smart cognoscenti brands such as PLAC, Brownbreath and Saturdays NYC. Clothes and kicks aside, you'll find anything from Shinola Detroit leathergoods to Balmain bedlinen.

EATING

For cheap, authentic local flavours spanning Chinese, Indian, Malay and Peranakan (Malay-style sauces with Chinese ingredients), head to the city's hawker centres and foodcourts, where memorable meals cost as little as S$3. The general rule: join the longest queues. Beyond these budget staples is a booming restaurant scene, from fine-dining institutions to trendy restaurant-bar hotspots run by innovative local and expat talent. You'll find many of the latter in Chinatown.

Colonial District, the Quays & Marina Bay

Satay by the Bay Hawker $

(www.gardensbythebay.com.sg; Gardens by the Bay, 18 Marina Gardens Dr; dishes from S$4; food stalls vary, drinks stall 24hr; M Bayfront) Gardens by the Bay's own hawker centre has an enviable location, alongside Marina Bay and far from the roar of city traffic. Especially evocative at night, it's known for its satay, best devoured under open skies on the spacious wooden deck. As you'd expect, prices are a little higher than at more local hawker centres, with most dishes between S$8 and S$10.

National Kitchen by Violet Oon Peranakan $$

(Map p242; National Gallery Singapore, 1 St Andrew's Rd; S$17-35; 11am-2.30pm & 6-9.30pm; M City Hall) Chef Violet Oon is a national treasure, much loved for her faithful Peranakan (Chinese-Malay fusion) dishes – so much so that she was chosen to open her latest venture inside Singapore's showcase National Gallery. Feast on made-from-scratch beauties like sweet, spicy *kueh pie tee* (prawn- and yam-bean-stuffed pastry cups), dry laksa and fried turmeric chicken wings with *chinchalok sambal*.

True to its name, the restaurant also touches on Singapore's other culinary traditions, from Indian and Eurasian to Hainanese.

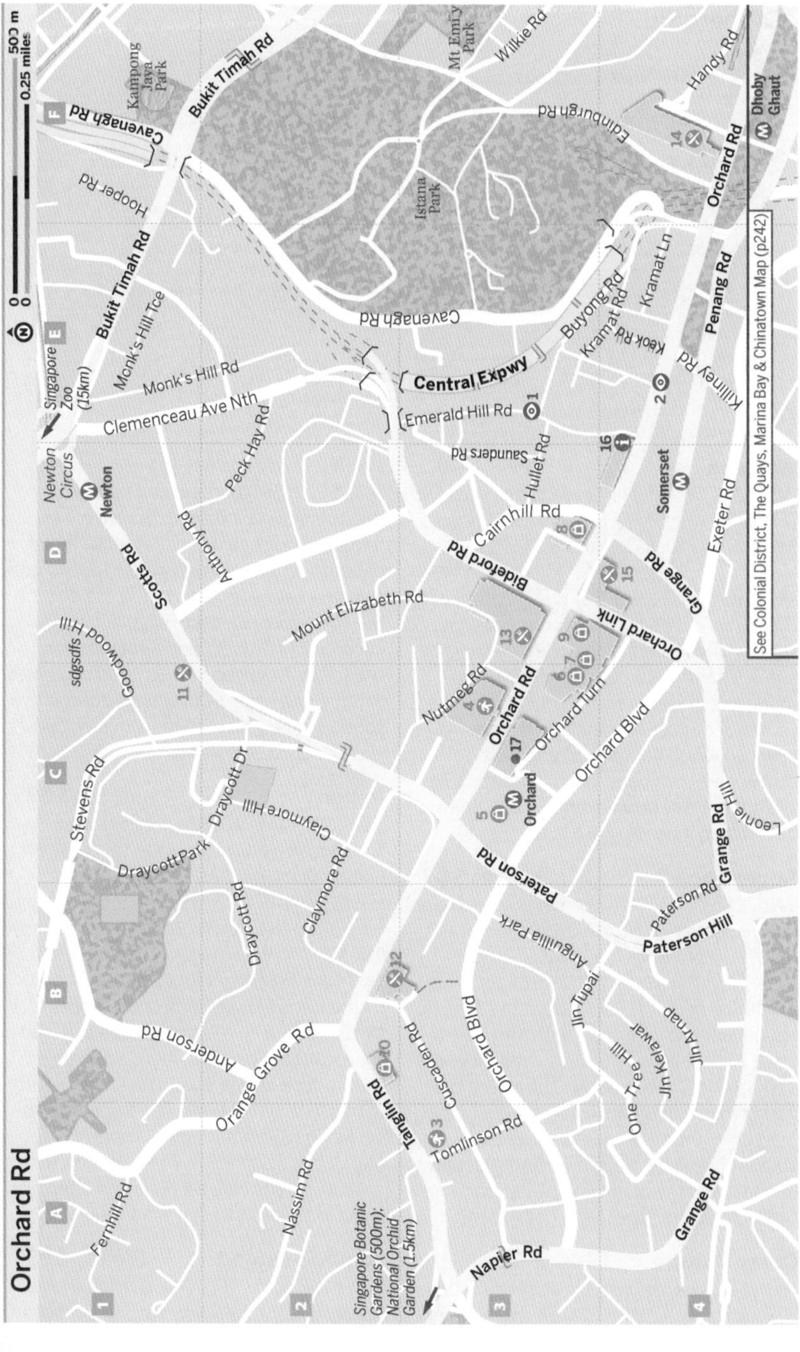
Orchard Rd
0.25 miles
500 m
Singapore Zoo (15km)
Singapore Botanic Gardens (500m); National Orchid Garden (1.5km)
See Colonial District, The Quays, Marina Bay & Chinatown Map (p242)
Newton Circus
Newton
Somerset
Orchard
Dhoby Ghaut
Kampong Java Park
Mt Emily Park
Istana Park
Bukit Timah Rd
Cavenagh Rd
Hooper Rd
Wilkie Rd
Edinburgh Rd
Handy Rd
Orchard Rd
Monk's Hill Tce
Monk's Hill Rd
Clemenceau Ave Nth
Central Expwy
Emerald Hill Rd
Buyong Rd
Kramat Rd
Kramat Ln
Keok Rd
Killiney Rd
Penang Rd
Saunders Rd
Hullet Rd
Peck Hay Rd
Anthony Rd
Scotts Rd
Cairnhill Rd
Bideford Rd
Mount Elizabeth Rd
Orchard Link
Grange Rd
Exeter Rd
Goodwood Hill
Nutmeg Rd
Orchard Turn
Orchard Blvd
Stevens Rd
Draycott Dr
Claymore Hill
Claymore Rd
Paterson Rd
Draycott Park
Draycott Rd
Anguillia Park
Paterson Hill
Leonie Hill
Anderson Rd
Orange Grove Rd
Cuscaden Rd
Tanglin Rd
Jln Tupai
One Tree Hill
Jln Kelawar
Jln Arnap
Tomlinson Rd
Nassim Rd
Fernhill Rd
Napier Rd

Orchard Rd

Wah Lok Chinese $$

(Map p242; 6311 8188; Level 2, Carlton Hotel, 76 Bras Basah Rd; dim sum S$4.80-6.90, mains S$12-36; 11.30am-2.15pm & 6.30-10.15pm Mon-Sat, 11am-2.15pm & 6.30-10.15pm Sun; ; City Hall, Bras Basah) This plush Cantonese classic serves one of Singapore's best dim-sum lunches. There's no trolley-pushing aunties here, just a dedicated yum-cha menu and gracious staff ready to take your order; must-eats include the *xiao long bao* (soup dumplings) and baked barbecued-pork buns. There are two lunch sittings per day on weekends; book three days ahead if heading in then.

Super Loco Mexican $$

(Map p242; 6235 8900; http://super-loco.com; 01-13, Robertson Quay; tacos S$9-11, quesadillas S$16-18; 5-10.30pm Mon-Fri, 10am-3.30pm & 5-10.30pm Sat & Sun; 51, 64, 123, 186) The only thing missing is a beach at this breezy hipster cantina, complete with Mexican party vibe, pink-neon Spanish and playful barkeeps in Cancún-esque shirts. Get the good times rolling with a competent frozen margarita, then lick your lips over the standout ceviche, zingy crab and avocado tostada, and the damn fine *carne asada* (grilled meat) and *pescado* (fish) tacos.

Curry Culture Indian $$

(Map p242; www.thecurryculture.com.sg; 01-10/11, 60 Robertson Quay; mains S$14-28; 5-10.30pm Mon-Thu, 12.30-2pm & 5-10.30pm Fri-Sun; ; 51, 64, 123, 186) Softly lit and semi-alfresco, this outstanding Indian restaurant offers flavour-packed, nuanced dishes like tangy *papdi chaat* (crisp dough wafers topped with spiced potato, yogurt and chutney), seductive *Hyderabadi Baingan* (eggplant, fresh coconut and peanut), and a spectacular *bhuna gosht* (spiced, slow-cooked lamb with caramelised onion). Cool things down with a soothing ginger *lassi*, made with fried curry leaf for added complexity.

Pollen European $$$

(Map p242; 6604 9988; www.pollen.com.sg; Flower Dome, Gardens by the Bay, 18 Marina Gardens Dr; mains S$32-70, 5-course dinner tasting menu S$170; restaurant noon-2.30pm & 6-9.30pm Wed-Mon, Pollen Terrace cafe 11am-9pm Mon-Thu, 9.30am-9pm Fri-Sun, afternoon tea 3-5pm; Bayfront) Right inside Gardens by the Bay's Flower Dome, posh Pollen is the Singapore spin-off of London's lauded Pollen Street Social. Its menus deliver artful, produce-driven European flavours with subtle Asian inflections. The three-course set lunch (S$50, available Wednesday to Monday) is good value, while Pollen's more casual upstairs cafe serves a fine afternoon high tea (book at least a week ahead).

Jumbo Seafood Chinese $$$

(Map p242; 6532 3435; www.jumboseafood.com.sg; 01-01/02 Riverside Point, 30 Merchant

Rd; dishes from S$12, chilli crab around S$78 per kg; ⌚noon-2.15pm & 6-11.15pm; MClarke Quay) If you're lusting after chilli crab – and you should be – this is a good place to indulge. The gravy is sweet and nutty, with just the right amount of chilli. Make sure to order some *mantou* (fried buns) to soak up the gravy. While all of Jumbo's outlets have the dish down to an art, this one has the best riverside location.

One kilo of crab (or 1.5kg if you're especially hungry) should be enough for two. Book ahead if heading in later in the week.

Chinatown & the CBD

Chinatown Complex Hawker $

(Map p242; 11 New Bridge Rd; dishes from S$3; MChinatown) Leave Smith St's revamped 'Chinatown Food Street' to the out-of-towners and join old-timers and foodies at this nearby labyrinth. The 25-minute wait for mixed claypot rice at **Lian He Ben Ji Claypot Rice** (Stall 02-198/199; dishes S$2.50-20, claypot rice from S$5; ⌚4.30-10pm Fri-Wed) is worth it, while the rich and nutty satay at **Shi Xiang Satay** (Stall 02-79; satay from S$6; ⌚3.30-9pm Fri-Wed) is insane. For a little TLC, opt for **Ten Tonic Ginseng Chicken Soup at Bonne Soup** (Stall 02-05; soups from S$3.70; ⌚10am-8pm).

Maxwell Food Centre Hawker $

(Map p242; cnr Maxwell & South Bridge Rds; dishes from S$2.50; ⌚stalls vary; ✍; MChinatown) One of Chinatown's most accessible hawker centres, Maxwell is a solid spot to savour some of the city's street-food staples. While stalls slip in and out of favour with Singapore's fickle diners, enduring favourites include **Tian Tian Hainanese Chicken Rice** (Stall 10; chicken rice from S$3.50; ⌚10am-5pm Tue-Sun) and **Rojak, Popiah & Cockle** (Stall 01-56; popiah S$2.50, rojak from S$3; ⌚noon-10.30pm).

Ding Dong Southeast Asian $$$

(Map p242; www.dingdong.com.sg; 23 Ann Siang Rd; dishes S$15-25, 'feed me' menus S$56-80; ⌚noon-3pm & 6pm-midnight Mon-Fri, 6pm-midnight Sat; MChinatown) From the graphic bar tiles to the meticulous cocktails to the wow-oh-wow modern takes on Southeast Asian flavours, it's all about attention to detail at this sucker-punch champ. Book a table and drool over zingtastic scallop ceviche with fresh coconut, sultry pork *bao* with smoked hoisin, or 48-hour beef-cheek *rendang* with wild puffed rice and crispy herbs.

Good-value options include a weekday three-course set lunch (S$25) and 'feed me' menus for indecisive gourmets.

Momma Kong's Seafood $$$

(Map p242; ☎6225 2722; www.mommakongs.com; 34 Mosque St; crab dishes S$48, set menu for two from S$107; ⌚5-10pm Mon-Fri, 11am-10pm Sat & Sun; MChinatown) Small, funky Momma Kong's is run by two young brothers and a cousin obsessed with crab. While the compact menu features numerous finger-licking, MSG-free crab classics, opt for the phenomenal chilli crab, its kick and non-gelatinous gravy unmatched in this town. One serve of crab and four giant, fresh *mantou* (Chinese bread buns) should happily feed two stomachs.

Unlike many other chilli-crab joints, you'll find fixed prices, which means no unpleasant surprises when it's payment time. Book two days ahead (three days for Friday and Saturday) or take a chance and head in late.

Burnt Ends Barbecue $$$

(Map p242; ☎6224 3933; www.burntends.com.sg; 20 Teck Lim Rd; dishes S$8-45; ⌚6-11pm Tue, 11.45am-2pm & 6-11pm Wed-Sat; MChinatown, Outram Park) The best seats at this perennial hot spot are at the counter, which offers a prime view of chef Dave Pynt and his 4-tonne, wood-fired ovens and custom grills. The affable Aussie cut his teeth under Spanish charcoal deity Victor Arguinzoniz (Asador Etxebarri), an education echoed in pulled pork shoulder in homemade brioche, and beef marmalade and pickles on char-grilled sourdough.

The produce-driven, sharing-style menu changes daily, while the drinks list showcases smaller wineries and microbreweries. Walk-ins only after 12.30pm at lunch and 6.30pm at dinner.

Chef preparing noodles in the foodcourt of Marina Bay Sands (p240)

> *For cheap, authentic local flavours head to the city's foodcourts*

Little India & Surrounds

Ananda Bhavan Indian $

(Map p246; www.anandabhavan.com; block 663, 01-10 Buffalo Rd; dosa S$2.60-4.60, set meals S$6-9; ⏰7am-10pm; 🌶; Ⓜ Little India) This super-cheap chain restaurant is a top spot to sample south Indian breakfast staples like *idly* (fermented-rice cakes) and *dosa* (thin, lentil-flour pancake; spelt 'thosai' on the menu). It also does great-value thali, some of which are served on banana leaves. Other outlets are at 58 Serangoon Rd, 95 Syed Alwi Rd and Changi Airport's Terminal 2.

Tekka Centre Hawker $

(Map p246; cnr Serangoon & Buffalo Rds; dishes S$3-10; ⏰7am-11pm; 🌶; Ⓜ Little India, Rochor) There's no shortage of subcontinental spice at this bustling hawker centre, wrapped around the sloshed guts and hacked bones of the wet market. Queue up for real-deal biryani, *dosa*, *roti prata* and *teh tarik* (pulled tea). Well worth seeking out is **Ah-Rahman Royal Prata** (Stall 01-248; murtabak S$4-8; ⏰7am-10pm, closed alternative Mon), which flips some of Singapore's finest *murtabak* (stuffed savoury pancake).

Lagnaa Barefoot Dining Indian $$

(Map p246; ☎6296 1215; www.lagnaa.com; 6 Upper Dickson Rd; dishes S$6-22; ⏰11.30am-10pm; 📶; Ⓜ Little India) You can choose your level of spice at friendly Lagnaa: level three denotes standard spiciness, level four significant spiciness, and anything above admirable bravery. Whatever level you opt for, you're in for finger-licking good homestyle cooking from both ends of Mother India, devoured at Western seating downstairs or on floor cushions upstairs. If you're indecisive, order chef Kaesavan's famous threadfin fish curry.

Kampong Glam & Surrounds

Zam Zam Malaysian $

(Map p246; 699 North Bridge Rd; murtabak from S$5, dishes S$4-20; ⏰7am-11pm; Ⓜ Bugis)

These guys have been here since 1908, so they know what they're doing. Tenure hasn't bred complacency, though – the touts still try to herd customers in off the street while frenetic chefs inside whip up delicious *murtabak*, the restaurant's speciality savoury pancakes, filled with succulent mutton, chicken, beef, venison or even sardines.

Servings are epic, so order a medium between two.

Warong Nasi Pariaman Malaysian, Indonesian $
(Map p246; ☎6292 2374; 742 North Bridge Rd; dishes from S$4.50; ⏰7.30am-2.30pm Mon-Sat; Ⓜ Bugis) This no-frills corner *nasi padang* (rice with curries) stall is the stuff of legend. Top choices include the *belado* (fried mackerel in a slow-cooked chilli, onion and vinegar sauce), delicate *rendang* beef and *ayam bakar* (grilled chicken with coconut sauce). Get here by 11am to avoid the hordes. And be warned: most of it sells out by 1pm (10am Saturday).

QS269 Food House Hawker $
(Map p246; block 269B, Queen St; ⏰stalls vary; Ⓜ Bugis) This is not so much a 'food house' as a loud, crowded undercover laneway lined with cult-status stalls. Work up a sweat with a bowl of award-winning coconut-curry noodle soup from **Ah Heng Curry Chicken Bee Hoon Mee** (Map p246; stall 01-236; dishes from S$4; ⏰8am-4.30pm Sat-Thu; Ⓜ Bugis) or join the queue at **New Rong Liang Ge Cantonese Roast Duck Boiled Soup** (Map p246; stall 01-235; dishes from S$2.50; ⏰7am-8pm; Ⓜ Bugis), with succulent roast-duck dishes that draw foodies from across the city.

Kilo Fusion $$$
(☎6467 3987; www.kilokitchen.com; 66 Kampong Bugis; sharing plates S$15-28, mains S$26-48; ⏰6-10.15pm Mon-Sat; Ⓜ Lavender) Despite Singapore's cut-throat restaurant scene, gastro geeks remain loyal to this swinging ode to fusion cooking. Expect the unexpected, from beef-tongue tacos with apple-miso slaw to goat-cheese and ricotta gnocchi in the pan with *maitake*, brown-miso butter and *shiso*. A little tricky to find, the restaurant occupies the 2nd floor of a lone industrial building on the Kallang River; take a taxi.

Bill settled, head up to level eight for cocktails at in-spot **Kilo Lounge** (⏰5.30pm-late Tue-Sat).

Afternoon Tea

It's hard to resist a long, slow, naughty session of high tea. Not only is it a civilised antidote to Singapore's high speed and higher temperatures, it's the perfect mid-afternoon recharge.

Singapore's best high tea is arguably at the plush **Landing Point** (Map p242; www.fullertonbayhotel.com; Fullerton Bay Hotel, 80 Collyer Quay; high tea per adult S$45, with glass of Champagne S$65, per child S$22; ⏰9am-midnight Sun-Thu, to 1am Fri & Sat, high tea 3-5.30pm; 📶; Ⓜ Raffles Pl). Book ahead (one day for Monday to Thursday, two weeks for Friday to Sunday), style up, and head in on an empty stomach.

Seafood and champagne rule the roost at the Westin's **Lobby Lounge** (Map p242; ☎6922 6888; www.thewestinsingapore.com/en/lobbylounge; level 32, The Westin, Asia Square Tower 2, 12 Marina View; high tea for two S$85; ⏰afternoon high tea 2.30-5pm daily; 📶; Ⓜ Downtown) good-value option. Book weekend sessions a fortnight in advance.

Orchard Road

Tim Ho Wan Dim Sum $$
(Map p259; Plaza Singapura, 68 Orchard Rd; dishes from S$3.80; ⏰10am-9.30pm Mon-Fri, 9am-9.30pm Sat & Sun; Ⓜ Dhoby Ghaut) Hong Kong's Michelin-starred dim-sum seller is steaming in Singapore, with the same Mong Kok queues (head in after 8.30pm) and tick-the-boxes order form. While nothing compares to the original (the Singapore branches need to import many

ingredients), the recipes are the same and the results still pretty spectacular. Must-trys include the sugary buns with barbecue pork and the perky prawn dumplings.

Paradise Dynasty Chinese $$

(Map p259; www.paradisegroup.com.sg; 04-12A, ION Orchard, 2 Orchard Turn; dishes S$4-25; ⌚11am-9.30pm Mon-Fri, from 10.30am Sat & Sun; Ⓜ Orchard) Preened staffers in headsets whisk you into this svelte dumpling den, passing a glassed-in kitchen where Chinese chefs stretch their noodles and steam their buns. Skip the novelty flavoured *xiao long bao* (soup dumplings) for the original version, which arguably beat those of legendary competitor Din Tai Fung. Beyond these, standouts include *la mian* (hand-pulled noodles) with buttery, braised pork belly.

Tambuah Mas Indonesian $$

(Map p259; ☎6733 2220; www.tambuahmas.com.sg; B1-44, Paragon, 290 Orchard Rd; mains S$7.50-29; ⌚11am-9.30pm; 📶; Ⓜ Orchard) Hiding shyly in a corner of the Paragon's food-packed basement, Tambuah Mas is where Indonesian expats head for a taste of home. Bright, modern and good value for Orchard Rd, it proudly makes much of what it serves from scratch, a fact evident in what could possibly be Singapore's best beef *rendang*. No reservations, so head in early if dining Thursday to Saturday.

Wild Honey Cafe $$

(Map p259; www.wildhoney.com.sg; 03-02, Mandarin Gallery, 333A Orchard Rd; dishes S$12-35; ⌚9am-9.30pm Sun-Thu, to 10.30pm Fri & Sat; 🖊; Ⓜ Somerset) Industrial-style windows, concrete floors and plush designer furniture: airy, contemporary Wild Honey serves scrumptious all-day breakfasts from around the world, from the smoked-salmon-laced Norwegian to the *shakshuka*-spiced Tunisian. Other options include muesli, gourmet sandwiches and freshly roasted coffee. Consider booking a day in advance if heading in on weekends. Second branch inside Scotts Square mall, just off Orchard Rd.

Iggy's Fusion $$$

(Map p259; ☎6732 2234; www.iggys.com.sg; level 3, Hilton Hotel, 581 Orchard Rd; 3-course

Night market

lunch S$85, set dinner menus S$195-275; ⊙noon-1.30pm & 7-9.30pm Mon, Tue & Thu-Sat; ✒; MOrchard) Iggy's dark, slinky design promises something special, and head chef Masahiro Isono delivers with his arresting, poetic takes on fusion flavours. Menus are tweaked according to season, though the knockout capellini with *sakura ebi* (shrimp), *konbu* (kelp) and shellfish oil is always on call to blow gastronomes away. Superlatives extend to the wine list, one of the city's finest.

Buona Terra Italian $$$

(Map p259; ☑6733 0209; www.scotts29.com/buonaterra; 29 Scotts Rd; 3-course set lunch S$38, 3-/4-/5-/6-course dinner S$88/108/128/148; ⊙noon-2.30pm & 6-10.15pm Mon-Fri, 6-10.15pm Sat; ☎; MNewton) This intimate, linen-lined Italian is one of Singapore's unsung glories. In the kitchen is young Lombard chef Denis Lucchi, who turns exceptional ingredients into elegant, modern dishes like Parmesan crème brûlée with truffle caviar and yellowtail carpaccio with pomegranate, blood orange and fennel. Lucchi's right-hand man is Emilian sommelier Gabriele Rizzardi, whose wine list, though expensive, is extraordinary.

If you're a gourmand on a budget, opt for the weekday set-lunch menu, which offers three courses for S$38. Book ahead if heading in on Friday or Saturday evening.

Eastern Singapore

East Coast Lagoon Food Village Hawker $

(1220 East Coast Parkway; dishes from S$3; ⊙generally 1-10pm; ☐36, 196, 197, 401) There are few hawker centres with a better location. Tramp barefoot off the beach, find a table (note the table number for when you order), then trawl the stalls for staples like satay, laksa, stingray, and the uniquely Singaporean *satay bee hoon* (rice noodles in a chilli-based peanut sauce). Cheap beer and wine (!) available.

328 Katong Laksa Peranakan $

(www.328katonglaksa.com.sg; 51/53 East Coast Rd; laksa from S$5; ⊙8am-10pm; ☐10, 14) For a bargain foodie high, hit this cult-status corner shop. The star is the namesake laksa: thin rice noodles in a light curry broth made with coconut milk and Vietnamese coriander, and topped with shrimps and cockles. Order a side of *otak-otak* (spiced mackerel cake grilled in a banana leaf) and wash it all down with a cooling glass of lime juice.

Southern Singapore

Tamarind Hill Thai $$$

(☑6278 6364; www.tamarindrestaurants.com; 30 Labrador Villa Rd; mains S$22-59, Sun brunch S$60; ⊙noon-2.30pm & 6.30-10.30pm; ☎; ☐408, MLabrador Park) In a colonial bungalow in Labrador Park, Tamarind Hill sets an elegant scene for exceptional Thai. The highlight is the Sunday brunch (noon to 3pm), which offers a buffet of beautiful cold dishes and salads, as well as the ability to order as many dishes off the à la carte menu as you like (the sautéed squid is sublime). Book ahead.

Sentosa Island

Knolls European $$$

(☑6591 5046; www.capellahotels.com/singapore; Capella, 1 The Knolls; Sun brunch from S$128, children from S$48; ⊙7am-11pm, Sun brunch 12.30-3pm; MHarbourFront, then monorail to Imbiah) Free-flow-alcohol Sunday brunch (S$148) is huge in Singapore, and this posh, secluded spot – complete with strutting peacocks and roaming band – serves one of the best. Style up and join the fabulous for scrumptious buffet bites like freshly shucked oysters, blue-cheese and pumpkin liégeois, spicy cappellini with quail egg and prawns and foie-gras brûlée. Leave room for Grand Marnier profiteroles and snow eggs.

Book one week ahead.

🍷 DRINKING & NIGHTLIFE

You'll find many of Singapore's hottest bars in Chinatown, especially on Club St and Ann Siang Rd, Duxton Hill, and up-and-coming Keong Saik Rd. Chinatown's Neil Rd is home to a handful of swinging gay venues. Other popular drinking spots include bohemian-spirited Kampong Glam, heritage-listed Emerald Hill Rd (just off Orchard Rd), leafy expat enclave Dempsey, and hyper-touristy Boat and Clarke Quays.

Colonial District, the Quays & Marina Bay

Lantern Bar

(Map p242; ☎6597 5299; Fullerton Bay Hotel, 80 Collyer Quay; ⌚8am-1am Sun-Thu, to 2am Fri & Sat; Ⓜ Raffles Pl) It may be lacking in height (it's dwarfed by the surrounding CBD buildings) and serves its drinks in plastic glasses (scandalous!), but Lantern remains a magical spot for a sophisticated evening toast. Why? There are the flickering lanterns, the shimmering, glass-sided pool (for Fullerton Bay Hotel guests only), and the romantic views over Marina Bay.

To avoid disappointment, consider booking a table two to three days ahead, especially on weekends.

Southbridge Bar

(Map p242; ☎6877 6965; level 5, 80 Boat Quay; ⌚5-11.30pm; Ⓜ Clarke Quay) Rising above the glut of mediocre Boat Quay bars, this discerning rooftop hangout delivers a panorama guaranteed to loosen jaws. Scan skyline and river with a Lust, Caution (Sichuan pepper–infused gin, Cynar, lemon and soda), or taste-test an interesting selection of spirits that include Nardini grappa and Nikka Taketsuru whisky. Entry is via the back alley, which runs off South Bridge Rd.

Zouk Club

(Map p242; www.zoukclub.com; 17 Jiak Kim St; ⌚Zouk & Phuture 11pm-late Wed, Fri & Sat, Velvet Underground 11pm-late Fri & Sat, Wine Bar 6pm-2am Tue, 6pm-3am Wed-Sat; 🚌5, 16, 75, 175, 195, 970) Set to move to Clarke Quay (at Block C, The Cannery, River Valley Rd) at the end of 2016, Singapore's premier club draws some of the world's biggest DJs. Choose between the multilevel main club, the hip-hop-centric Phuture or the plush Velvet Underground, slung with original artworks by Andy Warhol, Frank Stella and Takashi Murakami. Take a taxi, and prepare to queue.

Level 33 Microbrewery

(Map p242; www.level33.com.sg; level 33, Marina Bay Financial Tower 1, 8 Marina Blvd; ⌚noon-midnight Sun-Thu, noon-2am Fri & Sat; 📶; Ⓜ Downtown) In a country obsessed with unique selling points, this one takes the cake – no, keg. Laying claim to being the world's highest 'urban craft brewery', Level 33 brews its own lager, pale ale, stout, porter and wheat beer. It's all yours to slurp alfresco with a jaw-dropping view over Marina Bay. Bargain hunters, take note: beers are cheaper before 8pm.

Wine Connection Wine Bar

(Map p242; www.wineconnection.com.sg; 01-06 Robertson Walk, 11 Unity St; ⌚11am-2am Mon-Thu, to 3am Fri & Sat, to midnight Sun; 📶; 🚌64, 123, 143) Oenophiles love this savvy wine store and bar at Robertson Quay. The team works closely with winemakers across the world, which means no intermediary, an interesting wine list, and very palatable prices: glasses from S$7 and bottles as low as S$30. Edibles include decent salads and tartines, not to mention top-notch cheeses from Wine Connection's fabulously stinky, next-door Cheese Bar.

Ronin Cafe

(Map p242; 17 Hongkong St; ⌚8am-6pm Mon-Fri, to 7.30pm Sat & Sun; Ⓜ Clarke Quay) Ronin hides its talents behind a dark, tinted-glass door. Walk through and the brutalist combo of grey concrete, exposed plumbing and low-slung lamps might leave you expecting some tough-talking interrogation. Thankfully, the only thing you'll get slapped with is smooth Australian Genovese coffee and T2 speciality teas. Simple food options include jam and toast and gourmet panini. Cash only.

Orgo Bar

(Map p242; ☎6336 9366; www.orgo.sg; 4th fl, Esplanade Roof Tce, 8 Raffles Ave; ⌚6pm-1.30am; Ⓜ Esplanade, City Hall) It's hard not to feel like the star of a Hollywood rom-com at rooftop Orgo, its view of the skyline so commanding you'll almost feel obliged to play out a tear-jerking scene. Don't. Instead, slip into a wicker armchair, order a vino (you'll get better cocktails elsewhere) and Instagram the view to the sound of soft conversation and sultry tunes.

Chinatown & the CBD

Operation Dagger Cocktail Bar
(Map p242; operationdagger.com; 7 Ann Siang Hill; 6pm-late Tue-Sat; M Chinatown) From the 'cloud-like' light sculpture to the boundary-pushing cocktails, 'extraordinary' is the keyword here. To encourage experimentation, libations are described by flavour, not spirit, the latter shelved in uniform, apothecary-like bottles. Whether you sample the sesame-infused complexity of the Gomashio, the textural surprise of the Hot & Cold or the bar's raw-chocolate-infused vino, prepare to fall deeply in love.

Potato Head Folk Cocktail Bar
(Map p242; 6327 1939; www.pttheadfolk.com; 36 Keong Saik Rd; Studio 1939 & rooftop bar 5pm-midnight Tue-Sun; ; M Outram Park) Offshoot of the legendary Bali bar, this standout, multi-level playground incorporates three spaces, all reached via a chequered stairwell pimped with creepy storybook murals and giant glowing dolls. Skip the Three Buns burger joint and head straight for the dark, plush glamour of cocktail lounge Studio 1939 or the laidback frivolity of the rooftop tiki bar.

Tippling Club Cocktail Bar
(Map p242; 6475 2217; www.tipplingclub.com; 38 Tanjong Pagar Rd; noon-midnight Mon-Fri, 6pm-midnight Sat; M Outram Park, Tanjong Pagar) Tippling Club propels mixology to dizzying heights, with a technique and creativity that could turn a teetotaller into a born-again soak. The best seats are at the bar, where under a ceiling of hanging bottles, passionate pros turn rare and precious spirits into wonders like the Smokey Old Bastard, a mellow concoction of whisky, Peychaud's Bitters, cigar and orange.

Backstage Bar Bar, LGBT
(Map p242; www.backstagebar.moonfruit.com; 74 Neil Rd; 6pm-midnight; M Chinatown, Outram Park) Chinatown's veteran gay bar has found new life in a converted Neil Rd shophouse, complete with snug alfresco courtyard and a splash of Broadway posters. Much friendlier than neighbouring gay bar Tantric, it's a top spot to chat, flirt or just sit back and people watch. Entry is via the side alley.

Kyō Club
(Map p242; www.clubkyo.com; B2-01, Keck Seng Tower, 133 Cecil St; 9pm-3am Wed & Thu, 9pm-3.30am Fri, 10.30pm-4.30am Sat; M Telok Ayer, Raffles Pl) From boring bank to pulsating hot spot, this sprawling, Japanese-inspired playpen is home to Singapore's longest bar (expect the odd bar-top booty shake), suited eye-candy, and sharp DJs spinning credible electro, house, funk or disco. If you're itching for a little midweek hedonism, you know where to go.

Chinese Teahouses

For soothing cultural enlightenment, slip into one of Chinatown's atmospheric teahouses. Start at **Yixing Xuan Teahouse** (Map p242; www.yixingxuan-teahouse.com; 60 Tanjong Pagar Rd; 10am-9pm Mon-Sat, to 7pm Sun; M Tanjong Pagar), where reformed corporate banker Vincent Low explains everything you need to know about sampling different types of tea. Demonstrations with tastings last around 45 minutes to two hours (S$25 to S$35).

Once you know your green tea from your oolong, duck around the corner to **Tea Chapter** (Map p242; 6226 1175; www.teachapter.com; 9-11 Neil Rd; teahouse 11am-10.30pm Sun-Thu, to 11pm Fri & Sat, shop 10.30am-10.30pm daily; M Chinatown), where Queen Elizabeth dropped by for a cuppa in 1989. If you don't know the tea-making drill, the waiter will give you a brief demonstration. If you can't get enough, you'll find quality teas and tea sets for sale in the adjoining shop.

Fireworks over Marina Bay

🚇 Little India & Kampong Glam

Maison Ikkoku Cafe, Bar

(Map p246; www.maison-ikkoku.net; 20 Kandahar St; ⊙cafe 9am-10pm Mon-Thu, to midnight Fri & Sat, to 8pm Sun, bar 6pm-1am Mon-Thu, to 2am Fri-Sun; 🛜; ⓂBugis) Pimped with suspended dressers, Maison Ikkoku's cafe flies the flag for third-wave coffee, with brewing options including Chemex, siphon, cold drip, V60, AeroPress and seasonal-blend espresso. The real magic happens in the upstairs cocktail bar, where a request for something sour might land you a tart, hot combo of spicy gin, grape, lemon and Japanese-chilli threads. Not cheap but well worth it.

Chye Seng Huat Hardware Cafe

(Map p246; www.cshhcoffee.com; 150 Tyrwhitt Rd; ⊙9am-7pm Tue-Fri, to 10pm Sat & Sun; ⓂLavender) An art-deco former hardware store provides the setting and name for Singapore's coolest cafe and roastery, its third-wave offerings including on-tap Nitro Black Matter, a malty, cold-brew coffee infused with CO_2. Get your coffee geek on at one of the cupping sessions (S$25); see

www.papapalheta.com/education/classes for details.

Druggists Beer Hall

(Map p246; www.facebook.com/DruggistsSG; 119 Tyrwhitt Rd; ⊙4pm-midnight Tue-Sun; ⓂLavender) Druggists is indeed addictive for beer aficionados. Its row of 23 taps pour a rotating selection of craft brews from cognescenti brewers like Denmark's Mikkeller and Britain's Magic Rock. The week's beers are scribbled on the blackboard, with the option of 250mL or 500mL pours. Sud-friendly grub is also available, though the place is best for drinking, not eating.

A pared-back combo of trippy, vintage floor tiles, kopitiam chairs and marble-top tables, the space occupies the ground floor of the Singapore Chinese Druggists Association.

✪ ENTERTAINMENT

The city's performing arts hub is **Esplanade – Theatres on the Bay** (Map p242; ☑6828 8377; www.esplanade.com; 1 Esplanade Dr; ⊙box office noon-8.30pm; ⓂEsplanade), which also hosts regular free music performances. The venue is also home to the Singapore Symphony Orchestra. Broadway musicals take to the stage at Marina Bay Sands (p240), while independent theatre companies such as **Wild Rice** (Map p246; ☑6292 2695; www. wildrice.com.sg; 65 Kerbau Rd; MLittle India) and **Singapore Repertory Theatre** (Map p242; ☑6221 5585; www.srt.com.sg; DBS Arts Centre, 20 Merbau Rd; ᬐ64, 123, 143, MClarke Quay) perform at various smaller venues.

An enthusiastic local music scene thrives (to a point) and home-grown talent is sometimes showcased at unexpected venues, such as cafe **Artistry** (Map p246; ☑6298 2420; www.artistryspace.com; 17 Jln Pinang; ☺9am-11pm Tue-Fri, 9.30am-11pm Sat, 9.30am-4pm Sun; ☎; MBugis).

Clubs, which generally close at 3am and are strictly drug-free, often line up renowned local and visiting DJs. Most clubs have cover charges of around S$15 to S$40, often including at least one drink; women sometimes pay less (or even nothing).

Tickets to most events are available through **SISTIC** (Map p259; ☑6348 5555; www.sistic.com.sg). To see what's on, scan Singapore broadsheet *Straits Times* or click onto www.timeout.com/singapore.

Chinese Theatre Circle　　Opera

(Map p242; ☑6323 4862; www.ctcopera.com; 5 Smith St; show & snacks S$25, show & dinner S$40; ☺7-9pm Fri & Sat; MChinatown) Teahouse evenings organised by this nonprofit opera company are a wonderful, informal introduction to Chinese opera. Every Friday and Saturday at 8pm there is a brief talk on Chinese opera, followed by a 45-minute excerpt from an opera classic, performed by actors in full costume. You can also opt for a pre-show Chinese meal at 7pm. Book ahead.

Timbrè @ The Substation　　Live Music

(Map p242; www.timbre.com.sg; 45 Armenian St; ☺6pm-1am Sun-Thu, to 2am Fri & Sat; MCity Hall) Young ones are content to queue for seats at this popular live-music venue,

whose daily rotating roster features local bands and singer-songwriters playing anything from pop and rock to folk. Hungry punters can fill up on soups, salads, tapas and passable fried standbys like buffalo wings and truffle fries.

ⓘ INFORMATION

You'll also find tourist information desks in the arrivals hall of all three terminals at Changi Airport.

Singapore Visitors Centre @ ION Orchard (Map p259; level 1, ION Orchard Mall, 2 Orchard Turn; ☺10am-10pm; MOrchard) Inside ION Orchard shopping mall.

Singapore Visitors Centre @ Orchard (Map p259; ☑1800 736 2000; www.yoursingapore. com; 216 Orchard Rd; ☺9.30am-10.30pm; ☎; MSomerset) Singapore's main tourist-information centre, with brochures, customised itineraries and design-savvy souvenirs.

ⓘ GETTING THERE & AWAY

Singapore is one of Asia's major air hubs, serviced by both full-service and budget airlines. The city-state has excellent and extensive regional and international connections. You can also catch trains and buses to Malaysia and Thailand.

AIR

Changi Airport (☑6595 6868; www.changi airport.com), 20km northeast of Singapore Central Business District (CBD), has three main terminals, with a fourth terminal scheduled to open in 2017.

BUS

If you are travelling beyond Johor Bahru, the simplest option is to catch a bus straight from Singapore, though there are more options and lower fares travelling from JB.

Numerous private companies run comfortable bus services to Singapore from many destinations in Malaysia, including Melaka and Kuala Lumpur, as well as from destinations such as Hat Yai in Thailand. Many of these services terminate at the **Golden Mile Complex** (5001 Beach Rd;

MNicoll Hwy), close to Kampong Glam. You can book online at www.busonlineticket.com.

From Johor Bahru in Malaysia, Causeway Link (www.causewaylink.com.my) commuter buses run regularly to various locations in Singapore, including Newton Circus, Jurong East Bus Terminal and Kranji MRT station.

FERRY

Ferry services from Malaysia and Indonesia arrive at various ferry terminals in Singapore:

Changi Point Ferry Terminal (6545 2305; 51 Lorong Bekukong; MTanah Merah, then 2)

HarbourFront Cruise & Ferry Terminal (6513 2200; www.singaporecruise.com; MHarbourFront)

Tanah Merah Ferry Terminal (6513 2200; www.singaporecruise.com; MTanah Merah, then 35)

TRAIN

Malaysian railway system Keretapi Tanah Malayu Berhad (www.ktmb.com.my) operates commuter shuttle trains from **Woodlands Train Checkpoint** (11 Woodlands Crossing; 170, Causeway Link Express from Queen St Bus Terminal) in Singapore to JB Sentral in Johor Bahru (JB) in Malaysia.

From Singapore, shuttle trains (S$5) take five minutes to reach JB. Daily services depart at 6.30am, 8.00am, 9.30am, 5pm, 6.30pm, 8pm and 11pm. Note that shuttle services are not designed to connect with services from JB, so check transit times before travel. You can book tickets either at the station or via the KTM website (www.ktmb.com.my).

GETTING AROUND

Singapore is the easiest city in Asia to get around. For online bus information, including the useful IRIS service (which offers live next-bus departure times), see www.sbstransit.com.sg or download the 'SBS Transit iris' Smartphone app. For train information, see www.smrt.com.sg.

There's also a consolidated website at www.publictransport.sg.

BOAT

Visit the islands around Singapore from the Marina South Pier. There are regular ferry services from Changi Point Ferry Terminal to Pulau Ubin (S$2). To get there, take bus 2 from Tanah Merah MRT.

BUS

Singapore's extensive bus service is clean, efficient and regular, reaching every corner of the island. The two main operators are **SBS Transit** (1800 287 2727; www.sbstransit.com.sg) and SMRT (www.smrt.com.sg). Both offer similar services. For information and routes, check the websites.

Bus fares range from S$1 to S$2.10 (less with an EZ-Link card). When you board the bus, drop the exact money into the fare box (no change is given), or tap your EZ-Link card or Singapore Tourist Pass on the reader as you board, then again when you get off.

MASS RAPID TRANSIT (MRT)

The efficient MRT subway system is the easiest, quickest and most comfortable way to get around Singapore. The system operates from 5.30am to midnight, with trains running every two to three minutes at peak times, and every five to seven minutes off-peak. You'll find a map of the network at www.smrt.com.sg.

TAXI

Singapore taxis are fairly cheap if you're used to Sydney or London prices. Flag one on the street or find them at taxi stands. Good luck getting one on rainy days. Don't be surprised by hefty surcharges during peak hours and from midnight to 6am.

TRISHAW

There are only around 250 trishaws left in Singapore, mainly plying the tourist routes. Trishaws have banded together and are now managed in a queue-system by **Trishaw Uncle** (Map p246; www.trishawuncle.com.sg; Queen St; 30min tour adult/child from S$39/29, 45min tour S$49/39; MBugis).

You can also find freelance trishaw riders outside Raffles Hotel and outside the Chinatown Complex. Always agree on the fare beforehand: expect to pay about S$40 for half an hour, but you can haggle a little.

Where to Stay

Staying in Singapore is expensive, although hostel rooms can cost $20 a night. Newer midrange hotels are lifting the game with better facilities and good regular online deals. Luxury digs are among the world's best.

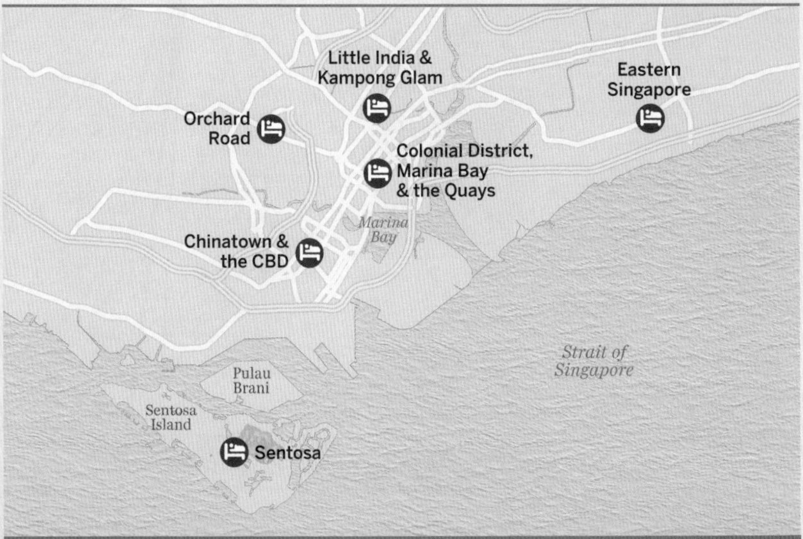

Neighbourhood	Atmosphere
Colonial District, Marina Bay & the Quays	Very central, with good transport options. Variety of accommodation, from flashpacker hostels to iconic luxury hotels, but some areas are noisy.
Chinatown & the CBD	A stone's throw from great eateries, bars and nightlife. Culturally rich, good transport links and an excellent range of accommodation, many in restored shophouses. Too touristy for some.
Little India & Kampong Glam	Singapore's largest choice of cheap accommodation. Has some lovely higher-end boutique hotels. Also has a unique atmosphere that is unlike any other district of Singapore. Fabulous food and good transport links.
Orchard Road	On the doorstep of Singapore's shopping mecca. Fine choice of quality hotels, including top-name international chains.
Eastern Singapore	Quiet (a relative concept in Singapore), close to the cooling breeze of East Coast Park, close to the airport.
Sentosa	Ideal for families, with a resort-like vibe and easy access to kid-friendly attractions, beaches and sporting activities.

SkyBridge, Panorama Langkawi (p124)

In Focus

Colourful building in Little India, Singapore (p247)

PAUL BIRIS/GETTY IMAGES ©

Malaysia & Singapore Today

Allegations of corruption have dogged Malaysia's Prime Minister Najib Razak for the last couple of years. In 2015, Singapore mourned the death of its founding father Lee Kuan Yew, then celebrated its 50th anniversary by re-electing his son as prime minister.

Najib Under Fire

In July 2015 the Wall St Journal and other media sources implicated Malaysia's Prime Minister Najib Razak in a corruption scandal involving the government's 1MBD sovereign investment fund that aims to turn Kuala Lumpur (KL) into a global financial hub. The fund has racked up huge debts at the same time as it appears that nearly US$700m had been transferred from it into Najib's personal bank accounts.

Najib claims that the transfer was a political donation from undisclosed Middle Eastern supporters. However, public opinion remains highly sceptical – particularly so after the PM sacked his deputy, who had publicly voiced his doubts about the situation, and removed the attorney general who had been conducting an investigation into the affair. That investigation was subsequently suspended. The government also blocked online access to

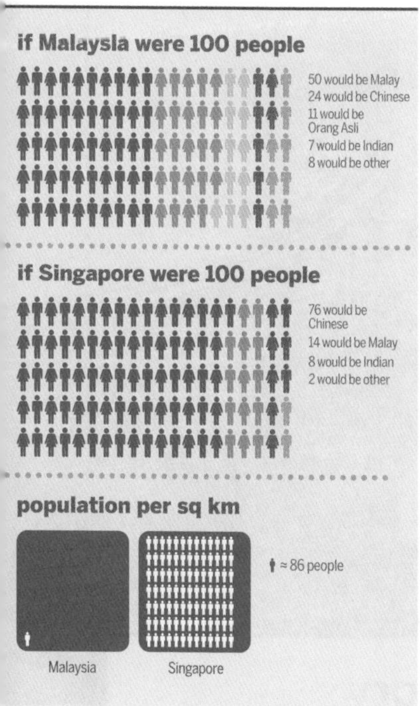
if Malaysia were 100 people
50 would be Malay
24 would be Chinese
11 would be Orang Asli
7 would be Indian
8 would be other
if Singapore were 100 people
76 would be Chinese
14 would be Malay
8 would be Indian
2 would be other
population per sq km
≈ 86 people
Malaysia
Singapore

the Sarawak Report (www.sarawakreport.org), which has covered the 1MDB scandal extensively.

Wither Malaysia's Opposition

At the end of August 2015 the Bersih movement organised a rally in KL and several other major cities across Malaysia. Bersih, which means 'clean', consists of 84 non-government organisations calling for free and fair elections in Malaysia. Their main demand at the rally was for Najib to resign, a call echoed by former PM Mohammad Mahathir who briefly joined the tens of thousands of yellow-T-shirt-clad Bersih supporters on KL's streets.

The rally passed without any major confrontations, as did a smaller 'red shirt' rally of government supporters on Malaysia Day, 16 September. Bersih supporters are painted predominantly as Chinese, while those on the ruling party side are mainly Malays, which has led to fears of any future demonstration escalating into the kind of ethnic-based riots that shook Malaysia's sense of national cohesion in 1969.

Meanwhile there has been disarray among the political opposition. In September 2015 a new coalition, Pakatan Harapan (PH), was formed; their prime ministerial candidate for the next general election (most likely to occur in 2018) is Anwar Ibrahim. However, it's unclear whether Anwar will have been released by then from jail, where he is currently serving time for sodomy, a conviction he and his supporters claim is politically motivated.

Singapore at 50

In March 2015, thousands of Singaporeans stood in pouring rain to pay their respects to Lee Kuan Yew as the funeral cortège for the country's first prime minister passed by. Not everyone was sad to see him go: when 16-year-old vlogger Amos Yee was jailed for 53 days for posting offensive comments about Lee on social media it highlighted the country's draconian record on freedom of speech and media censorship.

A few months later everyone reunited in celebration of their country's 50th birthday, proud of Singapore's ascent from a 'little red dot' with rocky prospects, to a global 'it' kid, more than punching its weight when it comes to business, the arts and urban sustainability. The wave of patriotism was one of the factors that is said to have aided the ruling People's Action Party (PAP) in winning 83 out of 89 seats and capturing almost 70% of the vote in the September 2015 general election. This was significantly up from the PAP's record low of 60.1% in 2011 and a severe blow for the opposition who for the first time had fielded candidates in all constituencies.

Khoo Kongsi (p99), George Town

History

The region's early history is hazy due of a lack of archaeological evidence and early written records. Events from the rise of the Melaka Sultanate in the 16th century, however, were well documented locally and by the nations which came to trade with, and later rule over, the peninsula and Borneo.

200
Langkasuka, one of the first Hindu-Malay kingdoms, is established on the peninsula around the area now known as Kedah.

1402
Hindu prince and pirate Parameswara (1344–1414) founds Melaka; seven years later he adopts the title Iskandar Shah.

1446
A naval force from Siam (Thailand) attacks Melaka. Such attacks encourage Melaka's rulers to develop closer relations with China.

Sarawak State Assembly (p207), Kuching

RICHARD I'ANSON/GETTY IMAGES ©

Early Trade & Empire

Traders from India and China stopped by the region from around the 1st century AD. By the 2nd century, Malaya was known as far away as Europe. From the 7th century to the 13th century, the area fell under the sway of the Buddhist Srivijaya empire, based in southern Sumatra. Under the protection of the Srivijayans, a significant Malay trading state grew up in the Bujang Valley area in the far northwest of the Thai–Malay peninsula. The growing power of the southern Thai kingdom of Ligor and the Hindu Majapahit empire of Java finally led to the demise of the Srivijayans in the 14th century.

The Melaka Empire

Parameswara, a renegade Hindu pirate prince from a little kingdom in southern Sumatra, washed up around 1401 in the tiny fishing village that would become Melaka. He

1511

Following the Portuguese conquest of Melaka, the sultan and his court flee, establishing two new sultanates: Perak and Johor.

1641

After a siege lasting several months, the Dutch take Melaka from the Portuguese. Melaka starts to decline as a major trading port.

1786

Captain Francis Light cuts a deal with the sultan of Kedah to establish a settlement on the largely uninhabited island of Penang.

immediately lobbied the Ming emperor of China for protection from the Thais in exchange for generous trade deals, and thus the Chinese came to Peninsular Malaysia.

Equidistant between India and China, Melaka developed into a major trading port. The Melaka sultans soon ruled over the greatest empire in Malaysia's history, which lasted a century, until the Portuguese turned up in 1509.

The Portuguese & the Dutch

In 1511 the Portuguese drove the sultan and his forces out of Melaka to Johor. While their rule lasted 130 years, unlike with Indian Muslim traders, the Portuguese contributed little to Malay culture. Attempts to introduce Christianity and the Portuguese language were never a big success, though a dialect of Portuguese, Cristang, is still spoken in Melaka.

In 1641 the Dutch formed an allegiance with the sultans of Johor, and ousted the Portuguese from Melaka, which fell under Dutch control for the next 150 years. Johor was made exempt from most of the tariffs and trade restrictions imposed on other vassal states of the Dutch.

Enter the East India Company

British interest in the region began with the East India Company (EIC) establishing a base on the island of Penang in 1786. Napoleon overran the Netherlands in 1795, prompting the British to take over Dutch Java and Melaka to protect their interests. When Napoleon was defeated in 1818, the British handed the Dutch colonies back.

The British lieutenant-governor of Java, Stamford Raffles, soon persuaded the EIC that a settlement south of the Malay peninsula was crucial to the India–China maritime route. In 1819 he landed in Singapore and negotiated a trade deal with Johor that saw the island ceded to Britain in perpetuity, in exchange for a significant cash tribute.

In 1824 Britain and the Netherlands signed the Anglo–Dutch Treaty, dividing the region into two distinct spheres of influence. The Dutch controlled what is now Indonesia, and the British controlled Penang, Melaka, Dinding and Singapore, which were soon combined to create the 'Straits Settlements'.

Borneo Developments

Britain did not include Borneo in the Anglo–Dutch Treaty, preferring that the EIC concentrate its efforts on consolidating their power on the peninsula. Into the breach jumped opportunistic British adventurer James Brooke. In 1841, having helped the local viceroy quell a rebellion, Brooke was installed as raja of Sarawak, with the fishing village of Kuching as his capital.

Through brutal naval force and skilful negotiation, Brooke extracted further territory from the Brunei sultan and eventually brought peace to a land where piracy, headhunting

1819
By backing the elder brother in a succession dispute in Johor, Stamford Raffles gains sole rights to build a trading base on Singapore.

1826
The British East India Company combines Melaka with Penang and Singapore to create the Straits Settlements.

1874
British start to take control of Peninsular Malaysia after the Pankor Treaty; Sir James Birch is installed as Perak's first British Resident.

and violent tribal rivalry had been the norm. The 'white raja' dynasty of the Brookes was to rule Sarawak until 1946 when the territory was ceded to the UK.

British Malaya

In Peninsular Malaya, Britain's policy of 'trade, not territory' was challenged when trade was disrupted by civil wars within the Malay sultanates of Negeri Sembilan, Selangor, Pahang and Perak. In 1874 the British started to take political control by appointing the first colonial governor of Perak and, in 1896, Perak, Selangor, Negeri Sembilan and Pahang were united under the banner of the Federated Malay States, each governed by a British resident.

Kelantan, Terengganu, Perlis and Kedah were then purchased from the Thais, in exchange for the construction of the southern Thai railway, much to the dismay of local sultans. The 'Unfederated Malay States' eventually accepted British 'advisers', though the sultan of Terengganu held out till 1919. By the eve of WWII, Malays were pushing for independence.

The Rise of Singapore

'It is impossible to conceive a place combining more advantages...it is the Navel of the Malay countries,' wrote a delighted Raffles soon after landing in Singapore in 1819. The statement proves his foresight, because at the time the island was an inhospitable swamp. Raffles returned to his post in Bencoolen, Sumatra, but left instructions on Singapore's development as a free port with the new British Resident, Colonel William Farquhar.

In 1822 Raffles returned to Singapore and governed it for one more year. He initiated a town plan that included erecting government buildings around Forbidden Hill (now Fort Canning Hill), building shipyards, churches and streets of shophouses with covered walkways, and planting a botanical garden. Raffles' blueprint also separated the population according to race, with the Europeans, Indians, Chinese and Malays living and working in their own delineated quarters.

WWII Period

A few hours before the bombing of Pearl Harbor in December 1941, Japanese forces landed on the northeast coast of Malaya. Within a few months they had taken over the entire peninsula and Singapore. The poorly defended Bornean states fell even more rapidly.

In Singapore, Europeans were slung into the infamous Changi Prison, and Chinese communists and intellectuals were targeted for Japanese brutality. Thousands were executed in a single week. In Borneo, early resistance by the Chinese was also brutally put down. The Malayan People's Anti-Japanese Army (MPAJA), comprising remnants of the British army and Chinese from the fledgling Malayan Communist Party, waged a weak, jungle-based guerrilla struggle throughout the war.

1941
The Japanese land on Malaya's northeast coast. Within a month they've taken KL, and a month later they are at Singapore's doorstep.

1946
The United Malays National Organisation (UMNO) is formed on 1 March, signalling a desire for political independence from Britain.

1957
On 31 August Merdeka (independence) is declared in Malaya; Tunku Abdul Rahman becomes the first prime minister.

★ **The Best Historical Sites**

Merdeka Square (p40)

Khoo Kongsi (p99)

Fort Margherita (p207)

National Museum of Singapore (p232)

Sultan Abdul Samad Building (p44), Merdeka Square

TOM BONAVENTURE/GETTY IMAGES ©

The Japanese surrendered to the British in Singapore in 1945. However, the easy loss of Malaya and Singapore to the Japanese had humiliated the empire and its days of controlling the region were now numbered.

Federation of Malaya

In 1946 the British persuaded the sultans to agree to the Malayan Union, which amalgamated all the Malayan peninsula states into a central authority with citizenship to all residents regardless of race. The sultans were reduced to the level of paid advisers and the system of special privileges for Malays was abandoned. Rowdy protest meetings were held throughout the country, leading to the formation of the first Malay political party, the United Malays National Organisation (UMNO). In 1948 the Federation of Malaya was created, which reinstated the sovereignty of the sultans and the special privileges of the Malays.

Merdeka & Malaysia

UMNO formed a strategic alliance with the Malayan Chinese Association (MCA) and the Malayan Indian Congress (MIC). The new Alliance Party led by Tunku Abdul Rahman won a landslide victory in the 1955 election and, on 31 August 1957, Merdeka (Independence) was declared. Sarawak, Sabah (then North Borneo) and Brunei remained under British rule.

In 1961 Tunku Abdul Rahman proposed a merger of Singapore, Malaya, Sabah, Sarawak and Brunei, which the British agreed to the following year. At the 11th hour Brunei pulled out of the deal.

When modern Malaysia was born, in July 1963, it immediately faced a diplomatic crisis. The Philippines broke off relations, claiming that Sabah was part of its territory (a claim upheld to this day), while Indonesia laid claim to the whole of Borneo, invading parts of Sabah and Sarawak before eventually giving up its claim in 1966.

Ethnic Chinese outnumbered Malays in both Malaysia and Singapore, and the new ruler of the island-state, Lee Kuan Yew, refused to extend constitutional privileges to the Malays

1963
In July the British Borneo territories of Sabah and Sarawak are combined with Singapore and Malaya to form Malaysia.

1965
In August, following refusals to extend constitutional privileges to the Malays on the island, Singapore is booted out of Malaysia.

1969
Following the general election, on 13 March race riots erupt in KL, killing hundreds.

in Singapore. Riots broke out in Singapore in 1964, and in August 1965 Tunku Abdul Rahman was forced to boot Singapore out of the federation.

Ethnic Tensions

In the 1969 general elections the Alliance Party lost its two-thirds majority in parliament. A celebration march by the opposition Democratic Action Party (DAP) and Gerakan (The People's Movement) in Kuala Lumpur led to a full-scale riot, which Malay gangs used as a pretext to loot Chinese businesses, killing hundreds of Chinese in the process.

Stunned by the savageness of the riots, the government decided that the Malay community needed to achieve economic parity for there to be harmony between the races. To this end the New Economic Policy (NEP), a socioeconomic affirmative action plan, was introduced. The Alliance Party invited opposition parties to join them and work from within, with the expanded coalition renamed the Barisan Nasional (BN; National Front).

The Emergency

While the creation of the Federation of Malaya appeased Malays, the Chinese felt betrayed, particularly after their massive contribution to the war effort. Many joined the Malayan Communist Party (MCP), and in 1948 many of their members took to the jungles and embarked on a protracted guerrilla war against the British. Even though the insurrection was on par with the Malay civil wars of the 19th century, it was classified as an 'Emergency' for insurance purposes.

The effects of the Emergency were felt most strongly in the countryside, where villages and plantation owners were repeatedly targeted by rebels. Almost 500,000 rural Chinese were forcibly resettled into protected *kampung baru* ('new villages') and the jungle-dwelling Orang Asli were brought into the fight to help the police track down the insurgents. In 1960 the Emergency was declared over, although sporadic fighting continued, and the formal surrender was signed only in 1989.

The Era of Mahathir

In the 1980s, under Prime Minister Mahathir Mohamad, Malaysia's economy went into overdrive. Multinationals were successfully wooed to set up in Malaysia, and manufactured exports began to dominate the trade figures, rather than traditional commodities such as rubber.

At the same time, the main media outlets became little more than government mouthpieces. The sultans lost their right to give final assent on legislation, and the independent judiciary appeared to become subservient to government wishes. The draconian Internal Security Act (ISA), a hangover from the Emergency, was used to silence opposition leaders and social activists.

1974
Following the formation of the Barisan Nasional (BN) in 1973, this new coalition led by Tun Abdul Razak wins the Malaysian general election.

1981
Dr Mahathir Mohamad becomes prime minister of Malaysia and introduces policies of 'Buy British Last' and 'Look East'.

1990
After more than three decades in the job, Lee Kuan Yew steps down as prime minister of Singapore, handing over to Goh Chok Tong.

Economic & Political Crisis

In 1997 Malaysia was hit by the regional currency crisis. Mahathir and his deputy prime minister and heir apparent Anwar Ibrahim disagreed on the best course of action. Their falling out was so severe that in September 1998 Anwar was sacked and soon after charged with corruption and sodomy.

Many Malaysians, feeling that Anwar had been falsely arrested, took to the streets chanting Anwar's call for '*reformasi*'. The demonstrations were harshly quelled and, in trials that were widely criticised as unfair, Anwar was sentenced to a total of 15 years' imprisonment. The international community rallied around Anwar, with Amnesty International proclaiming him a prisoner of conscience.

In the general elections the following year, BN suffered huge losses, particularly in the rural Malay areas. The gainers were the fundamentalist Islamic party, PAS (standing for Parti Islam se-Malaysia), which had vociferously supported Anwar, and a new political party, Keadilan (People's Justice Party), headed by Anwar's wife Wan Azizah.

Barisan Nasional on the Ropes

Prime Minister Mahathir's successor, Abdullah Badawi, was sworn into office in 2003 and went on to lead BN to a landslide victory in the following year's election. In stark contrast to his feisty predecessor, the pious Abdullah impressed voters by taking a nonconfrontational, consensus-seeking approach and calling time on several of the massively expensive megaprojects that had been the hallmark of the Mahathir era.

Released from jail in 2004, Anwar returned to national politics in August 2008, winning the bi-election for the seat vacated by his wife. However, sodomy charges were again laid against the politician in June and he was arrested in July.

In the March 2008 election, UMNO and its coalition partners in Barisan Nasional (BN) saw their parliamentary dominance slashed to less than the customary two-thirds majority. Pakatan Rakyat (PR), the opposition People's Alliance, led by Anwar bagged 82 of parliament's 222 seats and took control of three of Malaysia's 13 states including the key economic bases of Selangor and Penang. Abdullah Badawi resigned in favour of his urbane deputy Mohammad Najib bin Tun Abdul Razak (typically known as Najib Razak) in April 2008.

Five years later, Najib would lead BN to yet another victory in the polls, albeit with a reduced majority in parliament and less votes overall than those cast for PR coalition members. Protest rallies by opposition supporters were held before and after the election to little avail.

1998
Anwar Ibrahim is sacked, arrested, sent for trial and jailed following disagreements with Dr Mahathir.

2003
Dr Mahathir steps down as prime minister in favour of Abdullah Badawi. He remains very outspoken on national politics.

2008
BN retains power in general election but suffers heavy defeats to the opposition coalition Pakatan Rakyat (PR).

Government buildings, Putrajaya

Improved Relations

As in most divorces, relations between Singapore and Malaysia have been pretty touchy since their split in 1965 and reached a low in the 1990s. Former Malaysian prime minister Dr Mahathir and Singapore's 'Minister Mentor' Lee Kuan Yew parried insults back and forth across the Causeway, the former accusing Singaporeans of being the sort of people who 'urinate in lifts' and the latter retorting that the Malaysian town of Johor Bahru was 'notorious for shootings, muggings and car-jackings'.

Recently, however, relations have improved. Persistent squabbles over water (under a 1962 accord, Malaysia supplies Singapore with 250 million gallons of raw water daily) are becoming moot as Singapore develops alternative sources of supply. The 2011 land swap deal that ended a long-running dispute over the KTM railway line in Singapore was also heralded as a breakthrough in attitudes between the two countries.

2011
Elections in Sarawak return a BN state government but with a reduced majority; thousands rally in KL in support of fairer elections.

2013
General elections in May see BN hold on to power even though opposition parties in PR won a majority of votes overall.

2014
Malaysia suffers double blow as flight MH370 goes missing in March, and flight MH17 is shot down over Ukraine in July.

Asian Civilisations Museum (p232), Singapore

SAIKO3P/SHUTTERSTOCK ©

Multicultural Malaysia & Singapore

Although Malaysians and Singaporeans have a shared national identity, there are distinct cultural differences between the region's three main ethnic groups – Malays, Chinese and Indians. Peranakan (Straits Chinese) and scores of aboriginal tribal groups add yet another complex layer to the multicultural mix.

The Malays

All Malays who are Muslims by birth are supposed to follow Islam, but many also adhere to older spiritual beliefs and adat (Malay customary law). Adat, a Hindu tradition, places great emphasis on collective responsibility and maintaining harmony within the community.

The enduring appeal of the communal *kampung* (village) spirit cannot be underestimated. Many an urban Malay hankers after it, despite their affluent lifestyles. In principle, villagers are of equal status, though a headman is appointed on the basis of his wealth, greater experience or spiritual knowledge. Traditionally the founder of the village was appointed village leader *(penghulu* or *ketua kampung)* and often members of the same family would also become leaders. A *penghulu* is usually a haji, one who has made the pilgrimage to Mecca.

The Muslim religious leader, the imam, holds a position of great importance in the community as the keeper of Islamic knowledge and the leader of prayer, but even educated urban Malaysians periodically turn to *pawang* (shamans who possess a supernatural knowledge of harvests and nature) or *bomoh* (spiritual healers with knowledge of curative plants and the ability to harness the power of the spirit world) for advice before making any life-changing decisions.

The Peranakans

Peranakan means 'half-caste' in Malay, which is exactly what the Peranakans are: descendants of Chinese immigrants who, from the 16th century onwards, principally settled in Singapore, Melaka and Penang and married Malay women.

The culture and language of the Peranakans is a fascinating melange of Chinese and Malay traditions. The Peranakans took the name and religion of their Chinese fathers, but the customs, language and dress of their Malay mothers. They also used the terms Straits-born or Straits Chinese to distinguish themselves from later arrivals from China.

The Peranakans were often wealthy traders who could afford to indulge their passion for sumptuous belongings. Their terrace houses were brightly painted, with patterned tiles embedded in the walls for extra decoration, and heavily carved and inlaid furniture inside. Peranakan dress was similarly ornate.

The Chinese

In Malaysia, the Chinese represent the second-largest ethnic group after the Malays. In Singapore they are the largest. The Chinese immigrants are mainly, in order of largest dialect group, Hokkien, Hakka, Cantonese and Wu. They are predominantly Buddhist, but also observe Confucianism and Taoism, with a smaller number being Christian.

When Chinese people first began to arrive in the region in the early 15th century they came mostly from the southern Chinese province of Fujian and eventually formed one half of the group known as Peranakans. They developed their own distinct hybrid culture, whereas later settlers, from Guangdong and Hainan provinces, stuck more closely to the culture of their homelands, including keeping their dialects.

If there's one cultural aspect that all Chinese in the region agree on it's the importance of education. It has been a very sensitive subject among the Malaysian Chinese community since the attempt in the 1960s to phase out secondary schools where Chinese was the medium of instruction, and the introduction of government policies that favoured Malays in the early 1970s. The constraining of educational opportunities within Malaysia for the ethnic Chinese has resulted in many families working doubly hard to afford the tuition fees needed to send their offspring to private schools within the country and to overseas institutions.

The Indians

Like the Chinese settlers, Indians in the region hail from many parts of the subcontinent and have different cultures depending on their religions – mainly Hinduism, Islam, Sikhism and Christianity. Most are Tamils, originally coming from the area now known as Tamil Nadu in South India where Hindu traditions are strong. Later, Muslim Indians from northern India followed, along with Sikhs. These religious affiliations dictate many of the home life customs and practices of Malaysian Indians, although one celebration that all Hindus and much of the rest of the region takes part in is Deepaval.

A small, English-educated Indian elite has always played a prominent role in Malaysian and Singaporean society, and a significant merchant class exists. However, a large percentage of Indians remain a poor working class in both countries.

★ The Best Museums for Cultural Understanding

Asian Civilisations Museum (p232)

Islamic Arts Museum (p55)

Pinang Peranakan Mansion (p99)

Chinatown Heritage Centre (p245)

Indian Heritage Centre (p248)

Inner courtyard, Pinang Peranakan Mansion (p99)

The Orang Asli

The indigenous people of Malaysia are known collectively as Orang Asli (Original People). According to the most recent government data published in December 2004, Peninsular Malaysia had just under 150,000 Orang Asli; 80% live below the poverty line, compared with an 8.5% national average. The tribes are generally classified into three groups: the Negrito; the Senoi; and the Proto-Malays, who are subdivided into 18 tribes, the smallest being the Orang Kanak with just 87 members. There are dozens of different tribal languages and most Orang Asli follow animist beliefs, though there are attempts to convert them to Islam.

Since 1939 Orang Asli concerns have been represented and managed by a succession of government departments, the latest iteration being Jakoa (www.jakoa.gov.my), which came into being in 2011. The main goals of Jakoa are to provide protection to the Orang Asli and their way of life from exploitation by external parties and to ensure there are adequate facilities and assistance for education, health and socio-economic development.

In the past, Orang Asli land rights have often not been recognised, and when logging, agricultural or infrastructure projects require their land, their claims are generally regarded as illegal. Between 2010 and 2012 the Human Rights Commission of Malaysia (SUHAKAM; www.suhakam.org.my) conducted a national enquiry into the land rights of indigenous peoples and made various recommendations. This was followed up by a government task force to study the findings and look at implementing the recommendations. The report was presented to government in September 2014, but the government is yet to respond.

Dayaks & the People of Borneo

The term 'Dayak', first used by colonial authorities in about 1840, means upriver or interior in some local languages, human being in others. Only some of Borneo's indigenous tribes refer to themselves as Dayaks, and none of them are particularly keen on the term, but the term usefully groups together peoples who have a great deal in common.

In Sarawak, Dayaks make up about 48% of the population. About 29% of Sarawakians are Iban. Also known as Sea Dayaks for their exploits as pirates, the Iban are traditionally rice growers and longhouse dwellers. A reluctance to renounce head-hunting enhanced the Iban's ferocious reputation. The Bidayuh (8% of the population) are concentrated in the hills south and southwest of Kuching. Few Bidayuh still live in longhouses, and adjacent villages sometimes speak different dialects.

Upland groups such as the Kelabit, Kayan and Kenyah are often grouped under the term Orang Ulu ('upriver people'). There are also the Penan, originally a nomadic hunter-gatherer group living in northern Sarawak.

The state's largest ethnic group, the Kadazan-Dusun, make up 18% of the population. Mainly Roman Catholic, the Kadazan and the Dusun have a similar language and customs.

Masjid Asy-Syakirin, KLCC Park (p39)

DASHUKI MOHD/GETTY IMAGES ©

Religion

Hinduism's roots in the region long predate Islam, and the various Chinese religions are also strongly entrenched. Christianity has a presence, more so in Singapore than Peninsular Malaysia, where it has never been strong. In Malaysian Borneo many of the indigenous people have converted to Christianity, yet others still follow their animist traditions.

Islam

Islam most likely came to the region in the 14th century with South Indian traders. It absorbed rather than conquered existing beliefs, and was adopted peacefully by Malaysia's coastal trading ports. Islamic sultanates replaced Hindu kingdoms – though the Hindu concept of kings remained – and the Hindu traditions of adat continued despite Islamic law dominating.

Malay ceremonies and beliefs still exhibit pre-Islamic traditions, but most Malays are ardent Muslims – to suggest otherwise would cause great offence. With the rise of Islamic fundamentalism, the calls to introduce Islamic law and purify the practices of Islam have increased; yet, while the federal government of Malaysia is keen to espouse Muslim ideals, it is wary of religious extremism.

★ The Best Temples & Mosques

Thian Hock Keng Temple (p245)
Sultan Mosque (p248)
Kek Lok Si Temple (p109)
Sri Veeramakaliamman Temple (p247)

Roof sculpture, Thian Hock Keng Temple (p245)

Key Beliefs & Practices

All Malays are Muslim by birth and most are Sunnis. All Muslims share a common belief in the Five Pillars of Islam. The first is Shahadah (the declaration of faith): 'There is no God but Allah; Mohammed is his Prophet'. The second is salat (prayer), ideally done five times a day; the muezzin (prayer leader) calls the faithful from the minarets of every mosque. Third is akat (tax), usually taking the form of a charitable donation, and fourth, sawm (fasting), which includes observing the fasting month of Ramadan. The last pillar is ishajj (the pilgrimage to Mecca), which every Muslim aspires to do at least once in their lifetime.

Muslim dietary laws forbid alcohol, pork and all pork-based products. Restaurants where it's OK for Muslims to dine will be clearly labelled halal; this is a more strict definition than places that label themselves simply 'pork-free'.

A radical Islamic movement has not taken serious root in Malaysia, but religious conservatism has grown over recent years. For foreign visitors, the most obvious sign of this is the national obsession with propriety, which extends to newspaper polemics on female modesty and raids by the police on 'immoral' public establishments, which can include clubs and bars where Muslims may be drinking.

Chinese Religions

The Chinese in the region usually follow a mix of Buddhism, Confucianism and Taoism. Buddhism takes care of the afterlife, Confucianism looks after the political and moral aspects of life, and Taoism contributes animistic beliefs to teach people to maintain harmony with the universe. But to say that the Chinese have three religions is too simplistic a view of their traditional religious life. At the first level Chinese religion is animistic, with a belief in the innate vital energy in rocks, trees, rivers and springs. At the second level people from the distant past, both real and mythological, are worshipped as gods. Overlaid on this are popular Taoist, Mahayana Buddhist and Confucian beliefs.

On a day-to-day level most Chinese are much less concerned with the high-minded philosophies and asceticism of the Buddha, Confucius or Lao Zi than they are with the pursuit of worldly success, the appeasement of the dead and the spirits, and seeking knowledge about the future. Chinese religion incorporates elements of what Westerners might call 'superstition' – if you want your fortune told, for instance, you go to a temple. The other thing to remember is that Chinese religion is polytheistic. Apart from the Buddha, Lao Zi and Confucius, there are many divinities, such as house gods, and gods and goddesses for particular professions.

Hinduism

Hinduism in the region dates back at least 1500 years and there are Hindu influences in cultural traditions, such as *wayang kulit* (shadow-puppet theatre) and the wedding ceremony. However, it is only in the last 100 years or so, following the influx of Indian contract labourers and settlers, that it has again become widely practised.

Hinduism has three basic practices: puja (worship), the cremation of the dead, and the rules and regulations of the caste system. Although still very strong in India, the caste system was never significant in Malaysia, mainly because the labourers brought here from India were mostly from the lower classes.

Hinduism has a vast pantheon of deities, although the one omnipresent god usually has three physical representations: Brahma, the creator; Vishnu, the preserver; and Shiva, the destroyer or reproducer. All three gods are usually shown with four arms, but Brahma has the added advantage of four heads to represent his all-seeing presence.

Major Religious Festivals

The high point of the Islamic calendar is **Ramadan**, when Muslims fast from sunrise to sunset. Ramadan always occurs in the ninth month of the Muslim calendar and lasts between 29 and 30 days, based on sightings of the moon. The start of Ramadan and all other Muslim festivals is 11 days earlier every year, as dates are calculated using the lunar calendar. **Hari Raya Puasa** (also known as Hari Raya Aidilfitri) marks the end of the month-long fast, with two days of joyful celebration and feasting.

The Hindu festival of **Thaipusam**, famously involving body piercing, falls between mid-January and mid-February. Enormous crowds converge at the Batu Caves north of Kuala Lumpur, Nattukotai Chettiar Temple in Penang, and in Singapore for the celebrations.

From mid- to late August, the region's Chinese communities mark the **Festival of the Hungry Ghosts** with street performances of traditional Chinese opera.

Animism

The animist religions of Malaysia's indigenous peoples are as diverse as the peoples themselves. While animism does not have a rigid system of tenets or codified beliefs, it can be said that animists perceive natural phenomena to be animated by various spirits or deities, and a complex system of practices is used to propitiate these spirits.

Ancestor worship is also a common feature of animist societies; departed souls are considered to be intermediaries between this world and the next. Examples of elaborate burial rituals can still be found in some parts of Sarawak, where the remains of monolithic burial markers and funerary objects still dot the jungle around longhouses in the Kelabit Highlands. However, most of these are no longer maintained and they're being rapidly swallowed up by the fast-growing jungle.

In Malaysian Borneo, Dayak animism is known collectively as Kaharingan. Carvings, totems, tattoos and other objects (including, in earlier times, head-hunting skulls) are used to repel bad spirits, attract good spirits and soothe spirits that may be upset. Totems at entrances to villages and longhouses are markers for the spirits.

Woodcarving

Arts & Architecture

Malaysia and Singapore are not widely known for their arts, which is a shame, as there is much creativity here. Traditional performance arts and crafts are practised alongside contemporary art, drama and filmmaking. There's also a distinctive look to Malaysia's vernacular architecture, as well as a daring originality in modern constructions.

Literature

Tash Aw's debut novel *The Harmony Silk Factory,* set in Malaysia of the 1930s and '40s, won the 2005 Whitbread First Novel Award. Tan Twan Eng's debut novel *The Gift of Rain,* set in Penang prior to WWII, was long-listed for the Man Booker literature prize. His follow up, *The Garden of Evening Mists,* winner of the Man Asian Literary Prize in 2012, takes the reader deep into the Cameron Highlands and the 1950s era of the Emergency.

Catherine Lim's *Little Ironies* (1978) is a series of keenly observed short stories about Singaporeans from a writer who has also published five novels, poetry collections and political commentary. Singapore-born Kevin Kwan has garnered much praise for his witty satire on the lives of the island state's megarich in *Crazy Rich Asians* (2013).

Other celebrated novels by Singaporean writers include *The Shrimp People* (1991) by Rex Shelly, *Abraham's Promise* (1995) by Philip Jeyaretnam, *Heartland* (1999) by Daren Shiau, and *Ministry of Moral Panic* (2013) by Amanda Lee Koe. More are likely on the way as the National Arts Council of Singapore has beefed up its program with competitions, and events such as the Singapore Writers Festival (www.singaporewritersfestival.com).

Dance & Drama

Traditional Malay dances include *menora*, a dance-drama of Thai origin performed by an all-male cast dressed in grotesque masks, and the similar *mak yong*, in which the participants are female. These performances often take place at Puja Ketek, a Buddhist festival celebrated at temples near the Thai border in Kelantan. There's also the *rodat*, a dance from Terengganu, and the *joget* (better known in Melaka as *chakunchak*), an upbeat dance with Portuguese origins, often performed at Malay weddings by professional dancers.

When it comes to contemporary drama and dance, Singapore tends to have the edge, with theatre companies such as Necessary Stage and Singapore Repertory Theatre producing interesting work. Singapore's leading dance company, Singapore Dance Theatre, puts on performances ranging from classical ballet to contemporary dance.

Traditional Crafts

Basketry & weaving Materials include rattan, bamboo, swamp nipah grass and pandanus palms. While each ethnic group has certain distinctive patterns, hundreds or even thousands of years of trade and interaction has led to an intermixing of designs.

Batik Produced by drawing or printing a pattern on fabric with wax and then dyeing the material.

Kain songket This hand-woven fabric with gold and silver threads through the material is a speciality of Kelantan and Terengganu.

Kites & puppets *Wau bulan* (moon kites) are made from paper and bamboo, while *wayang kulit* (shadow puppets) are made from buffalo hide in the shape of characters from epic Hindu legends.

Woodcarving In Malaysian Borneo the Kenyah and Kayan peoples are skilled woodcarvers, producing hunting charms and ornate knife hilts known as *parang ilang*.

Music

Traditional Malay music is based largely on *gendang* (drums), but other percussion instruments include the gong and various tribal instruments made from seashells, coconut shells and bamboo. The Indonesian-style *gamelan* (a traditional orchestra of drums, gongs and wooden xylophones) also crops up on ceremonial occasions. The Malay *nobat* uses a mixture of percussion and wind instruments to create formal court music.

Islamic and Chinese influences are felt in the music of *dondang sayang* (Chinese-influenced romantic songs) and *hadrah* (Islamic chants, sometimes accompanied by dance and music). The Kuala Lumpur–based Dama Orchestra (www.damaorchestra.com) combines modern and traditional Chinese instruments and play songs that conjure up the mood of 1920s and 1930s Malaysia. In Singapore, catch the well-respected Singapore Chinese Orchestra, which plays not only traditional and symphonic Chinese music, but also Indian, Malay and Western pieces.

★ The Best Contemporary Architecture

Petronas Towers (p38)

Marina Bay Sands (p240)

Esplanade – Theatres on the Bay (p268)

Esplanade – Theatres on the Bay (p268)

Cinema

In the 1950s and '60s, the Malay director, actor and singer P Ramlee dominated the silver screen. His directorial debut *Penarik Becha* (The Trishaw Man; 1955) is a classic of Malay cinema. Yasmin Ahamad is considered to be the most important Malaysian filmmaker since Ramlee. Her film *Sepet* (2005), about a Chinese boy and Malay girl falling in love, cut across the country's race and language barriers, upsetting many devout Malays, as did her follow up, *Gubra* (2006), which dared to take a sympathetic approach to prostitutes. Set in Kelantan, Dain Said's action-drama *Bunohan* (2012) did well at film festivals around the world, gaining it an international release – rare for a Malaysian movie.

Singapore's film industry began to gain international attention in the 1990s with movies such as Eric Khoo's *Mee Pok Man* (1995). Khoo's films, including the animated drama *Tatsumi* (2011), have since featured in competition at Cannes. Royston Tan's *881* (2007) is a campy musical comedy about the *getai* (stage singing) aspirations of two friends. Anthony Chen's *Ilo Ilo* (2013) explores the relationship between a Singaporean family and their Filipino maid, topical given the recent tension between locals and foreign workers. The film has garnered a number of awards, including the Camera d'Or at Cannes.

Traditional Architecture

Vividly painted and handsomely proportioned, traditional wooden Malay houses are also perfectly adapted to the hot, humid conditions of the region. Built on stilts, with high, peaked roofs, they take advantage of even the slightest cooling breeze. Further ventilation is achieved by full-length windows, no internal partitions, and lattice-like grilles in the walls.

Although their numbers are dwindling, this type of house has not disappeared altogether. The best places to see examples are in the *kampung* (villages) of Peninsular Malaysia, particularly along the east coast in the states of Kelantan and Terengganu. Here you'll see that roofs are often tiled, showing a Thai and Cambodian influence. In Melaka, the Malay house has a distinctive tiled front stairway leading up to the front verandah – examples can be seen around Kampung Morten.

Few Malay-style houses have survived Singapore's rapid modernisation. Instead, the island state has some truly magnificent examples of Chinese shophouse architecture, particularly in Chinatown, Emerald Hill (off Orchard Rd) and around Katong. There are also the distinctive 'black and white' bungalows built during colonial times; find survivors lurking in the residential areas off Orchard Rd.

Hawker stall in Kota Kinabalu (p188)

KONG FOO MEE GORENG / SHANGHAI MEE GORENG /
FISHBALL MEE / SEAFOOD MEE / KEPALA IKAN MEE /
TUARAN MEE GORENG / CHASAU YUN TUN MEE / KANLAU MEE

TOM COCKREM/GETTY IMAGES ©

Food

Centuries of trade, colonisation and immigration have left their culinary mark on Malaysia and Singapore in the form of cuisines so multifaceted and intertwined it would take months of nonstop grazing to truly grasp their breadth. You'll soon understand why locals live to eat, not eat to live.

Rice & Noodles

The locals would be hard-pressed to choose between *nasi* (rice) and *mee* (noodles) – one or the other features in almost every meal. Rice is boiled in water or stock to make porridge (*congee* or *bubur*), fried with chillies and shallots for *nasi goreng,* and packed into banana-leaf-lined bamboo tubes, cooked, then sliced and doused with coconut-and-vegetable gravy for the Malay dish *lontong*. Glutinous (sticky) rice – both white and black – is also common, particularly for desserts such as *kuih* (cakes).

Rice flour, mixed with water and allowed to ferment, becomes the batter for Indian *idli,* steamed cakes to eat with *dhal* (stewed lentils), and *apam,* crispy-chewy pancakes cooked in special concave pans. Rice-flour-based dough is transformed into sweet dumplings such

★ The Best Local Restaurants

Laksa

as *onde-onde,* coconut-flake-dusted, pandanus-hued balls hiding a filling of semi-liquid *gula Melaka* (palm sugar).

Many varieties of noodle are made from rice flour, both the wide, flat *kway teow* and *mee hoon* (or *bee hoon;* rice vermicelli). *Chee cheong fun* – steamed rice flour sheets – are sliced into strips and topped with sweet brown and red chilli sauces; stubby *loh see fun* (literally 'rat-tail noodles') are stewed in a claypot with dark soy sauce.

Round yellow noodles form the basis of the Muslim Indian dish *mee mamak*. The Chinese favourite *won ton mee,* found anywhere in the region, comprises wheat-and-egg vermicelli, a clear meat broth and silky-skinned dumplings.

Meat

In Malaysia, religion often dictates a diner's choice of protein. *Haram* (forbidden) to Muslims, *babi* (pork) is the king of meats for Chinese; some hawkers even drizzle noodles with melted lard. Whether roasted till crispy-skinned *(char yoke)* or marinated and barbecued till sweetly charred *(char siew),* the meat is eaten with rice, added to noodles, and stuffed into steamed and baked buns.

Ayam (chicken) is tremendously popular in Malaysia and Singapore. Malay eateries offer a variety of chicken curries, and the meat regularly turns up on skewers, grilled and served with peanut sauce for satay. Another oft-enjoyed fowl is *itik* (duck), roasted and served over rice, simmered in star-anise-scented broth and eaten with yellow *mee,* or stewed with aromatics for a spicy Indian Muslim curry.

Tough local *daging* (beef) is best cooked long and slowly, for dishes such as coconut-milk-based rendang. Chinese-style beef noodles feature tender chunks of beef and springy meatballs in a rich, mildly spiced broth lightened with pickled mustard. Indian Muslims do amazing things with mutton; it's worth searching out *sup kambing,* stewed mutton riblets (and other parts, if you wish) in a thick soup, flavoured with loads of aromatics and chillies that's eaten with sliced white bread.

Fish & Seafood

Lengthy coastlines and abundant rivers and estuaries mean that seafood forms much of the diet for many of the region's residents. The region's wet markets devote whole sections to dried seafood, with some stalls specialising in *ikan bilis* – tiny dried anchovies that are deep-fried till crispy and incorporated into sambal or sprinkled atop noodle and rice dishes – and others displaying an array of salted dried fish.

Vegetables & Fruit

Every rice-based Malay meal includes *ulam*, a selection of fresh and blanched vegetables – wing beans, cucumbers, okra, eggplant and the fresh legume *petai* (or stink bean, so-named for its strong garlicky taste) – and fresh herbs to eat on their own or dip into sambal. Indians cook cauliflower and leafy vegetables such as cabbage, spinach and roselle (sturdy leaves with an appealing sourness) with coconut milk and turmeric. The humble *jicama* is particularly versatile: it's sliced and added raw to *rojak;* grated, steamed and rolled into *popiah* (soft spring rolls); and mashed, formed into a cake and topped with deep-fried shallots and chillies for Chinese *oh kuih*.

Tahu (soy beans) are consumed in many forms. Soy-milk lovers can indulge in the freshest of the fresh at Chinese wet markets, where a vendor selling deep-fried *crullers* (long fried-doughnut sticks) for dipping is never far away. *Dou fu* (soft fresh bean curd), eaten plain or doused with syrup, makes a great light snack. *Yong tauhu* is a healthy Hakka favourite of firm bean curd and vegetables such as okra and eggplant stuffed with ground fish paste and served with chilli sauce. Malays often cook with *tempeh*, a fermented soy bean cake with a nutty flavour, stir-frying it with *kecap manis* (sweet soy sauce), lemongrass and chillies, and stewing it with vegetables in mild coconut gravy.

Pineapples, watermelon, papaya and guava are abundant. In December, January, June and July, follow your nose to sample notoriously odoriferous love-it-or-hate-it durian. Should the king of fruits prove too repellent, consider the slightly smelly but wonderfully sweet yellow flesh of the young *nangka* (jackfruit).

Tips on Tipples

- Look out for tea wallahs toss-pouring an order of *teh tarik* ('pulled' tea) from one cup to the other.
- *Kopi* (coffee), an inky, thick brew owes its distinctive colour and flavour to the fact that its beans are roasted with sugar.
- Also try freshly squeezed or blended vegetable and fruit juices, fresh sugar-cane juice and *kelapa muda* (coconut water), drunk straight from the fruit with a straw.
- Other, more unusual drinks, include *ee bee chui* (barley boiled with water, pandanus leaf and rock sugar), *air mata kucing* (made with dried longan) and *cincau* or herbal grass jelly.
- Alcohol is pricey; for a cheap, boozy night out stick to locally brewed beers such as Tiger and Carlsberg.

Regional Cuisines

Penang is known for its Peranakan (also known as Nonya) cuisine, a fusion of Chinese, Malay and Indian ingredients and cooking techniques. This is also the home of *nasi kandar,* rice eaten with a variety of curries, a *mamak* (Indian Muslim) speciality named after the *kandar* (shoulder pole) from which ambulant vendors once suspended their pots of rice and curry.

Culinary fusion is also a theme in Melaka, the former Portuguese outpost where you'll find Cristang (a blend of Portuguese and local cooking styles) dishes such as *debal,* a fiery Eurasian stew that marries European originated red wine vinegar, Indian black-mustard seeds, Chinese soy sauce and Malay candlenuts.

The peninsular east coast is the heartland of traditional Malay cooking. Local cooks excel at making all manner of *kuih* (sweet rice cakes) and even savoury dishes have a noticeably sweet edge.

If you're looking to diverge from the local cuisine altogether, look no further than Singapore; its high-end dining scene is second to none in Southeast Asia.

Deer Cave, Gunung Mulu National Park (p209)

Environment

Home to thousands of natural species (with more being discovered all the time), Malaysia and Singapore are a dream come true for budding David Attenboroughs. Tropical flora and fauna is so abundant that this region is a 'megadiversity' hot spot. You don't need to venture deep into the jungle to see wildlife either.

Malaysia

Large parts of Peninsular Malaysia are covered by dense jungle, particularly its mountainous, thinly populated northern half, although it's dominated by palm oil and rubber plantations. On the western side of the peninsula there is a long, fertile plain running down to the sea, while on the eastern side the mountains descend more steeply, and the coast is fringed with sandy beaches.

Jungle features heavily in Malaysian Borneo, along with many large river systems, particularly in Sarawak. Mt Kinabalu (4095m) in Sabah is Malaysia's highest mountain.

Singapore

Singapore, consisting of the main, low-lying Singapore island and 63 much smaller islands within its territorial waters, is a mere 137km north of the equator. The central area is an igneous outcrop, containing most of Singapore's remaining forest and open areas. The western part of the island is a sedimentary area of low-lying hills and valleys, while the southeast is mostly flat and sandy. The undeveloped northern coast and the offshore islands are home to some mangrove forest.

Environment Trivia

- Over half of Malaysia's total of 329,758 sq km is covered by East Malaysia, which takes up 198,847 sq km of Borneo.
- Malaysia includes 877 islands. Popular isles with visitors include Penang, Langkawi and Pulau Pangkor off the west coast of the peninsula; and Pulau Tioman, Pulau Redang and Pulau Perhentian off the east coast.
- There's a disparity between government figures and those of environmental groups, but it's probable that 60% of Peninsular Malaysia's rainforests have been logged, with similar figures applying to Malaysian Borneo.
- Singapore island is 42km long and 23km wide; with the other islands, the republic has a total landmass of 714.3 sq km (and this is growing through land reclamation).

National Parks & Protected Areas

Fancy seeing what life was possibly like 100 million years ago? Trekking into the deepest parts of Malaysia's jungles will give you a clue, as they were largely unaffected by the far-reaching climatic changes brought on elsewhere by the ice age. Significant chunks of these rainforests have been made into national parks, in which all commercial activities apart from tourism are banned.

The British established the region's first national park in 1938 and it is now included in Taman Negara, the crowning glory of Malaysia's network of national parks, which crosses the state borders of Terengganu, Kelantan and Pahang. In addition to this and the 27 other national and state parks across the country (23 of them located in Malaysian Borneo), there are various government-protected reserves and sanctuaries for forests, birds, mammals and marine life.

Though little of Singapore's original wilderness is left, growing interest in ecology has seen bird sanctuaries and parkland areas created, with new parks in the Marina Bay development as well as a series of connectors that link up numerous existing parks and gardens around the island.

Mega-Diversity Areas

The wet, tropical climate of this region produces an amazing range of flora, some unique to the area, such as certain species of orchid and pitcher plants. A single hectare of rainforest (or dipterocarp forest) can support many species of tree, plus a vast diversity of other plants, including many thousands of species of orchid, fungi, fern and moss – some of them epiphytes (plants that grow on other plants).

Other important vegetation types include mangroves, which fringe coasts and estuaries and provide nurseries for fish and crustaceans; the stunted rhododendron forests of Borneo's high peaks, which also support epiphytic communities of orchids and hanging lichens (beard moss); and the *kerangas* of Sarawak, which grows on dry, sandy soil and can support many types of pitcher plant.

★ **The Best National Parks**

Taman Negara (p142)

Gunung Mulu National Park (p209)

Kinabalu National Park (p182)

Bako National Park (p208)

Rhinoceros beetle, Taman Negara (p142)

STUART WILSON/GETTY IMAGES ©

Jungle Life

The region's lush natural habitats, from steamy rainforests to tidal mangroves, teem with mammals, birds, amphibians, reptiles and insects, many of them found nowhere else on earth.

Well over 1000 species of birds and 100 species of bats can be spotted in this part of the world. The most easily recognisable species in Malaysia are the various types of hornbill, of which the rhinoceros hornbill is the flashiest. Other birds that easily catch the eye include the brightly coloured kingfishers, pitas and trogons, as well as the spectacularly named racket-tailed drongo.

Orangutans, Asia's only great apes, are at the top of many visitors' wish lists. The World Wildlife Fund (WWF) estimates that between 45,000 and 69,000 live in the dwindling forests of Borneo, a population that has declined by 50% in the last 50 years. Orangutans can be viewed at Sarawak's Semenggoh Wildlife Rehabilitation Centre and Singapore Zoo.

Wildlife Conservation

Malaysia's Wildlife Conservation Act includes fines of up to RM100,000 and long prison sentences for poaching, smuggling animals and other wildlife-related crimes. Even so, smuggling of live animals and animal parts remains a particular problem in the region. In July 2010 police looking for stolen cars also uncovered an illegal 'mini zoo' in a KL warehouse containing 20 species of protected wildlife, including a pair of rare birds of paradise worth RM1 million.

After serving 17 months of a five-year sentence, Malaysia's most notorious animal smuggler, Alvin Wong – described as 'the Pablo Escobar of wildlife trafficking' in Bryan Christy's *The Lizard King* – was allegedly back in business in 2013 according to a documentary screened by Al Jazeera that same year.

It's not just live animals that are being smuggled. Malaysia has been fingered as a transit point for illegally traded ivory on its way to other parts of Asia. In August 2015 authorities busted a syndicate in KL that claimed to be trading in tiger and other wildlife parts.

Dragon statue, Thean Hou Temple (p58)

Survival Guide

Directory A–Z

Accommodation

Malaysia and Singapore's accommodation possibilities range from rock-bottom flophouses to luxurious five-star resorts. In Malaysia, inquire about homestays with Tourism Malaysia (www.malaysia.travel) or each of the state tourism bodies. In Sarawak it's also possible to stay in longhouses, the traditional dwellings of many (but not all) of the region's indigenous people.

Costs & Payment

Budget options (denoted with a $) offer a double room with attached bathroom or a dorm bed for under RM100/S$100; midrange properties ($$) have double rooms for RM100–400/S$100–250; top end places ($$$) charge over RM400/S$250.

Where a room rate is expressed as ++ (plus, plus) it means that service of 10% and tax of 6% is added in Malaysia; in Singapore it's 10% service plus 7% tax.

Outside the peak holiday seasons (around major festivals such as Chinese New Year in January/February) big discounts are frequently available.

Credit cards are widely accepted at midrange and top-end hotels; cash payment may be expected at cheaper places.

Book Your Stay Online

For accommodation reviews by Lonely Planet authors, check out http://hotels.lonelyplanet.com/malaysia. You'll find independent reviews, as well as recommendations on the best places to stay. Best of all, you can book online.

Climate

Kuala Lumpur

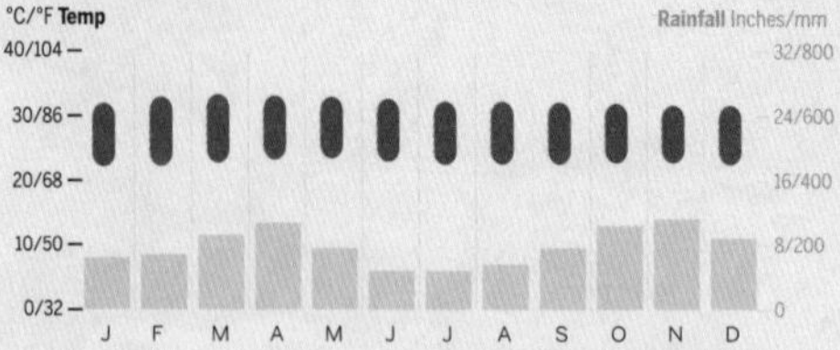

Kuching

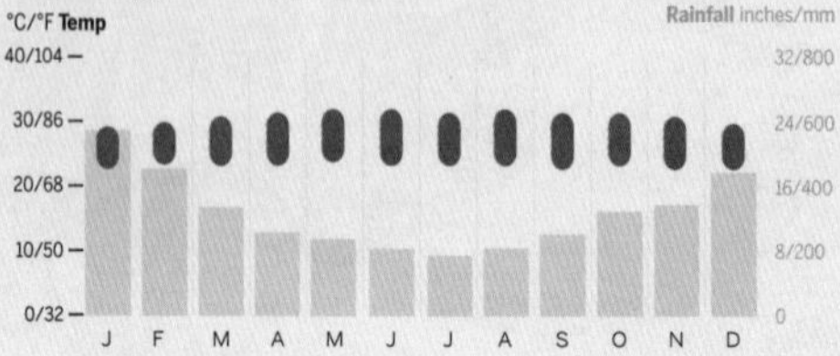

Singapore

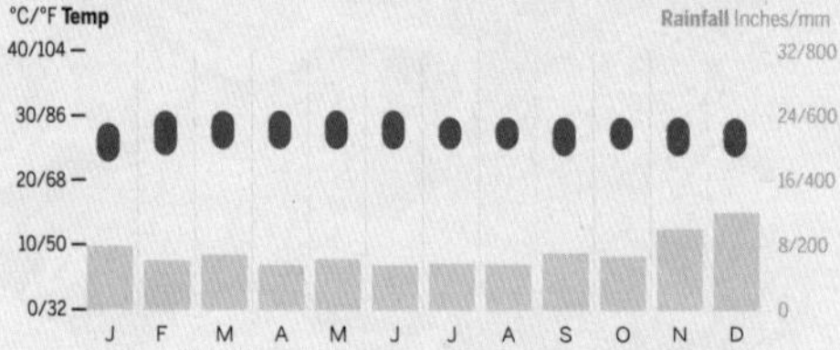

Hotels

Standard rooms at top-end hotels are often called 'superior' in the local parlance. Most hotels have slightly more expensive 'deluxe' or 'club' rooms, which tend to be larger, have a better view and include extras such as breakfast or free internet access. Many also have suites.

At the low end of the price scale are the traditional Chinese-run hotels usually offering little more than simple rooms with a bed, table and chair, and sink. The showers and toilets may be down the corridor. The main catch with these hotels is that they can sometimes be terribly noisy. They're often on main streets, and the cheapest ones often have thin walls that stop short of the ceiling – great for ventilation but terrible for acoustics and privacy.

Customs Regulations

Malaysia

The following can be brought into Malaysia duty free: 1L of alcohol, 225g of tobacco (200 cigarettes or 50 cigars), and souvenirs and gifts not exceeding RM200 (RM500 when coming from Labuan or Langkawi).

Cameras, portable radios, perfume, cosmetics and watches do not incur duty. Prohibited items include weapons (including imitations), fireworks, 'obscene and prejudicial articles' (pornography, for example, and items that may be considered inflammatory or religiously offensive) and drugs. Drug smuggling carries the death penalty in Malaysia.

Visitors can carry only RM1000 in and out of Malaysia; there's no limit on foreign currency.

Singapore

You are not allowed to bring tobacco into Singapore unless you pay duty. You will be slapped with a hefty fine if you fail to declare and pay.

You are permitted 1L each of wine, beer and spirits duty free. Alternatively, you are allowed 2L of wine and 1L of beer, or 2L of beer and 1L of wine. You need to have been out of Singapore for more than 48 hours and to anywhere but Malaysia.

It's illegal to bring chewing gum, firecrackers, obscene or seditious material, gun-shaped cigarette lighters, endangered species or their by-products and pirated recordings or publications with you.

Electricity

250V/50Hz

Food

In our listings, the following price ranges refer to the all-inclusive price of a single dish or main course:

$ less than RM15/S$10

$$ RM15–60/S$10–30

$$$ more than RM60/S$30

Bear in mind that most restaurant prices in Malaysia will have a 6% government sales tax (GST) added. In Singapore the extra cost can add up to 17% (including a 10% service charge, plus 7% for GST). You'll see this indicated by ++ on menus.

Health

In Malaysia the standard of medical care in the major centres is good, and most problems can be adequately dealt with in Kuala Lumpur.

Singapore has excellent medical facilities. Note that you cannot buy medication over the counter without a doctor's prescription.

Before You Go

- Take out health insurance.
- Pack medications in their original, clearly labelled containers.
- Carry a signed and dated letter from your physician describing your medical conditions and medications,

Drinking Water

- Never drink tap water unless you've verified that it's safe (many parts of Malaysia, Singapore and Brunei have modern treatment plants).
- Bottled water is generally safe – check the seal is intact at purchase.
- Avoid ice in places that look dubious.
- Avoid fruit juices if they have not been freshly squeezed or you suspect they may have been watered down.
- Boiling water is the most efficient method of purification.
- The best chemical purifier is iodine. It should not be used by pregnant women or those with thyroid problems.
- Water filters should also filter out viruses. Ensure your filter has a chemical barrier such as iodine and a small pore size (less than 4 microns).

including their generic names.

- If you have a heart condition bring a copy of your ECG taken just prior to travelling.
- Bring a double supply of any regular medication in case of loss or theft.

Recommended Vaccinations

Proof of yellow fever vaccination will be required if you have visited a country in the yellow-fever zone (such as Africa or South America) within the six days prior to entering the region. Otherwise the World Health Organization (WHO) recommends the following vaccinations:

Adult diphtheria & tetanus Single booster recommended if none have been had in the previous 10 years.

Hepatitis A Provides almost 100% protection for up to a year. A booster after 12 months provides at least another 20 years' protection.

Hepatitis B Now considered routine for most travellers. Given as three shots over six months. A rapid schedule is also available, as is a combined vaccination with Hepatitis A.

Measles, mumps & rubella (MMR) Two doses of MMR are required unless you have had the diseases. Many young adults require a booster.

Polio There have been no reported cases of polio in recent years. Only one booster is required as an adult for lifetime protection.

Typhoid Recommended unless your trip is less than a week and is only to developed cities. The vaccine offers around 70% protection, lasts for two to three years and comes as a single shot. Tablets are also available, but the injection is usually recommended as it has fewer side effects.

Varicella If you haven't had chickenpox, discuss this vaccination with your doctor.

Infectious Diseases

The following are the most common for travellers:

Dengue fever Increasingly common in cities. The mosquito that carries dengue bites day and night, so use insect avoidance measures at all times. Symptoms can include high fever, severe headache, body ache, a rash and diarrhoea. There is no specific treatment, just rest and paracetamol – do not take aspirin as it increases the likelihood of haemorrhaging.

Hepatitis A This food- and water-borne virus infects the liver, causing jaundice (yellow skin and eyes), nausea and lethargy. All travellers to the region should be vaccinated against it.

Hepatitis B The only sexually transmitted disease (STD) that can be prevented by vaccination, hepatitis B is spread by body fluids, including sexual contact.

Hepatitis E Transmitted through contaminated food and water and has similar symptoms to hepatitis A, but it is far less common. It is a severe problem in pregnant women and can result in the death of both mother and baby. There is currently no vaccine, and prevention is by following safe eating and drinking guidelines.

HIV Unprotected sex is the main method of transmission.

Influenza Can be very severe in people over the age of 65 or in those with underlying medical conditions such as heart disease or diabetes; vaccination is recommended for these individuals. There is no specific treatment, just rest and paracetamol.

Malaria Uncommon in the region and antimalarial drugs are rarely recommended for travellers. However, there may be a small risk in rural areas. Remember that malaria can be fatal. Before you travel, seek medical advice on the right medication and dosage for you.

Rabies A potential risk, and invariably fatal if untreated, rabies is spread by the bite or lick of an infected animal – most commonly a dog or monkey. Pre-travel vaccination means the post-bite treatment is greatly simplified. If an animal bites you, gently wash the wound with soap and water, and apply iodine-based antiseptic. If you are not pre-vaccinated you will need to receive rabies immunoglobulin as soon as possible.

Typhoid This serious bacterial infection is spread via food and water. Symptoms include high and slowly progressive fever, headache, a dry cough and stomach pain. Vaccination, recommended for all travellers spending more than a week in Malaysia, is not 100% effective so you must still be careful with what you eat and drink.

Traveller's diarrhoea Commonly caused by a bacteria, diarrhoea is by far the most common problem affecting travellers. Treat by staying well hydrated, using a solution such as Gastrolyte. Antibiotics such as Norfloxacin, Ciprofloxacin or Azithromycin will kill the bacteria quickly. Loperamide is just a 'stopper', but it can be helpful in certain situations, such as if you have to go on a long bus ride. Seek medical attention quickly if you do not respond to an appropriate antibiotic. **Giardiasis** is also relatively common. Symptoms include nausea, bloating, excess gas, fatigue and intermittent diarrhoea. The treatment of choice is Tinidazole, with Metroniadzole being a second option.

Environmental Hazards

Air pollution If you have severe respiratory problems, speak with your doctor before travelling to any heavily polluted urban centres. If troubled by the pollution, leave the city for a few days to get some fresh air. Consult the Air Polutant Index of Malaysia (http://apims.doe.gov.my/v2) for the current situation across the region.

Diving & surfing If planning on diving or surfing, seek specialised advice before you travel to ensure your medical kit also contains treatment for coral cuts and tropical ear infections. Have a dive medical before you leave your home country – there are certain medical conditions that are incompatible with diving. Hyperbaric chambers are located in Kuantan and Lumut on Peninsular Malaysia, Labuan on Malaysian Borneo, and in Singapore.

Heat It can take up to two weeks to adapt to the region's hot climate. Swelling of the feet and ankles is common, as are muscle cramps caused by excessive sweating. Prevent these by avoiding dehydration and excessive activity in the heat. Prickly heat – an itchy rash of tiny lumps – is caused by sweat being trapped under the skin. Treat it by moving out of the heat and into an air-conditioned area for a few hours and by having cool showers. Avoid creams and ointments as they clog the skin.

Skin problems There are two common fungal rashes that affect travellers in the Tropics. The first occurs in moist areas that get less air, such as the groin, armpits and between the toes. It starts as a red patch that slowly spreads and is usually itchy. Treatment involves keeping the skin dry, avoiding chafing and using an antifungal cream such as Clotrimazole or Lamisil. Tinea versicolour is also common – this fungus causes small, light-coloured patches, most commonly on the back, chest and shoulders. Consult a doctor. Take meticulous care of any cuts and scratches to prevent infection. Immediately wash all wounds in clean water and apply antiseptic. If you develop signs

Further Resources

Consult your government's travel-health website, if one is available, before departure:

Australia (http://smartraveller.gov.au)

Canada (www.phac-aspc.gc.ca)

New Zealand (www.safetravel.govt.nz)

UK (www.gov.uk/foreign-travel-advice)

USA (wwwnc.cdc.gov/travel)

of infection (increasing pain and redness), see a doctor. Divers and surfers should be particularly careful with coral cuts.

Snakes Assume all snakes are poisonous. Always wear boots and long pants if walking in an area that may have snakes. First aid in the event of a snake bite involves pressure immobilisation via an elastic bandage firmly wrapped around the affected limb, starting at the bite site and working up towards the chest. The bandage should not be so tight that the circulation is cut off; the fingers or toes should be kept free so the circulation can be checked. Immobilise the limb with a splint and carry the victim to medical attention. Don't use tourniquets or try to suck out the venom. Antivenin is available for most species.

Sunburn Even on a cloudy day, sunburn can occur rapidly. Always use a strong sunscreen (at least SPF 30), making sure to reapply after a swim, and always wear a wide-brimmed hat and sunglasses outdoors. Avoid lying in the sun during the hottest part of the day (10am to 2pm). If you're sunburnt, stay out of the sun until you've recovered, apply cool compresses and take painkillers for the discomfort. Applied twice daily, 1% hydrocortisone cream is also helpful.

Travelling With Children

There are specific health issues you should consider before travelling with your child:

- All routine vaccinations should be up to date, as many of the common childhood diseases that have been eliminated in the West are still present in parts of Southeast Asia. A travel-health clinic can advise on specific vaccines, but think seriously about rabies vaccination if you're visiting rural areas or travelling for more than a month, as children are more vulnerable to severe animal bites.
- Children are more prone to getting serious forms of mosquito-borne diseases such as malaria, Japanese B encephalitis and dengue fever. In particular, malaria is very serious in children and can rapidly lead to death – you should think seriously before taking your child into a malaria-risk area. Permethrin-impregnated clothing is safe to use, and insect repellents should contain between 10% and 20% DEET.
- Diarrhoea can cause rapid dehydration and you should pay particular attention to keeping your child well hydrated. The best antibiotic for children with diarrhoea is Azithromycin.
- Children can get very sick, very quickly, so locate good medical facilities at your destination and make contact if you are worried – it's always better to get a medical opinion than to try to treat your own children.

Insect Bites & Stings

Bedbugs Live in the cracks of furniture and walls and migrate to the bed at night to feed on you; they are a particular problem in cheapter hotels in the region. Treat the itch with antihistamines.

Lice Most commonly inhabit your head and pubic area. Transmission is via close contact with an infected person. Treat with numerous applications of an anti-lice shampoo such as Permethrin.

Ticks Contracted after walking in rural areas. If you are bitten and experience symptoms – such as a rash at the site of the bite or elsewhere, fever or muscle aches – see a doctor. Doxycycline prevents tick-borne diseases.

Leeches Found in humid rainforest areas. Don't transmit any disease, but their bites can be itchy for weeks afterwards and can easily become infected. Apply an iodine-based antiseptic to any leech bite to help prevent infection.

Bees or wasps If allergic to their stings, carry an injection of adrenaline (eg an Epipen) for emergency treatment.

Jellyfish Most are not dangerous. If stung, pour vinegar onto the affected area to neutralise the poison. Take painkillers, and seek medical advice if your condition worsens.

Women's Health

- In urban areas, supplies of sanitary products are readily available. Birth-control options may be limited so bring adequate supplies of your own form of contraception.
- Heat, humidity and antibiotics can all contribute to thrush. Treatment is with antifungal creams and pessaries such as clotrimazole. A practical alternative is a single tablet of Fluconazole (Diflucan).
- Urinary-tract infections can be precipitated by dehydration or long bus journeys without toilet stops; bring suitable antibiotics.

Pregnant travellers should consider the following advice:

- Find out about quality medical facilities at your destination and ensure you continue your standard antenatal care at these facilities. Avoid travel in rural areas with poor transport and medical facilities.
- Ensure your travel insurance covers all pregnancy-related possibilities, including premature labour.
- Malaria is a high-risk disease in pregnancy. The World Health Organization recommends that pregnant women do not travel to areas with malaria resistant to chloroquine. None of the more effective antimalarial drugs is completely safe in pregnancy.
- Traveller's diarrhoea can quickly lead to dehydration and result in inadequate blood flow to the placenta. Many of the drugs used to treat various diarrhoea bugs are not recommended in pregnancy. Azithromycin is considered safe.

Insurance

It's always a good idea to take out travel insurance. Check the small print to see if the policy covers potentially dangerous sporting activities such as caving, diving or trekking, and make sure that it adequately covers your valuables. Health-wise, you may prefer a policy that pays doctors or hospitals directly rather than your having to pay on the spot and claim later. If you have to claim later, make sure that you keep all documentation. Check that the policy covers ambulances, an emergency flight home and, if you plan trekking in remote areas, a helicopter evacuation.

A few credit cards offer limited, sometimes full, travel insurance to the holder.

Worldwide travel insurance is available at www.lonelyplanet.com/travel-insurance. You can buy, extend and claim online anytime – even if you're already on the road.

Internet Access

Malaysia and Singapore are blanketed with hot spots for wi-fi connections (usually free). Internet cafes are less common these days, but do still exist if you're not travelling with a wi-fi enabled device. Only in the jungles and the most remote reaches of the peninsula and Malaysian Borneo are you likely to be without any internet access.

Legal Matters

In any dealings with the local police it will pay to be deferential. You're most likely to come into contact with them either through reporting a crime (some of the big cities in Malaysia have tourist police stations for this purpose) or while driving. Minor misdemeanours may be overlooked, but don't count on it.

Drug trafficking carries a mandatory death penalty. A number of foreigners have been executed in Malaysia, some of them for possession of amazingly small quantities of heroin. Even possession of tiny amounts can bring down a lengthy jail sentence and a beating with the *rotan* (cane). Just don't do it.

LGBT Travellers

Sex between males is illegal in both Malaysia and Singapore. Prosecution is rare, however, and in Kuala Lumpur and Singapore, in particular, there are fairly active gay scenes.

Malaysians and Singaporeans are fairly conservative about public affection. Although same-sex hand-holding is fairly common for men and women, this is rarely an indication of sexuality; an overtly gay couple doing the same would attract attention, though there is little risk of vocal or aggressive homophobia.

The websites Travel Gay Asia (www.travelgayasia.com), PLUguide (www.pluguide.com) and Utopia (www.utopia-asia.com) provide coverage of venues and events.

Money

ATMs & Credit Cards

Mastercard and Visa are the most widely accepted brands of credit card. You can make ATM withdrawals with your PIN, or banks such as Maybank (Malaysia's biggest bank), HSBC and Standard Chartered will accept credit cards for over-the-counter cash advances. Many banks are also linked to international banking networks such as Cirrus (the most common), Maestro and Plus, allowing withdrawals from overseas savings or cheque accounts.

If you have any questions about whether your cards will be accepted in Malaysia, ask your home bank about its reciprocal relationships with Malaysian and Singaporean banks.

Currency

Malaysia

The ringgit (RM) is made up of 100 sen. Coins in use are 1 sen (rare), 5 sen, 10 sen, 20 sen and 50 sen; notes come in RM1, RM5, RM10, RM20, RM50 and RM100.

Older Malaysians sometimes refer to ringgit as 'dollars' – if in doubt ask if people mean US dollars or 'Malaysian dollars' (ie ringgit).

Carry small bills with you when venturing outside cities.

Singapore

The Singapore dollar, locally referred to as the 'singdollar', is made up of 100 cents. Singapore uses 5¢, 10¢, 20¢, 50¢ and $1 coins, while notes come in denominations of $2, $5, $10, $50, $100, $500 and $1000.

Taxes & Refunds

Malaysia

Since 2015, a goods and sales tax (GST) of 6% has been levied on most goods and services in Malaysia. There are some exemptions (mainly for fresh and essential foods), but generally you'll now find this tax added to most things you buy including restaurant meals and souvenirs. Some establishments, if their turnover is low or if they have decided to absorb the GST into their regular prices, will not add the tax on top of the bill – it's always worth checking in advance if you're unsure.

If you spend in excess of RM300 at any one government-approved outlet, it is possible for international visitors to claim a refund of GST on certain goods they are taking out of the country. Full details of how to do this can be found at http://gst.customs.gov.my.

Singapore

Departing visitors can get a refund of the 7% GST on their purchases, under the following conditions:

- Minimum spend of S$100 at one retailer on the same day for no more than three purchases.
- You have a copy of the eTRS (Electronic Tourist Refund Scheme) ticket issued by the shop.
- You scan your eTRS ticket at the self-help kiosks at the airport or cruise terminal. If physical inspection of the goods is required as indicated by the eTRS self-help kiosk, you will have to present the goods, together with the original receipt and your boarding pass, at the Customs Inspection Counter.

Smaller stores may not participate in the GST refund scheme.

Travellers Cheques & Cash

Banks in the region are efficient and there are plenty of moneychangers. For changing cash or travellers cheques, banks usually charge a commission (around RM10 per transaction, with a possible small fee per cheque), whereas moneychangers have no charges, but their rates vary more. Compared with a bank, you'll generally get a better rate for cash at a moneychanger – it's usually quicker, too. Away from the tourist centres, moneychangers' rates are often poorer and they may not change travellers cheques.

All major brands of travellers cheques are accepted across the region. Cash in major currencies is also readily exchanged, though like everywhere else in the world the US dollar has a slight edge.

Practicalities

Newspapers English-language newspapers in Peninsular Malaysia include the *New Straits Times*, the *Star* and the *Malay Mail*. In Malaysian Borneo you'll also find the *Borneo Post*, the *New Sarawak Tribune* and the *New Sabah Times*. In Singapore there's the *Straits Times*, *Business Times* and *New Paper*.

Radio Try Traxx FM (http://traxxfm.rtm.gov.my; 90.3FM), HITZ FM (www.hitz.fm; 92.9FM), MIX FM (www.mix.fm; 94.5FM) and Power FM (www.power98.com.sg; 98FM) for pop music, and BFM (www.bfm.my; 89.9FM), Fly FM (www.flyfm.com.my; 95.8FM) or 938LIVE (www.938live.sg; 93.8FM) for news.

TV Watch Malaysia's two government channels (TV1 and TV2) and four commercial stations (TV3, NTV7, 8TV and TV9), as well as a host of satellite channels within both Malaysia and Singapore.

Weights & Measures Both Malaysia and Singapore use the metric system.

Opening Hours

Opening hours can vary between individual businesses. General opening hours are as follows.

Malaysia

Banks 10am–3pm Monday to Friday, 9.30am–11.30am Saturday

Bars & clubs 5pm–5am

Cafes 8am–10pm

Restaurants noon–2.30pm and 6pm–10.30pm

Shopping malls 10am–10pm

Shops 9.30am–7pm

Singapore

Banks 9.30am–4.30pm Monday to Friday, with some branches open at 10am and some closing at 6pm or later; 9.30am–noon Saturday

Bars & clubs 3pm–1am or 3am

Cafes 10am–7pm

Restaurants noon–2pm and 6pm–10pm

Shops 10am–9pm or 10pm.

Photography

Locals usually have no aversion to being photographed, although of course it's polite to ask permission before photographing people or taking pictures in mosques or temples. For advice on taking better photos, Lonely Planet's *Travel Photography: A Guide to Taking Better Pictures* is written by travel photographer Richard I'Anson.

Public Holidays

In addition to national public holidays, each Malaysian state has its own holidays, usually associated with the sultan's birthday or a Muslim celebration. Muslim holidays move back 10 or 11 days each year. Hindu and Chinese holiday dates also vary, but fall roughly within the same months each year.

Malaysia

Fixed annual holidays include the following:

New Year's Day 1 January

Federal Territory Day 1 February (in Kuala Lumpur and Putrajaya only)

Good Friday March or April (in Sarawak & Sabah only)

Labour Day 1 May

Yang di-Pertuan Agong's (King's) Birthday 1st Saturday in June

Governor of Penang's Birthday 2nd Saturday in July (in Penang only)

National Day (Hari Kebangsaan) 31 August

Malaysia Day 16 September

Christmas Day 25 December

Singapore

The only holiday that has a major effect on the city is Chinese New Year, when virtually all shops shut down for two days.

New Year's Day 1 January

Chinese New Year Three days in January/February

Good Friday April

Labour Day 1 May

Vesak Day May

Hari Raya Puasa July

National Day 9 August

Hari Raya Haji September

Deepavali November

Christmas Day 25 December

Safe Travel

Animal Hazards

Rabies does occur in Malaysia, so any bite from an animal should be treated very seriously. In the jungles and mangrove forests, living hazards include leeches (annoying but harmless), snakes (some kinds are highly venomous), macaques (prone to bag-snatching in some locales), orangutans (occasionally aggressive) and, in muddy estuaries, saltwater crocodiles (deadly if they drag you under).

Theft & Violence

Theft and violence are not particularly common in either country. Nevertheless, it pays to keep a close eye on your belongings, especially your travel documents (passport, travellers cheques etc), which should be kept with you at all times.

Muggings do happen, particularly in KL and Penang, and physical attacks have been known to occur, particularly after hours and in the poorer, rundown areas of cities. Thieves on motorbikes particularly target women for grab raids on their handbags. Also keep a watch out for sleazy local 'beach boys' in Langkawi and the Perhentians.

Credit-card fraud is a growing problem in Malaysia. Use your cards only at established businesses and guard your credit-card numbers closely.

A small, sturdy padlock is well worth carrying, especially if you are going to be staying at any of the cheap huts found on Malaysia's beaches, where flimsy padlocks are the norm.

Telephone

Malaysia

Local Calls

Landline services are provided by the national monopoly, Telekom Malaysia.

International Calls

The easiest and cheapest way to make international calls is to buy a local SIM card for your mobile (cell) phone. Only certain payphones permit international calls. You can make operator-assisted international calls from local TM offices. To save money on landline calls, buy a prepaid international calling card (available from convenience stores).

Mobile Phones

If you have arranged global roaming with your home provider, your GSM digital phone will automatically tune into one of the region's networks. If not, buy a prepaid SIM card (passport required) for one of the local networks on arrival. The rate for locals calls and text messages is around 36 sen.

There are three main mobile-phone companies, all with similar call rates and prepaid packages:

Celcom (www.celcom.com.my) This is the best company to use if you'll be spending time in remote regions of Sabah and Sarawak.

DiGi (www.digi.com.my)

Maxis (www.maxis.com.my).

Singapore

Local & International Calls

There are no area codes within Singapore; telephone numbers are eight digits unless you are calling toll-free (☎1800).

You can make local and international calls from public phone booths.

Most phone booths take phonecards. Singapore also has credit-card phones that can be used by running your card through the slot.

Calls to Malaysia (from Singapore) are considered to be STD (trunk or long-distance) calls. Dial the access code ☎020, followed by the area code of the town in Malaysia that you wish to call (minus the leading zero) and then the phone number. Thus, for a call to ☎346 7890 in Kuala Lumpur (area code 03) you would dial ☎02-3-346 7890.

Mobile Phones

Mobile-phone numbers start with 9 or 8.

You can buy a local SIM card for around $18 (including credit) from post offices, convenience stores and local telco stores – by law you must show your passport to get one.

Time

Malaysia and Singapore are eight hours ahead of GMT/UTC (London). Noon in the region is 8pm in Los Angeles, 11pm in New York, 4am in London, and 2pm in Sydney and Melbourne.

Toilets

Western-style sit-down loos are the norm, but there are some places with Asian squat toilets. Toilet paper is not usually provided; instead, you will find a hose or a spout on the toilet seat, which you are supposed to use as a bidet, or a bucket of water and a tap. If you're not comfortable with the 'hand-and-water' technique, carry packets of tissues or toilet paper wherever you go. Public toilets in malls usually charge an entry fee, which often includes toilet paper.

Tourist Information

Malaysia

Tourism Malaysia (www.malaysia.travel) has a good network of overseas offices, which are useful for pre-departure planning. Unfortunately, its domestic offices are less helpful and are often unable to give specific information about destinations and transport. Nonetheless, they do stock some decent brochures as well as the excellent *Map of Malaysia*.

Within Malaysia there are also a number of state tourist-promotion organisations, which often have more detailed information about specific areas. These include the following:

Pahang Tourism (www.pahangtourism.org.my)

Penang Tourism (www.visitpenang.gov.my)

Perak Tourism (www.peraktourism.com.my)

Sabah Tourism (www.sabahtourism.com)

Sarawak Tourism (http://sarawaktourism.com)

Tourism Selangor (www.tourismselangor.my)

Tourism Terengganu (http://tourism.terengganu.gov.my)

Singapore

Before your trip, a good place to check for information is the website of the Singapore Tourism Board (www.yoursingapore.com).

There are several tourism centres offering a wide range of services, including tour bookings and event ticketing, plus a couple of electronic information kiosks:

Chinatown Visitor Centre (2 Banda St; ⏲9am-9pm Mon-Fri, to 10pm Sat & Sun; Ⓦ; ⓂChinatown)

Singapore Visitors Centre @ Ion Orchard (level 1, ION Orchard Mall, 2 Orchard Turn; ⏲10am-10pm; ⓂOrchard)

Singapore Visitors Centre @ Orchard (☎1800 736 2000; www.yoursingapore.com; 216 Orchard Rd; ⏲9.30am-10.30pm; Ⓦ; ⓂSomerset)

Travellers with Disabilities

Before setting off, get in touch with your national support organisation (preferably with the travel officer, if there is one). Also try the following:

Accessible Journeys (www.disabilitytravel.com) In the US.

Mobility International USA (www.miusa.org) In the US.

Nican (www.nican.com.au) In Australia.

Tourism For All (www.tourismforall.org.uk) In the UK.

Malaysia

For the mobility impaired, KL, Melaka and Penang can be a nightmare. There are often no footpaths, kerbs can be very high, construction sites are everywhere, and crossings are few and far between. On the upside, taxis are cheap, and both Malaysia Airlines and KTM (the national rail service) offer 50% discounts for travellers with disabilities.

Singapore

A large government campaign has seen ramps, lifts and other facilities progressively installed around the island. The footpaths in the city are nearly all immaculate, MRT stations all have lifts, and there are some buses and taxis equipped with wheelchair-friendly equipment.

Visas

Malaysia

Visitors must have a passport valid for at least six months beyond the date of entry into Malaysia. The following gives a brief overview of other requirements – full details of visa regulations are available at www.kln.gov.my.

Nationals of most countries are given a 30- or 60-day visa on arrival, depending on the expected length of stay. As a general rule, if you arrive by air you will be given 60 days automatically, though coming overland you may be given 30 days, unless you specifically ask for a 60-day permit. It's possible to get an extension at an immigration office in Malaysia for a total stay of up to three months. This is a straightforward procedure that is easily done in major Malaysian cities.

Only under special circumstances can Israeli citizens enter Malaysia.

Both Sabah and Sarawak retain a certain degree of state-level control of their borders. Tourists must go through passport control and have their passports stamped whenever they arrive in Sabah or Sarawak from Peninsular Malaysia or the federal district of Pulau Labuan, exit Sabah or Sarawak on their way to Peninsular Malaysia or Pulau Labuan, or travel between Sabah and Sarawak.

When entering Sabah or Sarawak from another part of Malaysia, your new visa stamp will be valid only for the remainder of the period left on your original Malaysian visa. In Sarawak, an easy way to extend your visa is to make a 'visa run' to Brunei or Indonesia (through the Tebedu–Entikong land crossing).

Singapore

Citizens of most countries are granted a 90-day entry on arrival. Citizens of India, Myanmar, the Commonwealth of Independent States and most Middle Eastern countries must obtain a visa before arriving in Singapore. Visa extensions can be applied for at the **Immigration & Checkpoints Authority** (☎6391 6100; www.ica.gov.sg; 10 Kallang Rd; MLavender).

Women Travellers

The key to travelling with minimum hassle in Malaysia and Singapore is to blend in with the locals, which means dressing modestly and being respectful, especially in areas of stronger Muslim religious sensibilities. Regardless of what local non-Muslim women wear, it's better to be safe than sorry – we've had reports of attacks on women ranging from minor verbal aggravation to physical assault. Hard as it is to say, the truth is that women are much more likely to have problems in Malay-dominated areas, where attitudes are more conservative.

In Malay-dominated areas you can halve your hassles just by tying a bandanna over your hair (a minimal concession to the headscarf worn by most Muslim women). When visiting mosques, cover your head and limbs with a headscarf and sarong (many mosques lend these at the entrance). At the beach, most Malaysian women swim fully clothed in T-shirts and shorts, so don't even think about going topless.

Be proactive about your own safety. Treat overly friendly strangers, both male and female, with a good deal of caution. In cheap hotels check for small peepholes in the walls and doors; when you have a choice, stay in a Chinese-operated hotel. On island resorts, stick to crowded beaches, and choose a chalet close to reception and other travellers. After dark, take taxis and avoid walking alone in quiet or seedy parts of town.

Transport

Getting There & Away

Flights, tours and rail tickets can be booked online at www.lonelyplanet.com/bookings.

Entering Malaysia & Singapore

The main requirements are a passport that's valid for travel for at least six months, proof of an onward ticket and adequate funds for your stay, although you will rarely be asked to prove this.

Air

Malaysia

The bulk of international flights arrive at **Kuala Lumpur International Airport** (KLIA; ☎03-8777 7000; www.klia.com.my; KLIA), 55km south of Kuala Lumpur; it has two terminals with KLIA2 being used mainly by budget airlines (including AirAsia). There are also direct flights from Asia and Australia into Penang, Kuching, Kota Kinabalu and a few other cities.

Singapore

Changi Airport (☎6595 6868; www.changiairport.com), 20km northeast of the Singapore Central Business District (CBD), has three main terminals, with a fourth terminal scheduled to open in 2017. Regularly voted the world's best airport, Changi Airport is a major international gateway, with frequent flights to all corners of the globe. You'll find free internet, courtesy phones for local calls, foreign-exchange booths, medical centres, left luggage, hotels, day spas, showers, a gym, a swimming pool and no shortage of shops.

Land

The Causeway linking Johor Bahru (JB) with Singapore handles most traffic between the countries. Trains and buses run from all over Malaysia straight through to Singapore, terminating at Woodlands, or you can take a bus to JB and get a taxi or one of the frequent buses from JB to Singapore.

A shuttle train (RM5/S$5, five minutes) operated by Malaysia's Keretapi Tanah Melayu (KTM) ferries commuters between the Woodlands Checkpoint and JB Sentral seven times a day.

A good website with details of express buses between Singapore, Malaysia and Thailand is the Express Bus Travel Guide (www.singaporemalaysiabus.com).

There is also a causeway linking Tuas, in western Singapore, with Geylang Patah in JB. This is known as the Second Link, and some bus services to Melaka and up the west coast head this way; be prepared for delays at the immigration section on the Singapore side. If you have a car, tolls on the Second Link are much higher than those on the main Causeway.

Getting Around

Air

The main domestic operators are **Malaysia Airlines** (MAS; ☎1300 883 000, international 03-7843 3000; www.malaysiaairlines.com), **Singapore Airlines** (www.singaporeair.com) and **AirAsia** (☎600 85 8888; www.airasia.com).

The MAS subsidiary **Firefly** (☎03-7845 4543; www.fireflyz.com.my) has flights from KL's **SkyPark Subang Terminal** (Sultan Abdul Aziz Shah Airport; ☎03-7842 2773; www.subangskypark.com; M17, Subang) to Ipoh, Kota Bharu,

Climate Change & Travel

Every form of transport that relies on carbon-based fuel generates CO_2, the main cause of human-induced climate change. Modern travel is dependent on aeroplanes, which might use less fuel per kilometre per person than most cars but travel much greater distances. The altitude at which aircraft emit gases (including CO_2) and particles also contributes to their climate change impact. Many websites offer 'carbon calculators' that allow people to estimate the carbon emissions generated by their journey and, for those who wish to do so, to offset the impact of the greenhouse gases emitted with contributions to portfolios of climate-friendly initiatives throughout the world. Lonely Planet offsets the carbon footprint of all staff and author travel.

Langkawi and Penang. It also runs connections between Penang and Langkawi, Kuantan and Kota Bharu, Ipoh and JB, and JB and Kota Bharu.

Malindo Air (☎03-7841 5388; www.malindoair.com) also has a wide range of connections between many Malaysian cities and towns. Jetstar (www.jetstar.com) and Tiger Airways (www.tigerairways.com) also fly around the region.

In Malaysian Borneo, Malaysia Airlines' subsidiary **MASwings** (☎1300-88 3000; www.maswings.com.my) offers local flights within and between Sarawak and Sabah; its main hub is Miri. These services, especially those handled by 19-seat Twin Otters, are very much reliant on the vagaries of the weather. In the wet season (October to March in Sarawak and on Sabah's northeast coast; May to November on Sabah's west coast), small towns can be isolated for days at a time, so don't venture into those areas if you have a tight schedule. These flights are completely booked during school holidays. At other times it's easier to get a seat at a few days' notice, but always book as far in advance as possible.

Bicycle

Malaysia

Bicycle touring around Malaysia is an increasingly popular activity. The main road system is well engineered and has good surfaces, but the secondary road system is limited. Road conditions are good enough for touring bikes in most places, but mountain bikes are recommended for forays off the beaten track.

Top-quality bicycles and components can be bought in major cities, but generally 10-speed (or higher) bikes and fittings are hard to find. Bringing your own is the best bet. Bicycles can be transported on most international flights; check with the airline about extra charges and shipment specifications.

Useful websites:

Kuala Lumpur Mountain Bike Hash (http://klmbh.org) Details of the monthly bike ride out of KL.

Bicycle Touring Malaysia (www.bicycletouringmalaysia.com) Mine of information about cycling around the region, run by Mr David and his son Suresh, who also offer tour packages.

Malaysia Cycling Events & Blogs (www.malaysiacycling.blogspot.co.uk) Includes listings of cycle shops around the country.

Cycling Kuala Lumpur (http://cyclingkl.blogspot.co.uk) Great resource for cycling adventures in and around KL

Singapore

Avoid cycling on roads. Drivers are aggressive and the roads themselves uncomfortably hot. A much safer and more pleasant option for cyclists is Singapore's large network of parks and park connectors, not to mention the dedicated mountain-biking areas at Bukit Timah Nature Reserve, Tampines and Pulau Ubin.

Only fold-up bikes are allowed on trains and buses, and only during the following hours: 9.30am to 4pm and 8pm onwards Monday to Friday, and all day Saturday, Sunday and public holidays. Note that only ONE fold-up bike is allowed on a bus at any one time, so you might as well ride if you have to.

Boat

Malaysia

There are no services connecting Peninsular Malaysia with Malaysian Borneo. On a local level, there are boats and ferries between the peninsula and offshore islands, and along the rivers of Sabah and Sarawak. Note that some ferry operators are notoriously lax about observing safety rules, and local authorities are often nonexistent. If a boat looks overloaded or otherwise unsafe, *do not board it* – no one else will look out for your safety.

Singapore

Visit the islands around Singapore from the Marina South Pier. There are regular ferry services from Changi Point Ferry Terminal to Pulau Ubin ($2). To get there, take bus 2 from Tanah Merah MRT.

Bus

Bus travel in Malaysia is economical and generally comfortable. Seats can be paid for and reserved either directly with operators or via online sites such www.easybook.com. Some bus drivers speed recklessly, resulting in frequent, often fatal, accidents.

Konsortium Transnasional Berhad (www.ktb.com.my) is Malaysia's largest bus operator running services under the **Transnasional** (1300 888 582; www.transnasional.com.my), **Nice** (013-220 7867; www.nice-coaches.com.my; Kuala Lumpur), **Plusliner** (013-220 7867; www.plusliner.com.my) and **Cityliner** (03-4047 7878; www.cityliner.com.my) brands. Its services tend to be slower than rivals, and its buses have also been involved in several major accidents. It has competition from a variety of privately operated buses on the longer domestic routes, including Aeroline (www.aeroline.com.my) and Supernice (www.supernice.com.my). There are so many buses on major runs that you can often turn up and get a seat on the next bus.

Most long-distance buses have air-con, often turned to frigid, so bring a sweater!

In larger towns there may be a number of bus stations; local and regional buses often operate from one station and long-distance buses from another; in other cases, KL for example, bus stations are differentiated by the destinations they serve.

Bus travel off the beaten track is relatively straightforward. Small towns and *kampung* (villages) all over the country are serviced by public buses, usually rattlers without air-con. Unfortunately, they are often poorly signed and sometimes the only way to find your bus is to ask a local. These buses are invariably dirt cheap and provide a great sample of rural life. In most towns there are no ticket offices, so buy your ticket from the conductor after you board.

Car & Motorcycle

A valid overseas license is needed to rent a car in both Malaysia and Singapore. It is also recommended that you bring an International Driving Permit (a translation of your state or national driver's license and its vehicle categories). Most rental companies also require that drivers are at least 23 years old (and younger than 65) with at least one year of driving experience.

Malaysians and Singaporeans drive on the left-hand side of the road and it is compulsory to wear seat belts in the front and back of the car.

Malaysia

Driving in Malaysia is fantastic compared with most Asian countries. There has been a lot of investment in the country's roads, which are generally of a high quality. New cars for hire are commonly available and fuel is inexpensive (around RM1.95 per litre).

It's not all good news though. Driving in the cities, particularly KL, can be a nightmare, due to traffic and confusing one-way systems. Malaysian drivers aren't always the safest when it comes to obeying road rules – they mightn't be as reckless as drivers elsewhere in Southeast Asia, but they still take risks. For example, hardly any of the drivers keep to the official 110km/h speed limit on the main highways and tailgating is a common problem.

The Lebuhraya (North–South Hwy) is a six-lane expressway that runs for 966km along the length of the peninsula from the Thai border in the north to Johor Bahru in the south. There are quite steep toll charges for using the expressway and these vary according to the distance travelled. As a result the normal highways remain crowded, while traffic on the expressway is light.

Major rent-a-car operations include Avis (www.avis.com.my), Hertz (www.simedarbycarrental.com), Mayflower (www.mayflower-carrental.com.my) and Orix (www.orixcarrentals.com.my). There are many others, though, including local operators only found in one city.

Unlimited distance rates for a 1.3L Proton Saga, one of the cheapest and most popular cars in Malaysia, are posted at around RM190/1320 per day/week, including insurance and collision-damage waiver. The Proton is basically a Mitsubishi assembled under licence in Malaysia.

You can often get better prices, either through smaller local companies or when the major companies offer special deals. Rates drop substantially for longer rentals. The advantage of dealing with a large company is that it has offices all over the country, giving better backup if something goes wrong and allowing you to pick up in one city and drop off in another.

The best place to look for car hire is KL, though Penang is also good. In Sabah and Sarawak there is less competition and rates are higher, partly because of road conditions; there's also likely to be a surcharge if you drop your car off in a different city from the one you rented it in.

Rental companies will provide insurance when you hire a car, but always check what the extent of your coverage will be, particularly if you're involved in an accident. You might want to take out your own insurance or pay the rental company an extra premium for an insurance excess reduction.

Singapore

While Singapore's roads are immaculate, aggressive driving is common, speeding and tailgating endemic, use of signals rare and wild lane-changing universal.

In short, we don't recommend driving in Singapore, but if you do, practice extreme defensive driving and have your road rage under control.

Motorcycles are held in low esteem and some drivers display little regard for bike safety. Be alert.

If you want a hire car for local driving only, it's worth checking smaller operators, where the rates are often cheaper than the big global rental firms. If you're going into Malaysia, you're better off renting in Johor Bahru, where the rates are significantly lower (besides, Malaysian police are renowned for targeting Singapore licence plates).

Rates start from around S$60 a day. Special deals may be available, especially for longer-term rental. Most rental companies require that drivers be at least 23 years old.

All major car-hire companies, including **Avis** (☎6737 1668; www.avis.com.sg; 01-07 Waterfront Plaza, 390A Havelock Rd; 🚌5, 16, 75, 175, 195, 970) and **Hertz** (☎6542 5300; www.hertz.com; Terminals 2 & 3, Changi Airport) have booths at Changi Airport, as well as in the city.

Local Transport

Malaysia

Taxis are found in all large cities, and most have meters – although you can't always rely on the drivers to use them.

Bicycle rickshaws (trishaws) supplement the taxi service in George Town and Melaka and are definitely handy ways of getting around the older parts of town, which have convoluted and narrow streets.

In major cities there are also buses, which are extremely cheap and convenient once you figure out which one is going your way. KL also has commuter trains, a Light Rail Transit (LRT) and a monorail system.

In Malaysian Borneo, once you're out of the big cities, you're basically on your own and must either walk or hitch. If you're really in the bush, of course, riverboats and airplanes are the only alternatives to lengthy jungle treks.

Singapore

The efficient MRT subway system is the easiest, quickest and most comfortable way to get around Singapore. The system operates from 5.30am to midnight, with trains at peak times running every two to three minutes, and off-peak every five to seven minutes.

In the inner city, the MRT runs underground, emerging overground out towards the suburban housing estates. It consists of five colour-coded lines: North–South (red), North-East (purple), East–West (green), Circle Line (yellow) and Downtown (blue). Extensions of the Downtown line – known as Downtown 2 and Downtown 3 – are scheduled to open in 2016 and 2017 respectively.

You'll find a map of the network at www.smrt.com.sg.

You can flag down a taxi any time, but in the city centre taxis are technically not allowed to stop anywhere except at designated taxi stands.

Finding a taxi in the city at certain times is harder than it should be. These include during peak hours, at night, or when it's raining. Many cab drivers change shifts between 4pm and 5pm, making it notoriously difficult to score a taxi then.

The fare system is also complicated, but thankfully it's all metered, so there's no haggling over fares. The basic flagfall is $3 to $3.40 then $0.22 for every 400m.

There's a whole raft of surcharges to note, among them:

- 50% of the metered fare from midnight to 6am.
- 25% of the metered fare between 6am and 9.30am Monday to Friday, and 6pm to midnight daily.
- S$5 for airport trips from 5pm to midnight Friday to Sunday, and S$3 at all other times.
- S$3 city-area surcharge from 5pm to midnight.
- S$2.30 to S$8 for telephone bookings.
- Payment by credit card incurs a 10% surcharge. You can also pay using your EZ-Link transport card.

For a comprehensive list of fares and surcharges, visit www.taxisingapore.com.

Local companies include Comfort Taxi & CityCab (☎6552 1111), Premier Taxis (☎6363 6888) and SMRT Taxis (☎6555 8888).

Train

Malaysia's national railway company is **Keretapi Tanah Melayu** (KTM; ☎1300 885 862; www.ktmb.com.my). It runs a modern, comfortable and economical railway service, although there are basically only two lines and for the most part services are slow.

One line runs up the west coast from Singapore, through KL, Butterworth and on into Thailand. The other branches off from this line at Gemas and runs through Kuala Lipis up to the northeastern corner of the country near Kota Bharu in Kelantan. Often referred to as the 'jungle train', this line is properly known as the 'east-coast line'.

In Sabah, the North Borneo Railway (www.suteraharbour.com/north-borneo-railway), a narrow-gauge line running through the Sungai Padas gorge from Tenom to Beaufort, offers tourist trips lasting four hours on Wednesday and Saturday.

Services & Classes

There are two main types of rail services: express and local. Express trains are air-conditioned and have 'premier' (1st class), 'superior' (2nd class) and sometimes 'economy' (3rd class) seats and, depending on the service, sleeping cabins. Local trains are usually economy class only, but some have superior seats.

Express trains stop only at main stations, while local services, which operate mostly on the east-coast line, stop everywhere, including the middle of the jungle, to let passengers and their goods on and off. Consequently local services take more than twice as long as the express trains and run to erratic schedules, but if you're in no hurry they provide a colourful experience and are good for short journeys.

Train schedules are reviewed a few times a year, so check the KTM website, where you can make bookings and buy tickets.

Language

In Malay most letters are pronounced the same as their English counterparts, except for *c* which is always pronounced as the 'ch' in 'chair'. The second-last syllable is lightly stressed, except for the unstressed *e* – eg in *besar* (big) – which sounds like the 'a' in 'ago'.

To enhance your trip with a phrasebook, visit **shop.lonelyplanet.com**, or you can buy Lonely Planet's Fast Talk app through the Apple App store.

Basics

Hello.	*Helo.*
Goodbye.	*Selamat tinggal/jalan.* (by person leaving/staying)
Yes./No.	*Ya./Tidak.*
Excuse me.	*Maaf.*
Sorry.	*Maaf.*
Please.	*Silakan.*
Thank you.	*Terima kasih.*
You're welcome.	*Sama-sama.*
How are you?	*Apa kabar?*
I'm fine.	*Kabar baik.*
What's your name?	*Siapa nama kamu*
My name is ...	*Nama saya ...*
Do you speak English?	*Adakah anda berbahasa Inggeris?*
I don't understand.	*Saya tidak faham.*

Accommodation

Do you have any rooms available?	*Ada bilik kosong?*
How much is it per day/person?	*Berapa harga satu malam/orang?*
Is breakfast included?	*Makan pagi termasukkah?*

Eating & Drinking

A table for (two), please.	*Meja untuk (dua) orang.*
I'd like (the menu).	*Saya minta (daftar makanan).*
What's in that dish?	*Ada apa dalam masakan itu?*
The bill, please.	*Tolong bawa bil.*
I don't eat ...	*Saya tak suka makan ...*
fish	*ikan*
(red) meat	*daging (merah)*
nuts	*kacang*

Shopping

I'd like to buy ...	*Saya nak beli ...*
Can I look at it?	*Boleh saya tengok barang itu?*
How much is it?	*Berapa harganya?*
It's too expensive.	*Mahalnya.*

Emergencies

Help!	*Tolong!*
Go away!	*Pergi!*
Call the police!	*Panggil polis!*
Call a doctor!	*Panggil doktor!*
I'm ill.	*Saya sakit.*
I'm lost.	*Saya sesat.*

Transport & Directions

When's the (next bus)?	*Jam berapa (bis yang berikutnya)?*
I want to go to ...	*Saya nak ke ...*
I'd like a ... ticket.	*Saya nak tiket ...*
one-way	*sehala*
return	*pergi balik*
Where is ...?	*Di mana ...?*
Can you show me (on the map)?	*Tolong tunjukkan (di peta)?*
hotel	*hotel*
internet cafe	*cyber cafe*
market	*pasar*
post office	*pejabat pos*
public phone	*telpon awam*
restaurant	*restoran*
station	*stasiun*
toilets	*tandas*
tourist office	*pejabat pelancong*

Behind the Scenes

Acknowledgements

Climate map data adapted from Peel MC, Finlayson BL & McMahon TA (2007) 'Updated World Map of the Koppen-Geiger Climate Classification', *Hydrology and Earth System Sciences*, 11, 163344

This Book

This book was curated by Simon Richmond and researched and written by Simon, Isabel Albiston, Brett Atkinson, Greg Benchwick, Cristian Bonetto, Austin Bush, Anita Isalska, Robert Scott Kelly and Richard Waters.

This guidebook was produced by the following:

Destination Editor Sarah Reid
Product Editor Kathryn Rowan
Senior Cartographer Julie Sheridan
Book Designer Jessica Rose
Assisting Editors Bruce Evans, Victoria Harrison, Saralinda Turner
Cartographer Hunor Csutoros
Assisting Book Designer Lauren Egan
Cover Researcher Naomi Parker
Thanks to Liz Heynes, Indra Kilfoyle, Katherine Marsh, Kate Mathews, Campbell McKenzie, Wayne Murphy, Catherine Naghten, Kirsten Rawlings, Dianne Schallmeiner, Angela Tinson, Juan Winata

Send Us Your Feedback

We love to hear from travellers – your comments keep us on our toes and help make our books better. Our well-travelled team reads every word on what you loved or loathed about this book. Although we cannot reply individually to postal submissions, we always guarantee that your feedback goes straight to the appropriate authors, in time for the next edition. Each person who sends us information is thanked in the next edition, the most useful submissions are rewarded with a selection of digital PDF chapters.

Visit lonelyplanet.com/contact to submit your updates and suggestions or to ask for help. Our award-winning website also features inspirational travel stories, news and discussions.

Note: We may edit, reproduce and incorporate your comments in Lonely Planet products such as guidebooks, websites and digital products, so let us know if you don't want your comments reproduced or your name acknowledged. For a copy of our privacy policy visit lonelyplanet.com/privacy.

A—Z

Index

000 Map pages

000 Map pages

N

O

P

R

Symbols & Map Key

Look for these symbols to quickly identify listings:

- Sights
- Activities
- Courses
- Tours
- Festivals & Events
- Eating
- Drinking
- Entertainment
- Shopping
- Information & Transport

These symbols and abbreviations give vital information for each listing:

Sustainable or green recommendation

FREE No payment required

- Telephone number
- Opening hours
- Parking
- Nonsmoking
- Air-conditioning
- Internet access
- Wi-fi access
- Swimming pool
- Bus
- Ferry
- Tram
- Train
- English-language menu
- Vegetarian selection
- Family-friendly

Find your best experiences with these Great For... icons.

- Budget
- Food & Drink
- Drinking
- Cycling
- Shopping
- Sport
- Art & Culture
- Events
- Photo Op
- Scenery
- Family Travel
- Short Trip
- Detour
- Walking
- Local Life
- History
- Entertainment
- Beaches
- Winter Travel
- Cafe/Coffee
- Nature & Wildlife

Sights

- Beach
- Bird Sanctuary
- Buddhist
- Castle/Palace
- Christian
- Confucian
- Hindu
- Islamic
- Jain
- Jewish
- Monument
- Museum/Gallery/Historic Building
- Ruin
- Shinto
- Sikh
- Taoist
- Winery/Vineyard
- Zoo/Wildlife Sanctuary
- Other Sight

Points of Interest

- Bodysurfing
- Camping
- Cafe
- Canoeing/Kayaking
- Course/Tour
- Diving
- Drinking & Nightlife
- Eating
- Entertainment
- Sento Hot Baths/Onsen
- Shopping
- Skiing
- Sleeping
- Snorkelling
- Surfing
- Swimming/Pool
- Walking
- Windsurfing
- Other Activity

Information

- Bank
- Embassy/Consulate
- Hospital/Medical
- Internet
- Police
- Post Office
- Telephone
- Toilet
- Tourist Information
- Other Information

Geographic

- Beach
- Gate
- Hut/Shelter
- Lighthouse
- Lookout
- Mountain/Volcano
- Oasis
- Park
- Pass
- Picnic Area
- Waterfall

Transport

- Airport
- BART station
- Border crossing
- Boston T station
- Bus
- Cable car/Funicular
- Cycling
- Ferry
- Metro/MRT station
- Monorail
- Parking
- Petrol station
- Subway/S-Bahn/Skytrain station
- Taxi
- Train station/Railway
- Tram
- Tube Station
- Underground/U-Bahn station
- Other Transport

Greg Benchwick

Greg's been writing about travel both near and far for the better part of the past two decades. He's written dozens of travel guides for Lonely Planet, and is a recognised expert on sustainable tourism. For this edition, he jungle-boated down from Taman Negara, got nuclear drunk in his search for the perfect bar in Cherating and nearly fell off the planet in Tioman.

Cristian Bonetto

Cristian has been chowing his way across Singapore for well over a decade. Countless calories later, the Australian-born writer remains deeply fascinated by the Little Red Dot's dramatic evolution. To date, Cristian has contributed to more than 30 Lonely Planet guides, including *New York City, Italy, Denmark* and both the Singapore city and pocket guides. His musings have also appeared in a string of publications, including Britain's *The Telegraph* and San Francisco's *7X7*. Follow Cristian on Twitter (@CristianBonetto) and Instagram (rexcat75).

Austin Bush

Austin came to Thailand in 1999 on a language scholarship, and has remained in Southeast Asia ever since. This is his second time contributing to this region, a gig that is arguably Lonely Planet's most delicious. Austin is a native of Oregon and a writer and photographer who often focuses on food; samples of his work can be seen at www.austinbushphotography.com.

Anita Isalska

Anita is a freelance travel journalist, editor and copywriter. Formerly a Lonely Planet digital editor, Anita surprised no one when she swapped office life for taste-testing street food and prowling beach resorts. Previous Malaysia travels took Anita from leechy Sabah hikes to Ipoh's red bean frappés. Returning to research her most-adored regions, Perak and Melaka, was a joy. Anita writes about travel, adventure, food and culture for a host of international publications; check out some of her work at www.anitaisalska.com.

Robert Scott Kelly

A resident of Kuala Lumpur since 2013, Robert enjoyed the opportunity to explore the states surrounding his home in more detail to update this guidebook. His favourite discoveries: the megaliths of Negeri Sembilan and the traditional wood houses of Kampung Pantai. Robert, a freelance writer, photographer, documentary filmmaker and, now, fledgling podcaster, has contributed to other Lonely Planet titles including *Kuala Lumpur, Taiwan, China, Alaska and Tibet*. Check out his latest work on www.robertscottkelly.com.

Richard Waters

Richard is an award-winning journalist and writes about travel for *The Daily Telegraph, The Independent* and *Sunday Times, Sunday Times Travel Magazine, Elle* and *National Geographic Traveller*. He lives with his family in the Cotswolds, UK, and when he's not travelling, loves surfing and diving. Exploring Sabah was an absolute joy, his favourite moments being watching sharks in Sipadan, and seeing the sun rise over the jungle in the Danum Valley. He also writes a family wellbeing, adventure blog called Soul Tonic for Sanlam Bank. Check it out on www.sanlam.co.uk/Media/Blogs/Soul-Tonic.asp

Our Story

A beat-up old car, a few dollars in the pocket and a sense of adventure. In 1972 that's all Tony and Maureen Wheeler needed for the trip of a lifetime – across Europe and Asia overland to Australia. It took several months, and at the end – broke but inspired – they sat at their kitchen table writing and stapling together their first travel guide, *Across Asia on the Cheap*. Within a week they'd sold 1500 copies. Lonely Planet was born. Today, Lonely Planet has offices in Dublin, Melbourne, Franklin, London, Oakland, Beijing and Delhi, with more than 600 staff and writers. We share Tony's belief that 'a great guidebook should do three things: inform, educate and amuse'.

Our Writers

Simon Richmond

Simon first travelled in the region back in the early 1990s. A lot has changed since, but Malaysia and Singapore remain among Simon's favourite destinations for their easily accessible mix of cultures, landscapes, adventures and, crucially, delicious food. An award-winning travel writer and photographer, Simon has helmed Lonely Planet's *Malaysia, Singapore & Brunei* guide for five editions. He's also the author of Lonely Planet's *Kuala Lumpur, Melaka & Penang* guide as well as a shelf-load of other titles for this and other publishers. Read more about Simon's travels at www.simonrichmond.com and on Twitter and Instagram @simonrichmond.

Isabel Albiston

Since her first trip to Malaysia, travelling the length of the peninsula by train on an overland journey from Singapore to Nepal, Isabel has grown to love shimmying across rickety bamboo bridges on rainforest hikes. The pursuit of laksa keeps luring her back and she can now confirm Sarawak to be the clear winner in the countrywide contest for the best broth. Isabel is a journalist who has written for a number of newspapers and magazines including the UK's *Daily Telegraph*.

Brett Atkinson

Following past sojourns in the west of Malaysia, this was Brett's first exploration of the peninsula's eastern edge. Highlights included island hopping from the Perhentians to Pulau Kapas, the street food and night markets of Kota Bharu, and the compact heritage appeal of Chinatown in Kuala Terengganu. Brett is based in Auckland, New Zealand and has covered more than 50 countries as a guidebook author and travel and food writer. See www.brett-atkinson.net for his most recent work and upcoming travels.

More Writers

STAY IN TOUCH LONELYPLANET.COM/CONTACT

EUROPE Unit E, Digital Court, The Digital Hub, Rainsford St, Dublin 8, Ireland

AUSTRALIA Levels 2 & 3 551 Swanston St, Carlton, Victoria 3053 ☎ 03 8379 8000, fax 03 8379 8111

USA 150 Linden Street, Oakland, CA 94607 ☎ 510 250 6400, toll free 800 275 8555, fax 510 893 8572

UK 240 Blackfriars Road, London SE1 8NW ☎ 020 3771 5100, fax 020 3771 5101

twitter.com/lonelyplanet
facebook.com/lonelyplanet
instagram.com/lonelyplanet
youtube.com/lonelyplanet
lonelyplanet.com/newsletter